ATHENS, ADEN, ARIKAMEDU

Essays on the interrelations between India, Arabia and the Eastern Mediterranean

edited by
Marie-Françoise Boussac
Jean-François Salles

MANOHAR

CENTRE DE SCIENCES HUMAINES
NEW DELHI
2005

First published in India 1995
Reprinted from *Topoi*, vol. 3/2 (1993), pp. 387-623
Lyon, France
Reprinted 2005

ISBN 81-7304-079-6

Published by
Ajay Kumar Jain *for*
Manohar Publishers & Distributors
4753/23 Ansari Road, Daryaganj
New Delhi 110 002

Printed at
Lordson Publishers Pvt Ltd
Delhi 110 007

Distributed in South Asia by
FOUNDATION BOOKS
4381/4, Ansari Road
Daryaganj, New Delhi 110 002
and its branches at Mumbai, Hyderabad,
Bangalore, Chennai, Kolkata

CONTENTS

List of maps

PREFACE

The deliberately cryptic title of this book, *Athens, Aden, Arikamedu* is intended to enlighten the objectives of the editors of the present dossier, which was published in Lyon in 1993,[1] and is reprinted here with the necessary corrections and a minimum of additions. Our purpose was not, indeed, to undertake a revised and thorough approach on the topic of the relations between India and the Mediterranean area during the Greek, Hellenistic and Roman periods ; a large amount of studies and publications have been carried on in India, in Europa and in America since the pioneering works of W.W. Tarn and Sir M. Wheeler, and any concerned scholar should be really pleased by the vivid and recent revival of the « Graeco-Indica » and « Indo-Roman » studies.

A wide avenue of the renewed research consists in a re-reading of the ancient texts, both Classical and Indian — although the 1901's compilation by J.W. McCrindle is still often quoted in the latest bibliographies. Indeed, the purely linguistic problem remains a basic one, and M. Casevitz's contribution emphasizes several borrowings of the Greek language which are definitely of Indian origin ; the process by which such Indian words reached the Eastern Mediterranean/ Greek world maybe as early as the VIIth or VIth cent. B.C. is still a matter of fascinating investigation. Several groups of Europaean scholars have also nourished the path of historical interpretation with great efficiency and produced a large number of high valued contributions, for example the Belgians on Alexander's campaigns in India and « Hellenistic » northeastern India — not to mention A. Dihle's important contributions.[2] More remarkable was the attempt

1. The journal *Topoi. Orient-Occident* from which the present volume is extracted with the kind cooperation of our publisher in India, is an annual publication of the *Société des Amis de la Bibliothèque Salomon Reinach* (Institute of Classical Archaeology, University Lumière Lyon-2), Maison de l'Orient Méditerranéen, 7, rue Raulin, 69007, Lyon, France. More information on the journal can be obtained from the Editor, Professor Marie-Françoise Boussac, at the Maison de l'Orient, address above.

2. See the references cited by K. KARTTUNEN in his contribution in this volume, and his « Graeco-Indica — A Survey of Recent Work » (1), *Arctos* 20 (1986) : 73-86.

Athens, Aden, Arikamedu
New Delhi, 1994
J.-F. SALLES, p. 5-10

The title of A. Tchernia's review of the recent book *Rome and India. The Ancient Trade* seems to be the most promising window on further research : *Rome and India. Archaeology alone* ? It is now an obvious evidence that the Indo-Roman studies have to rely on a tight cooperation between Indian and Europaean/ American archaeologists, and historians, and numismats, and epigraphers, and philologists, and historians of art, and historians of the religions, and philosophers, and many other specialists. It was an unpretentious aim of the *Topoi* dossier to open such a path, and we hope it would be able to create new opportunities and determinations of collaboration.

The Indo-Roman trade cannot be conceived without ships and sailors. A lot has been written on the Roman traditions of navigation and ship-building, although the Roman naval reality in the Red Sea and eastwards remains almost totally unknown in the literary sources — and archaeology is not very helpful yet in this region. On the other hand, a common *topos* used to assume that India was not a maritime country, for many reasons none of which could be actually substantiated. The only possible response to this contradiction had to come from ethnographical studies of the Indian maritime traditions, and L. Varadarajan's paper in this volume is a major contribution in a way which is being more and more explored in India.[7]

But the most important renewal of the past few years definitely came from archaeological research. We have just mentioned the vigorousness of the Indian archaeologists — new excavations at Arikamedu, explorations in Southern India, excavations at Ter, Chandraketugarh, Sonkh, etc.[8] The fringes of the Indian subcontinent are not neglected, indeed, and recent works in the area of and at Banbhore, in the mouth of the Indus, and at Mahasthan, in Eastern Bengal (Bangladesh) will certainly provide us with fresh and important data on the badly known archaeology of these regions in the late 1st millennium B.C./ early 1st millennium A.D.

Most determining were the results of the French excavations at Ai Khanum, in Afghanistan [9]. They allowed, under the direction of P. Bernard, a critical

---

studies, see also H.P. Ray, « The western Indian Ocean and the early maritime links of the Indian subcontinent », *The Indian Economic and Social History Review*, 31, 1 (1994) : 65-88.

7. This was one of the main field of inquiry during the Indo-French Seminar « Techno-archaeological perspectives... » cited above. The proceedings will include several contributions on the traditional techniques of navigation and ship-building in India.

8. It would be too long to list here the numerous sites or collections of objects presently under study in India. See for example *Rome and India*, reviewed by A. Tchernia in this volume.

9. The latest publication in the Ai Khanum series, Cl. Rapin, *Fouilles d'Aï Khanoum,* VIII, *La trésorerie du palais hellénistique d'Aï Khanoum. L'apogée et la chute du royaume grec de Bactriane*, De Boccard, Paris, 1992, presents Indian objects found in Ai Khanum and their interpretation.

revision of the traditional W.W. Tarn's *Greeks in Bactria and India* (1951), a better appreciation of the Greek presence in Central Asia,[10] and a thorough and new interpretation of the relations between the Graeco-Bactrians and their Indian neighbours. The history of the Indo-Greek kingdoms is being now seriously revised and revived by several historical and numismatic studies,[11] and O. Bopearachchi offered to this volume a nice and very clear example of what should not be done and what should be done when writing the history of the Indo-Greek kingdoms.

What we consider as a true innovation in the dossier of the relations between India and the Eastern Mediterranean Sea is the introduction of Arabia into the general scheme. Looking at a map obviously shows that the Arabian peninsula and its bordering seas — the Red Sea and the Persian Gulf — appear as the natural and ineludible bridge between the western coasts of India, from Cape Cormorin to Karachi, and the eastern coast of the Mediterranean, from Antioch to Alexandria — assuming, indeed that continental routes were existing through Iran and Central Asia.

Archaeological research has been vigourous in the Persian Gulf for the last tewnty years and is still going on ; new data are overnumerous, and their interpretation needs a large amount of further study. However, a global approach was presented recently,[12] which places the Persian Gulf into the true perspective of its role between the Mesopotamian world and India. For the periods under consideration in the present book, we would just emphasize that the Gulf was the main artery of the Seleucid trade with India from the IVth to the IInd cent. B.C., with the help of Arabian traders and sailors, the Gerrhaeans and later the Characenians and the Palmyraneans. After any western presence — and influence — had disappeared from the area, at the end of the Seleucid period, the Gulf remained busy and operative as a major maritime lane between Mesopotamia and India, through the Arabian kingdoms of its western shores or in the Shatt el-Arab, through the new Persian power and, probably, through some Indian presence in the area.[13]

---

10. See P. BERNARD, « L'Asie centrale et l'empire séleucide », *Topoi* 4/2 (1994), p. 473-511. This article is part of a larger dossier on the recent book by S. SHERWIN-WHITE and A. KUHRT, *From Samarkhand to Sardis. A new approach of the Seleucid Empire,* London, 1993, which gives a priority to the eastern provinces of the Seleucids, including India (p. 91-102). The *Topoi* dossier includes thirteen contributions on this book, p. 431-610.

11. See O. BOPEARACHCHI, *Monnaies gréco-bactriennes et indo-grecques. Catalogue raisonné,* Bibliothèque Nationale, Paris, 1991.

12. D.T. POTTS, *The Arabian Gulf in Antiquity,* Oxford, 1990 (2 vols.).

13. See J.-F. SALLES, « India and the Near East. The bridge of Arabia », in press, *Journal of the Asiatic Society of Bangladesh* ; ID. , « *Fines Indiae - Ardh el Hind* », *The Roman and Byzantine Army in the East,* Proceedings of a colloquium held at the

The southern coast of Arabia, from Aden to the Ras Musandam, has also yielded a large amount of archaeological data. In Oman, sites like Suhar of Khor Rori show strong relations with the Indus mouth area and the Gujarat, on the opposite side of the Sea of Oman.[14] In South Arabia/ Yemen, A.V. Sedov, who is presenting here the preliminary results of his survey of the Socotra island, is now excavating one of the major sites cited by *The Periplus of the Erythraean Sea*, Kana : the first results are remarkable, and this Arabian site is revealing critical evidence of the relations between India and the Mediterranean area.[15] Finally, mention should be made of several explorations and excavations in the Red Sea, especially on the Egyptian shores, which prove a closer integration of the area into the Arabian networks.

Adding Aden as a symbol of maritime Arabia, to the pair Rome (or Athens) and India appears as a new and provocative perspective of scholarship. Serious revisions of ancient and modern evidence (texts, archaeological finds, etc.) have to be undertaken with a renewed point of view, and the objective is far from being reached. It was the purpose of the *Topoi* dossier to make a first step in this direction.

Jean-François SALLES
Institut F. Courby, Lyon

Jagiellonian University, Krakow, 7-9 sept. 1992, ed. by E. Dabrowa, Krakow, 1994 : 165-187.

14. Recently, P. YULE and M. KERVRAN (M.), 1993, « More than Samad in Oman : Iron Age pottery from Suhar and Khor Rori », *Arabian Archaeology and Epigraphy*, 4/2 (1993) : 69-106.

15. Several preliminary reports on Kana excavations were published in the journal *Arabian Archaeology and Epigraphy*, Munsksgaard, Copenhagen. Another report will be included in the proceedings of the Indo-French Seminar « Techno-archaeological perspectives... », see above.

GRAECO-INDICA (2)

Graeco-Indian studies, as I like to call them, have recently gained much attention. Their fascination lies in the fact that we here have to deal with a contact between two different ancient civilizations, which both are rather well documented. In a superficial view this contact always seems to have been marginal, and to many Greeks and Indians it probably was, but a closer look reveals many phases and levels of contact and interaction. Although Indian literature only contains brief notes on the Yavanas, the western classical sources include a few lengthy accounts and a great amount of scattered notes. Outside literary traditions such disciplines as archaeology, numismatics and epigraphy are often able to considerably elucidate these contacts. Important is further the study of other neighbouring civilizations, of Iranian and even Arabian.

Six years ago I published a kind of survey of recent philological work on Graeco-Indian studies.[1] I have been asked by several colleagues to continue it, and now I have been offered an occasion to do that in a place, where it perhaps better reaches all that are interested in it. As in 1986 I shall again concentrate my attention on the philological side, and only occasionally give attention to such fields as archaeology and numismatics.[2]

---

1. « Graeco-Indica — A Survey of Recent Work », *Arctos* 20 (1986) : 73-86. For an earlier summary, see F.F. SCHWARZ, « Neue Perspektiven in den griechisch-indischen Beziehungen », *OLZ* 67 (1972) : 5-26.

2. This leaves the Indo-Greek history oustide my scope. It will be discussed elsewhere in this volume. At present, I would only like to mention two contributions of major importance viz. Paul BERNARD's *Fouilles d'Aï Khanoum.* IV. *Les monnaies hors trésors. Questions d'histoire gréco-bactrienne*, MDAFA 28, Paris 1985, and Osmund BOPEARACHCHI's *Monnaies Gréco-Bactriennes et Indo-Grecques : catalogue raisonné*, Paris 1991. In art history, a remarkable new find was reported by Nazir Ahmad KHAN, « A New Relief from Gandhara Depicting the Trojan House », *East and West* 40 (1990) : 315-319. See further the bibliographical accounts by Frank L. HOLT in the *Ancient World* 9 (1984) : 2-12, and 15 (1987) : 3-15.

Athens, Aden, Arikamedu
New Delhi, 1994
K. KARTTUNEN, p. 11 - 20

Perhaps the most important work published during the 1980s was the *L'Inde vue de Rome. Textes latins de l'Antiquité relatifs à l'Inde* by J. ANDRÉ & J. FILLIOZAT (Paris 1986).[3] A nearly complete (not quite) collection of all references to India in Latin literature — including even a great amount of poetic references to Hercules and Bacchus in India — up to the end of the sixth century A.D., accompanied by a French translation and copious notes by the Indologist Filliozat, it is an extremely useful tool for further studies. We can only hope that somebody would take the laborious task to make a similar collection of the much more numerous Greek sources. A good beginning was made, more than 50 years ago, by B. BRELOER and F. BÖMER (*Fontes historiae religionum Indicarum*, Bonn 1939), who gave an excellent collection of *loci* dealing with Indian religion and philosophy.

Two felicitation volumes have more or less concentrated on Graeco–Indian studies, those for K. FISCHER and P. H. L. EGGERMONT.[4] In the first one, dedicated to the well-known art historian, the emphasis is naturally on art and archaeology. The second, too, contains much on archaeology (*e.g.* Narain on foundation of Ai Khanum) and Indology, but also some interesting philological contributions (Dihle on Dionysus in Indien and Puskás on Indo-Roman trade). Eggermont himself, a veteran in the field, has again published several articles on related questions.[5] While some of his ingenious solutions to old questions (*e.g.* an Arabian etymology, *'awâlî* « southwestern monsoon wind », for the name Hippalus) are certainly not accepted by all, a study of his contributions always gives new insights.

In India the main interest of Graeco-Indian studies lies in their importance for ancient Indian history. Too often the results have been marred by the fact

---

3. See my review in *Arctos* 23 (1989) : 282f. and those by R. SCHMITT in *Gymnasium* 94 (1987) : 282-284 and W. SCHMITTHENNER in *Gnomon* 60 (1988) : 551-553.

4. J. OZOLS & V. THEWALT (eds.), *Aus dem Osten des Alexanderreiches : Völker und Kulturen zwischen Orient und Occident, Iran, Afghanistan, Pakistan, Indien*, Festschrift zum 65. Geburtstag von Klaus Fischer, Köln 1984 ; G. POLLET (ed.), *India and the Ancient World. History, Trade and Culture before A.D. 650*, Prof. P. H. L. Eggermont Volume, Orientalia Lovaniensia Analecta 25, Leuven 1987. For the latter, see my review in *Arctos* 21 (1987) : 203f.

5. EGGERMONT, « The Kushan Dynasty and Alexandreia Bucephalus », *Studia Paulo Naster oblata* II, Orientalia antiqua, Orientalia Lovaniensia Analecta 13, Leuven 1982 : 53-68 ; « Ptolemy, the geographer, and the people of the Dards », *Orientalia Lovaniensia Periodica* 15 (1984) : 191-233 (also published in *JCA* 7 [1984] : 73-123) ; « Indien und die hellenistischen Königreiche. Zusammenschau einer west-östlichen Gesellschaft zwishen 550 und 150 v. Chr. », *Fischer Volume* 1984 : 74-83 ; « Heracles-Dorsanes and Priyadarsin-Asoka », *OLP* 17 (1986) : 159-168 ; « Sanchi-Kakanada and the Hellenistic and Buddhist sources », G. BHATTACHARYA (ed.), *Deyadharma. Studies in memory of Dr. D.C. Sircar*, Delhi 1986 : 11-27 ; « Hippalus and the discovery of the Monsoons », A. THÉODORIDÈS, P. NASTER & J. RIES (eds.), *Humour, travail et science en Orient*, Leuven 1988 : 343-364.

that Indian scholars rarely have a command of classical languages. An exception in this respect is U. P. ARORA, who is independently culling out from Greek sources even such material as was ignored in the classic surveys of McCrindle. In addition to several articles,[6] he has lately edited a commemoration volume to the memory of the Greek Indologist Demetrius Galanos,[7] and the first volume of a new periodical *Yavanika*, published by the Indian Society for Greek and Roman Studies.

The *Galanos Volume* contains no less than 28 articles, a majority of which deals with Graeco-Indian questions, arranged under headings of art and archaeology, classical sources, history, literature and philosophy. While some are just repeating well-known general facts or suggesting untenable interpretations, there are also several important contributions included. Among philological, we can mention the attempt of ARORA (86–108) to show how the Greek literary background is reflected in the accounts of India reducing their value as information.

The *Yavanika* (vol. 1, 1991) is a meagre volume of 128 pages, although we are promised to have more in the future (vol. 2 came out in 1992, but cannot be discussed here). Contributions are mostly written by South Asian scholars, the most interesting being those by ARORA (« Roman-Age Authors on Ancient India » : 21–46) and WEERAKODDY (« Sri Lanka's Diplomatic Mission to Rome in the First Century A.D. » : 47–67). In addition to this, Dr. Weerakkody has published a long series of articles in Sri Lankan journals dealing with the contacts between the classical world and ancient Sri Lanka.[8]

---

6. ARORA, « Greek Attitude Towards the Indians », *Prof. Baldeva Upadhyaya Felicitation Volume, Journal of the Ganganatha Jha Research Institute* 37 (1983) : 97-109 ; « On Nearchos' discovery of the Sea-route between India and the Persian Gulf », *Proceedings of the Thirty-First International Congress of Human Science in Asia and North Africa. Tokyo-Kyoto 31st Aug-7th Sept.* Vol. 1, Tokyo 1984 : 411-413 ; « Metamorphoses in Myth », S. JOSHI (ed.), *India and Greece : connections and parallels*, Bombay 1985 : 43-52 ; « The Folklore of Ancient India and Greek literature », S.D. TRIVEDI (ed.), *Essays on Indology, Polity and Administration. In the Honour of Padmabhushan Shri R. K. Trivedi*, Vol. 2, Delhi 1989 : 341-349 ; « Problem of Understanding Greek Nomenclatures in Classical Accounts on India », N. C. GOSH & S. CHAKRABARTI (eds.), *Adaptation and Other Essays (Proceedings of the Archaeological Conference)*, Shantiniketan 1990 : 287-295 ; « Form of State Power in Mauryan India — Megasthenes' Evidence », S.P. GUPTA & K.S. RAMACHANDRAN (eds.), *Facets of Indian History, Culture and Archaeology*, New Delhi 1991 : 164-172.

7. ARORA (ed.), *Graeco-Indica. India's Cultural Contacts with the Greek World. In Memory of Demetrius Galanos (1760-1833), A Greek Sanskritist of Benares*, Heritage of Ancient India, New Delhi 1991.

8. « Ancient Sri Lanka as described by Cosmas », *The Sri Lanka Journal of the Humanities* 7 : 1-2 (1981), 107-127 ; « Some observations on Ptolemy's description of Sri Lanka », *Kalyani Journal of Humanistics and Social Science of the University of Kelaniya* 1 : 1-2 (1962), 31-47 ; « Adventures of a Theban Lawyer on his Way to

Much interest has been given to Graeco-Indian questions by Russian scholars. In addition to G. M. BONGARD-LEVIN,[9] we may quote such names as I. V. P'JANKOV,[10] V. K. ŠOHIN,[11] and J. J. VASIL'KOV.[12] Still more has been done in the field of archaeology. As the name reveals, the emphasis of Šohin's book is in contacts between India and Medieval Russia, but in most cases he is just dealing with the afterlife of classical conception of India (*e.g.* the tradition of Indian Gymnosophists).

Another « geographical school » is flourishing in Argentina. The collaboration of Fernando TOLA and Carmen DRAGONETTI has resulted in a new

---

Sri Lanka », *JRAS Sri Lanka* N.S. 26 (1982), 23-42 ; « The Earliest Greek Notices on Sri Lanka », *The Sri Lanka Journal of the Humanities* 10 (1984), 1-26 ; « Classical references in the interlinear inscriptions from Sri Lanka », *Ancient Ceylon. Journal of the Archaeological Survey Department of Sri Lanka* 6 (1986), 259-273 ; « Sri Lanka in Greek and Latin Verse », *Nava Samskriti Cultural Quaterly* 1 : 1 (1986), 39-46 ; « The Foreign Relations and Trade of Ancient Sri Lanka from Greek and Latin Sources », *Silver Jubilee Commemoration Volume of the University of Kelaniya, Sri Lanka* (1986), 21-32 ; « Sri Lanka's Diplomatic Mission to Rome, 1st century A.D. », *Palma II. Commemoration Volume of the Classical Association of Ceylon Golden Jubilee 1935-1985* (1989), 66-80 ; « Sri Lanka through Greek and Roman Eyes », S. BANDARANAYAKE *et al.* (eds.), *Sri Lanka and the Silk Road of the Sea*, Colombo, 1990, 163-173 ; « Sri Lanka as Known to Strabo », *The Sri Lanka Journal of the Humanities* 15 : 1-2 (1992), 55-64 ; *Some Reflections on Roman Coins from Sri Lanka*, Ceylon Studies Seminar Discussion Paper, 1992 ; « A note on the Greek names from Sri Lanka », *The Sri Lanka Journal of the Humanities* 16 : 1-2 (1990, pub. 1992), 118-130.

9. BONGARD-LEVIN, « Drevnjaja Indija i anticnost' (obšaja harakteristika tradicij) », *Drevnij vostok i mirovaja kul'tura*, Moscow 1981 : 107-111 ; « Graeco-Roman tradition and religious-philosophical currents in Mauryan India », *ALB* 44-45 (1980-81) : 50-62 ; « Indijskij brahman Čanak'ja v antičnoj tradicii », *VDI* 1982 : 1 : 13-26 (with English summary) ; « Ancient India and the Graeco-Roman World », *The Indian Historical Review* 10 (1984) : 21-31 and, again, *I T* 13 (1985-86) : 169-185 ; « Palladij o brahmanah i dispute Aleksandra », *Kul'turnoe nasledenie vostoka. Problemy, poiski, suždenija* (B.B. Piotrovskij Volume), Leningrad 1985 : 66-72.

10. P'JANKOV, « Vostočnyj Turkestan v svete antičnyh istočnikov », B.A. LITVINSKIJ (ed.), *Vostočnyj Turkestan i Srednjaja Azija v sisteme kul'tur drevnego i srednevekovogo Vostoka*, Moskva 1986 : 6-23 ; « Drevnejšee antičnoe izvestie o puti v vostočnyj Turkestan », B.A. RANOV (ed.), *Prošloe srednej Azii (arheologija, numizmatika i èpigrafica, ètnografija)*, Dušanbe 1987 : 261-267.

11. ŠOHIN, *Drevnjaja Indija v kul'ture Rusi (XI-seredina XV v.). Istocnikovedčeskie problemy*, Moscow 1988.

12. VASIL'KOV, « O vozmožnosti grečeskogo vlijanija na 'Voprosy Milindy' », *Buddiszm, istorija i kul'tura*, Moscow 1989 : 91-103 ; and « Buddijskie sjužety v hritianskoj literature : konflikt mirovozzrenij », *Vostok* 1991 : 3 : 42-51 (a review of Šohin's book).

survey of western sources on India,[13] and their pupil Rosalía C. VOFCHUK has carried on her author-oriented studies on western sources.[14] It would be interesting to see the contents of her doctoral thesis (*Las doctrinas brahmánicas a través de las fuentes griegas y latinas*), too, in printed form.

In the previous article I was still able to more or less silently pass over my own work in the field. This time I feel myself bound to mention it, although the evaluation must be left to others. Thus I can be brief with the early Greek sources (of the period before Alexander's campaigns) on India, which I have myself discussed in a monograph and in several articles.[15] In addition, there are only few articles to be mentioned here.[16]

After the vague notes on India in early Greek sources a turning point in western knowledge of India was clearly Alexander's Indian campaign. Ever since the historians of Alexander were among the most used sources on India. On the history of Alexander a major work is now A. B. BOSWORTH's *Conquest and Empire. The reign of Alexander the Great* (Cambridge 1988), a calm and reasonable survey of the sources.[17] The eastern part of the campaigns has been dealt separately, too.[18] An important contribution, though not strictly speaking

---

13. TOLA & DRAGONETTI, « India and Greece before Alexander », *ABORI* 67 (1986) : 159-194 ; « India and Greece from Alexander to Augustus », ARORA (ed.), *Graeco-Indica (Galanos Volume)*, New Delhi 1991 : 119-149.

14. VOFCHUK, « Los informes de Onesicrito, cronista de Alejandro Magno sobre la India », *Bol. As. Esp. des Orientalistas* 22 (1986) : 187-202 (revised version of Vofchuk 1984) ; « La India en Ciceron y los liricos latinos », *Argos* 9-10 (1985-86) : 143-158 ; « The Woman of India as pictured by Greek and Latin Authors », *ABORI* 59 (1988) : 141-154. See also note 49, below.

15. *India and Early Greek Literature*, Studia Orientalia 65, Helsinki 1989. Articles : « The reliability of the *Indica* of Ctesias », *Proceedings of the Nordic South Asia Conference*, held in Helsinki June 10-12 1980, *Studia Orientalia* 50 (1981) : 105-107 ; « Κυνοκέφαλοι and Κυναμολγοί in classical ethnography », *Arctos* 18 (1984) : 31-36 ; « A miraculous fountain in India », *Arctos* 19 (1985) : 55-65 ; « Expedition to the end of the world - An ethnographic τόπος in Herodotus », *St. Or.* 64 (1988) : 177-181 ; « The *Indica* of Ctesias and its criticism », *Galanos Volume* 1991 (see above) : 74-85. See further « On the contacts of South India with the Western world in ancient times, and the mission of the Apostle Thomas », A. PARPOLA & B. SMIDT HANSEN (eds.), *South Asian Religion and Society*, Studies on Asian Topics (Scandinavian Institute of Asian Studies), Copenhagen & London 1986 : 189-204 ; « Taxila. Indian City and a Stronghold of Hellenism », *Arctos* 24 (1990) : 85-96 ; and note 53, below.

16. P. BERNARD, « Les Indiens de la liste des tributs d'Hérodote », *Studia Ir.* 16 (1987) : 175-191 ; J.M. BIGWOOD, « Ctesias' *Indica* and Photius », *Phoenix* 43 (1989) : 302-316 : P. DAFFINÀ, « Semiramide in India », *Indo-Sino-Tibetica. Studi in Onore di Luciano Petech*, Roma 1990 : 91-101 ; and Dilhe 1990 in note 26 below. In addition, several studies on Achaemenian history are important here.

17. See my review in *Arctos* 23 (1989) : 279f.

18. I would like to mention here Paul GOUKOWSKY's *Essai sur les origines du mythe d'Alexandre (336-270 av. J.-C.)*. I. *Les origines politiques*, Annales de l'Est publiées

dealing with India, is F. L. HOLT's book *Alexander the Great and Bactria. The Formation of a Greek Frontier in Central Asia* (Leiden 1989).[19] There was much intercourse between Bactria and northwestern India even before the Macedonian conquest, and after it the two countries were often sharing the same fate. *Mutatis mutandis* Holt's comments on Alexander's politics towards local people, in arrangement of the government and in founding colonies are very useful for the Indian part of his history, too.

To the historians of Alexander must be added the name of Megasthenes, the ambassador. Nobody denies his importance, but still we are without a full and up-to-date evaluation of him. Nevertheless, some important work can be noted. Unfortunately the dissertation of Joanna SACHSE is available only in Polish,[20] but from the summary and from her one article[21] we learn that this pupil of L. SKURZAK has followed the « Indian » viewpoint of his master. The western view has been interestingly represented in a long study by A. ZAMBRINI,[22] who emphasizes the relation of the *Indica* to the slightly earlier *Aegyptiaca* by Hecataeus of Abdera. Both are seen in the light of the political tension between Ptolemies and Seleucids, serving the propaganda of their respective masters. An attempt to make a critical evaluation of different views on Megasthenes and of his value for Indian history has been made by Romila THAPAR.[23]

Of the so-called « epitome of Megasthenes » in the *Historical Library* of Diodorus Siculus (2, 35–42) a new translation with notes has been published by

---

par l'Université de Nancy, Mémoire 60, Nancy 1978, & II. *Alexandre et Dionysos*, Nancy 1981.

19. See *e.g.* F.F. SCHWARZ, « Flammen über Baktrien. Zu einem wichtigen Thema wichtiger Mission », *Grazer Beiträge* 16 (1989) : 125-142 ; and P. BERNARD, « Alexandre et l'Asie centrale : réflexions à propos d'un ouvrage de F.L. Holt », *Studia Ir.* 19 (1990) : 21-38.

20. J. SACHSE, *Megasthenes o Indiach*, Classica Wratislaviensia VIII, Acta Universitatis Wratislaviensis 587, Wroclaw 1981.

21. SACHSE, « Le mythe des Sila, fleuve indien (Mégasthène, *FGrHist.* 715 7 10) », *Eos* 70 (1982) : 237-241. This is the only publication known to me by Mrs Sachse which is not in Polish.

22. ZAMBRINI, « Gli *Indiká* di Megastene », *Annali della Scuola Norm. Sup. di Pisa* Serie 3, vol. 12 : 1 (1982) : 71-149 and vol. 15 : 3 (1985) : 781-853 ; see further his « Idealizzazione di una terra : etnografica e propaganda negli *Indiká* di Megastene », *Forme di conttato e processi di transformazione nelle società antiche*, Atti del convegno di Cortona (24-30 maggio 1981), Collection de l'École française de Rome, Pisa & Roma 1983 : 1105-1118 ; « A proposito degli *Indika* di Arriano », *ASNP* Serie 3, vol. 17 : 1 (1987) : 139-154.

23. THAPAR, *The Mauryas Revisited. S.G. Deuskar Lectures on Indian History, 1984*, Calcutta 1987.

Edwin MURPHY.[24] Another author, too rarely mentioned in Graeco-Indian studies, Pomponius Mela, can now be consulted from the annotated edition of Piergiorgio PARRONI.[25]

For the western accounts on India of the Hellenistic and Roman period Albrecht DIHLE has for a long time been a most reliable guide. Again, there are several new contributions by him.[26] The first one contains an attempt of re-evaluation of classical tradition of Dionysus connected with India, beginning with historians of Alexander. The second takes again a theme already discussed by the author in an earlier article,[27] while the third takes up the earliest western accounts of India.

During last decade, our understanding of Romano-Indian trade relations has greatly expanded, and through it the *Periplus of the Erythraean Sea*, too, has got some fresh light. An annotated reprint, with occasional changes, of Frisk's text (the only useful one), together with a translation and notes has been prepared by Lionel CASSON,[28] and this specialist of ancient trade and travel has also contributed several articles.[29] Our general knowledge of the trade dealt with in the *Periplus* has been added to, in addition to fresh views and interpretations, by important archaeological and numismatic finds, and even by a new papyrus

---

24. MURPHY, *The Antiquities of Asia. A Translation with Notes of Book II of the* Library of History *of Diodorus Siculus*, New Brunswick & Oxford 1989.

25. *Pomponii Melae de Chorographia libri tres*. Introduzione, edizione critica e commento a cura di Piergiorgio Parroni, Storia e letteratura raccolti di studi et testi 160, Roma 1984.

26. DIHLE, « Dionysos in Indien », *Eggermont Volume* 1987 : 47-57 ; « L'ambassade de Théophile l'Indien ré-examinée », T. FAHD (ed.), *L'Arabie préislamique et son environnement historique et culturel. Actes du Colloque de Strasbourg 24-27 juin 1987*, Université des Sciences Humaines de Strasbourg, Travaux du Centre de Recherche sur le Proche-Orient et la Grèce antique 10, Leiden 1987 : 461-468 ; and « Arabien und Indien », *Hérodote et les peuples non grecs*, Entretiens sur l'Antiquité classique 35, Genève 1990 : 41-67 ; and a review of my own book in *JESHO* 35 (1992) : 96-101.

27. DIHLE, « Die Sendung des Inders Theophilos », *Palingenesia* 4 (1969) : 330-336.

28. *The Periplus Maris Erythraei*. Text with introduction, translation and commentary by L. CASSON, Princeton 1989.

29. CASSON, « *Periplus Maris Erythraei* : three notes on the text », *CQ*, N.S. 30 (1980) : 495-497 ; « *Periplus Maris Erythraei* 36 : teak, not sandalwood», *CQ*, N.S. 32 (1982) : 181-183 ; « *Periplus Maris Erythraei* : Notes on the text », *JHS* 102 (1982) : 204-206 ; « Sakas versus Andhras in the *Periplus Maris Erythraei* », *JESHO* 26 (1983) : 164-177 ; « Egypt, Africa, Arabia and India : patterns of seaborne trade in the first century A.D. », *Bulletin of the American Society of Papyrologists* 21 (1984) : 39-47 ; « The sea route to India : *Periplus Maris Erythraei* 57 », *CQ* 34 (1984) : 473-479.

dealing with India[30] and a few Indian inscriptions found in Egypt.[31] As it is not my intention to give here a summary of studies on the history of this trade itself (it has been discussed elsewhere in the present volume), I list only the most important contributions in order to round up my bibliographical account : Steven E. SIDEBOTHAM, *Roman Economic Policy in the Erythra Thalassa 30 B.C.–A.D. 217*, Mnemosyne, Supplementum 91, Leiden 1986 ;[32] Raphaela DREXHAGE, *Untersuchungen zum römischen Osthandel.* Bonn 1988 ; Ajoy Kumar SINGH, *Indo-Roman Trade. An Archaeological Perspective*, New Delhi 1988 ; Paula J. TURNER, *Roman Coins from India*, London 1989 ;[33] Vimala BEGLEY & R. D. DE PUMA (eds.), *Rome and India. The ancient sea trade*, Madison 1991 (discussed elsewhere in this volume) ; further many articles like those by J. BOUZEK & S. DERANIYAGALA ;[34] F. DE ROMANIS ;[35] B.G. GOKHALE ;[36] M.H. PANHWAR ;[37] Fritz PAULI ;[38] I. PUSKÀS ;[39] and I. SIDDIQUI.[40]

A question closely related to the history of maritime trade, and extending from the Near Eastern prehistory of Graeco-Indian studies to the end of the classical antiquity, is the history of seafaring in the Indian (Erythraean) Sea. The early phases I have discussed myself in the second chapter of my *India in Early Greek Literature*, but now there are also several more extensive discussions. In a valuable collection of seminary articles (*L'Arabie et ses mers bordières*. 1.

30. H. HARRAUER & P. SIJPESTEIJN, « Ein neues Dokument zu Roms Indienhandel, P. Vindob. G 40822 », *Anzeiger der Österreichischen Akademie der Wissenschaften, Philosophisch-hist. Klasse* 122 (1985) : 124-155.

31. R. SALOMON, « Epigraphic Remains of Indian Traders in Egypt », *JAOS* 111 (1991) : 731-736.

32. See my review in *Arctos* 22 (1988) : 237f.

33. See my review in *Arctos* 24 (1990) : 204-207.

34. B. & D., « Tessons de vases hellénistiques trouvés en Sri Lanka », *BCH* 109 (1985) : 589-596.

35. DE ROMANIS, « Roma ei nótia dell'India. Ricerche sui rapporti tra Roma et l'India dravidica dal 30 a.C. all'età flavia », *Helikon* 22-27 (1982-1987) : 143-210 (not seen by myself).

36. GOKHALE, « Bharukaccha/Barygaza », *Eggermont Volume* 1987 (see above) : 67-79.

37. PANHWAR, « International trade of Sind from its port Barbaricon (Banbhore), 200 B.C. to 200 A.D. », *Sindhological Studies (Institute of Sindhology, University of Sind, Jamshoro, Sind)*, 1981 : 8-35.

38. PAULI, « Nahapana / Μανβαν.ς vor 78 n. Chr. ? Ein epigraphischer Neufund aus Indien und seine Bedeutung für die antike Südasien-Chronologie », *Studien zur alten Geschichte. Siegfried Lauferr... dargebracht* 2, 1986 : 743-753.

39. PUSKÀS, « Trade contacts between India and the Roman Empire », *Eggermont Volume* 1987 (see above) / 141-156.

40. SIDDIQUI, « The Ware-House Theory of Indo-Roman Trade Between First and Fourth Century A.D. », *Yavanika* 1 (1991) : 68-81.

Itinéraires et voisinages, Travaux de la Maison de l'Orient 16) published in Lyon in 1988, J. ROUGÉ has given a summary of its history, while J.-F. SALLES subjects the explorations arranged by Darius (Scylax and the expedition indicated in Suez inscriptions — being two separate instances) and Alexander under a more detailed examination.[41] SALLES has further written a long review of the second volume of the important new book by D.T. POTTS on *The Arabian Gulf in the Antiquity* (II. *From Alexander the Great to the Coming of Islam*, Oxford 1990).[42] Unfortunately I have not yet been able to read the book myself, and must postpone my opinion to another occasion.

The vexed problem of interaction and influence between ancient India and the West in the field of religion and philosophy has been a cause of much speculation, quite often of a questionable value. Now we can hope that the important contribution of Wilhelm HALBFASS[43] perhaps could make the air little clearer. On the idea and legend of India in the West some further light is given by John DREW, *India and the Romantic Imagination* (Delhi 1987).

The special question of the knowledge of Buddhism in the West has been discussed in several articles by P. C. ALMOND,[44] Alain CHRISTOL,[45] Carsten

---

41. ROUGÉ, « La navigation en mer Érythrée dans l'Antiquité » : 59-74 ; SALLES, « La circumnavigation de l'Arabie dans l'Antiquité classique » : 75-102 ; see also SALLES, « Les échanges commerciaux dans le golfe arabo-persique au 1er millénaire avant J.-C. », T. FAHD (ed.), *L'Arabie préislamique et son environnement historique et culturel. Actes du Colloque de Strasbourg 24-27 juin 1987*, Université des Sciences Humaines de Strasbourg, Travaux du Centre de Recherche sur le Proche-Orient et la Grèce antique 10, Leiden 1987 : 67-96 ; and « Les Achéménides dans le golfe arabo-persique », H. SANCISI-WEERDENBURG & A. KUHRT (eds.), *Achaemenid Workshop. IV. Centre and Periphery*, Proceedings of the Groningen 1986 Achaemenid Workshop, Leiden 1990 : 111-130.

42. SALLES, *TOΠOI* 2 (1992) : 201-235 ; for the first volume (*From Prehistory to the Fall of the Achaemenid Empire*) see P. LOMBARD, *Ibid.* : 195-199.

43. HALBFASS, *India and Europe. An Essay in Understanding*, Albany, N.Y. 1988 (original edition in German in 1981, now also published in a cheap Indian edition).

44. ALMOND, « The Buddha in the West : from Myth to History », *Religion* 16 (1986) ; and « Buddhism in the West : 300 BC-AD 400 », *Journal of Religious History* 14 (1987) : 235-245.

45. CHRISTOL, « Le nom des bouddhistes en grec », *Lalies* (Paris) 3 (1981) : 37-43.

COLPE,[46] André DUPONT-SOMMER,[47] David SCOTT,[48] and Rosalía VOFCHUK.[49] Among these, Colpe gives a survey of the history of western relations to and knowledge of Buddhism. The discussion proceeds from Megasthenes to the Manichaeans, and, despite some questionable speculations (like the supposed Indian origin of Ammonius Sakkas), it is an useful introduction. A more cautious and methodically preferable, though also shorter, approach is given by Almond. Vofchuk, too, gives a brief survey of classical accounts possibly related to Buddhism. Christol argues for an early conversion of the Indo-Greeks in Buddhism, an idea hardly supported by archaeological and numismatical evidence.

Late classical and Christian literature contain new versions of old tales about India, but also some fresh ideas, which often became important in the medieval conception of India. Several aspects of this have been dealt with in articles by J. Duncan M . DERRETT,[50] R. M. DZANPOLADJAN,[51] Gianfranco FIACCADORI,[52] and myself.[53]

Klaus KARTTUNEN
University of Helsinki

46. COLPE, « Heidnischer und christlicher Hellenismus in ihren Beziehungen zum Buddhismus », *Vivarium. Festchrift Theodor Klauser*, Jahrbuch für Antike und Christentum 11 (1984) : 57-81.

47. DUPONT-SOMMER, « Essénisme et bouddhisme », *CRAI* 1980 : 698-715.

48. SCOTT, « Christian responses to Buddhism in pre-medieval times », *Numen* 32 (1985) : 88-100.

49. VOFCHUK, « Primeras menciones des Budismo en el mundo-greco-romano », *Revista de Estudios Budistas* 1: 2 (1991-92) : 117-137.

50. DERETT, « Jewish Brahmins and the tale of Zosimus : a theme common to three religions », *Cl. & Med.* 34 (1983) : 75-90.

51. DŽANPOLADJAN, « Armjanskie istočniki V-VII vv. ob Indii », V.M. MASSON (ed.), *Drevnie kul'tury Srednej Azii Indii*, Leningrad 1984 : 141-146.

52. FIACCADORI, « Teofilo Indiano. Parte I. Le origini », *Studi Classici e Orientali* 23 (1983) : 295-331 (English summary on p. 340) ; « Teofilo Indiano. Parte II. Il viaggio », *Studi Cl. e Or.* 24 (1984) : 271-308 (E. s. on p. 322f.).

53. KARTTUNEN, « The country of fabulous beasts and naked philosophers — India in classical and medieval literature », *Arctos* 21 (1987) : 43-52 ; « A Thousand Years of Contamination — India in the Dictionary of Stephanus of Byzantium », *Berliner indologische Studien* 4/5 (1989) : 95-110 ; and « Distant Lands in Classical Ethnography », *Grazer Beiträge* 18 (1992) : 195-204.

« MOTS VOYAGEURS »
FROM INDIA TO GREECE *

Over a century ago, Arsène Darmesteter compared the history of words with natural history in the light of Darwinian theory and set out to study the « birth, life and death of words ». His contention was : « Even if it (the Darwinian theory) is replaced by other new theories, transformism in language will still remain a fact. Vocal sounds which constitute the materials of language are continually and imperceptibly transformed by human thought due to the automatic action of vital competition and natural selection ».[1] The author was concerned primarily with linguistic stocks. Lexical borrowings were treated summarily as he considered them to be more a matter of style than anything else. He felt that words borrowed from neighbouring peoples were corrupted by « coarse irony » or contempt.[2] As a point of fact, when just the signifier was borrowed, the loan word only added a derogatory nuance to a concept (signified) already existent in the borrowing language, at least at the beginning of its life on a foreign soil. But there are other kinds of borrowings. For instance, when a language travelled to an alien land, it

---

* Translation into English : Miss Poonam PURI.

1. A. DARMESTETER, *La vie des mots étudiée dans leurs significations*, Paris, 1887 (reprinted Paris, 1979), p. 31. For an interesting critique of this work, see J. VENDRYES, *Le langage, introduction linguistique à l'histoire*, Paris, 1923 (reprinted Paris, 1968, with bibliographical additions), pp. 216-218 ; the author warns against the ambiguity that results from the analogy between words and living beings, asserting that the specific aim of the linguist as far as etymology is concerned is: to collect « as many semantic processes as possible in order to arrive at the general laws which govern the way the meaning of words changes » (p. 218) ; he also reminds us that « the laws are never in the words themselves » *(ibid)*.

2. *Ibid.*, p. 94. See also, more qualified, J. VENDRYES, *op. cit*, pp. 231-233. For a comprehensive study on loan words, see L. DEROY, *L'emprunt linguistique*, (Bibliothèque de la Faculté de Philosophie et de Lettres, University of Liège), Paris, 1956, which includes an extensive bibliographical appendix, pp. 345-425.

Athens, Aden, Arikamedu
New Delhi, 1994
M. CASEVITZ, p. 21 - 26

was at times obliged to draw upon resources other than its own :[3] words which were the remainders of an old « substratum » language were incorporated in the new dominant language that went on to become an indigenous language.[4] Some words denote objects of no initial usefulness but which acquired utility in the course of time. Such words have remained loan words ; the traveller carrying exotic goods brought along with him both the word and what it denoted.[5] While some words stay rooted to the native soil, others travel and come into use wherever they go, all along the way from the place of production to the place of export. We shall attempt to see, with the help of a few examples, from where these words came into Greek, how they were assimilated, and whether they possess any distinctive characteristics by which they can be identified with certainty.

From the very first Greek attestations, words which are not of Greek origin appear in the Mycenaean tablets. This is particularly true of anthroponomy and onomastics, but also holds good for aromatics (perfumes, ointments, aromas). In the first case, the words may well have been borrowed within the country ; in the second, it seems natural to assume that the names of products not produced on the Greek mainland or its islands entered the language after of a long journey. In the Mycenaean tablets, the seven tablets of the Ge-series of Mycenae provide some words of this type :[6] *ka-da-mi-ja* (Ge 604, 5) should be interpreted as καρδάμια

---

3. See L. DEROY, *op. cit*., p. 138 (with bibliography, note 2).

4. For a discussion on substrata in general, see A. MEILLET, *Linguistique historique et linguistique générale*, Paris, 1965, pp. 82-83, and M. COHEN, *Matériaux pour une sociologie du langage*, Paris, 1956 (reprinted in two volumes, Paris, 1971), II, pp. 57-60. In the case of Greek, the concept of substratum or « Pelasgic » Indo-European substratum, borrowed from an Aegean or Mediterranean stock, has been used ; recourse to such assumptions is, for the most part, an admission of ignorance, as has been shown by P. CHANTRAINE in relation to the Aegean in the preface of *Dictionnaire Étymologique de la Langue Grecque, Histoire des mots*, Paris, 1968, p. 6 (we shall subsequently refer to this work by its acronym *DELG*). L. DEROY (*op. cit.* p. 316) reminds us that παλλακίς , σῦκον, ῥόδον, for example, when compared with words of the same meaning in different languages, whether Indo-European or not, attest to the existence of a Mediterranean substratum (for the last two words cited, see also A. MEILLET, *Aperçu d'une histoire de la langue grecque*, 7th ed., Paris, 1965, pp. 68-69).

5. « Rem verba sequantur », as we are reminded by J. VENDRYES, *op. cit*., p. 252.

6. See M. VENTRIS - J. CHADWICK, *Documents in Mycenaean Greek*, 2nd edition, Cambridge, 1973, pp. 225-231 (an additional commentary p. 442). For the spices in Knossos (series Ga and Og), see pp. 221-225. See especially the article by M. WYLOCK, « Les aromates dans les tablettes Ge de Mycènes », *Studi Micenei ed Egeo-Anatolici*, 15, 1972. p. 105-146.

(plural neutral)[7] and denotes garden cress[8] (alphabetic Greek : κάρδαμον) ; the final -αμον is found in many borrowed plant names.[9] One is inclined to think that the word is indeed a « mot voyageur » as the Sanskrit name *kardama* [10] does not denote the same plant, and later Greek sources[11] attribute Persian origins to a *cardamon* recipe. Besides, had the plant come from India, words similar to its original form ought to have been found in the countries on the trade routes; now this does not seem to be the case. Accordingly, we would do better to treat it as a simple borrowing without identifying the origin, common perhaps to both the Greek and the Sanskrit word.

The interpretation of *kanako* (Ge 602, 603, 604) is at issue ;[12] be it yellow or red, it certainly does not denote saffron in Mycenaean (L.*Cathamus tinctorius*), as is the case in Greek for κνῆκος. The word does not appear to have been borrowed from any one country, and perhaps Indo-European equivalents can be found in the adjectives meaning « yellow ».[13] As for *kono* (Ge 602, 603, 604, and *koino* Ge 606) = σχοῖνος, rush, (aromatic rush in Mycenaean), it has no equivalent and could well be a substratum word.

On the other hand, it is very likely that *korijadana* (Ge 605),[14] which should be interpreted as κορίαδνα, plural neutral, is an authentic « mot voyageur » ; the Greeks must have learnt of coriander[15] from Egypt, the Egyptians having received

---

7. Or feminine singular, as suggested by C.J. RUIJGH, *Études sur la grammaire et le vocabulaire du grec mycénien*, Amsterdam, 1967, p. 105 (§ 84).

8. See the remarks of J. ANDRÉ, « Notes sur une édition récente d'Athénée », *Revue de Philologie*, 34, 1960, pp. 51-57, especially p. 51-52 : « ... κάρδαμον is always garden cress (*Lepidium sativum* L.) and one must be careful not to translate it as 'cress' alone, which for us is always watercress (*Nasturtium officanle* L.), in Greek σισύμβριον ».

9. See P. CHANTRAINE, *La formation des noms en grec ancien*, Paris, 1933, p. 133 ; for the etymology of κάρδαμον, see *DELG, sv*. Though not explicitly stated, the hypothesis of R. STROMBERG, *Griechische Wortstudien*, Goteborg, 1944, p. 28 (quoted by H. FRISK, *Griechiches Etymologisches Worterbuch*, I, Heidelberg, 1960), which supposes *κάρδος = κράδος, is considered improbable.

10. See M. MAYRHOFER, *Kurzgefasstes etymologisches Worterbuch des Altindischen*, Heidelberg, 1965, I, 173, *sv kardamah 1* : « masculine, a certain plant... *karadamī*, feminine, a kind of jasmine ». As this is a purely Indian word, it is not found in his latest work : MAYRHOFER, *Etymologisches Worterbuch des Altindoarischen*, I, Heidelberg, 1992, in which the lemma *kardama-* (p. 317) corresponds to *kardama-*[2] in *Kurzgefasstes Worterbuch*.

11. Athenaeus, 3, 114 F and lexicographers.

12. See M. WYLOCK, *op. cit*., pp. 118-125.

13. See *DELG*, *sv* κνῆκος.

14. Or *koria$_2$dana* in Mycenae also (Ge 605) and in Pylos (Un 267), and *korijadono* (singular) in Knossos (Ga 415, 418), perhaps *korijodana* (Pylos An 616).

15. For the different forms of the word in Greek, see *DELG*, *sv* κορίαννον.

it from India.[16] Its varied forms in Greek suggest that even the word continued to be perceived as foreign. As for *kumino* (Ge 602, 603, 604), plural *kumina* (Ge 605), the word must be a « Semitic borrowing » that Greek took from the Phoenicians,[17] even though the plant itself[18] might have been gathered in Greece.[19] *Sasani*, alphabetic Greek σάσαμον (Ion.-Att. σήσαμον), is a name of Accadian origin and is attested in all Semitic dialects ; the Greeks too borrowed it from the Phoenicians.[20] In the case of *Maratuwo* (Ge 602), which ought to be understood as *marathwon* and corresponds to the Greek μάραθϝον = μάραθον (other form μάραθρον), both the name and the plant (fennel)[21] are native, just like *mita* (= μίνθα, Ion.-Att. μίνθη). The condiment attested in Knossos *kuparo* (Ga 463, 517 ; in Pylos, Un 249, 267, $kuparo_2$), alphabetic Greek κύπειρος, sage[22], may be a substratum name. As for *serino*, alphabetic Greek σέλινον,[23] it too is undoubtedly a substratum or loan word.

With regard to precious substances, *erepa*, alphabetic Greek ἐλέφας, ivory, must have originated from Asia. The name came perhaps through Hittite,[24] as the animal was unknown till the time of Alexander.

As far as animal names are concerned, *rewo*, alphabetic Greek λέων,[25] lion, corresponds to one of the three types of lions, « the most common whose name is found in practically every language of the Mediterranean basin ».[26] This may be a lion of Asian origin ; in fact it could well have come from India, from a periphrase which denotes the animal as « the roarer » (cf. Sanskrit *rauti* « it roars »), though there is a name in Sanskrit, which too has no doubt been borrowed, *simmah*. At

16. See M. Wylock, *op. cit.*, pp. 135-138.

17. See É. Masson, *Recherches sur les plus anciens emprunts sémitiques en grec*, Paris, 1967, pp. 51-52.

18. *Lagoecia cuminoïdes* L.

19. M. Wylock, *op. cit.*, pp. 114-115 (*contra* Ventris-Chadwick, *Documents*², p. 227).

20. See É. Masson, *op. cit.*, pp. 57-58 ; M. Wylock, *op. cit.*, pp. 115-118.

21. *Foeniculum vulgare* L.

22. See M. Wylock, « La fabrication des parfums à l'époque mycénienne, d'après les tablettes Fr de Pylos », *Studi Micenei ed Egeo-Anatolici*, 11, 1970, pp. 116-133 ; É. Masson, *op. cit.*, pp. 111-112.

23. *Apium graveolens* L. See M. Wylock, *op. cit.*, pp. 129-133.

24. See É. Masson, *op. cit.*, pp. 80-83 (with mention of this explanation due to E. Laroche).

25. The instrumental plural *rewopi* = λέον(τ)φι in Pylos (Ta 708) must denote table legs carved « in lion shape ». A nominative *rewo* = Λέων, attested in Knossos (Xd 7663), could be an anthroponym.

26. See É. Masson, *op. cit.*, p. 87. The other name for lion in Greek, λῖς, which has a rare equivalent in Semitic, is of unknown origin.

any rate, the various names of the lion are « noms voyageurs », as shown by É. Masson.[27]

After the Mycenaean era, a number of commercial travellers came to Greece, either by sea from Arabia or by land from Persia. As they brought in new wares, so new words were also brought in.[28] Before Alexander's time, this is how kasiva, *cinnamomum iners*, attested since Sappho, and κιννάμωμον, a variety of *cinnamomum*, name attested since Herodotus, entered the language. Such merchandise came mainly from India and their names appear in the Semitic field as borrowings transmitted by these traders. The form of the second word in Greek must have been influenced by the term ἄμωμον, also of Indian origin, denoting an aromatic plant, amomum ;[29] nard, Greek νάρδος, known since the 4th century B.C., also came from India (cf. Sanskrit *nalada*) through Semitic languages from where it got its Greek name ; this is yet another example of a typical « mot voyageur ». Another word which travelled from India, from the Hellenistic era, is the word for sugar, Greek σάκχαρ (or σάκχαρι) and spread to all parts taking on various forms (*DELG*). The red product used in painting and medicine, σάνδυξ (attested since Strabo), may also have come from India ; the same can be said for ζιγγίβερι, ginger (Dioscoridus, Galenus).

Among the names of animals, the camel, κάμηλος, appears in the writings of Aeschylus where it is associated with the Indians (*Supplices*, 284-285 : « I have heard it said that there are Indian nomads who ride camels, Ἰνδούς τ'ἀκούω νομάδας ἱπποβάμοσιν | εἶναι καμήλοις ἀστραβιζούσας...) ;[30] the name itself comes from Occidental Semitic languages.[31]

Among the names of precious stones, lapis-lazuli, σάπφειρος, which appears in the works of Theophrastus, entered Greek through the Semitic (cf. Hebrew *sappīr*, with a long i). But as the stone came from India, it is possible that the name itself is of Indian origin ;[32] the word for opal, ὀπάλλιος, must come from Sanskrit *upalah*, stone. Σμάραγδος , « the word for emerald and other green stones », (*DELG*) is also a « mot voyageur », and even in Greek, there is an alternative term μάραγδος. This is a more recent word which may correspond to the Sanskrit *marak(a)tam* ; in Semitic languages the word has taken different forms.

---

27. *Op. cit.*, p. 87. We are of the opinion that, as soon as one supposes a euphemistic designation, the association with the Sanskrit *rauti* should not be excluded (*contra DELG*, *sv* λέων).

28. See É. MASSON, *op. cit.*, pp. 46-47.

29. See J. ANDRÉ, *Les noms de plantes dans la Rome antique*, Paris, 1985, *sv* amomum.

30. See my contribution, « L'Inde des poètes, d'Eschyle à Nonnos », to be published in the Proceedings of the Symposium on India, held in Besançon in December 1992.

31. See É. MASSON, *op. cit.*, pp. 66-67.

32. But the Sanskrit *sanipriya* is a modern term, see É. MASSON, *op. cit.*, p. 66, n. 2.

Apart from the words that came to Greece from India through the trade routes, often deformed due to the many adaptations they underwent on their way, there are some words which were introduced directly by men with a taste for the picturesque, Ctesias being the most famous of them. These are not « mots voyageurs » but more or less faithful transcriptions which, when adopted by the language, can transcend time and language. A case in point is *martichora*, the man eater, a derivation from an old Iranian prototype which was to fire the imagination till the Middle Ages.[33]

Michel CASEVITZ
Université Lumière-Lyon 2

33. See Ch. MALAMOUD's preface in *Ctésias, histoires de l'Orient*, Paris, 1991, pp. XIV-XV, and J. AUBERGER's forward, pp. XVII-XIX.

ARISTOTLE, INDIA AND THE ALEXANDER HISTORIANS

Few subjects have aroused so much speculation on so little evidence as Aristotle's relations with Alexander the Great.[1] It inspired one of Fritz Schachermeyr's most rhapsodic passages in which he traced a journey of imagination through the curriculum devised for the young prince at Mieza.[2] In addition to the studies in ethics and politics, which Plutarch infers took place,[3] Schachermeyr hypothesised wide-ranging instruction in geography which (he alleged) formed Alexander's world-view and fuelled his lifelong curiosity for exploration. This geographical grounding is based on speculation,[4] some of it misplaced. The world maps displayed in the lecture halls of the Peripatos, for instance, are only attested in the will of Theophrastus (c. 286 B.C.)[5] and cannot readily be retrojected half a century to serve as an inspiration for the young

1. Bibliography is provided by J. SEIBERT, *Alexander der Grosse* (Darmstadt, 1972) : 72-3. See particularly W. JAEGER, *Aristotle* ² (Oxford, 1948) : 105-23 ; V. EHRENBERG, *Alexander and the Greeks* (Oxford, 1938) : 62-102 ; J.R. HAMILTON, *Plutarch Alexander* (Oxford, 1969) : 16-20. A.-H. CHROUST, *Aristotle* (London, 1973) : 125-132, denied that there was any association.

2. F. SCHACHERMEYR, *Alexander der Grosse : das Problem seiner Persönlichkeit und seines Wirkens* (Sb. Oesterreich. Akad. d. Wiss. 285 : Vienna, 1973) : 81-93, esp. 87-9, an exposition largely unchanged from his *Alexander der Grosse : Ingenium and Macht* (Graz, 1949) : 66-77.

3. Plut. *Al.* 7.5. Cf. P. MERLAN, « Isocrates, Aristotle and Alexander the Great » *Historia*, 3 (1954) : 60-81, esp. 73-4 ; HAMILTON (above, n.1) : 17-18.

4. So SCHACHERMEYR (88, n. 70) admitted with outraged passion, responding to HAMILTON's characterisation of his account as « rather speculative » (HAMILTON [above, n. 1], 18) and demanding whether we should abjure rational thought whenever we do not run nose first upon explicit textual evidence. « Dann lebe wohl, du arme Altertumswissenschaft, denn du sinkst erneut in Scholastik ! ».

5. Diog. Laert. 5.51. There is no hint that these maps were an inheritance from Aristotle. One could argue that they were the response to Alexander's conquests, representing the new discoveries.

Athens, Aden, Arikamedu
New Delhi, 1994
A.B. BOSWORTH, p. 27 - 44

Alexander. However, Schachermeyr's picture despite its rococo excrescences has some intrinsic plausibility. World geography, particularly the geography of the Persian empire, ought to have been a subject of intense discussion at Mieza, particularly on the eve of the proclamation of Philip's war of revenge,[6] and that discussion presumably generated expectations in the minds of Alexander and his staff. They acquired a world view which affected their strategic planning and which they constantly tested against the body of empirical fact as it accrued during the campaign. The problem is to delineate Aristotle's contribution and find traces of its impact in the historical tradition of Alexander's reign.

Geography does not bulk large in the extants works of Aristotle. It is practically confined to two passages in the *Meteorologica*, which certainly assumed its final shape in the late 340s B.C. and contains at least one abstruse fact of Macedonian topography (an acid spring in Lyncestis) which presumably derives from his stay at Philip's court.[7] The most important passage for our purposes is an illustration of the general principle that the largest rivers spring from the greatest mountain ranges. Aristotle here refers to the conventional gazetteers compiled, he alleges, from autopsy at first or second hand,[8] and he is clearly retailing material which he considered authoritative. One detail is rightly famous. The Hindu Kush, which Aristotle terms Parnassus (a Greek rendering of the Akkadian *Paruparaessana*), is the greatest watershed in Asia from which the greatest rivers flow, including the greatest of all, the Indus, and, among others, the Araxes, from which the Tanais (Don) branches and flows into Lake

6. Plut. *Al.* 5.1-2 (so *Mor.* 342 B-C) depicts the young Alexander quizzing a Persian embassy about routes and distances within the Empire. Whether the anecdote is true (so SCHACHERMEYR) or false (so TREVES), it shows that geographical curiosity was conventionally expected of Alexander even before his accession.

7. Arist. *Mete.* 2.359b17. Other internal references include 1.345a1 (dating by the archonship of Nicomachus, 341/40 B.C.) and 3.371a31 (burning of the temple of Artemis at Ephesus [356] in the recent past [καὶ νῦν ἐθεωροῦμεν]. For a very speculative late dating see JAEGER (above, n. 1) : 307, n. 1. What cannot be doubted (*pace* JAEGER) is that the *Meteorologica* reveals no knowledge of Alexander's conquests.

8. Arist. *Mete.* 1.350a16-19 : δῆλον δ' ἐστι τοῦτο θεωμένοις τὰς τῆς γῆς περιόδους. Ταῦτας γὰρ ἐκ τοῦ πυνθάνεσθαι παρ' ἑκάστων οὕτως ἀνέγραψαν, ὅσων μὴ συμβέβηκεν αὐτόπτας γενέσθαι τοὺς λέγοντας. The key word περίοδοι cannot be translated « maps » (as at *Mete.* 2.362b12). The wording used refers best to written descriptions, as found in the standard *periodoi* (cf. *Pol.* 2.1262a18-21 ; *Rhet.* 1.1360a33-5, where *periodoi* are the source of anthropological material), the most famous of which was probably Eudoxus' (cf. Plut. *Mor.* 1093 C ; the numerous extant fragments are most conveniently consulted in F. LASSERRE, *Die Fragmente des Eudoxos von Knidos* [Berlin, 1966] : 96-127).

Maeotis.[9] Aristotle's Araxes, it is agreed, is to be identified with the modern Syr-Darya, which rises in the Pamirs and discharges into the Aral Sea. Its banks marked the north-eastern limit of the Achaemenid empire, and Cyrus founded a frontier city there before crossing the river for his fateful campaign against the Massagetae.[10] Herodotus (1.202.3-4) had equated the river with the Caucasian Araxes (Araks), which he believed split into forty streams. One discharged into the Caspian while the rest lost themselves in stagnant lakes and marshland. There is no indication that Herodotus associated the river with the Hindu Kush or even with Bactria. The Araxes which Cyrus crossed is localised vaguely in the wastes east of the Caspian.[11]

Further illumination came in the course of the fourth century, thanks probably to the repeated campaigns fought by the Achaemenids against the Cadusii, who occupied the coastland of the Caspian south of the mouth of the Araxes.[12] Returning Greek mercenaries may have brought details of the actual course of the Araxes and reported that there were no subsidiary streams. But the river crossed by Cyrus was still named Araxes and it was still associated with a major river of the west, the Tanais (Don). Some authentic reports of the geography of Sogdiana had percolated to the west. It was confirmed that the local name of the Syr-Darya approximated to the Greek Araxes, and possibly it was also noted that the general word for « river » was something like *danu* (a common root word for water in Iranian and related languages).[13] The inference

9. Arist. *Mete.* 1.350a19-26, esp. 23-5 : ἐκ μὲν οὖν τούτου ῥέουσιν ἄλλοι τε ποταμοὶ καὶ ὁ Βάκτρος καὶ ὁ Χοάσπης καὶ ὁ 'Αράξης. τούτου δ' ὁ Τάναϊς ἀποσχίζεται μέρος ὢν εἰς τὴν Μαιῶτιν λίμνην. From the context it is clear that major rivers are at issue. The Bactrus can only be the Oxus ; the Choaspes, it seems, was a southern affluent of the Hindu Kush, probably to be identified with the Kabul river and its main tributary, the Swat/Panjkora (cf. Strab. 15.1.25 [697] ; Curt. 8.10.22 ; Sir A. STEIN, *Serindica* [Oxford, 1921], I. 2, n. 3). The Araxes must be the Syr-Darya (A. HERRMANN's denial of the equation [*RE*, IX, 1183] is singularly unconvincing).

10. Arr. 4.2.2 ; Curt. 7.6.16, 19-20 ; Strabo 11.11.4 (517) ; cf. E. BENVENISTE, « La ville de Cyreschata », *Journal Asiatique*, 324 (1943/5) : 163-6.

11. Cf. Hdt. 1.201, 204 (Massagetae located in a vast plain east of the Caspian), 205.2, 211.1-2. There is no reference to Bactria in the whole of Herodotus' account of the Massagetic campaign.

12. Campaigns are attested under Artaxerxes II (Diod. 15.8.5, 10.1 ; Nepos *Datames* 1.2) and Artaxerxes III (Diod. 17.6.1 ; Justin 10.3.3). The latter campaign, fought at the outset of Artaxerxes' reign (c. 359/8), must have employed a fair number of mercenaries.

13. Cf. A.B. BOSWORTH, *A Historical Commentary on Arrian's History of Alexander*, I (Oxford, 1980) : 379-380. G. HUXLEY, « Sogdian Tanais and Aristobulus », *BASP*, 22 (1985) : 117-21, argues that Tanais actually was a local name of the Syr-Darya and that Aristobulus (at Arr. 3.30.7) reported it as such. But Arrian's wording cannot be pressed to the conclusion that Aristobulus stated that the locals named the river « Orxantes» *as well as* Tanais (ὃν δὴ καὶ 'Ορξάντην..... καλεῖσθαι). Arrian elsewhere uses δὴ καί with a relative on some ten occasions, and in no case does it have the

was accordingly drawn that the eastern Araxes was in fact the same river as the western Don/Tanais. [14] Herodotus' forty arms were replaced by a single bifurcation ; one arm of the Araxes became the European Tanais while the other (probably) discharged into the Caspian.

Aristotle, as we have seen, adopted the revised scheme, and he may well have been foreshadowed by Callisthenes. Strabo reports that Callisthenes addressed the problem and to some degree followed Herodotus. [15] It was not a simple adaptation of Herodotus' account, for Strabo alleges that Herodotus made the Araxes the boundary between Bactria and the Sacae.[16] That, as we have observed, Herodotus never even suggests. The connection with Bactria is presumably Callisthenes' addition. Like Herodotus he used the name Araxes ; but he went further and stated that it formed the frontier of the Persian Empire to the north-east. Given Strabo's brevity and vagueness we cannot reconstruct the remainder of Callisthenes' account. He may have followed Herodotus completely, equating the Caucasian Araxes with the Syr-Darya[17] and adding that it was the boundary river of Bactria. Alternatively he may simply have stated that the frontier of Bactria followed the Araxes, perhaps adding that it was the river crossed by Cyrus when he attacked the Massagetae. That would have been enough for Strabo to infer that Callisthenes had adopted Herodotus' framework. All we can state with confidence is that Callisthenes used the name Araxes when

---

force of « also » (1.7.7, 14.6 ; 5.13.2, 18.3 ; 7.13.2, 20.9, 24.3 ; *Tact.* 4.4, 4.6 ; *Succ.* F 27 [Roos]) ; the καὶ appears to strengthen δή, meaning something like « in fact ». For Aristobulus the Syr-Darya was the Tanais, and he noted that the natives actually termed it « Orxantes ». Despite this flaw, HUXLEY's exposition, particularly the etymological discussion (119-120), is pertinent and informative.

14. Herodotus himself may have helped the equation by his note (1.201) that the Massagetae were alleged to be Scythian and faced the Issedones, whom he placed to the east of the European Scyths (4.25.2-27 ; cf. J.O. THOMSON, *History of Ancient Geography*, Cambridge, 194 : 62-4).

15. Strab. 11.14.13 (531) = *FgrH* 124 F 38. Cf. L. PEARSON, *The Lost Histories of Alexander the Great* (New York, 1960) : 49, n. 135 ; L. PRANDI, *Callistene. Uno storico tra Aristotele e i re macedoni* (Milan, 1985) : 89-91.

16. Φησὶ γὰρ ἐκ Ματιηνῶν αὐτὸν ῥέοντα εἰς τετταράκοντα ποταμοὺς σχίζεσθαι, μερίζειν δὲ Σκύθας καὶ Βακτριανούς. Καὶ Καλλισθένης δὲ ἠκολούθησεν αὐτῷ. JACOBY (*FGrH* II D. 430 ; X. 1699) observed that the Araxes is not a frontier river in Herodotus and that Callisthenes cannot have been copying Herodotus. PRANDI (above, n. 15) : 90-1, notes that Bactria and Scythia were not coterminous ; Sogdiana is omitted. However, Bactria could be used in an extended sense to include Sogdiana (cf. Arr. III.8.3, 21.1, where Bessus is described merely as satrap of the Bactrians, even though Sogdiana clearly fell within his command).

17. That is unlikely if he wrote during Alexander's campaigns. Strabo makes it clear that Medeius of Larisa was reasonably well informed about the lower course of the Araxes (*FGrH* 129 F 1 ; cf. PEARSON [above, n. 15] : 69) and did not share Herodotus' delusion.

he referred to the frontier of Bactria/Sogdiana and, in part at least, shared Aristotle's geographical conceptions. Callisthenes' observations cannot be placed in any specific context. The universal assumption that he mentioned the Araxes in his Alexander history is totally ungrounded.[18] His *Hellenica* impinged on Persian affairs, notably the abortive invasion of Egypt (374 B.C.),[19] and it could well have included a « gazetteer of Empire » which dealt in passing with the Bactrian frontier area and summarised the state of knowledge before Alexander's campaigns.

If Callisthenes' contribution is vague, the views of Alexander and his men are crystal clear. There is no doubt that they identified the Syr-Darya and the European Don.[20] They realised that the local name of the river did not exactly conform to the Greek Araxes and gave various approximations (Iaxartes was later approved by Eratosthenes and became canonical). But the standard name of the Syr-Darya in all the Alexander sources is Tanais. Alexander's men understood it to be the European Tanais, seizing on the abundance of silver fir, believed unique in Europe, as proof that they had reached the limits of Asia.[21] The Saka tribes north of the river are repeatedly described as « European » Scyths[22] and Alexander believed the Maeotis to be relatively close, even within reconnaissance range. It was a delusion encouraged by the locals. Aware of Alexander's passionate curiosity about Amazons, the Chorasmian king, Pharasmanes (whose realm lay due south of the Aral) claimed to have a common border with Colchis and hospitably offered to lead the king on a career of

---

18. Strabo gives no hint of the location of the material he resumes, and JACOBY (above, n. 16) can reach no conjectural conclusion regarding its position within the *Praxeis Alexandrou*. It is unlikely that the work continued as late as 329, when Alexander entered Bactria, and, if the reference to the Araxes came in an anticipatory digression, there is no reason to limit that digression to the Alexander history. On the other hand the *Hellenica*, written before Alexander's accession (*FGrH* 124 T 26), would naturally retain the older nomenclature of the Sogdian rivers, before Alexander's campaigns had canonised the Syr-Darya as the Tanais.

19. *FGrH* 124 F 12 ; see below, p. 38.

20. Explicitly stated by Plut. *Al.* 45.6, representing the river name as « Orexartes ». For the other variants see BOSWORTH (above, n. 13) : 378.

21. Strabo 11.7.4 (510) = Polycleitus, *FGrH* 128 F 7. Theophrastus (*HP* 4.4.1 ; cf. 1.3.3) associates ivy and silver fir as plants not found within Asia beyond five days' journey from the Syrian coast (AMIGUES' recent Budé rightly retains the MS reading ἐλατῆν at *HP* 4.4.1). The discovery of silver fir was in due course capped by the sighting of ivy growths north of the Syr-Darya (Curt. VII.9.15).

22. Arr.4.1.1, 15.1 ; Curt. 1.6.12 ; 8.1.7. According to Curtius Alexander's emissary received instructions « to inspect the Scythians who live above the Bosporus ». His later report may have helped disabuse the king of the geographical fantasy.

conquest down to the Black Sea.[23] He was supplying « information » and using it for his material advantage, much as later the Indian natives responded to Macedonian enquiries about Herodotus' giant gold-digging ants by bringing what they alleged were the skins of the insects into camp — and (no doubt) offering them for sale.[24]

Alexander himself seems to have become sceptical. By the end of his reign he had commissioned Heracleides to explore the Caspian to determine whether it was connected with the Black Sea or simply a gulf of the circumambient Ocean (Arr. 7.16.1-2). The first alternative had been suggested by Polycleitus of Larisa, in the entourage of Alexander[25] and was a variant of Aristotle's theory of the link between the Don and the Syr-Darya. The second, however, was totally incompatible with it. If the Caspian was a gulf of Ocean there could be no east-west river connection. The fact that Alexander was grappling with such conflicting theories suggests strongly that he had garnered information which shed doubt on the equation of the Don and Syr-Darya.[26] Now he was conducting an experiment which could have determined its truth or falsehood for all time. It looks as though he had entered the great satrapy of Bactria/Sogdiana with fixed geographical expectations which were gradually undermined by experiences in the field. The geographical theory was inevitably modified in the light of pragmatic observation.

In the case of the Syr-Darya/Don equation Alexander clearly had accepted the geographical framework propounded by Aristotle's in the *Meteorologica*. We cannot prove Aristotle's direct influence. It could be argued that the equation was common currency in the latter part of the fourth century and that it could have been accepted among Alexander's staff irrespective of any teaching by Aristotle. The geography of India, however, permits us to refine the picture.

---

23. Arr. 4.15.4. On this passage see now A.B. BOSWORTH, *From Arrian to Alexander* (Oxford, 1988) : 66-7.

24. Strabo 15.1.44 (705) ; Arr. *Ind.* 15.4 (= *FGrH* 133 F 8). For the remarkable history of this fantasy, in which modern commentators have surpassed the ancients in credulity, see K. KARTTUNEN, *India in Greek Literature* (Helsinki, 1989) : 171-6.

25. Strabo 11.7.4 (510) = *FGrH* 128 F 7. For discussion see J.R. HAMILTON, « Alexander and the Aral », *CQ*, 21 (1971) : 106-11. Polycleitus seems to have been dealing with local reports that the Tanais flowed into an inland sea, which the Macedonians were led to identify with the Caspian. If that was true and the Tanais was the European Don, then the only conclusion was that the Caspian in its upper reaches was identical with the Sea of Azov (Maeotis). The major premise was that the Syr-Darya and Don were the same river, and that entailed the conclusion that the Caspian and Maeotis were identical.

26. The abundance of silver fir later discovered in Sogdiana far to the south of the Syr-Darya (Arr. 4.21.3 : winter 328/7) may have evoked doubts, as would its appearance in the forests north of the Punjab (Diod. 17.89.4 ; Strabo 15.1.29 [698]) ; and for silver fir the civilising influence of Dionysus could not be invoked, as it was for the appearance of ivy in India.

Aristotle presumably had views on the geography, ethnography and natural history of India, but it is unlikely that they bulked large in the curriculum at Mieza. In the extant works of the philosopher India appears rarely. It is an area of proverbial remoteness, as far from practical reality, the material under our control, as is the squaring of the circle ;[27] and much of the zoological data compiled in the *Historia Animalium* is acknowledged fantasy from the pages of Ctesias. Admittedly Aristotle is well informed about the characteristics of the Indian elephant,[28] but it is dubious whether his information comes from India. The elephant stables of the Persian king were close enough to satisfy the empirical curiosity of Greek tourists,[29] and it can be plausibly argued that our texts of the *Historia Animalium* (particularly the latter books) contain early reports from Alexander's campaigns.[30] Aristotle can have imparted little information about India. However, it can be argued that geographical theory obtained from Aristotle influenced Alexander's thinking in India, and in particular that the perennial debate about the flooding of the Nile had an immediate impact on Macedonian views of the course of the Indus. For most of this material our primary source is Nearchus of Crete, Alexander's admiral and boyhood friend. He belonged to the select group of Alexander's intimates which was exiled by Philip during the dynastic convulsions of his final years,[31] and there can be no doubt that he had the benefit of Aristotle's instruction along with his royal patron. If, then, Aristotle's influence can be traced in the extant fragments of Nearchus, it can elicit little surprise.

---

27. Arist. *EE* 2.1226a28-30 ; *MM* 1.1189a20-22.

28. The passages are usefully assembled (with comment) by H.H. SCULLARD, *The Elephant in the Greek and Roman World* (London, 1974) : 37-52. Cf. J.S. ROMM, « Aristotle's elephant and the myth of Alexander's scientific patronage », *AJP*, 110 (1989) : 566-75, arguing that Aristotle's observations refer primarily to the African elephant.

29. The elephants which participated at Gaugamela may have been summoned specially for the campaign (Arr. 3.8.6, cf. 11.6, 15.6), but it is hardly likely that these were the first beasts to have been used in Persian armies. Curtius (5.2.10) attests that there were reserves at Susa, and there was presumably accommodation for them there.

30. In particular the use of tame elephants to break wild ones (*HA* 9.610a25-33) is reminiscent of (but not identical to) Megasthenes' famous description (*FGrH* 715 F 20 ; cf. BOSWORTH [above, n. 23] : 43-5). Aristotle's informant may have witnessed Alexander's elephant hunt by the Indus (Arr. 4.30.8). It is also significant that for one detail (exceptional consumption of food and water), Aristotle gives measurements in Macedonian units (*HA* 7.596a3-9), which again suggests an eye-witness report (cf. P. BERNARD, « Le monnayage d'Eudamos », in *Orientalia Iosephi Tucci Memoriae Dicata* [ed. G. Gnoli & L. Lanciotti, Rome, 1985] : 93-4).

31. Arr. 3.6.5 ; Plut. *Al.* 10.4. Cf. H. BERVE, *Das Alexanderreich auf prosopographischer Grunglage*, II (Munich, 1926) : 269, n° 544 ; G. WIRTH, *Studien zur Alexandergeschichte* (Darmstadt, 1985) : 53-4.

According to Nearchus Alexander was for a short time convinced that the Indus and Nile were interconnected in the same way that Aristotle had represented the Syr-Darya and Don. His discussion is independently digested by Strabo and Arrian and can be reconstructed in some detail.[32] It deals with the river fleet which Alexander had originally commissioned in the summer of 326, in the aftermath of the battle of the Hydaspes. The king, states Nearchus, was eager to explore the course of the Indus. He had already confirmed the report of Herodotus that crocodiles were found in the Indus as well as the Nile.[33] This observation was strengthened when he crossed the Acesines (Chenab) at the time of the summer solstice and discovered stands of the Egyptian bean on its banks. Alexander was convinced of a connection between the Nile and Indus and believed that he had discovered the sources of the Nile. The river fleet was to establish the truth of the theory. This is on the surface a bizarre story, but there is no doubt that Nearchus retailed it as sober fact. Alexander clearly believed in an interconnection between the great rivers. What, we may ask, inspired him to make the inference, and why was he so convinced by proofs which Arrian justly terms weak and insubstantial ?[34]

The lesser question is the more easily answered. According to Nearchus the crucial find was the growths of the Egyptian bean. Now the Egyptian bean, as the Greeks called it, was the sacred lotus (*nelumbo nucifera* or *nelumbo speciosa*), a tall river plant rising up to two metres above the water with characteristic pink or rose-coloured flowers. What the Greeks called beans are its edible seeds, « differing only in size and taste from the bean as we know it ».[35] Theophrastus gave a careful description,[36] and, as we shall see, the plant was almost certainly familiar to Aristotle. For Greeks of the fourth century it was pre-eminently associated with the Nile, and Herodotus had carefully described it as quite distinct from the white and blue lotuses of the Nile.[37] But

---

32. Strabo 15.1.25 (696) ; Arr. 6.1.2-6 (*FGrH* 133 F 20). From Arrian's account it seems that Nearchus placed his discussion in the context of the commissioning of the Indus fleet, whereas in Strabo the passage is placed in a general discussion of analogies between the Nile and Indus. This grouping is likely to be Strabo's own rather than reflect the original arrangement in Nearchus (cf. BOSWORTH [above, n. 23] : 41-2). Arrian probably preserves the proper context.

33. Hdt. 4.44.1. Aristobulus also reported the appearance of a few innocuous crocodiles in the Indus (*FGrH* 139 F 38).

34. Arr. 6.1.4 μικροῖς δή τισι καὶ φαύλοις ὑπὲρ τῶν τηλικούτων τεκμαιρόμενον.

35. So Strabo 17.1.15 (799). Strabo comments on the density of the plant, which gave shade to water-borne picnic parties, and its leaves supported a flourishing bowl manufacture at Alexandria.

36. Theophr. *HP* 4.8.8. Cf. S. AMIGUES, « Phytonomes grecs et morphologie végétale », *JS*, 1984 : 172-3 with fig. 13, and pp. 266-7 of her Budé edition.

37. Hdt. 2.92.4. Cf. A.B. LLOYD, *Herodotus Book II* (Leiden, 1976) : 372-5.

the sacred lotus was an intruder in Egypt, never appearing in any landscape of the native kingdom. In all probability it was introduced from India under Persian auspices around 500 B.C.[38] and, like so many introduced species, entrenched itself indelibly upon the landscape. By Alexander's day its Indian origins, if they had ever been known, were long forgotten. But why did its appearance at the Acesines make such an impression upon him ? The answer may be provided by Theophrastus, who mentioned unsuccessful attempts to cultivate the plant outside Egypt. One stand of sacred lotus, however, did mature and bear fruit —in a lake near Torone.[39] This was obviously a familiar local curiosity, particularly familiar, one might think, to Aristotle. His native Stageira lay within easy visiting distance of Torone, and the *Historia Animalium* has three references which suggest that he was closely acquainted with the city.[40] Aristotle could well have informed his royal pupil about the rarity of the sacred lotus and its apparent uniqueness to Egypt. In that case the discovery of the sacred lotus on the Acesines in what was (unbeknown to Alexander) its natural habitat will have caused considerable interest. If he was predisposed to see a connection between the Indus and the Nile, it is not surprising that it confirmed him in his convinction.

Why should Alexander have been inclined to make the connection ? For elucidation we must turn to an obscure and tantalising work, the Aristotelian treatise on the flooding of the Nile.[41] It survives in the barbarous Latin

38. Representations of the Indian lotus are first found in the Graeco-Roman period and continue till the Christian era. Herodotus in fact appears to provide the first evidence. Cf. STEIER, *RE* XIII : 1517-18 ; LLOYD (above, n. 37) : 372. The Persian influence is conjectural but plausible. The interest of Persian kings (and Darius I in particular) in transplanting trees and crops is well known (cf. MEIGGS/LEWIS : 12 for Darius' encouragement of the cultivation of the plants of Syria in western Asia Minor), and the Indian lotus could well have been introduced to Egypt after the annexation of the Indus valley.

39. Theophr. *HP* 4.8.8 (it ripens and bears mature fruit in a modest lake near Torone). The plants must have been notorious. When a similar growth appeared in Epirus (c. 260 B.C.) it generated such curiosity that a royal guard was installed to protect it — after which it failed to reach maturity (Phylarchus, *FGrH* 81 F 65).

40. Arist. *HA* 3.523a7 ; 4.530b10 ; 5.548b14-15.

41. Edited and translated by D. BONNEAU, « Liber Aristotelis de inundatione Nili », *Études de Papyrologie*, 9 (1971) : 1-33. The most accessible text is provided by JACOBY, *FGrH* 646 F 1. Most scholars opt for the conclusion that the work is in some sense derived from a genuine treatise of Aristotle (so BONNEAU, following J. PARTSCH, « Das Aristoteles Buch "Uber das Steigen des Nil" », *Abh. Leipzig*, 27 (1909) : 554-600 ; JAEGER [above, n. 1] : 331 n. 2, and, more recently, S. BURSTEIN, « Alexander, Callisthenes and the sources of the Nile », *GRBS*, 17 [1976] : 135-46). The main sceptic has been JACOBY. Undecided but inclined to disbelief in 1910 (*RE* X. 1688-9), he had hardened into rejection by 1958, when in *FGrH* 646 he labelled the work « Pseudo-Aristoteles » and dated it around 125-100 B.C.

translation of the thirteenth century A.D., and presents a critical review of explanations of the Nile flood propounded since the time of Thales. Whether this is an extract from or epitome of a genuine work of Aristotle must be reserved for discussion later. What matters for our purpose is that it is a critical compilation of views current in the fourth century B.C. and deals with a subject Aristotle is known to have addressed. One particularly curious detail concerns the Red Sea, which (it is claimed) could be an enclosed body of water. In that case the Nile might possibly run to the south and join the Indus. Indeed the Persian king, Artaxerxes III Ochus, twice made inquiries.[42] The appearance of crocodiles in the Indus inspired him to take soundings about its course. On learning that it discharged into the southern Ocean he subsequently investigated a second river which rose from the same watershed as the Indus and allegedly flowed south of the Ocean.[43] This material is wretchedly transmitted and the names are deeply corrupt, but it preserves a tradition of speculation. The Nile may have been connected to the Indus, in which case the monsoonal summer rains of India were responsible for the flooding of the Nile in Egypt. Whether Artaxerxes Ochus ever contemplated diverting the Indus, as the treatise claims, is more than dubious,[44] but at least there was a tradition which accredited him with such a project — reminiscent of Herodotus' report of Cyrus' punishment of the River Gyndes (Hdt. 1.189.2-190.1). Persian kings, it was thought, had a short way with rivers. However, underlying the story is a conviction that it was possible that the Indus and Nile could be interconnected. Alexander was clearly aware of the possibility and for a few heady moments beside the Acesines he thought that he had proved the theory.

One serious objection can be formulated. Could Alexander possibly have been unaware of the voyage of Scylax of Caryanda, who was commissioned by Darius to sail down the Indus and along the coast of the Indian Ocean to and

---

42. *FGrH* 646 F 1.4 (BONNEAU : 4-5). The information is apparently unique and there is no possibility of testing its factual basis.

43. *Hunc autem dicebant habere crocodillos et circumfluere exterius Rubrum Mare* (F 1.4 = BONNEAU : 4).

44. SCHACHERMEYR (above, n. 2), 446 n. 540 accepted that Ochus actually believed in the possibility of a Nile-Indus connection, but he did not address the story of Ochus' grandiose plan to divert the Indus and drain the Nile. That can surely never have been a serious project. On the other hand, given the tradition of Ochus' megalomania and near madness (Cf. Deinon, *FGrH* 690 F 21), it is not impossible that Greeks of Aristotle's day considered him capable to such a plan, which would have destroyed the country he aspired to conquer (*maiorem destruit regionem quam accipit*).

beyond the Persian Gulf ?[45] Aristotle knew and cited Scylax's work,[46] and it is grossly implausible that it was unknown among Alexander's staff. Two explanations suggest themselves, by no means mutually exclusive. In the first place Scylax may have been somewhat discredited, tarnished by the reputation for fiction which accrued to the early writers on India.[47] His report may have been discounted. Secondly, even if Scylax was accepted, all he had apparently done was elicit that one mouth of the Indus impinged on the southern Ocean. It was possible that the Indus threw off a second branch, as the Syr-Darya was thought to do, and diverged to the east and south of the great inland sea which the Indian Ocean was conceived to be. That explains the detailed report Nearchus gave of the topographical information that Alexander obtained. Not merely the Indus but all the Indian rivers discharged into the ocean.[48] There was no possibility of any offshoot encircling the sea to the south. Empirical observation in this case definitively refuted the intellectual construct. All waters comprising the Indus ended in the southern Ocean. No connection with the Nile could now be envisaged.

If the Indus did not provide the answer to the origins of the Nile, it suggested a solution to the problem of its flooding. Nearchus had the mixed pleasure of experiencing the monsoon rains in the Punjab during the summer of 326, and in particular witnessed the flooding of the Acesines about the time of the solstice.[49] That confirmed a solution to the age-old dilemma of the Nile floods. In India, in a proverbially hot climate, there was prolonged summer rainfall and general flooding, so that one could reasonably posit analogous

---

45. Hdt. 4.44.1-2. For other testimonia and fragments see JACOBY, *FGrH* 709. P.A. BRUNT in his Loeb edition of Arrian (I. 546, II. 520-1) has argued that Alexander's staff had no knowledge of Scylax precisely because of their apparent ignorance of the lower Indus.

46. Arist. *Pol.* 7.1332b23-5 = *FGrH* 709 F 5 (superiority of Indian rulers over their subjects). BRUNT (see above) is right to be sceptical that Alexander « took geographical lessons [...] about a land he probably never then thought of entering », but it is stretching credulity to assume that *nobody* on Alexander's staff had knowledge of Scylax.

47. On the fantastic nature of much of Scylax's material see Philostr. VA 3.4 (= FGrH 709 F 7). The meagre harvest of citations in JACOBY suggests that his influence, particularly on fourth century thinking, was small (Cf. SCHACHERMEYR [above, n. 2] : 443-6, with n. 540).

48. Strabo 15.1.25 (696) :'Ὠκεανὸς μὲν πρῶτον, εἰς ὃν ἐκδιδόασιν οἱ 'Ινδικοὶ πάντες ποταμοί. Arrian (6.1.5) is not so explicit, but he claims that Alexander elicited (a) that all tributaries of the Indus coalesced in a single stream and (b) that there were only two outlets, both into the Ocean.

49. Strabo 15.1.18 (692) = *FGrH* 133 F 18 ; cf. Arr. *Ind.* 6.3 ; *Anab.* 5.20.8-9 (= Ptolemy, *FGrH* 138 F 22).

conditions in Ethiopia.[50] Summer rains could be expected there if they also occurred in India. Once again we have the echoes of Aristotelian doctrine. It is clear that Aristotle nailed his colours fast to the mast and declared himself firmly in favour of the theory of summer rainfall in Ethiopia. According to Poseidonius the theory went back to Thrasyalces of Thasos and was disseminated by Callisthenes under the influence of Aristotle.[51] This passage of Poseidonius was adopted by Seneca in a lost section of *Naturales Quaestiones* and reproduced by John the Lydian.[52] It has been sadly garbled in transmission. John alleges that Callisthenes himself gave eye-witness reports of the rains in Ethiopia ; he actually viewed the phenomenon while he was with Alexander. That is a total travesty. In the first place there is hardly time for Callisthenes to have been dispatched on a fact-finding mission up the Nile on what must have been a year-long expedition (if he witnessed the summer rains of 331),[53] catch up with the rapidly moving entourage of Alexander and write the definitive propagandist account of the reign down to at least the victory of Gaugamela. Nor could he have written up his report in Book IV of the *Hellenica*, as John states, unless it was a revision for a second edition produced after 331.[54] Callisthenes' expedition

---

50. Strabo 15.1.25 (696) = *FGrH* 133 F 20. The material is also excerpted by Arr. *Ind.* 6.6-7, where the inductive nature of the argument is emphasised (ἀπὸ τῶνδε ἔξεστι τεκμηριοῦσθαι... εἰκὸς [εἶναι] ὕεσθαι). Aristobulus was to continue the analogy and observe that there was no summer rain in the lower courses of the Nile between Meroe and the Thebaid and in the Indus below the Hydaspes (Strabo 15.1.19 [692-3] = *FGrH* 139 F 35). He may have been correct about the Nile (cf. BURSTEIN [above n. 41] : 41), but he is in error about the Indus, generalising from his experience in 325, when (unusually) no rain fell during the summer (Strabo 15.1.15 [691]). Autopsy in this instance provided misleading data.

51. Strabo 17.1.5 (790) = *FGrH* 87 F 79, 646 T 2 (b).

52. Lyd. *mens.* 4.107 (Wuensch) = *FGrH* 124 F 12 (a) : ὡς καὶ Καλλισθένης ὁ Περιπατητικὸς ἐν τῷ τετάρτῳ βιβλίῳ τῶν Ἑλληνικῶν φησιν ἑαυτὸν συστρατεύσασθαι Ἀλεξάνδρῳ τῷ Μακεδόνι, καὶ γενόμενον ἐπὶ τῆς Αἰθιοπίας εὑρεῖν τὸν Νεῖλον ἐξ ἀπείρων ὄμβρων κατ' ἐκείνην γενομένων καταφερόμενον. On the general accuracy of Lydus' reproduction of Seneca see BURSTEIN (above, n. 41) : 138 with the notes of P. OLTRAMARE in his Budé edition (1929) of the *Naturales Quaestiones* : 170-1.

53. The rains fell (as is universally attested) between the risings of Sirius and Arcturus (July to September). During that period in 331 Alexander was moving fast, and he continued to do so throughout 330. If Callisthenes was away in the Sudan during the latter part of 331, it is hardly possible that he rejoined the main army before 329. PRANDI's chronology (above, n. 15, 157) which gives him a four month absence and has him return in time for Gaugamela, would have him miss the summer rains, the very thing (Lydus alleges) he claims to have witnessed.

54. This was argued by PARTSCH (above, n. 41) : 584, n. 3, and restated by PRANDI (above, n. 15) : 157. But, as BURSTEIN (138) himself admits, the anonymous Florentine work on the flooding of the Nile (*FGrH* 647 F 1.3) also cites Callisthenes' account of the Nile floods and gives the theory of the summer rains simply as his

is a near absurdity, and indeed it is impossible to countenance any new discoveries in Alexander's reign. Otherwise Nearchus' approach to the problem is inexplicable. He works from inference, arguing that the flooding from the monsoonal rains in India shows that the same conditions could be obtained in Ethiopia. Had the rains at the source of the Nile been verified by an expedition commissioned by Alexander, inference was superfluous,[55] and there was no point in drawing an analogy from the rivers of the Punjab.

Nearchus was clearly out to confirm Aristotelian doctrine on the Nile floods. Callisthenes, we are told, used inductive reasoning to conclude that rains prevailed in Ethiopia between the risings of Sirius and Arcturus,[56] and, according to Poseidonius, he borrowed the argumentation from Aristotle himself, who in the *Meteorologica* linked together Ethiopia and Arabia as areas of high summer rainfall.[57] It seems that Aristotle's argumentation was theoretical. Eratosthenes mentioned the geographical discoveries of the early Ptolemaic period which established by autopsy the summer rainfall in Ethiopia and claimed that this recent information confirms the conclusion which had previously been obtained by conjecture.[58] In this context Aristotle is mentioned

---

gnome, without any suggestion of autopsy. PRANDI's argument (157) that this does not exclude additional eye-witness knowledge smacks of special pleading.

55. BURSTEIN (above, n. 41) : 138 n. 17 skirts around this fatal objection without addressing it explicitly. It is totally ignored by PRANDI.

56. See above, n. 54. According to the Florentine anonymous (*FGrH* 647 F 1.3) Callisthenes wrote in ignorance of the monsoonal winds from the Indian Ocean and inferred that the etesian winds from the Mediterranean drove an accumulating mass of rain clouds south to deposit their contents upon the Ethiopian mountains.

57. Strabo 17.1.5 (790) = *FGrH* 87 F 79 (παρὰ 'Αριστοτέλους λαβόντα) ; cf. Arist. *Met.* 1.349a5-9. Theophrastus (*CP* 3.3.3) was later to associate Ethiopia with India rather than Arabia and may well have modified Aristotle's theory in the light of Nearchus' discussion.

58. Strabo 17.1.5 (789) ; Proclus *in Tim.* 22 E (οὐδὲ ζητεῖν χρῆναι περὶ τῆς αὐξήσεως τοῦ Νείλου, σαφῶς καὶ ἀφικομένων τινῶν εἰς τὰς τοῦ Νείλου πηγὰς καὶ τοὺς ὄμβρους γιγνομένους ἑωρακότων ὥστε κρατύνεσθαι τὴν 'Αριστοτέλους ἀπόδοσιν). Despite the interpretation of the last clause which has recently been propounded by BURSTEIN (above, n. 41 : 142, following PRÉAUX) and PRANDI (above, n. 15 : 154), it seems to me that the ὥστε clause can only be understood in a consecutive sense : « some people reached the sources of the Nile and observed the existence of the rains, so as to confirm the explanation of Aristotle ». A purposive interpretation « in order to confirm » is most implausible and weakened by the parallel passage of Strabo which is explicit that eye-witness knowledge of the Ethiopian rains first accrued in the Ptolemaic period. It is not beyond the realm of possibility that Alexander commissioned an expedition up the Nile (without Callisthenes' participation).
Curtius (4.8.3-4) alleges that Alexander considered a visit to Ethiopia in person but lacked the time for it. He *may* have sent others ; but apart from the suspect evidence of John the Lydian the only suggestion that he did comes from Lucan (*Phars.* 10.272-

by name ; the eye-witness reports confirm his (theoretical) explanation. That sheds considerable doubt upon the authenticity of the Aristotelian treatise on the flooding of the Nile, which echoes Eratosthenes in claiming that there was no longer a problem and that eye-witness reports were available confirming the summer rains in Ethiopia between Sirius and Arcturus.[59] It might conceivably be an over-optimistic reaction by Aristotle to reports from travellers who had penetrated south of Egypt, perhaps mercenaries in the service of the last Pharaoh, Nectanebos II, who fled with him to Nubia[60] and in time returned to the Greek world (after 340). Such reports may not have reached Macedon before Philip's death, and they could have been eventually discounted through lack of corroboration. In that case Nearchus will have absorbed Aristotelian doctrine at an earlier point when the master relied on induction alone. But the evidence of Eratosthenes suggests that Aristotle never within his knowledge claimed anything other than inferential support for his theory, and the more prudent course would be to deny the authenticity of the treatise.

The influence of Aristotle is by now undeniable. It can be traced further in Nearchus' discussion of the alluvial plain of the Indus, which is again excerpted by Arrian and Strabo.[61] Nearchus gives us another argument from analogy. The plainland of the Indus is compared with that of the Nile and the four major rivers of western Asia Minor. All were the creation of their rivers and were appropriately named after their creators. Their names symbolised their origins. In this argument Nearchus deploys familiar material. Herodotus had discussed the alluvial nature of the rivers of Asia Minor and compared them with the Nile.[62] His exposition was adapted and refined by Nearchus, and brought to bear upon the question of the Indian plain. For the origins of Egypt Nearchus appealed to the most traditional of authorities, Homer. Homer had repeatedly referred to the Nile as the river Aegyptus — proof, Nearchus claimed, that the country was named after its river. Now the line Nearchus chose to quote (*Od.* 4.581) was famous in scientific literature. It was adduced by both Eudoxus and

---

5), who notes that Alexander dispatched chosen explorers to Ethiopia. Driven back by the heat, they merely saw the Nile evaporating (*calentem*). Whether any genuine historical information underlies this statement may be justly doubted. Even if it does, Lucan's expedition did *not* witness the Ethiopian rains, and Nearchus is surely unimpeachable evidence that Alexander's men had no eye-witness knowledge of them.

59. Phot. *Bibl.* 249.441b2-12 ; *FGrH* 646 F 1.10 (BONNEAU [above, n. 41] : 7, § 12).

60. Diod. 16.51.1. Since Nectanebos took the majority of his treasure with him, it is hardly likely that he dispensed with an escort — and he is accredited with 20,000 Greek mercenaries (Diod. 16.47.6).

61. Arr. 5.6.3-7 ; Strabo 15.1.16 (691) = *FGrH* 133 F 17.

62. Hdt. 2.10. The passage is also used by Pliny, *NH* 2.201, but in connection with the alluvial plain of the Nile. It was Nearchus' innovation, it seems, to use the Herodotean examples to explain the origins of the Indus plain.

Aristotle in their proofs that the Nile flooded as a result of summer rainfall[63] It was not the name that attracted their attention but the epithet διιπετής, which Homer used of the river. It was rendered « rain-fed » and used as evidence that the flooding originated from precipitation. Nearchus on the other hand based his argument on Homer's name for the river. He was presumably aware of the importance of the line in the Nile debate and adduced it for a different purpose, to prove the alluvial origins of the Indus plain.

The use of Herodotus may equally have been inspired by Aristotle. There is a comparable passage of the *Meteorologica* (1.351b28-352a8), which argues that the Egyptian plain was created by progressive silting and uses material from both Homer and Herodotus. Aristotle makes much of Homer's failure to mention Memphis as a place of importance, and he evidently draws upon Herodotus. Like Herodotus he whimsically maintains that Lower Egypt did not exist in Homer's time,[64] and he exploits Herodotus' statement that the old name of Egypt was Thebes.[65] The use of Herodotus was probably an example to Nearchus, as was the general method of combining inductive reasoning with citations of approved authorities. Aristotle's argumentation on the origins of the Egyptian plain was applied to a comparable problem, and evidence previously adduced in the context of the Nile was adapted to the Indus. This is not regurgitation of rote learning, but judicious application of acquired knowledge to new material.

Nearchus, then, had been imbued with the doctrine of his master. Even if Alexander had not been so deeply affected, Nearchus was in his close entourage and (after Callisthenes' death) could remind him of the geographical lessons of his youth. Others could doubtless do the same. In that case we may address the perennial problem of Alexander's ambitions in India with somewhat more confidence. When he reviews received opinion in his *Meteorologica*, Aristotle alludes to the remarkable proximity of the Parnassus (Hindu Kush) range to the Ocean. When one has crossed it, he avers, the outer sea appears to view.[66] Aristotle is clearly referring to the eastern ocean, for he notes the fact that the Indus is the largest of all rivers and could not believe that the Indian ocean at its mouth was in any sense close to the range in which the river rises. In his view

63. Arr. 5.6.5. For the use of the Homeric quotation by Aristotle and Eudoxus see Schol. *Od* 4.477 (LASSERRE [above, n. 8] : 100, F 287). Poseidonius (*FGrH* 87 F 79) also took the argument back to Homer via Aristotle, Callisthenes and Thrasyalces of Thasos.

64. Arist. *Mete.* 1.351b25. Herodotus (2.10) had argued that the land north of Memphis was once a gulf of the Mediterranean.

65. Hdt. 2.15.3 (τὸ δ' ὦν πάλαι αἱ Θῆβαι Αἴγυπτος ἐκαλέετο). Aristotle (*Mete.* 351b34-5) reproduces Herodotus' wording and though he does not quote him directly, he must surely be aware of his discussion. Aristotle in effect accepts Herodotus' archaeology of the Nile valley and buttresses it with additional inductive arguments.

66. Arist. *Mete.* 1.350a19-23 : ὑπερβάντι γὰρ ἤδη τοῦτο φαίνεται ἡ ἔξω θάλαττα.

the Indus valley was close to the outer ocean, and in that case he can have known nothing of the Ganges river system. That was probably Alexander's view when he entered India, and it appears that he still held it in the immediate aftermath of the battle of the Hydaspes. Then he had commissioned the building of his Indus fleet to explore the course of the river. A note in the vulgate tradition, common to Curtius, Diodorus and the *Metz Epitome*, has it that Alexander intended to use the fleet to sail down to the Ocean and planned to do so after he had returned from the eastern boundary of India and the outer ocean.[67] There is no doubt about the chronology of the order to construct the fleet. Diodorus (17.89.4) mentions the cutting of timber in the forests north of the Hydaspes plain and does so immediately after the battle, while Strabo gives a vivid description of an encounter with baboons in that forest and states that Taxiles was personally present.[68] Taxiles, it is attested, returned to his domains shortly after the battle and before Alexander moved on to the Acesines ; and he was clearly present when the first timber for the fleet was felled. Alexander may already have gone on reconnaissance to the Acesines, made his sensational discovery of the Egyptian bean and commissioned the fleet in the flush of experimental fervour. Alternatively he could have intended the fleet for a voyage to the Ocean from the very start and modified his plans to take account of the Nile-Indus link.

The sources state explicitly that the Indus voyage was a secondary objective, to take place after the penetration of India to its eastern limits. Alexander still believed that the ocean was relatively close and that he could overrun the territory to the east in a relatively short time. To what extent he retained that conviction is impossible to determine. Both Arrian and Curtius represent him at the Hyphasis arguing that the Ganges and eastern sea were not far removed,[69] and they *may* be drawing upon an authentic tradition. If so it is a meagre grain of fact in a stubble of imaginative rhetoric, and a theme Alexander will have used to cajole his weary troops whether or not he believed what he said. What seems undeniable is that Alexander received reports of the eastern lands in increasing detail as he moved towards the Hyphasis. Arrian's sources reported rich country and populous nations beyond the river, while the vulgate

---

67. Diod. 17.89.4-5 ; Curt. 9.1.3-4 ; *Metz Ep*. 63. On this tradition the best discussion remains that of SCHACHERMEYR, « Alexander und die Ganges-Länder », *Innsbrücker Beitr. zur Kulturgeschichte*, 3 (1955) : 123-35 = G.T. Griffith (ed.), *Alexander the Great : the Main Problems* (Cambridge, 1966) : 137-49 (esp. 140-2). See also his *Alexander der Grosse* (above, n. 2) : 429.

68. Strabo 15.1.29 (699) : the incident is explicitly located in the Emodi mountains, where Alexander had his ships' timber felled. For Taxiles' return shortly after the battle of the Hydaspes see Arr. 5.20.4 with BERVE (above, n. 31), II. 371, n° 739.

69. Arr. 5.26.1 ; Curt. 9.2.26. On the dubious nature of this tradition see D. KIENAST, « Alexander und der Ganges », *Historia*, 14 (1965) : 180-8, esp. 181-2 ; BOSWORTH (above, n. 23) : 124-33.

tradition states that he was given detailed (and somewhat inaccurate) information about the Thar desert, the river Ganges and the heartland of the Nanda monarchs around Patna.[70] Whether precise or accurate distances were given is dubious, but it is clear that as local information accrued the eastern ocean receded. It was not proved a chimera like the Nile-Indus connection, and Alexander's appetite for conquest was not blunted by the increasing distances. Arrian (5.24.8) can still remark that there was no term for him until there was nothing left to conquer. It was his men who jibbed at crossing yet another river in monsoonal spate and pursuing an indefinitely receding ocean against the opposition of ever more formidable elephant armies. The geographical presuppositions had been fateful. They had engendered the idea of extending conquest to the outer ocean, and the ambition was not relinquished even when its factual underpinning was proved to be inadequate. The course of the Indus was a different matter. Its connection with the Nile was disproved, and Alexander had to abandon the plans predicated upon its existence. The eastern ocean remained a reality and a practical, if remote, objective.

We must conclude that current geographical theory had considerable, if indirect influence upon Alexander and his entourage. In this area of speculation Aristotle himself may have been little more than an intermediary, expounding the conventional views of Eudoxus and others. His own personal contribution was not large, and his thinking, even on the problem of the Nile floods, was not strikingly original. But he certainly provided a conceptual framework against which the raw data of exploration was interpreted. It was a framework rich of

70. Arr. 5.25.1 ; cf. Diod. 17.93.2-3 ; Curt. 9.2.2-7 ; *Metz Ep.* 68 (common tradition) ; Plut. *Al.* 61.1-3. KIENAST (above, n. 69) : 182-7 argues that the reports of the Ganges are a late accretion to the tradition, largely on account of the manifold discrepancies from Arrian's description of the land beyond the Hyphasis. However, Arrian's report is written from a perspective different from that of the vulgate. It concentrates upon the government of eastern India at city level, and emphasizes the size of the elephant armies which the Macedonians would encounter. The vulgate tradition, on the other hand, gives geographical background, including information about the Ganges, which Arrian omits. The omission hardly proves that Alexander received *no* detailed reports of the eastern river system. It might be conceded that his Indian hosts had some interest in minimising the eastward extension of India. If they were encouraging Alexander to expand his empire in their interest, it was sensible to confirm him in the impression that the Ocean was relatively close. The vulgate does indeed gloss over the fact that the capital of the eastern kingdom was more than 1,000 km from the district where Alexander would first impinge upon the Ganges (Diod. 93.2 ; Curt. 9.2.3). But, however vague and imprecise his information may have been, Alexander cannot have been unaware of the existence of the Ganges. At first he may have considered it close to the outer Ocean, but, once he turned back from the Hyphasis and it became prudent to assure him that his judgment had been correct, he probably obtained a more realistic picture of the length of the river and the remoteness of the Nanda capital.

delusion. Continents were viewed as narrowly separated, great river systems as interconnected, and in general the size of the physical world was minimised. The results of the expedition exploded a number of cherished hypotheses, now refuted by geographical fact, and the new material itself was subjected to inductive reasoning, as we can see from the speculations of Nearchus. The change in theoretical perspective was not always for the better. The exploration of the Caspian unleashed by Alexander and continued by Seleucus resulted in the firm conclusion that the Caspian was a gulf of ocean, and only in the second century A.D. did knowledge accrue to change the picture back to the earlier and accurate Aristotelian view that it was an inland sea.[71] However, the geographical results of the campaigns were dramatic, nowhere more strikingly than in the Greek conception of India, where for the first time authentic measurements and observations could be brought to bear. Alexander's reign is seen as the crucial dividing line, the moment when fantasy was ousted by autopsy. It is ironical that much of this autopsy came about through a geographical error, the supposed proximity of the eastern ocean. However, the irony may appear less gross in a year when we celebrate the quincentenary of another pursuit of an Aristotelian chimera, the belief that a narrow belt of ocean separated the Indian lands from the Pillars of Heracles.[72] A certain Genoese admiral followed unwittingly in the footsteps of Alexander the Great.

A. Brian BOSWORTH
University of Western Australia
Perth

---

71. Cf. A. HERRMANN, *RE* X. 2280 ; THOMSON (above, n. 14) : 127-9, 293-4 ; BOSWORTH (above, n. 23) : 30-1.

72. [Arist.] *Cael.* 2.298a10-15 ; cf. THOMSON (above, n. 14) : 119, 326-7.

ON THE SO-CALLED EARLIEST REPRESENTATION OF GAṆEŚA *

A Pakistani numismatist, Agha Inayat Ali Shah, published in 1955 a silver drachm issued in the name of the Indo-Greek Hermaios, and pretended that the Greek god Zeus on the reverse has been indianised by wearing an elephant trunk like the Hindu deity Gaṇeśa (1955, pp. 16-7). He further argued : « The symbolic representation of the enthroned Zeus as tutelary elephant-deity of Kapisa, like the square copper coin of Eukratides, furnishes local influence on foreign currency ». However, A.K. Narain apparently unaware of Agha Inayat Ali Shah's article and claiming the credit to be the first scholar to identify the earliest representation of Gaṇeśa, repeated, many years later, the same argument : « The Pi-lo-sho-lo mountain in Kapisi was so called after its presiding deity who had the Greek god Zeus of the Indo-Greeks and the elephant deity of the local population of a part of Afghanistan » (1978, pp. 142-144). [1] Narain then wrote a series of articles on the same subject, repeating more or less the same initial

---

* The subject of this paper has been presented in August 1992, first at the National Museum of New Delhi, at the Department of History and Culture, Rohilkand University, Bareilly, then at the Indian Coin Society, Bombay ; it was proposed to the Journal *Yavanika*, see O. Bopearachchi, 1992. Since then I have accumulated a number of numismatic data during my visits to Russia, England and U.S.A. which enabled me to take up the whole question in detail. I wish to extend my warmest thanks to Mr. Joe Cribb, Curator of South Asian Coins, Department of Coins and Medals, British Musem, to Dr. Michel Amandry, Director of the Cabinet des Médailles, Bibliothèque Nationale, to Dr. Carmen Arnold-Biucchi, Margaret Thompson Curator of Greek Coins, American Numismatic Society, to Uri Dukov, Curator of Greek Coins, State Hermitage Musem, to Fr. Widemann (CNRS) and to Mr. Harry Fowler, former President of the American Numismatic Society, who very kindly allowed me to reproduce certain coins.

1. This coin in the British Museum (see no 46) was donated in 1961 by A.D.H. Bivar (inv. no 1961. 3.2.1.).

Athens, Aden, Arikamedu
New Delhi, 1994
O. Bopearachchi, p. 45-74

arguments. [2] Since then scholars who dealt with this question gave a place of eminence to A.K. Narain, ignoring Agha Inayat Ali Shah who was the first to put forward this hypothesis.

Joe Cribb, in 1982, contested A.K. Narain's identification and showed that the photograph of the same coin, lit from a different angle gives a different picture (1982, pp. 30-32). He further argued that what Narain interpreted as the trunk of an elephant is a badly copied Zeus-Mithra's nose, beard and a fold in his gown. Curiously P.L. Gupta, in his editorial note to Cribb's paper, wrote : « Only photo-technician can provide us true answer. Only they can guide us about the light and angle for photographying coins to produce reliable and incontrovertible images », as if a problem of such importance can be solved by the verdict of a photo-technician, but not by historians of art and numismatists. A.K. Narain on several occasions repeated the same initial arguments until 1988, without making much of an attempt to answer the objections raised by J. Cribb. Three years later, A.K. Narain, in the collection of studies edited by R.L. Brown on the Hindu deity Gaṇeśa, without even referring to the objections raised by Cribb, talks about the so-called « elephant-headed » divinity on the Hermaios' coin as a well established fact (1991, pp. 19-48). To my surprise, R.L. Brown and M.K. Dhavalikar take A.K. Narain's identification very seriously into consideration. [3]

According to us, the hypothesis put forward by Agha Inayat Ali Shah and A.K. Narain is based on a mistaken identity. The aim of this paper is to develop further the arguments put forward by J. Cribb and to show that the coins in question with the so called « elephant-headed divinity » were not struck by the Greeks but by their nomadic successors, and to argue that the deity represented on this coin is Zeus-Mithra, and certainly not Gaṇeśa.

Firstly the coins on which Agha Inayat Ali Shah and A.K. Narain seemed to have identified the earliest representation of Gaṇeśa were not lifetime issues of Hermaios, but imitations issued by the nomads who occupied the Kabul Valley after the death of this Greek king. K. W. Dobbins clearly showed in 1970

2. A.K. NARAIN has first presented this idea in 1973, in his paper presented at the Paris session of the International Congress of Orientalists and in his presidential address at the Diamond Jubilee Conference of the Numismatic Society of India 1973 (*Journal of the Numismatic Society of India*, 1974, pp. 180-191). His initial article also appeared in 1982 (1982, pp. 26-29) and in 1984 (1984, pp. 9-14) [I shall not refer to this article since A.K. Narain considers it as an incomplete paper and forbids the using of it without his consent, *ibid.* p. 14] ; also in 1988 (1988, pp. 1007-1019), and in 1991 (1991, pp. 19-48).

3. See also M.K. DHAVALIKAR, 1990, pp. 38-46 ; and 1991, pp. 49-68). R.L. BROWN in his introduction to the above-mentioned volume on Gaṇeśa, does not take a firm standard on Narain's hypothesis, and avoids the discussion by saying : « Likewise some early artistic depictions of an elephant-headed therianthropomorphic figure, such as Narain's own first-century B.C. coin image, is while an incipient Ganeśa, not yet Gaṇeśa », 1991, p. 4.

that the coins of this group should be considered as posthumous issues (1970, pp. 307-326). Quoting K.W. Dobbins, J. Cribb correctly referred to these coins as posthumous issues of Hermaios (1982, pp. 30, n. 2). [4] Dobbins' hypothesis does not seem to have convinced A.K. Narain, because in his article (1978, pp. 142-144), these coins struck in the name of Hermaios are presented as lifetime issues. Curiously enough, even in 1991 A.K. Narain, in spite of Cribb's opposition, continues to talk about these coins as lifetime issues of Hermaios (1991, pp. 19-48). I wonder whether A.K. Narain is unaware of the importance of this hypothesis or if he purposely avoids the discussion which puts very seriously into question his reconstruction of Indo-Greek history.

The key to our understanding of the conquest of the Indo-Greek kingdoms, in the regions of the Paropamisadae and Gandhara, by the Yuezhi, who later came to be known as the Kushans, lies in the different coinages struck in the name of Hermaios. Hermaios was a contemporary of Archebios but in different territories, as is revealed by his monograms. While Archebios was ruling in West Panjab (Taxila ), Hermaios occupied the Paropamisadae (Alexandria of the Caucasus ) and the Gandhara (Charsadda ). [5] Although the kingdom of Archebios in the Indus valley centered on Taxila was taken over by a Scythian king named Maues, and the Greeks under the leadership of Apollodotos II were subsequently able to regain these lost territories for a short period, on the contrary after the death of Hermaios, the Greek power in the Paropamisadae and Gandhara came to an end.

The Yuezhi who invaded Bactria crossed a few years later the Hindu Kush mountains, the natural rampart which once protected the Mauryan empire from Greek expansion, and later the Indo-Greek kingdom from the nomad invasion, and conquered the Paropamisadae and Gandhara dethroning Hermaios. [6] They were no doubt the same nomads who, having conquered Bactria, copied the silver tetradrachms of Heliocles I, the last Greek king to rule north of the Hindu Kush. Having penetrated into the Paropamisadae, the same nomad conquerors began, as they were accustomed to, to imitate the coins of Hermaios, the last Greek king to rule in these regions. This is also revealed by the find spots of his coins, both lifetime and posthumous, found in large quantities in the Paropamisadae, Gandhara and the region of Gardez-Ghazni. On the basis of the total absence of coins of Maues and Azes I in the Paropamisadae and the abundance of coins minted in the name of Hermaios in the same region,

---

4. However, I learnt from J. Cribb that in his article the contradictory remark which follows the reference to Dobbin's article : « This is Dobbins' personal view and not acceptable to many scholars » was added, without the author's permission, by P.L. Gupta, the editor of the *Numismatic Digest*.

5. Regarding the attribution of these monograms to different geographical regions, see O. Bopearachchi, *BN*, pp. 84, 111, 116.

6. See O. Bopearachchi, 1990 b, pp. 93-103.

D.W. MacDowall (1985, pp. 555-566) correctly suggested that neither Maues nor Azes I ever occupied that region. In the Mir Zakah deposit, the lifetime and posthumous coins in the name of Hermaios alone or with that of his wife Calliope are represented by 928 coins, against only one coin of Maues (R. Curiel et D. Schlumberger, 1953, pp. 79 and 96). In the collection of J. Hackin gathered mainly in Begram and Peshawar and now in the Musée Guimet and the Cabinet des Médailles in Paris, not a single coin of Maues or of Azes I is attested. Furthermore out of 7000 coins collected by Ch. Masson (mostly in the region of Begram) during the years 1833, 1834 and 1835, none belonged to Azes I (1834, pp. 152-175 ; 1836, pp. 1-28 ; 1836 a, pp. 537-547). The total absence of Azes I's coins in the Paropamisadae is explained by the presence of imitations of Hermaios, minted in large number by the nomads who occupied that region for a long period. For these reasons A. K. Narain's hypothesis according to which Azes I conquered the Paropamisadae after the death of Hermaios c. 55 B.C. cannot be upheld anymore (1957, p. 162-164). The Greek power in the Paropamisadae and Gandhara came to an end with the penetration of the Yuezhi. This conquest may have taken place a few years after the time when Archebios lost his territories in the West Panjab to the Indo-Scythian Maues. It is very important to underline that the Taxila excavations did not yield any of the silver denominations of Hermaios. The 263 bronze coins in the name of Hermaios found in the excavations belong to later posthumous series. The absence of Hermaios' lifetime and of his very first posthumous issues in the Taxila excavations is counterbalanced by the presence of hundreds of coins of Maues and Azes I on this site.

The most difficult question here is to establish convincing criteria to differentiate the lifetime issues of Hermaios from the posthumous imitations. I have discussed this question in detail elsewhere and classified them into several groups on the basis of style, monograms, legends and metal. [7] I have no intention to discuss here once again all these groups, which were successively issued during nearly hundred years. I am mainly interested in the very first imitations minted by the nomads in the name of Hermaios.

All the coins of Hermaios characterized by a good style and workmanship and bearing the monograms : 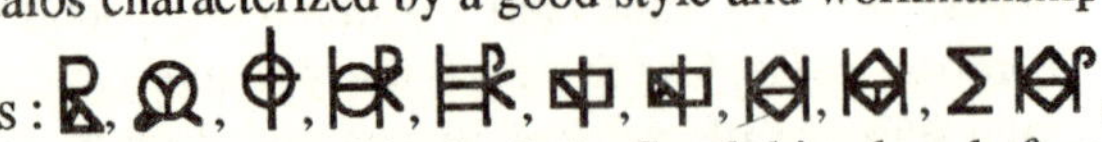 , frequently found on the coins that circulated in the Indo-Greek kingdom before him, belong to the first group. I consider them as the lifetime issues of Hermaios. There are several series that can be attributed to this group :

1. A first series, known today by three coins, consists of an Attic-standard monolingual tetradrachm, with a diademed bust of the king on the obverse and enthroned Zeus-Mithra on the reverse (see n° 20). [8]

7. O. Bopearachchi, *BN*, pp. 113-125.

8. O. Bopearachchi, 1990 b, p. 93, pl. 9, n° 20-21 ; *BN*, Hermaios, série 1.

2. The bilingual, Indian-standard tetradrachms and drachms bearing the same types belong to the second series (see n° 21). [9]

3. The third series has the same characteristics as the preceding one, except for the helmeted bust of the king on the obverse (see n° 22 and 23). [10]

4. On the fourth series, the bust of the king on the obverse is replaced by the mounted king on a horse prancing to right. The reverse types and both Greek and kharoshthi legends remain the same as on the two preceding ones. [11]

5. The fifth series is represented by three coins, one in the British Museum and two in the Cabinet des Médailles in Paris ; on these coins the mounted king is replaced by an amazon-queen on horseback on the obverse. On the reverse, the enthroned Zeus-Mithra, instead of making a gesture with his right hand, holds a scepter. [12]

6. We may also integrate the tetradrachms and drachms bearing the joint diademed busts of Hermaios and Calliope in the first group, in spite of the fact that both Greek and kharoshthi legends are in the name of Hermaios and Calliope (see n° 24). [13]

7. The last series of the lifetime issues is composed of bronze coins, with Zeus-Mithra on the obverse and a horse to right on the reverse (see n° 25-27). [14]

The coins bearing the following principal monograms ,  (see n° 28),  (see n° 29),  (see n° 30), ,  (see n° 31),  (n° 32-54), , 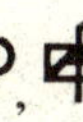, , 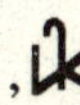, 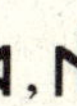, , 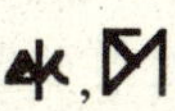, , , 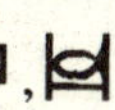, 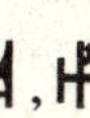,  belong to the first series of imitations of Hermaios. [15] These posthumous imitations of Hermaios are characterized by a stereotyped portrait of the king whose hair is represented by parallel streaks (see n° 28-48).

I have proposed this classification in my catalogue published by the Bibliothèque Nationale (*BN*, pp. 112-125), on the basis of style, monograms, legends and metal, judging only from the external appearance of the patina. Now I am in a position to justify further this sequence thanks to the results obtained from the neutron activation analysis carried out by J.N. Barrandon in Orléans, on several specimens belonging to the coins issued in the name of Hermaios. This

---

9. *BN*, Hermaios, séries 2-3. Since MITCHINER's arrangement of coins in the name of Hermaios (1975, pp. 229-237) does not tally with mine, I have only referred to the classification adopted in my catalogue published by the Bibliothèque Nationale.

10. *BN*, Hermaios, séries 4-5.

11. *BN*, Hermaios, séries 7-8.

12. *BN*, Hermaios, série 6 ; also see O. BOPEARACHCHI, 1989, pp 453-456.

13. *BN*, Hermaios et Calliope, série 1.

14. *BN*, Hermaios, série 9.

15. *BN*, Hermaios, séries 10-11.

non-destructive technique is performed on the whole coin to avoid errors due to corrosion and surface enrichment. [16] According to the results of this analysis, like all the Indo-Greek coins the coin of the first group (*BN*, Hermaios, n° 2) which I consider as a lifetime issue of Hermaios, is marked by a good percentage of silver. It contains 94.1 % silver against 4.68 % copper. The silver content of the coin of the second group, that is to say, the first series of posthumous imitations of Hermaios, is reduced to 85.4 % (*BN*, Hermaios, n° 23). The 13.6 % copper content of this coin is quite high compared to that of 4.68 % of the previous sample.

What are the arguments for differentiating the imitations from the lifetime coins ?

The first criterion is stylistic. Upon close examination one may observe that the first series of imitations — our second group — is characterized by a stereotyped royal portrait where the king's hair takes the form of parallel streaks. These coins are also marked by a degenerate treatment of the reverse type. One may compare the poor quality of the engraving of this reverse type with that of the lifetime issues of Hermaios — our first group — where Zeus-Mithra wearing the Phrygian cap with a solar crown shows good workmanship (see n° 20-23). When copying the genuine types the nomads engraved their dies in a less sophisticated manner, leaving out many details and introducing new elements, and I shall further discuss this point a little later.

There are a few cases where such stylistic differences can be observed on the coinage issued by the same king, the best example being the coins of Apollodotos II. The royal portrait on silver coins of Apollodotos II bearing the monograms  and  attributed to western Panjab is of relatively good workmanship, whereas the portrait on the coins with the monograms of eastern Panjab , ,  is larger and coarser. [17] However the context in the Hermaios coinage is different. The degeneration of style which can be observed on the coins of Apollodotos, as G.K. Jenkins (1955, pp. 1-26) clearly showed, is due to the difference of the geographical regions. But one cannot apply the same argument to underestimate the stylistic differences between the imitations and the lifetime issue of Hermaios, because both series of coins were found in the same geographical regions.

Secondly the reappearance of the monograms , , , 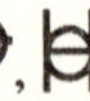, , , , 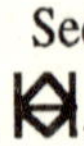, , Σ 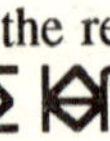, that already existed before Hermaios, is another criterion

16. For more details about this method, see J.N. BARRANDON, 1982, pp. 3-15 ; ID., 1989, pp. 12-15. The complete results of this analysis will be published in the near future by J.N. Barrandon and by myself.

17. Compare *BN*, Apollodote II, n° 1 & 16 with 2-11.

to distinguish the genuine coins of this king from the posthumous issues. [18] All the monograms found on the lifetime issues of Hermaios are characterized by an uninterrupted continuity. The most long-lived monogram in this respect is : inaugurated by Antimachos (II) Nikephoros, it was used without interruption by the Greek kings who, like Hermaios, reigned in the Paropamisadae and Gandhara. A similar case is the monogram , which first appeared on Strato's coins and reappears on the coinage of many of his successors including Hermaios. The fundamental point that should be stressed here is the continuity of the monetary system.

In this context, it should be emphasized that the composition of the so-called Charsadda hoard, found in 1917, carries valuable information to illustrate this point. This hoard contained 96 bilingual tetradrachms and a single bronze, issued by ten different Indo-Greek kings. Out of the 97 coins there were 10 specimens in the name of Hermaios and 2 of Hermaios and Calliope. These issues give a clear *terminus post quem* for the burial of the hoard. According to the description given by R. B. Whitehead who published this hoard (1923, p. 315 ; 1947, pp. 41, 42), the coins of Hermaios were characterized by the following monograms (1), (4), (5). The absence of monograms that characterises the second group is significant. Out of 63 tetradrachms that I have seen in various museums and private collections, 40 belong to the very early posthumous imitations (our second group) ; in other words they are superior in number to those of the first group. If the coins of the second group were issued during the lifetime of Hermaios, there should have been at least a few coins of the second group in the Charsadda hoard. It seems that this hoard was buried just after the death of Hermaios, and it is the only way to explain the absence of posthumous imitations of Hermaios. One may yet argue by saying that the second group of coins in the name of Hermaios was minted by Hermaios himself but towards the end of his life. Two more arguments can be added to

18. Although the monogram is only found on the coins of Hermaios and of his immediate predecessor Amyntas, the continuity is attested by the fact that both kings have identical monetary types on their bronzes (*BN*, Amyntas, séries 13-14 ; Hermaios, série 9). We have catalogued the coin bearing the monogram under the genuine series ; this same monogram appears for the first time on two coins of Strato I (MITCHINER, 1975, 2 : 308, d ; 320, d ; O. BOPEARACHCHI, 1991, Straton I, séries 1 A, 9 A). Dobbins, 1970, p. 308 had some doubts in considering the coins with this monogram as imitations, yet he admits that « there is nothing in its internal evidence of style to prove it as such ». It is reasonable to assume that the two monograms and that appear for the first time on the Indo-Greek coinage should be considered as variations of and which were first introduced by Euthydemus I *ca.* 210 B.C. *BN*, Euthydème I, séries 9 A, 10 A, 12 A, 13 A, 14 A, 22 c, 23 B and 24 A.

prove that the coins of the second group were indeed posthumous, and that will explain clearly why the Charsadda hoard contained only lifetime issues of Hermaios.

Certain monograms on the second group of coins that I have catalogued as posthumous imitations are also attested on certain bronze coins of Apollodotos I :  (see n° 18),  (see n° 19), , ,  [19] and Eucratides I, found mainly in the Paropamisadae ; ,  (see n° 13), , 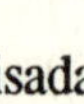 and 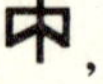 (also see n° 12). [20] These coins are no doubt barbarous imitations of the lifetime issues of these two kings. Most of the genuine bronzes of Eucratides bear the monograms which were also attested on the coins of his predecessors ; the two monograms  and  are noteworthy in this respect (n° 10 and 11). [21]

One may add the following remarks :

A. The flans of the lifetime issues are very regular in shape, [22] whereas those of the imitations are irregular (compare n° 10, 11 with n° 13, 14). [23]

B. The dies of some of the imitations are adjusted at 3 o' clock instead of the usual 12 o' clock.

C. Perhaps the most evident characteristic of the imitations is the extremely poor quality of the engraving (see n° 13, 14). When we compare the lifetime issues with the imitations, one cannot miss the fact that they are much superior in style. The stylistic features of the royal portrait are quite similar to the one on his silver (see n° 8) and gold (see n° 9) coins. The poor workmanship of the imitations misled A.N. Lahiri (1965, p. 129) in describing the obverse type : « Diademed bust of king to r. wearing "flat kausia" ; palm behind head ». It is unnecessary to emphasize here that what Lahiri identified as a flat kausia is the badly copied helmet, and the palm-branch the barbarous engraving of the plume. These features are also found on the bronzes of Apollodotos I bearing the same monograms as those of the posthumous imitations of Hermaios. [24] The barbarous rendering of the tripod and the crooked lines of irregular dots around it are some of the characteristics that enable us to identify these coins as posthumous imitations (compare n° 16, 17 with n° 18, 19).

Let us add another argument to reinforce this hypothesis. One may notice that the eleven bilingual bronze coins of Eucratides I found in the Ai Khanum

19. *BN*, Apollodote I, séries 6 P, 7, D ; 6 Q ; 6 R ; 6 U, 7 E ; 6 V.

20. *BN*, Eucratide I, série 19 U ; 21 A, B, C, D, E ; 23 A ; 24 A.

21. *BN*, Eucratide I, série 19 D, L ; 20 C.

22. See also *BN*, Apollodote I, n° 95-99, 101-104 ; Eucratide I, n° 76-97, 106-107.

23. *BN*, Apollodote I, n° 73-94, 100 ; Eucratide I, n° 98-105, 108-113 ; also see C. KIRKPATRICK, 1973, p. 423.

24. *BN*, Apollodote I, séries 6 O-W ; 7 C-E.

excavations in Afghanistan are all of good style. [25] The results obtained from the excavations conducted by the French Archaeological Delegation in Afghanistan under the directorship of P. Bernard (1985, pp. 96-105) show that the existence of this Greek city came to an end with the nomadic invasion *ca.* 145 B.C., and once driven away, the Greek settlers never returned to their city, which was then completely abandoned.

The fact that the coins found in the hoards and the stray finds of the Ai Khanum territory stop suddenly with Eucratides I's reign, proves that the life of the Greek city came to an end with his death. [26] Since the excavations did not yield any of the coins characterized by poor quality of style and none bearing monograms found also on the posthumous issues of Hermaios, the sensible conclusion one may draw is that such coins were not minted during the lifetime of Eucratides I. We do not believe that one could invoke the *ex absentia* argument, because, out of 256 bronze coins in the name of Eucratides that I have

---

25. P. BERNARD, (1985), p. 69, n 173-183, pl. 8.

26. P. BERNARD, 1985, pp. 97-105 ; also see Cl. RAPIN, 1983, pp. 315-381 ; ID., 1987, pp. 41-70 ; ID., 1992, pp. 95-114 ; O. BOPEARACHCHI, 1990 a, pp. 79-104 ; *id.*, 1990 b, pp. 39-85. The first Ai Khanum hoard was found in 1970, in room 20 of the administrative quarter of the palace situated in the centre of the lower city. It had been hidden after the pillage of the near-by treasury and during the last phase of the destruction of the palace, just before the arrival of a second wave of nomads. It contained 677 silver punch-marked coins and 6 bilingual drachms of Agathocles, but no issues of other Graeco-Bactrian kings were present : see R. AUDOUIN and P. BERNARD, 1973, pp. 238-289 ; ID, 1974, pp. 7-41. The second hoard was found in 1973, in the ruins of the kitchen of a large private house situated outside the northern wall of the city. It comprised 63 silver tetradrachms of Attic standard, 49 of which are Graeco-Bactrian coins : 7 Diodotos in the name of Antiochos, 1 Diodotos in the name of Diodotos, 27 Euthydemos I, 3 Demetrios I, 1 Euthydemos II, 3 Agathocles, 2 Antimachos (I) Theos, 1 Apollodotos I, 1 Eucratides I, see C.-Y. PETITOT-BIEHLER, 1975, pp. 23-57. The third hoard was found in the winter 1973/4 by an Afghan farmer very probably near the site itself. It was quickly sold in Kabul and a large portion of it passed by commerce through New York. It was published by Fr. HOLT, 1981, pp. 7-43, from a rapid inventory completed by Dr. N. Waggoner, former curator at the American Numismatic Society. As Holt himself correctly said, doubts must be expressed about the integrity of any hoard of valuable coins which has been passed from dealer to dealer over a period of years. Except for a few suspicious coins, like the drachm of Lysias, the composition of this hoard is similar to the one published by Petitot-Biehler. It may have comprised 142 silver coins of Attic standard, 120 of which were Graeco-Bactrian : 7 Diodotos in the name of Antiochos, 4 Diodotos in the name of Diodotos, 81 Euthydemos I, 8 Demetrios I, 3 Euthydemos II, 6 Agathocles, 2 Antimachos (I) Theos, 9 Eucratides I. The excavations have also yielded 274 stray coins. There were 224 legible specimens of which 77 were Graeco-Bactrian and Indo-Greek.
The stray finds are almost exclusively bronzes. The Seleucid coins are represented by a great quantity (68 specimens of which 62 of Antiochos I). Then come Euthydemos I with 49 coins, Diodotos with 26 coins and Eucratides I with 12 coins of which 11 were bilingual : see P. BERNARD, 1985, pp. 17-71.

seen personally in various collections, his posthumous imitations represent 114 specimens against 142 of lifetime issues, the proportion being 7 : 9. [27] If our calculation is exact, and if both series had been minted during the lifetime of Eucratides, the probability would be to find at least a few imitations at Ai Khanum.

A bronze coin of Eucratides I in the Smithsonian collection overstruck on a coin of Spalirises with Spalagadames enables us to solve once and for all the question of posthumous coins of Eucratides (see n° 15). Two thirds of the monogram is out of the flan, the visible one third is situated to the right side of the horses at the right edge of the flan. It is quite close, in appearance, to the monogram  found on the posthumous series of Eucratides. [28] Other than the monogram, the barbarous rendering of the royal portrait of Eucratides I, and the reverse type show clearly that this is a posthumous imitation of Eucratides. [29] When the coin is rotated 90°, on the obverse under the royal portrait, one can read three Greek letters ΔΕΛ, and just under them a line of pearls characterized by four dots. These pearls disappear under the shoulders of the king's bust and reappear over the legend [ΒΑΣΙ]ΛΕΩΣ of the overtype of Eucratides. On the reverse, once the coin is rotated 90°, one is able to read a part of the kharoshthi legend of the undertype : [*Spa*]*lagadama*[*sa*] 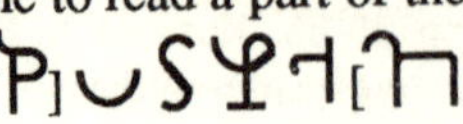. Thus the legible parts of the obverse and reverse legends of the undertype give a clear indication for identifying the original coin. The wording and the position of the legends : on the obverse : 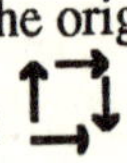 [CΠΑΛΑΥΡΙΟC / ΔΙΚΑΙΟΥ / Α]ΔΕΛ[ΦΟΥ ΤΟΥ /ΒΑCΙΛΕΩC] ; on the reverse :  [*Spalahoraputrasa* / *dhramiasa* / *Spa*]*lagadama*[*sa*], enable us to recognize without difficulty the undertype of Spalirises with Spalagadames' coin (cf. M. Mitchiner 5, 691). This coin proves beyond all doubt that the dies which were used to overstrike the coin of Spalirises with Spalagadames do not belong to a mint which was in activity during the lifetime of Eucratides I. As we have seen earlier, we know now that the reign of Eucratides came to an end around 145 B.C. and the overstruck coin belongs to the Indo-Scythian Spalirises who did not begin to reign before 70 B.C. So, the conclusion is that the overstriking was done at least 75 years after the death of Eucratides I.

In the light of this development we can also discuss the question of two bronze series of Eucratides, which Dobbins correctly considered as posthumous

27. *BN*, Eucratide I, série 19 et 20.

28. *BN*, Eucratide I, série 19 S.

29. A coin very close in style to our specimen and bearing the same monogram is in the British Museum collection, see MITCHINER, 1975, series 190, last illustration.

imitations. The first series bearing one of the posthumous monograms  has a reverse type of Nike to left. [30] In addition to the monogram and the poor execution of the engraving, this series has a peculiar title in kharoshthi, *rajadirajasa*, and we know that this title was never used by any of the Indo-Greek kings, its earliest use being attested on the coins of the Indo-Scythian Maues who ruled at least 60 years after Eucratides I. The second series is the bronzes with the legend *Kavisie nagara devata*, bearing the unique monogram  (see n° 12). [31] P. Gardner (1886, p. 19), judging from the peculiar features of this series, assumed that it was issued after the death of Eucratides. A. K. Narain (1957, pp. 123) argued that this series was struck by a third Eucratides. I believe that this series like the preceding one was struck by the same nomads, most probably to celebrate their victory over Alexandria of the Caucasus.

The gap between the reigns of Eucratides I and Hermaios is more than 60 years. The fact that these coins of Eucratides, Apollodotos and Hermaios that we consider as imitations have common monograms, were found in the same geographical regions and are characterized by a very poor quality of workmanship allows us to assume that all these coins were minted at about the same time by the same nomads who conquered the Greek Paropamisadae and Gandhara.

The conclusion that one may draw from all these arguments is that our second group of coins was struck by the nomads who conquered the Paropamisadae and Gandhara to the detriment of Hermaios. It was on two of these coins that Agha Inayat Ali Shah and A.K. Narain were convinced that they saw an « elephant's head » that they interpreted as evidence for the earliest form of Gaṇeśa. So, it is now very clear that it was not a Greek king but nomads who are responsible for issuing these coins with a so-called « Gaṇeśa head ».

It is interesting to analyze, at this point, what made A.K. Narain to interpret the « elephant's trunk » effect as the very first iconographic representation of Gaṇeśa. A.K. Narain, quoting the authorities on the question of Gaṇeśa, R.G. Bhandarkar, A.K. Coomaraswamy and A. Getty, admits that there is no literary evidence to attest Gaṇeśa cult in India before the sixth century A.D. [32] Narain further accepts : « Yet it is true that no image of an elephant-headed deity has been discovered which could be placed unquestionably earlier than the 5th

30. *BN*, Eucratide I, série 22.

31. *BN*, Eucratide I, série 24.

32. Narain, 1988, pp. 1007-1009 ; et 1991, pp. 19-20, 39. R.G. Bhandarkar, 1931, has shown that the cult of *Gaṇapati-Vināyaka* may have been set up by the end of the sixth century. Also see A. K. Coomaraswamy, 1931, et 1978, pp. 30-31. A. Getty, 1936, pp. 13, 35..

century » (1988, p. 1007). Although Narain presents his identification of a « elephant-headed » deity as an important discovery, he never attempts to bridge the gap between the earliest mention of *Gaṇapati-Vināyaka* in the sixth century A.D. and the isolated representation of the god on a coin dated as early as the first century B.C. A.K. Narain admits that although he first came across the coin with an « elephant face » in 1953-54, he was not much enthusiastic about publishing it because he thought that it was a freak or one of the degenerate piece of the last days of the Indo-Greeks. He goes on to say that he was waiting for either more specimens to appear or some weighty reason to shake his reluctance. Narain then explains very clearly that his reluctance gave way when he saw the photographs of some rectangular coins of Agathocles found in Ai Khanum. According to Narain, the discovery of these silver coins depicting two Brahmanic deities (see n° 1) encouraged him to present the Hermaios coin with an elephant faced Zeus, at the Paris session of the International Congress of Orientalists in 1973, suggesting that it could be the beginning of Gaṇeśa's iconography (1988, p. 1009). A.K. Narain correctly assumed that the Ai Khanum coins were very positive evidence to show the role of the Indo-Greeks in the formulation of Indian cults and icons. However as far as the coins with the so-called « elephant-headed » deity is concerned the context is extremely different.

Firstly as we have seen, these imitations (our second group) in the name of Hermaios were struck by nomads but not by Greeks, so one cannot use these coins, as Narain did, as evidence to show the role of the Indo-Greeks in the formulation of Indian cults and icons.

Secondly, the two male figures, identical in pose and dress, on the Agathocles' silver bilingual coins were correctly identified as Balarāma-Saṃkarṣaṇa and his brother Vāsudeva-Kṛṣṇa by J. Filliozat thanks to the attributes held by each god (1973, pp. 113-121). The divinity on the obverse, who flourishes a miniature plough is Balarāma « plough-Carrier » (*halabhṛt*) or Saṃkarṣaṇa « Ploughman ». The large wheel of six spokes, the disc (*cakra*) and the conch held by the god depicted on the reverse are distinctive attributes of Vāsudeva-Kṛṣṇa (see n° 1). On the contrary, other than the illusory « elephant's trunk », there is no trace of any symbol on the coins published by Agha Inayat Ali Shah and A.K. Narain which can be attributed to Gaṇeśa. [33]

Thirdly, the representation of two Brahmanic deities on the coins of Agathocles alone does not justify the existence of Gaṇeśa cult as early as the first century A.D. J. Filliozat clearly pointed out that literary texts as early as the

---

33. For the identification of these divinities, see also R. AUDOUIN and P. BERNARD, 1974, pp. 7-41 ; for the English translation of the same article see « The Aï Khanoum Coins : The 1970 Hoard (II) », in *Graeco-Bactrian and Indian Coins from Afghanistan*, edited and compiled by O. Guillaume, translated from the French by O. Bopearachchi, Delhi, 1991, pp. 80-116.

fourth-third centuries B.C. make allusions to the two Brahmanic divinities, Balarāma-Saṃkarṣaṇa and Vāsudeva-Kṛṣṇa represented on the coins (1973, pp. 116-8). Agathocles' silver bilingual coins give us a perfectly clear and explicit illustration of what was the first form of Vishnuism, the *Bhāgavata* religion. The grammarians Pāṇini (fourth-third centuries B.C.) and Patañjali (second century B.C.) mention several times Vāsudeva or Kṛṣṇa. [34] The oldest of the inscriptions relating to the *Bhāgavata* cult is the famous Besnagar column which stands near the ancient site of Vidiṣa. This monument which, as its designation (*garudadhvaja*) indicates, originally supported a statue of Garuḍa, Vishnu's sacred bird, was erected in honour of Vāsudeva, the god of gods (*devadeva*), by a Greek from Taxila, Heliodorus, ambassador of the Greek king Antialcidas to the local king Bhāgabhadra. In his dedication, the Greek proclaims himself a « devotee of the lord god » (*bhāgavata*). The existence of the *Bhāgavata* cult in Taxila during the reign of Antialcidas *ca.* 100 B.C. is thus confirmed by the Agathocles' coins depicting the two main gods of this religion. [35] As P. Bernard clearly pointed out, Agathocles should be credited with creating the first bilingual coinage reflecting the originality and the boldness of his monetary policy (1974, pp. 36-7). Agathocles first remained true to the traditional Greek Attic standard coinage in Bactria with his reverses of monolingual legend, and type : Zeus holding Hecate, [36] but when he introduced a bilingual coinage meant for circulation in Indian territories, he decided not only to proclaim himself king to them in their own language and in the two native scripts (brahmi and kharoshthi), but also to represent in these issues images of their gods (see also n° 1, 2). The conclusion one may draw from this analysis is that the fact that the two divine brothers are invoked in the coins of Agathocles is not accidental, but certainly reflects the political, religious and cultural policy adopted by the Greeks when they conquered the Indian territories. As we have underlined earlier, contrary to the *Bhāgavata* cult well attested as early as the fourth century B.C., there is no trace of a Gaṇeśa cult in India before the fifth century A.D. For these reasons, I believe that it is clearly dangerous to exploit the bilingual coins depicting the gods of *Bhāgavata* cult with so many cultural and religious implications, to justify the identification of a god like Gaṇeśa, whose cult did not develop before the fifth century A.D., on isolated coins which date back to the first century B.C.

Let us now come back to the coins on which both Agha Inayat Ali Shah and A.K. Narain have identified an « elephant-headed » deity. First of all we observe that these two coins (see n° 46) along with the one in the American

34. Patañjali in his *Māhabhaṣya* mentions several times Vāsudeva (III.I. 26, III. 2. 1111, IV.3.98) or Kṛṣṇa (II.2.24).

35. For the chronology of these kings, see *BN*, pp. 56-59.

36. *BN*, Agathocle, séries 1-4.

Numismatic Society (n° 40) that J. Cribb had mentioned (1982, p. 30), bear the same monogram : . Although all the posthumous imitations issued in the name of Hermaios are engraved in a less sophisticated manner, all known specimens with the monogram are of extremely crude style (see n° 32-48). Furthermore, the « elephant's trunk » effect can only be seen exclusively on some of the coins bearing this monogram , but never on the specimens of the same class bearing various other monograms , (n° 28), (n° 29), , , , , , (n° 30), , , , , , , (n° 31).

It should be well noted that the deity depicted on lifetime issues of Hermaios recalls the Olympian Zeus on the coins of Alexander the Great (see n° 3). The same enthroned Zeus reappeared in various forms on the coins of some Indo-Greek kings. Pantaleon reproduced a Zeus holding Hecate. [37] Heliocles depicted on his coins an enthroned Zeus holding a Nike (see n° 4). [38] Zeus on the coins of Antialcidas holds a scepter in his left hand and a winged Nike on his right palm, he is accompanied by the forepart of a small elephant turned to the left or to the right (see n° 5 and 6). This particular reverse type of Antialcidas served as a prototype for many of his Indo-Greek successors. Zeus on Amyntas' coins holds an armed Athena (see n° 7). The same god on the coins of Hermaios is shown enthroned, holding a sceptre which is reclined over his left shoulder and his right hand making a gesture or holding a curved object (see n° 20-23). E.T. Newell correctly called the deity depicted on the lifetime issues of Hermaios « Zeus-Mithra » in the guise of Zeus because of his Phrygian cap, like the Iranian Mithra (1938, pp. 89-91). The cap of Mithra can be identified very clearly on the square bronze coins of Amyntas and Hermaios (see n° 25-27). Zeus-Mithra on the bronze coins, like the one on the silver issues, is bearded and wears a solar crown. A.D.H. Bivar, has confirmed Newell's identification of this deity represented on both silver and bronze coins (1979, pp. 741-752).

Several factors should be taken into account regarding the coins in question. Since all of these coins are posthumous imitations of Hermaios, one should not forget the fact that the local engravers were not as experienced as the Greeks, and for this reason the execution of dies was done in a less sophisticated manner.

When Agha Inayat Ali Shah and A.K. Narain presented their identification of « Gaṇeśa », each of them drew their evidence from single specimen, without referring to the other coins with the same monogram. I would like to draw

37. *BN*, Pantaléon, séries 1-3.

38. *BN*, Hélioclès I, séries 3-4.

attention to a very interesting collection of coins bearing the monogram : ten from the French Cabinet des Médailles, (Bibliothèque Nationale) (see n° 33-39, 41-43), another specimen, other than the one published by A.K. Narain (n° 46), in the British Museum (n° 44), two in the American Numismatic Society (n° 32 and 40), one in the private collection of H. Fowler (n° 45) and one tetradrachm in the State Hermitage Museum in St. Petersburg (n° 48), which would enable us to show that the « elephant's trunk » effect partly visible on certain coins was not purposely introduced into the coinage, but was purely an accident of an inexperienced engraver.

In order to illustrate this phenomenon we have classified the drachms, in a sequence. The first three coins of our classification (see n° 32-34) are quite close in style to the deity depicted on the other posthumous imitations of Hermaios. We see on them a badly copied Zeus-Mithra with sun-ray crown, Phrygian cap, beard and two folds in his gown (see n° 32-34). On the next three coins (see n° 35-37), his nose and beard are engraved so crudely that they take the form of a compact bulk giving the impression of a half-cut trunk of an elephant. Zeus-Mithra on the next four coins is coarser (n° 38-41). The top fold of his drapery can only be vaguely differentiated from the awkwardly large nose and the beard. On the last four coins (see n° 42-45), the compact bulk of the nose and the beard join the fold of Zeus-Mithra's drapery giving the impression of an elephant's trunk.

It is in this context that our specimens bearing the monogram should be compared with Agha Inayat Ali Shah's and A.K. Narain's coins with the so-called « elephant-headed » deity (n° 46). We begin to understand that, what A.K. Narain (1988, p. 1010) calls the curved trunk (the *vakratunda*) of Gaṇeśa is nothing other than a fold of Zeus-Mithra's drapery (see n° 53 and 54). On the other hand, it is very easy to distinguish, on Narain's coin, the extremities of the nose and then the beard of the deity, which disrupt the continuity of the so-called « elephant's trunk » (see n° 53 and 54). It goes without saying that it was the die engraver's hand which had created this confusing effect. As J. Cribb (1982, p. 32) clearly demonstrated, the elephant's trunk effect disappears when the same coin is held to the light at a different angle. We made the same experiment on the tetradrachm still unpublished, bearing the same monogram , now in the State Hermitage Museum, St. Petersburg (n° 48). We have illustrated four photographs of the same coin lit from different angles. The first two photographs of the reverse of this coin lit from the right (n° 49) and from the top (n° 50) angles give the impression that the top fold of his drapery is almost linked by the nose and the beard. But the same coin lit from the left, makes us see better that, on the contrary, the nose and the fold of the deity's gown are well separated (n° 51). Once the same reverse lit from the bottom, one can distinguish the face of Zeus-Mithra with the sun-ray crown and Phrygian cap from the fold of his drapery (n° 52). When Narain's coin viewed alongside with the reverse of this tetradrachm, and the other drachms bearing the same monogram : , it can be seen that the « elephant's trunk » effect is just an illusion but not a reality.

Upon close examination, one would also realize that the reverse type of the coins in question, other than the illusory « elephant's trunk » effect, has no particular feature distinguishable from the type represented on the coins with the same monogram (see n° 53 and 54). It is the same deity shown enthroned, holding a sceptre which is reclined over his left shoulder and making a gesture with his right hand. It is now clear that the « elephant's trunk » is an illusion resulting from the dies cut in a less sophisticated manner, by an unskilled engraver of the officina represented by the monogram .

For these reasons, I believe that it is extremely dangerous to interpret the confusing « elephant's trunk » effect involuntarily created by an inexperienced die engraver, as the most ancient representation of a deity whose existence is only attested six centuries after the issuing of these isolated coins.

Osmund BOPEARACHCHI
C.N.R.S., UMR 126/5
Hellénisme et civilisations orientales
ENS, Paris

SELECT BIBLIOGRAPHY

AUDOUIN (R.) et BERNARD (P), 1973, 1974, « Trésor de monnaies indiennes et indo-grecques d'Aï Khanoum (Afghanistan) », *Revue numismatique*; 1973 : pp. 238-289 ; *ibid*, 1974 : pp. 8-41.

BARRANDON (J. N.), 1982, « Méthodes nucléaires d'analyse et numismatique », *Proceedings of the 9th International Congress of Numismatics, Berne September 1979*, edited by T. Hackens & R. Weiller, Louvain-la-Neuve, pp. 3-15.

BARRANDON (J. N.), 1989, « Les analyses en numismatique. Quelles méthodes ? et pourquoi ? », *Les Nouvelles de l'Archéologie*, 33 (1989), pp. 12-15.

BERNARD (P.), 1985, *Fouilles d'Aï Khanoum*. IV. *Les Monnaies hors trésors. Questions d'histoire gréco-bactrienne*, Mémoires de la Délégation Archéologique Française en Afghanistan, 27, Paris.

BHANDARKAR (R.G), 1913, *Vaiṣṇavism, Śaivism, and Minor Religious Systems*, Strasburg.

BIVAR (A.D.H), 1979, « Mithraic Images of Bactria : Are they related to Roman Mithraism ? », *Mysteria Mithrae, E.P.R.O.*, vol. 80, Rome, pp. 741-752.

BOPEARACHCHI (O.), 1989, « Roi-cavalier ou Reine-amazone ? », *Bulletin de la Société Française de Numismatique*, Nov. 1989, pp. 453-456.

BOPEARACHCHI (O.), 1990 a, « Ménandre Sôter, un roi indo-grec. Observations chronologiques et géographiques », *Studia Iranica*, 19 (1990), pp. 39-85.

BOPEARACHCHI (O.), 1990 b, « Graeco-Bactrian coins issued by the later Indo-Greek kings », *Numismatic Chronicle*, pp. 79-103, pl. 7-9.

BOPEARACHCHI (O.), 1991, *Monnaies gréco-bactriennes et indo-grecques. Catalogue raisonné*, Bibliothèque Nationale, Paris, [abbreviated hereafter : *BN*].

BOPEARACHCHI (O.), 1992, « Elephant-Headed Gaṇeśa or Zeus Mithra », *Yavanika* 2 (1992) [now in print].

COOMARASWAMY (A. K.), 1931, *Yaksas*, Washington.

COOMARASWAMY (A. K.), 1978, « Gaṇeśa », *Bulletin of the Museum of Fine Arts*, pp. 30-31.

CRIBB (J.), 1982, « The Earliest Ganeśa : a Case of Mistaken Identity », *Numismatic Digest*, pp. 30-32.

CURIEL (R.) et SCHLUMBERGER (D.), 1953, *Trésors monétaires d'Afghanistan*, Mémoires de la Délégation Archéologique Française en Afghanistan, 14, Paris.

DHAVALIKAR (M.K.), 1990, « The Elephant-Headed Gana at Mihintale », *Ancient Ceylon*, 7, vol. 2 (1990), pp. 38-46.

DHAVALIKAR (M.K.), 1991, « Gaṇeśa : Myth and Reality », *Ganesh. Studies of an Asian God*, edited by R.L. Brown, New York, pp. 49-68.

DOBBINS (K.W.), 1970, « The Question of the Imitation Hermaios Coinage », *East and West*, 20 (1970), pp. 307-326.

FILLIOZAT (J.), 1973, « Représentation de Vāsudeva et Saṃkarṣaṇa au IIe siècle av. J.-C. », *Arts Asiatiques*, 26 (1973), pp. 113-121.

GARDNER (P.), 1886, *A Catalogue of Indian Coins in the British Museum. The Coins of the Greek and Scythic Kings of Bactria and India*, London, 1886, reprint 1968.

GETTY (A.), 1936, *Gaṇeśa. A Monograph on the Elephant-faced God*, Oxford.

HOLT (Fr.), 1981, « The Euthydemid Coinage of Bactria : Further Hoard Evidence from Aï Khanum », *Revue numismatique*, pp. 7-44.

JENKINS (G.K.), 1955, « Indo-Scythic Mints », *Journal of the Numismatic Society of India*, pp. 1-26.

KIRKPATRICK (C.), 1973, « Some New Barbarous Coins of Eucratides I of Lahiri Type 21 », *Numismatic Circular*, 81 (Nov. 1973), pp. 423.

LAHIRI (A.N.), 1965, *Corpus of Indo-Greek Coins*, Calcutta.

MAC DOWALL (D.W.), 1985, « The Successors of the Indo-Greeks at Begram », in *South Asian Archaeology 1983*, ed. J. Schotmans and M. Taddei, Naples, pp. 555-566.

MASSON (C.), 1834, « Memoir on the Ancient Coins Found at Beghréam in the Kohistan of Kéabul », *Journal of the Asiatic Society of Bengal*, 3 (1834), pp. 152-175.

MASSON (C.), 1836, « Second Memoir on the Ancient Coins Found at Beghréam in the Kohistan of Kéabul », *Journal of the Asiatic Society of Bengal*, 5 (1836), pp. 1-28.

MASSON (C.), 1836 a, « Third Memoir on the Ancient Coins Found at Beghréam in the Kohistan of Kéabul », *Journal of the Asiatic Society of Bengal*, 5 (1836), pp. 537-547.

MITCHINER (M.), 1975, 1976, *Indo-Greek and Indo-Scythian Coinage*, vols. 1-8, London.

NARAIN (A.K.), 1957, *The Indo-Greeks*, Oxford.

NARAIN (A.K.), 1978, « On the Earliest Gaṇeśa », *Senerat Paranavitana Commemorative Volume*, Leiden, pp. 142-144.

NARAIN (A.K.), 1982, « On the Earliest Gaṇeśa », *Numismatic Digest*, pp. 26-29.

NARAIN (A.K.), 1984, « Some Brahmanicle Divinities on the Indo-Greek Coinage revisited », *Indian Institute of Research in Numismatic Studies, Inaugural Seminar, 8th to 10th January 1984*, Nasik, pp. 9-14

NARAIN (A.K.), 1988, « Iconographic Origins of Gaṇeśa and the Evidence of the Indo-Greek Coinage », in *Orientalia Iosephi Tucci Memoriae Dicta*, edited by G. Gnoli and L. Lanciotti, *Serie Orientale Roma*, LVI, 3 (1988), p. 1007-1019.

NARAIN (A.K.), 1991, « Gaṇeśa : A Protohistory of the Idea and the Icon », in *Ganesh. Studies of an Asian God*, edited by R.L. Brown, New York, pp. 19-48.

NEWELL (E.T.), 1938, *Miscellanea Numismatica : Cyrene to India*, ANS, Numismatic Notes and Monographs, 82, New York.

PETITOT-BIEHLER (C.Y.), 1975, « Le trésor d'Aï Khanoum », *Revue numismatique*, pp. 23-57.

RAPIN (Cl.), 1983, « Les inscriptions économiques de la trésorerie hellénistique d'Aï Khanoum (Afghanistan) », *Bulletin de Correspondance Hellénique*, 107 (1983), pp. 315-381.

RAPIN (Cl.), 1987, « La trésorerie hellénistique d'Aï Khanoum », *Revue Archéologique*, pp. 41-70.

RAPIN (Cl.), 1992, *Fouilles d'Aï Khanoum*. VII. *La Trésorerie du palais hellénistique d'Aï Khanoum*, Mémoires de la Délégation Archéologique Française en Afghanistan, 33, Paris.

SHAH (Agha Inayat Ali), 1955, « A Notable Numismatic Discovery », *The Museums Journal, Organ of the Museums Association of Pakistan*, August 1955, pp. 16-17.

TARN (W.W.), 1951, *The Greeks in Bactria and India*, 2nd ed., Cambridge, reprint Chicago 1984.

WHITEHEAD (R.B.), 1923, « Notes on Indo-Greek Numismatics », *Numismatic Chronicle*, pp. 294-34.

WHITEHEAD (R.B.), 1947, « Notes on the Indo-Greeks : Part II », *ibid*, 1947, pp. 28-51.

ILLUSTRATIONS

1. Agathocles. AR. (enlargement). Ai Khanum hoard I, P. BERNARD, 1974, pl. VII, 1-6. *BN*, série 9.
2. Agathocles. AE. *BN*, n° 14.
3. Alexander. AR. Tetradrachm. Bibliothèque Nationale.
4. Heliocles I. AR. Tetradrachm. Bibliothèque Nationale. *BN*, n° 23.
5. Antialcidas. AR. Tetradrachm. Bibliothèque Nationale. *BN*, n° 1.
6. Antialcidas. AR. Tetradrachm. Bibliothèque Nationale. *BN*, n° 2.
7. Amyntas. AR. Tetradrachm. Fr. Widemann collection. *BN*, pl. 47, D.
8. Eucratides I. AR. Tetradrachm. Bibliothèque Nationale. *BN*, n° 3.
9. Eucratides I. AV. Stater. Bibliothèque Nationale. *BN*, n° 26.
10. Eucratides I. AE. Bibliothèque Nationale. *BN*, n° 90.
11. Eucratides I. AE. Bibliothèque Nationale. *BN*, n° 92.
12. Eucratides I (posthumous). AE. Bibliothèque Nationale. *BN*, n° 122.
13. Eucratides I (posthumous). AE. Bibliothèque Nationale. *BN*, n° 103.
14. Eucratides I (posthumous). AE. Bibliothèque Nationale. *BN*, n° 102.
15. Eucratides I (posthumous) over Spalirises with Spalagadames. AE. Smithsonian Institution.
16. Apollodotos I. AE. British Museum. *BN*, série 6, F.
17. Apollodotos I. AE. British Museum. *BN*, série 6, F.
18. Apollodotos I (posthumous). AE. British Museum. *BN*, série 6, Q.
19. Apollodotos I (posthumous). AE. British Museum. *BN*, série 7, D.
20. Hermaios. AR. Tetradrachm (enlargement). Bibliothèque Nationale. *BN*, n° 1.
21. Hermaios. AR. Tetradrachm. Bibliothèque Nationale. *BN*, n° 2.
22. Hermaios. AR. Tetradrachm. British Museum. *BN*, pl. 53, H.
23. Hermaios. AR. Tetradrachm. State Hermitage, St. Petersbourg. *BN*, séries 4, D.
24. Hermaios and Calliope. AR. Tetradrachm. British Museum. *BN*, pl. 52, F.
25. Hermaios. AE. British Museum (BMC, n° 55). *BN*, série 9, A.
26. Hermaios. AE. British Museum (BMC, n° 54). *BN*, série 9, A.
27. Hermaios. AE. British Museum (inv. n° 1888. 12. 8. 404). *BN*, série 9, A.

Hermaios (posthumous imitations)

28. AR. Tetradrachm (enlargement). Bibliothèque Nationale. *BN*, n° 19.
29. AR. Tetradrachm (enlargement). Bibliothèque Nationale. *BN*, n° 20.
30. AR. Tetradrachm (enlargement). Bibliothèque Nationale. *BN*, n° 23.
31. AR. Drachm (enlargement). Bibliothèque Nationale. *BN*, n° 43.
32. AR. Drachm. American Numismatic Society, (ex-R.F. Kelley), *BN*, série 11, C.
33. AR. Drachm (enlargement). Bibliothèque Nationale. *BN*, n° 37.
34. AR. Drachm (enlargement). Bibliothèque Nationale. *BN*, n° 40.
35. AR. Drachm (enlargement). Bibliothèque Nationale. *BN*, n° 39.
36. AR. Drachm (enlargement). Bibliothèque Nationale. *BN*, n° 41.
37. AR. Drachm (enlargement). Bibliothèque Nationale. *BN*, n° 34.
38. AR. Drachm (enlargement). Bibliothèque Nationale. *BN*, n° 35.
39. AR. Drachm (enlargement). Bibliothèque Nationale. *BN*, n° 42.
40. AR. Drachm. American Numismatic Society, (ex-W.F. Spengler). *BN*, série 11, C.
41. AR. Drachm (enlargement). Bibliothèque Nationale. *BN*, n° 33.
42. AR. Drachm (enlargement). Bibliothèque Nationale. *BN*, n° 36.
43. AR. Drachm (enlargement). Bibliothèque Nationale. *BN*, n° 38.
44. AR. Drachm (enlargement). British Museum (*BMC*, 14). *BN*, série 11, C.
45. AR. Drachm (enlargement). Coll. H. Fowler (ex-R.C. Senior). *BN*, série 11, C.
46. AR. Drachm . British Museum (inv. n° 1961. 3.2.1.). *BN*, série 11, C.
47. Enlargement of the previous coin.
48. Hermaios. AR. Tetradrachm (enlargement). State Hermitage, St. Petersbourg. *BN*, série 10.
49. Same coin (1x1) lit from the top.
50. Same coin (1x1) lit from the left.
51. Same coin (1x1) lit from the right.
52. Same coin (1x1) lit from the bottom.
53. AR. Drachm (enlargement). British Museum (inv. n° 1961. 3.2.1.). *BN*, série 11, C.
54. Drawing of the same coin by G. Lecuyot.

1

2

3

4

5

6

7

8

9

10

11

12

13

14

15

16

17

18

19

20

21

22

23

24

25

26

27

28

29

30

31

32

33

34

35

36

37

38

39

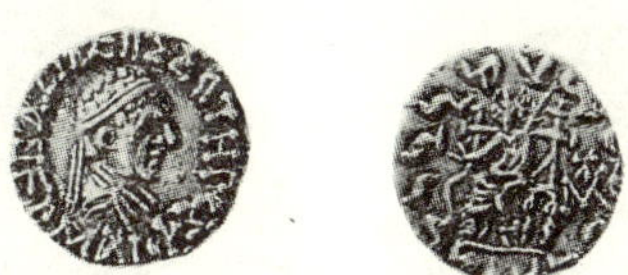

40

41

42

43

44

45

46

47

48

49

50

51

52

53

54

THE YAVANA PRESENCE IN ANCIENT INDIA *

It has often been assumed that the social structure in ancient India was neatly divided and compartmentalized in accordance with the four-fold *varṇa* hierarchy with very little scope for mobility. This picture, based solely on evidence from the *Dharmaśāstras*, fails to take into account the dichotomy and at times the contradiction that existed between the ritual status and actual status, and the constant attempts of the law-makers to reconcile the two. This is nowhere clearer than in the theory of the mixed-castes propounded by the *Dharmaśāstras* and the gradual increase in their number. This theory was an ingenious means by which new categories could be formed as and when the need arose and by which exterior groups could be accommodated in the *varṇa* fold. According to the *Gautama Dharma Sūtra* the number of mixed-castes was eleven, *Baudhāyana* increased it to fourteen and by the time of the *Manusmṛti*, chapter X being ascribable to the late Gupta period, the number had risen to sixty-one.[1] This process of legitimisation of non-Aryan groups was made much more complex by the gradual Sanskritisation of tribal areas and by the influx of foreigners such as the Indo-Greeks, the Śakas and the Kuṣāṇas into northern and western India in the early centuries of the Christian era.

This paper considers the presence of the *Yavanas* in the subcontinent in the early centuries of the Christian era and their involvement in the trading network. While inscriptions and literary references provide useful information on the subject, numismatic data affords further evidence of contacts. An effective barometer of the prosperity and economic power of a community is the social status accorded to it by the *Dharmaśāstras*.

---

* First published in the *Journal of the Economic and Social History of the Orient*, Leiden, vol. XXXI, 1988 : 311-325. Reproduced here with the kind permission of the Editors of *JESHO* (letter 5.01.1994), to whom we express our due thanks.

1. V.N. JHA, « Varnasamkara in the Dharmasūtras : Theory and Practice », *Journal of the Economic and Social History of the Orient*, 1970, XIII : 287.

The word *Yavana* is a back-formation from the Prakrit term *Yona* which is in turn derived from the old Persian form *Yauna* originally denoting the Ionian Greeks who were conquered by Cyrus in 545 B.C. It first occurs in the Behistun inscription of Darius I dated to 519 B.C.[2] As the Ionian Greeks were the first to have come into contact with India, the term was initially used for them. It was gradually extended to include not only the Greeks of West Asia but any group of people coming either from West Asia or the eastern Mediterranean.[3] In medieval Indian literature the word *yavana* was used as a synonym of *mleccha* and indicated any foreigner.[4]

Because of historical factors, the earliest *Yavana* settlements were located in the north-western region of the subcontinent. Excavations at Taxila have shown that the city of Sirkap at that site was founded by the Indo-Greeks and extended and fortified by a masonry wall built by the Indo-Parthians.[5] More recently work at Kandahar and at Aï Khanum has been very fruitful. At the latter site, the remains of a city said to have been founded either by Alexander or an officer of Seleucus have been unearthed.[6] Early Classical writers refer to a Greek colony named Nysa in the north-west, whose inhabitants, claimed to be the descendants of a troop led by Dionysus in an earlier period.[7] The thirteenth major rock edict of Aśoka refers to kingdoms situated along his borders and includes the country of the *Yavanas* [8] A bilingual rock edict of Aśoka in Greek and Aramaic has been found near Kandahar and another fragmentary epigraph in Greek at Kandahar itself. The Junagadh inscription of Rudradaman, recounting the history of the Sudarśana lake, states that it was created by the Vaiśya Pusyagupta during the reign of Candragupta Maurya and endowed with conduits by Yavanarāja Tuṣāspha on behalf of Aśoka.[9] The Greek Heliodorus records his devotion to Visnu in his Besnagar pillar inscription and speaks of himself as a member of the Bhāgavata sect.[10]

---

2. D.C. SIRCAR, *Select Inscriptions bearing on Indian History and Civilisation*, Calcutta, 1964 : 3.

3. R. THAPAR, *Ancient Indian Social History*, Orient Longman, 1978 : 164.

4. D. C. SIRCAR, *Select Inscriptions, op. cit.* : 101.

5. J. MARSHALL, *Taxila*, Cambridge, 1952.

6. P. BERNARD *et. al.*, *Fouilles d'Aï Khanoum*, 2 vols., Paris, 1973 ; A. K. NARAIN, « On the Greek Epigraphs from Ai Khanum », *Studies in Indian Epigraphy*, I, 1974 : 97-103

7. J. W. MCCRINDLE, *Ancient India as Described by Megasthenes and Arrian*, New Delhi, 1972 : 179.

8. D.C. SIRCAR, *Inscriptions of Aśoka*, New Delhi, 1967 : 56-9.

9. *Epigraphia Indica* (hereafter *EI*), VIII, 1905-6 : 36-49.

10. *Journal of the Royal Asiatic Society*, 1909 : 1053.

In the epigraphs discussed so far, the term *Yavana* is used to denote Greeks and Indo-Greeks, and this is also reflected in early Indian literature. Foreigners such as the Pāradas, the Śakas, the Pārasīkas, the *Yavanas* and the like figure as participants in the Rājasūya sacrifice of Yudhisthira,[11] while some of them find mention as participants in the *svayamvara* of Draupadi.[12] The *Rāmāyaṇa* locates the country of the *Yavanas* and the city of the Śakas between the *janapadas* of the Kurus and the Madras and the Himalayas.[13] Pāṇini in his *Aṣṭādhyāyī* states that the feminine form of *yavana* is *yavanānī*.[14] This is further elaborated by Kātyāyana, who takes the term to denote Greek writing.[15] As an allusion to the connection of the *yavanas* with the north-west, the *Mahābharata* mentions *yauna-kāmboja-gāndhārāh* as *uttarāpathajanmānah* and the *Purānas* place them in the Udīcya country.[16] Patañjali refers to the *Yavanas* besieging Sāketa and Madhyamika,[17] and Pāṇini contemptuously mentions *yavanamunda* or with the head shaved like that of a *Yavana*.[18]

Pāli literature refers to *Yavana* settlements in the *dīpa* or *doab* of Alasanda, identified with the district around Alexandria near Kabul.[19] The *Milindapañha* associates Sāgalanagara with the *Yavanas*,[20] and the *Majjhima Nikāya* states that in the region of the *Yonas* and the Kambojas there are only two *varṇas*, the master and the slave, and these are interchangeable.[21] According to the Buddhist tradition incorporated in the *Mahāvamsa*, after the Third Council in 250 B.C., the Theravādin Sangha sent missions to the different regions of India and Sri Lanka to propagate Buddhism. Among the places mentioned are Aparānta (Konkan) to which Yonarakhita was sent and Mahārattha where Dhammarakhita was despatched.[22] An earlier tradition in the *Theragāthā* would, however, suggest that Buddhism had already been introduced into western India during

11. *Mahābhārata*, II.47.12.

12. *Ibid*., I.177.

13. *Rāmāyaṇa*, Kiṣkindhā kāṇḍa, IV.43.11.2.

14. *Aṣṭādhyāyī*, 4.1.49.

15. Vārttika 3 on Pāṇini.

16. D.C. SIRCAR, « Yavana and Parasika », *Journal of India History*, XIV, 1935 : 36.

17. B. C. LAW, *Tribes in Ancient India*, Poona, 1943 : 157.

18. *Aṣṭādhyāyī*, III.1.72.

19. D. C. SIRCAR, « The Yavanas », in R.C. Majumdar, ed., *The Age of Imperial Unity*, *Bombay*, 1951 : 102 ; *Mahāvaṁsa* 29, verse 30f refers to *yonanagara* Alasanda.

20. *Milindapañha*, 1.1.1.

21. *Majjhima Nikāya*, II.149.

22. *Mahāvaṁsa* 837-8.

the time of Buddha by Punna, a merchant from Sopara, and Vaddha, a *gahapati* from Bharuch.[23]

Thus references to *Yavanas* in early Pāli and Sanskrit literature are of a general nature, referring primarily to Greeks and Indo-Greeks and to their settlement in the north-western region. These do not provide any information on the professions of the *Yavanas* or their mode of livelihood. A vast body of Kharoshthi inscriptions found at several sites in the north-western region of the sub-continent are not much help either. The term *Yavana* seldom occurs in these records, dated to the first few centuries of the Christian era, but the names of the donors are undoubtedly of Greek origin. The Swat relic vase inscription of the first century B.C. records the establishment of the relics of the Śākyamuni by Theodoros, the meridarkh.[24] The Taxila copper plate inscription is also by a meridarkh, though the name of the donor is damaged.[25] An engraved stone from Bajaur, south-east of Jalalabad, reads « of king Theodamas ».[26] The Kaldarra inscription records the laying of a tank by Thaidora or Theodoros, the Datiaputra.[27] Several Kharoshthi inscriptions of the Śaka period mention wells of or presented by various companions or *sahayas*.[28] Stein has indicated that these may refer to corporations.[29] Tarn has assumed that there are several traces of the Greek *poleis* in India and that the *Yavanas* mentioned in inscriptions were the citizens of some Greek *polis*. This view has been contradicted by others.[30]

As contrasted to this group, in Sangam literature the term *Yavana* is applied to merchants from the Roman East. The earliest poems in Tamil that have survived to the present comprise eight anthologies and ten idylls, a work on grammar and eighteen minor works. Of these, the earliest corpus, dated between 100 B.C. and A.D. 250, includes poems of the six anthologies,[31] though other scholars assign a slightly later date, *i.e.* between the first and the third centuries A.D.[32] The upper limit for this literature is generally taken as the fifth-sixth centuries A.D.

References in the earliest stratum of this corpus of literature speak of the third category of *Yavanas*, *i.e.* the merchants coming from the Roman East.

---

23. B. G. GOKHALE, *Buddhism in Maharashtra — a History*, Bombay, 1976, 34, 37.

24. S. KONOW, ed., *Kharoshthi Inscriptions*, II, Varanasi, 1969 (reprint) : 1.

25. *Ibid* : 4.

26. *Ibid* : 6.

27. *Ibid* : 65-66.

28. *Ibid* : nos 12, 14, 18, 25, 28.

29. O. Stein, « Yavanas in Early Indian Inscriptions », *Indian Culture*, I, 1934-5 : 343.

30. A. K. NARAIN, *The Indo-Greeks*, Oxford, 1957 : 94.

31. K. ZVELEBIL, *The Smile of Murugan*, Leiden, 1973 : 41.

32. G. L. HART, *The Poems of Ancient Tamils*, Berkeley, 1975.

These *Yavanas* came with gold and wine in their ships and returned with pepper,[33] and one of the ports they frequently visited was Muciri.[34] References in later texts dated to the second century A.D.[35] onwards indicate a more varied role of the *Yavanas*, and, in addition to being traders, they also seem to have established regular *Yavana* settlements.[36] They were now employed as bodyguards to kings and as palace guards during the night.[37] While describing the military campaigns of the hero it is stated that the hero's chamber was specially constructed by the fierce eyed *Yavanas*.[38] Lamps introduced by the *Yavanas* were known for their fine workmanship and their innovative shapes resembling a swan or a woman.[39] Elsewhere the *Yavanas* are described as indulging in drinking, decorating themselves and walking along the streets at night.[40] In the suburbs of Puhar or Kaveripūmpattinam the onlooker's attention was arrested by the sight of the abode of the *Yavanas* whose prosperity never waned.[41]

Sangam literature thus provides interesting evidence of *Yavana* presence in south India and the gradual diversification in their activities. It would seem that while a majority participated in trading ventures, a few took up other occupations as well. This overwhelming evidence from literary sources does not find corroboration in epigraphic data.

Seventy-six inscriptions engraved in Brahmi characters of the early centuries of this era have been found at twenty-one sites in the southern districts of Tamil Nadu, mostly around Madurai. These record donations or gifts made to Jaina monks who resided in these natural caverns and caves. The donors belonged to a variety of occupational groups such as goldsmiths, sugar merchants, salt merchants, cloth merchants, ironmongers, stone masons and lapidaries, and included kings, chieftains and lay devotees.[42] Though names from Sri Lanka occur as donors, *Yavanas* are conspicuous by their absence,[43] which seems rather intriguing at first when one considers the large number of

---

33. *Akam* 149 ; *Puram* 56, 343.

34. *Akam* 57 ; *Puram* 343.

35. K. Zvelebil, *The Smile of Murugan*, *op. cit.* : 41.

36. *Patirruppattu* (Patikam 2).

37. *Mulaippāttu* 66, 61.

38. *Ibid.*

39. *Netunalvātai* 101-2; *Perumpanarruppatai* 316-9.

40. *Netunalvātai* 31-5.

41. *Pattinappālai* 214-7.

42. K. V. Raman, « Brahmi Inscriptions of Tamil Nadu : a Historical Assessment », *Studies in Indian Epigraphy*, I, 1974 : 104-5.

43. *Ibid.*

Yavana donations recorded in the epigraphs of the western Deccan caves. A possible explanation may be that the *Yavanas* directly participated in local transactions in south India and hence were not dependent on indigenous trade networks or religious institutions who permeated these. This aspect of local dependence will be dealt with in greater detail a little later.

On the authority of the Peutingeran Tables it has been suggested that a temple dedicated to Augustus existed at Muziris in the erstwhile State of Cochin.[44] This claim has been questioned on the grounds that though Augustus had been deified at Rome no one ever thought seriously of considering him a god. Besides a closer analysis of the Tables shows that the temple of Augustus was located not in the town of Muziris but in the country where Muziris stood, *i.e.* in the south of India and it may have been an important landmark to navigators. Thus most likely the temple referred to may have been one dedicated to Agastya and stood at Cape Comorin.[45]

Inscriptions from central and western India stand in marked contrast to those from the south. An epigraph at Sanchi records the gift of a *Yona* (*Yavana*) inhabitant of Setapatha.[46] The *caitya* at Karle situated at the head of the Bhorghat in the Sahyadris is important for our study. A majority of the donations made by *Yavanas* occur at Karle and were made by the inhabitants of Dhenukākata,[47] an exception being the *Yavana* Vītasamgata from Umehanakata, the place-name being unidentified so far.[48] The gifts are primarily in the form of pillars in the *caitya* at Karle and date from the first century A.D. : the donors have Indian names such as Dhamadhaya, Chūlayakha, Sīhadhaya and Yasavadhana. At Nasik cave XVII (dated after 110 A.D.). Indrāgnidatta, son of Dhammadeva the *Yavana*, a northerner (*otarāhasa*) from Dattamitri, donated a cave, a *caitya* and cisterns.[49] Inscriptions at Junnar record gifts by *Yavana* donors of the Gata country, corresponding to Sanskrit Garta, *i.e.* part of Trigarta or Kangra.[50] Unlike other donors of the western Deccan, the *Yavanas* do not mention their occupations. It has been suggested that such a reference may have been considered unnecessary, as the *Yavanas* were probably exclusively

44. G. JOUVEAU DUBREUIL, « The Temple of Augustus in the South of India », *The Quarterly Journal of the Mythic Society*, XIX, 1929 : 180.

45. *Ibid.*

46. G. BUEHLER, « Further Inscriptions from Sanchi », *EI,* II, 1894 : 395, no. 364.

47. M. S. VATS, « Unpublished Votive Inscriptions in the Caitya Cave at Karle », *EI,* XVIII, 1925-6, nos. 4, 6, 10 ; J. BURGESS & BHAGWANLAL INDRAJI, *Inscriptions from the Cave Temples of Western India*, Varanasi, 1976 (reprint), nos. 7, 10.

48. M. S. VATS, « Unpublished Votive Inscriptions », *op. cit.* : no. 1.

49. E. SENART, « The Inscriptions in the caves at Nasik », *EI,* VIII, 1905-6, no. 18.

50. J. BURGESS & BHAGWANLAL INDRAJI, *Inscriptions from the Cave Temples, op. cit.*, nos. 5, 7, 33.

traders.[51] Kosambi has read the name of one of the donors as Milinda the physician instead of Mitidāsa, and suggested that he may also have been a *Yavana*, though not following the usual profession.[52]

Stein has argued that from a social point of view « *Yavanas* whoever they might have been » were absorbed by Indian society and it is unlikely that Greek colonies existed around the beginning of the Christian era.[53] Kosambi has, however, opposed this view and suggested that Deogadh on the opposite curve of hills from Karle be identified as Dhenukākata as a majority of the *Yavana* donors were resident there. Kosambi has based his observations on the fact that a small hillock about 500 m. to the east of Deogadh has impressive rock-cut cisterns and an unusual concentration of carnelian microliths may still be picked up at the foot of the hillock. Other signs of settlement at the site include a large cave without cells in the hillock behind the village at Deogadh. This cave seems to have been abandoned before completion because of water leaking into it. A continuity of the ancient tradition has been seen in the special cult relation that Deogadh still maintains with the Karle caves. The great April *palkhi* procession of the goddess Yamai starts at Deogadh and proceeds directly to the shrine of the goddess at the entrance to the Karle *caitya* without visiting any other village in between.[54] Whatever the merits of this identification, it seems hard to accept a Greek or *Yavana* colony at Dhenukākata, though it was an important trading centre, as one of the epigraphs refers to the *vāniya-gāma* of Dhenukākata.[55] The site should not be confused with Dhānyakataka, the ancient name of Amaravati,[56] now known as Dharanikota in district Guntur, where archaeological excavations have unearthed remains of an ancient wharf.

An inscription important to our study is the one found at Alluru in Krishna district and dated to the second/third century A.D. It records various gifts to the *ṇikāya* of the *pūrvaśailīya āryas*. These include some *nivartanas* of land, cows, bullocks and carts, vessels and, most significant of all, lamps shaped like the mouth of a fish and manufactured by *Yavanas*.[57] The motif of an oil lamp held in the cupped hands of a figurine is one of the few vestiges of Roman influence that continue into medieval times in Tamil Nadu.

51. V. Dehejia, *Early Buddhist Rock Temples*, London, 1972 : 143.

52. D. D. Kosambi, « Dhenukākata », *Journal of the Asiatic Society of Bombay*, XXX, pt. 2, 1955 : 59.

53. O. Stein, « Yavanas in Early Indian Inscriptions », *op. cit* : 356.

54. D. D. Kosambi, « Dhenukākata », *op. cit.* : 59-60.

55. *Ibid.* : 66.

56. D. C. Sircar,« Some Problems of Early Indian History », *Journal of the Royal Asiatic Society*. 1976 : 130-5.

57. D. C. Sircar, *The Successors of the Sātavāhanas in the Lower Deccan*, University of Calcutta, 1939 : 228-30.

It would then seem that even around the beginning of the Christian era the term *Yavana* indicated three different categories of foreigners, viz. the Greeks, the Indo-Greeks, and the inhabitants of the Roman east. While the first two categories were resident in the north-western and western regions of the subcontinent, the third category settled in the peninsula and participated primarily in trading ventures. These regional divisions are more in the nature of generalisations and are not meant to indicate water-tight compartments. Within the peninsula, three regions may be broadly demarcated : the western Deccan, the east coast and the Malabar coast ; differences between these regions being due to both geographical and historical factors. To take up the western Deccan first ; the early trade impinging on the far south is said to have originated in Gujarat and Sindh and along the west coast,[58] and gold from the Deccan plateau reached the ports of the Konkan coast as early as the fourth century B.C.[59] The participation of ports like Bharuch and Sopara in the early maritime trade is further indicated by references in Buddhist literature. Archaeological evidence defines a cultural unit comprising the Narmada-Bombay region, including the Tapti and upper Godavari valleys ; a unit characterised by the use of the *Black-and-Red Ware* from a period slightly earlier than the *Northern Black Polished Ware*.[60] The prosperity of this region depended in substantial measure on the trade that passed through Bharuch in the Mauryan period, though, as has been shown above, some of it had earlier beginnings. This early trading network in the north Konkan and Narmada region continued under the Mauryans as testified by the recovery of their punch-marked coins, as well as after the decline of the dynasty, when numismatic evidence again indicates that cities like Mahismatī,[61] Tripurī,[62] and Ter[63] issued their own die-struck coins. It would be reasonable to conclude from these data that on acount of the long tradition of the existence of a trading network, the local merchants would have been in a fairly dominant position by the time of the early Sātavāhanas in the first century B.C.

The first century B.C. was also the period of increased commercial traffic between the west coast and the Mediterranean. The *Periplus of the Erythraean Sea* contains a mariner's account of the sea traffic between India, Arabia and Egypt in the early centuries of the Christian era. The *Periplus* states that large

58. C. MALONEY, *The Effect of Early Coastal Sea Traffic on the Development of Civilization in South India*, unpublished Ph. D. thesis, University of Pennsylvania, 1968 : 286.

59. *Ibid.*: 227.

60. M. MITCHINER, *The Origins of Indian Coinage*, Hawkins Publications, 1973 : 6.

61. P. L. GUPTA, « Coins of the city of Mahismatī », *Journal of the Numismatic Society of India* (hereafter *JNSI*), XV, 1953 : 70-3.

62. S. L. KATARE, « A New coin of Tripurī a city-state in ancient India », *JNSI*, XIII, 1951 : 40-5.

63. C. GUPTA. « A Coin of the city state of Tagara », *JNSI*, XXXIII, 1971 : 37-40.

vessels plied between the market towns of Persia and Bharuch,[64] and Indian vessels shared a considerable part of the commercial traffic between the ports on the west coast and the Arabian coastline as far as the entrance to the Red Sea. Beyond that trade was completely monopolised first by the Arabs and later by the Greeks from Egypt. Strabo states that since the Romans invaded Arabia Felix the merchants of Alexandria sailed with fleets by way of the Nile and of the Arabian Gulf as far as India and that as many as one hundred and twenty vessels sailed from Myos Hormos to India, whereas under the Ptolemys only very few ventured to undertake the voyage and to carry on traffic in Indian merchandise.[65] It would seem that in spite of this substantial commercial traffic, the Greeks or Romans did not gather in person the products of the subcontinent, as is evident from their vague knowledge of plants. Pliny hardly gives any exact localities of Indian commodities and Ptolemy adds only a few.[66] The seasonal pattern of trade influenced by the monsoon winds and the increasing demand for Indian commodities in the Mediterranean markets would have led to the dependence on the local trade network in regions where it was well established. Elsewhere, the *Yavanas* may have had a more direct role and may have used their own Roman coins as high value currency.

In pre-industrial societies, long-distance trade requires finding solutions to a number of technical problems : the regular exchange of information about the conditions of supply and demand ; the creation and maintenance of relations of trust between the traders and intermediaries who are involved in the chain of trade ; the creation of regular credit arrangements ; and the organization of an efficient system of arbitration and adjudication in business disputes. These problems can only be overcome by the formation of what has been described as a « trading diaspora » which creates a corporate identity and cultural unity among its members.[67] This is essential in order to prevent infiltration into its ranks, thus breaking its monopoly of the trade. The criteria chosen for the definition of this distinctiveness depend on a variety of factors, and a common religion has generally been recognised as a potent binding force.[68] The spread of Islam in West Africa has been seen as providing a blue-print of a politico-economic organisation which has overcome the many basic technical problems

---

64. *Periplus*, sec. 36.

65. *The Geography of Strabo,* 2.5.12.

66. E. H. WARMINGTON, *The Commerce between the Roman Empire and India,* Vikas. 1974 : 260.

67. A. COHEN, « Cultural Strategies in the organization of trading diasporas », C. Meillassoux, ed., *The Development of Indigenous Trade and Markets in West Africa*, Oxford University Press, 1971 : 266-70.

68. *Ibid.*

of long-distance trade.[69] In India, in the centuries around the Christian era, this need was perhaps fulfilled by both Buddhism and Jainism, with a constant tussle between the two. Owing to historical factors the Deccan formed a part of the Buddhist trading diaspora. Thus gifts and donations by the *Yavanas* in the western Deccan may be seen as attempts to participate in the cultural distinctiveness of the Buddhist trading diaspora on which the *Yavanas* were dependent. In the eastern Deccan and south India the situation was radically different. Though the ports along the Andhra coast had participated in the looping coastal trade, they did not develop as outlets for the Mediterranean markets owing to their remote geographical location vis-a-vis the sea-routes oriented towards the west. Thus the direction of commercial traffic in the Deccan was mainly overland towards Bharuch and the Konkan coast and this greatly enhanced the importance of Buddhist caves located at the heads of passes in the Sahyadris.

The *Periplus*, written in the first century A.D., mentions only the land of Masalia on the Andhra coast « where much muslin is produced », while it prominently describes the trans-peninsular overland route from the east coast to Ter, Paithan and Bharuch.[70] As contrasted to this Ptolemy's compilation in the middle of the second century A.D. exhibits a growing knowledge of the trade routes, especially of the east coast, thereby providing evidence for the extension of trade into new regions.

Perhaps an inhibiting factor in the development and organisation of trade in the Andhra region was the continuation of megalithic settlements well into the early historical period. The lower Krishna valley was intensively settled in the Megalithic period and there were fairly large clusters of megaliths in Anantapur and Chittoor districts in the vicinity of gold-bearing Dharwar schists.[71] To the north of the Andhra region, no megalithic remains have been found in Orissa and this would suggest that the inhabited corridor in this period extended via the Nalgonda and Medak districts of Andhra Pradesh to central India, past the sites of Pochampad and Peddabankur in the middle Godavari valley.[72] It is difficult to work out the exchange system at this time owing to a paucity of excavated data, but there is no evidence as yet for the existence of coinage or of a trade network in pre-Mauryan times. Though many of the Megalithic sites may have continued into the early centuries of the Christian era, there is sufficient evidence for Mauryan presence in the Andhra region in the form of Aśokan inscriptions,

---

69. *Ibid.*

70. *Periplus*, secs. 62, 51.

71. A. CHATTERJEE, *Socio-economic conditions in early Andhra, c. 200 B.C.-300 A.D.*, unpublished Ph. D. thesis, Jawarharlal Nehru University. 1976 : 216.

72. *Ibid.*

Mauryan remains and punch-marked coins of the Magadha-Mauryan series.[73] The centralised organisation of trade under the Mauryans may have hampered the development of a local trade network, and this appears to be generally true of the post-Mauryan period as well. One of the few exceptions is indicated in the inscriptions of Bhattiprolu dated about 100 B.C., which mention a *rājan* named Kuberaka who headed the *gothi* of *nigamaputa*.[74]

Thus the available evidence indicates that it was perhaps only in the late first-early second century A. D. that the circumpeninsular route developed and the ports of the Andhra coast entered into the maritime trade network with the Mediterranean region. This observation seems to be corroborated by Sātavāhana expansion into the Andhra region in the reign of Vāsiṣṭhīputra Śrī Pulumāvi, of whom an inscription has been found for the first time outside the limits of the western Deccan, at Amaravati.[75] This comparatively late entry of the east coast in the trade circuit and the near absence of a local commercial network is reflected in the distribution pattern of Roman coins in the subcontinent and the use of imitation Roman coins in Andhra. Another piece of evidence that seems to fit in is the minting of silver portrait coins by Vāsiṣṭhīputra Śrī Pulumāvi, who was also the first ruler to have introduced bilingual and biscriptual legends on his coins. The dialect on the reverse has been variously identified as Tamil or as Telugu.[76] Whatever the identification, the very fact that a need was felt to incorporate bilingual legends on coins suggests an urgent desire to integrate new areas.

A similar situation may have prevailed further south. Archaeological evidence indicates that the Megalithic culture had already permeated throughout Tamil Nadu, excluding the districts of north Arcot, Salem and Madurai, by the third century B.C. at the latest, and that this continued until and perhaps beyond the period of Indo-Roman trade and its cultural impact.[77] A majority of silver coins found in peninsular India belong to two classes : firstly the Magadha-Mauryan *Karṣāpaṇas* and their imitations ; and secondly Roman *denarii* and their imitations. Although the influx of Mauryan silver probably initiated the widespread use of silver coinage in the Pāndya country and prompted the issues

---

73. M. MITCHINER, *The Origins of Indian Coinage*, *op. cit.* : 103.

74. H. LUEDERS, *A List of Brahmi Inscriptions*, Calcutta, 1912, no. 1335.

75. J. BURGESS, *The Buddhist Stupas of Amaravati and Jaggayyapeta*, London, 1887 : 100.

76. P. R. K. PRASAD, « Silver Portrait Coins of the Sātavāhanas », A. M. Shastri, ed., *Coinage of the Sātavāhanas and Coins from Excavations*, Nagpur, 1972 : 68-74.

77. K. V. SOUNDARA RAJAN, « Culture. Megalithic-southern region », A. Ghosh, ed., *Encyclopaedia of Indian Archaeology*, 1989.

of the local Pāndyan punch-marked coins, these never attained a dominant role in the economy.[78]

The distribution of ceramic industries provides further evidence of the regional divisions within the peninsula. In Kathiawar, a distinctive pottery of fine fabric and a bright red surface came into use in the first century A.D. This ware, called the *Red Polished Ware*, gained wide currency and has been found extensively from Gujarat through the western Deccan to Urchan in district Gulbarga,[79] Kotalingala in district Karimnagar,[80] Satanikota in district Kurnool (the Kharosthi letters inscribed on these examples providing a link with the north-west),[81] Peddamarrur, district Mahbûbnagar,[82] and Yelleswaram in district Nalgonda.[83] That there was a separate communication network linking the entire east coast including northern Sri Lanka can be demonstrated on the basis of the distribution of the *Rouletted Ware*, the most distinctive ceramic associated with the Early Historical period.[84] This network extended from Korkai in the south to Tamluk and Chandraketugarh in the north and included inland centres along the major routes, such as Maski, Amaravati, etc. As distinct from the Coromandel coast, the Malabar coast had a network of its own, as indicated by the distribution of the *Russet-coated Painted Ware*. The concentration of this ware was in the area south of the Krishna and extended as far as Uraiyur, though it is generally absent on the Coromandel coast.[85]

The role of the *Yavanas* and the influence that they could exert was determined by two factors : the efficiency and complexity of these local trade networks, and the use of indigenous coinage in local transactions within these. As has been shown above, the available data indicates a fairly well established trade network in the western Deccan with its own coinage, though this was not the case along the east coast and further south. This is borne out by the distribution of Roman coins found in India. An analytical study of these shows a preponderance of *denarii*, a total of 5,400 *denarii* to 800 *aurei*. The *denarius* was the main silver coin of the Republican period, the gold *aureus* being an infrequent issue. As soon as Augustus established the Empire and restored peace

78. M. MITCHINER, *The Origins of Indian Coinage*, *op. cit.* : 103.

79. *Indian Archaeology-a Review* (hereafter *IAR*), 1960-1961 : 65.

80. *IAR 1980-81* : 2

81. R. S. SHARMA, *Perspectives in Social and Economic History of Early India.* New Delhi. 1983 : 142.

82. *IAR 1977-78* : 12-3.

83. *IAR 1962-63* : 2.

84. V. BEGLEY, « Arikamedu Reconsidered », *American Journal of Archaeology*, 87, 1983 : 462.

85. B. K. THAPAR, « Maski, 1954. A Chalcolithic site of the southern Deccan », *Ancient India*. XIII, 1957 : 73.

in 31 B.C. he reorganised the coinage — gold coins were issued regularly and the gold *aureus* was valued at 25 *denarii*. Nero (54-68 A.D.) debased the currency, lowered the weight of gold and silver coins and reduced the fineness of the latter. In India pre-Augustan issues are rare and a majority of the coin finds are those of the reigns of Augustus and Tiberius. Another prominent feature of the Roman hoards is the newness of the coins.[86]

The distribution map of Roman coins shows almost the whole of north India and the western Deccan as a blank, the exceptions being Taxila, where a single coin of Tiberius was found ; Manikyala where a few Republican coins were recovered in an extremely worn condition along with Kuṣāṇa coins ; and a few sites in Uttar Pradesh such as Allahabad, Kanauj, Mathura and Mirzapur where single coins have been found.[87] This paucity has been blamed on the Kuṣāṇas, who are said to have melted Roman gold coins for minting their own issues, but this still does not explain the absence of coins of silver. In eastern India only one hoard of Roman *aurei* is known and has been recovered from Singhbhum.[88] Similarly finds of Roman coins are scanty in western India as well. In 1840 a hoard was discovered near Sholapur which included *aurei* of Severus Antoninus Commodus and Geta.[89] An *aureus* of Septimus Severus was also found at Waghoda in district Dhule, while three other finds of Roman coins have been confined to the Vidarbha region.[90] Roman *denarii* were recovered during the excavation at Vadgaon-Madhavpur,[91] and a gold coin of Augustus was found at Kondapur.[92] Unfortunately no hoard of Roman coins has yet been found at Bharuch and only a single coin has been reported so far.[93]

---

86. P. L. GUPTA, « Roman Trade in India », *Dr. Satkari Mookerji Felicitation Volume*, Varanasi, 1969 : 169-80. For orientation, the dates of some Roman emperors are as follows : Augustus (27 B.C.-A.D. 14) ; Tiberius (14-37) ; Claudius (41-54) ; Nero (54-68) ; Vespasian (69-79) ; Domitian (81-96) ; Trajan (98-117) ; Hadrian (117-138) ; Antoninus Pius (138-161) ; Marcus Aurelius (161-180) ; Commodus (180-192) ; Caracalla (212-217) ; Diocletian (284-305).

87. R. F. M. WHEELER, A. GOSH & K. DEVA, « Arikamedu », *Ancient India*, II, 1946 : 116-21.

88. P. L. GUPTA, « Roman Trade in India », *op cit.* : 169-80.

89. *Indian Antiquary*. II, 1873 : 241-2.

90. P. L. GUPTA, « Roman Trade in India », *op. cit.* ; K. O. KAWADKAR, « Adam Hoard of Roman Coins », *JNSI, XXXII*, 1972 : 243-7.

91. A. SUNDARA, « A Two Thousand Year Old Town and its Architecture in Vadgaon-Madhavpur (Belgaum) in Karnataka », M. S. Nagaraja Rao, ed., *Madhu*, Delhi, 1981 : 91.

92. G. YAZDANI, Excavations at Kondapur an Andhra Town (c. 200 B.C. to 200 A.D.), *Annals of the Bhandarkar Oriental Research Institute*, XXII, 1941 : 180.

93. R. E. M. WHEELER, *Rome Beyond the Imperial Frontiers*. London, 1955 : 195.

This absence of coin finds is in marked contrast to the evidence from clay bullae. Bullae are a characteristic feature of Early Historical levels in the subcontinent and are often made in imitation of Roman coins. Produced in clay from a mould these bullae have a loop or perforation, straight or tubular, for threading. Surprisingly these are of widespread occurrence in the north starting from Taxila, the Ganga valley and including sites such as Sisupalgarh, Ujjain and further south to Kanchipuram and Uraiyur.[94] The general opinion is that these were used as neck ornaments and indicate widespread familiarity with Roman coins. Clay sealings found at Mathura and Ujjain bear the legend « *yavanikānām* » (of *Yavana* women).[95]

As compared to this, finds of Roman coins are more numerous in the eastern Deccan and are scattered in the districts of Bijapur, Cuddapah, Guntur, Krishna, Nalgonda and Visakhapatnam.[96]. A hoard from Nasthulapar in district Karimnagar yielded 39 Roman and 8 silver punch-marked coins, the former belonging to Augustus and Nero.[97] Two more Roman *aurei* of Nero and one of Faustina the elder were found at Nagarjunakonda.[98] One gold coin of Augustus with holes on top suggesting its use as a pendant was unearthed in the recent excavation at Kudavelli in district Mahbubnagar ;[99] the excavations at Peddabankur and Dhulikatta have yielded some more Roman coins.[100]

Of the known 78 finds of Roman coins, 57 were found south of the Vindhyas and of these 29 were from the Tamil region,[101] though large hoards are also known from the district of Bangalore, comprising 250 silver coins of Augustus.[102] Further, there is a concentration of Roman coins around Coimbatore in Tamil Nadu within a radius of about 50 kms. from the beryl mines at Padiyur. What is significant is that in the district of Coimbatore the Eastern Ghats swing westwards and terminate upon the line of the Western Ghats and that the valley of the Ponnani carries a natural trans-peninsular

94. C. MARGABANDHU, « Bullae », A. Ghosh, ed., *Encyclopaedia of Indian Archaeology*, 1989.

95. *IAR 1967-68* : 56 ; *1968-69* : 46.

96. P. L. GUPTA, *Roman Coins from Andhra Pradesh*. Hyderabad, 1965 : 43-5.

97. P. L. GUPTA, « Nasthulapur Hoard of Silver Roman and punch-marked coins », *JNSI*. XIX, 1957 : 1-4.

98. *IAR 1956-57* : 38.

99. N. C. GHOSH & K. ISMAIL, « Two foreign gold coins from the excavation at Kudavelli, district Mahbubnagar, Andhra Pradesh », *JNSI*. XLII, 1980 : 11.

100. B. K. GURURAJA RAO, ed., *A Decade of Archaeological Studies in South India*, Dharwar, 1978 : 62, 66.

101. B. SRIVASTAVA, « The Economic Significance of Roman Coins found in India », *JNSI*, XXVI, 1964 : 222-7.

102. *IAR 1964-65* : 71.

highway immediately south of the abutment. This highway must have provided a useful alternative to the long coastal route between the Malabar and Coromandel coasts.[103]

At Akkenapalle in the district of Nalgonda, a pot containing 1531 silver coins, broken pieces of ornaments and some strips of silver were found. A majority of the coins belonged to the reigns of Augustus and Tiberius, but most interesting was the inclusion of as many as 55 imitations.[104] Gupta reasons that Roman silver coins could have been used as legal tender. Incisions were made on the coins to deface the portrait of the Emperor and as the coins were approximately the same weight as the punch-marked coins (50 to 54 grams) most of them could be introduced into circulation by counter-marking with minute symbols similar to those used on punch-marked coins, such as *svastika*, *cakra*, etc. A similar phenomenon has also been noticed in the Nasthulapur and Eyyal hoards.[105] It has been suggested that imitations of Roman coins were struck from locally made dies.[106] An Ikṣvāku inscription found at Nagarjunakonda records donations of *dinaris* and their investment with different guilds. Sircar explains that the *dinari* is a derivative from the Roman coin *denarius*.[107]

Several hypotheses have been put forward to explain the distribution of Roman coins in the subcontinent. Gupta has used the evidence to indicate a shift in Roman trade from south India to the eastern Deccan in the second century A.D.[108] Warmington suggests that there was a « deliberate exportation » of Roman money to India to create a Roman currency there,[109] while Wheeler accepts that Roman coins may have been used not as currency but as bullion to be weighed out in exchange for gold and silver ornaments or goods.[110] The *Periplus*, sec. 49, states that gold and silver money was imported into Bharuch and could be « exchanged with much profit for the local currency ».

We should discount here the chronological value of Roman coins found in India. The newness of the coins recovered, the predominance of the issues of Augustus and Tiberius and the fact that Nero debased the currency, thus making it useless for foreign trade, are definite indicators which suggest that the coins of

103. R. E. M. WHEELER, *et. al.*, « Arikamedu », *op. cit.* : 116.

104. P. L. GUPTA, *Roman Coins from Andhra Pradesh*, *op. cit.* : 65.

105. *Ibid.* : 68.

106. M. G. RASCHKE, « New Studies in Roman Commerce with the East », *Aufstieg und Niedergang der Romischer Welt*, Berlin, 1978 : 672.

107. D. C. SIRCAR, « More Inscriptions from Nagarjunakonda », *EI*, XXXV : 5.

108. P. L. GUPTA, *Roman Coins from Andhra Pradesh*. *op. cit.* : 45-50.

109. E. H. WARMINGTON, *The Commerce between the Roman Empire and India*, *op. cit.* : 274.

110. R. E. M. WHEELER, *Rome beyond the Imperial Frontiers*, *op. cit*: : 167.

Augustus and Tiberius were specifically collected for exchange and use in India. On the evidence of the *Periplus* and other texts Indian commodities were sent either to ports along the Arabian coast or to Alexandria in Egypt. The coins found in India thus in no way reflect the coinage in circulation in the Roman Empire. It has been established that the Roman conquerors of Egypt permitted the continued circulation of Ptolemaic coinage and almost all the papyri attest only to the use of Alexandrian tetradrachma until A.D. 296 when Diocletian gave Egypt the same coinage as the rest of the Empire.[111] The evidence thus suggests that Roman coins cannot be used to indicate any shifts in trade.

The uneven distribution of Roman coins in the peninsula can be better understood when compared with the local coinage prevalent in this area. In the western Deccan there are sufficient indications of a well-established currency under the Sātavāhanas and coins of copper, lead and potin would have been widely used in local trade transactions. As a result Roman coins are likely to have been used as bullion and would not have entered the local commercial network, hence their near absence in the region. In contrast the eastern Deccan and south India do not provide evidence of a local currency in the early centuries of the Christian era. This would have led to the use of Roman coins as a high value currency and their subsequent introduction in local trade transactions. This explains why imitation Roman coins were made in the Andhra region and the mention of the use of *dinari* in Ikṣvāku epigraphs. Use in local commercial exchange also led to their survival in the beryl producing areas of Coimbatore district.

Archaeological excavations might have provided decisive information on the existence of *Yavana* colonies in the subcontinent. But there has been little success in this direction so far, though excavations have now been carried out at several important sites such as Arikamedu on the east coast, Uraiyur in district Tiruchirapalli, Kanchipuram, district Chingleput, Kaveripattinam, district Thanjavur and Cranganore or Muziris of the *Periplus*. Of these sites, Arikamedu yielded imported wares such as the *Arretine ware* as well as gems, one of which was untrimmed and has been taken to indicate the presence of Western craftsmen at the site.[112] Another promising site recently discovered is that of Kottaimedu, 28 kms. from Ramanathapuram.[113]

Sherds of *Arretine ware* and Roman amphorae have been found extensively in the peninsula from sites such as Kanchipuram,[114] Vasavasamudram, district Chingleput, at the mouth of the river Palar,[115]

---

111. M. G. RASCHKE, New Studies in Roman Commerce with the East *op. cit.* : 668-9.

112. R. E. M. WHEELER, *et. al.*, Arikamedu, *op. cit.* : 17.

113. *Hindustan Times*, 7 October 1983.

114. *IAR 1962-63* : 12 ; *1970-71* : 32 ; *1972-73* : 30.

115. *IAR 1970-71* : 33.

Uraiyur,[116] and Karaikadu 30 kms. south of Arikamedu on the east coast,[117] and in Gujarat at Dwarka,[118] Prabhas Patan,[119] Ajabpura on the Mahi, and Sathod, Jalat and Nagara.[120] Other objects of Roman workmanship include terracotta heads imitating Graeco-Roman art and typically Roman lamps from Arikamedu[121] and Ter.[122] These two sites have also provided interesting specimens of glass objects such as beads, bottles and bowls. A rich hoard of Roman and Sātavāhana metal objects was found at Brahmapuri a suburb of Kolhapur and included a statuette of Poseidon ; two handles of wine jugs intricately carved ; a cup ; a wine jug ; a candlestick base ; and a mirror with a slightly raised knob.[123] A handle of a bronze jug carved with a figure of Cupid was another significant discovery, this time from Akota. Investigations at Karvan, 30 kms. to the south of Akota revealed the existence of a cameo of a patrician lady from the Roman world.[124] Fragments of Roman amphorae, a copper dish with a boss in the centre and two human masks of terracotta used to decorate the sides of vessels have been found at Nevasa.[125] The conclusion seems to be inescapable that Roman contacts were extensive in the peninsula, yet archaeology has been of little help in indicating specific Roman settlements.

The *varṇa* status accorded to the *Yavanas* in Indian literature varied in consonance with their economic status. In the second half of the first millennium B.C. a major distinction was based on language and all those areas where a *mleccha bhāṣā* was spoken came to be designated as *mleccha deśa* and included the frontier areas such as the lands of the *Yavanas* and the *Kāmbojas*.[126] The *Gautama Dharma Sūtra* elevated them to the progeny of *kṣatriya* men and *śūdra* women.[127] By the time of the *Mahābhārata* an indigenous origin had been found for the *Yavanas* and they were described as the sons of Yayāti associated with

---

116. *IAR 1964-65* : 25.

117. *IAR 1966-67* : 21.

118. *IAR 1962-63* : 7.

119. *IAR 1971-72* : 13.

120. R. N. MEHTA, « Urban Centres of Western India and the Western World », J. Deppert, ed., *India and the West*, Manohar, 1983 : 142.

121. R. E. M. WHEELER, *et. al.*, « Arikamedu », *op. cit.*: 34, 101.

122. *IAR 1967-68* : 35.

123. K. KHANDALAVALA, « Brahmapuri », *Lalit Kala*, 7, 1960 : 56.

124. R. N. MEHTA, « Urban Centres of Western India », *op. cit.* : 142.

125. H. D. SANKALIA, *et. al.*, *From History to Prehistory at Nevasa (1954-56)*, Poona, 1960 : 398-99, 421.

126. Yāska's *Nirukta*, II. 2 ; *Atharvaveda*. V. 22. 14 ; *Chāndogya Upaniṣad*. VI. 14. 1. 2 ; R. THAPAR, *Ancient Indian Social History*, *op. cit.* : 159.

127. *Gautama Dharma Sūtra*, IV. 21.

one of the very early and important tribes of north India.[128] Elsewhere they are said to have sprung from the body of Vasiṣṭha's cow together with the Pahlavas, Drāvidas, Śakas, etc. in order to destroy the army of her attacker Viśvāmitra.[129] No less a personage than Indra says that the *Yavanas* can be admitted into the social pale provided they follow the *dharma* of the Śāstras.[130] Elsewhere in the *Mahābhārata* the *Yavanas* are degraded as *śūdras* along with the Drāvidas, Kalingas and Śakas.[131] The *Manusmṛti* also does not seem to be very clear about the position to be accorded to the *Yavanas*. At one point they are described as *vrātya kṣatriyas*, *i.e.* basically of *kṣatriya* origin but having become degenerate owing to the non-performance of sacred rites, while soon there after they are referred to as *dasyus*.[132] These contradictions no doubt arise from the need to compromise political status with ritual status within the *varṇa* hierarchy. It is perhaps complicated by the use of the term *Yavana* to indicate several categories of foreigners such as the Greeks, Indo-Greeks and merchants from the Roman East.

Our analysis thus indicates a significant *Yavana* presence in the subcontinent in the early centuries of the Christian era though their role seems to have varied in different regions. Their earliest settlements were in the north-western region of the subcontinent and these continued for a considerable time. In the western Deccan *Yavana* presence coincides with a spurt in external trade and judging from the donations to Buddhist monastic establishments it would seem that they were vying for acceptability and inclusion in the trading network. In the eastern Deccan and south India, the *Yavanas* appear to be direct participants in local trade transactions. This is also the reason why tangible proofs of their presence such as coins, lamps, pottery, etc. are abundantly found in these regions.

Himanshu P. RAY
Jawaharlal Nehru University

128. *Mahābhārata*, I. 80. 26.

129. *Ibid.* : I. 165.

130. *Ibid.* : XII. 65. 13.

131. *Ibid.* : XIII. 33. 21-3.

132. *Manusmṛti*, X. 43-5.

Postscript (1994)

Since the publication of this paper, the author has participated in the 1990-91 excavations at Arikamedu at the kind invitation of Dr. Vimala Begley and has also done extensive field-work in south India. An analysis of the antiquities generally termed « Roman » in archaeological literature and referred to as such in the paper, has shown that very few of these were actual imports, a majority being made in imitation of foreign prototypes. This is true of the terracotta figurines, moulded pots and lamps from Ter (RAY, forthcoming), as also the intaglios and gems with Classical motifs and glass objects (RAY, 1994 : 73-76). Khandalavala believed that the bronzes from Kolhapur were part of a hoard manufactured in Alexandria. Subsequent analysis by De Puma has suggested that the bronzes do not form a homogenous group, and though they may have been shipped from Alexandria, they were certainly not manufactured there. This motley collection could have been obtained from anywhere in the Roman Empire and its adjacent territories. Thus it is most likely that it was gathered together for smelting in a foundry (DE PUMA, 1992). It is also evident that Roman trade need not be invoked for explaining the innovations in techniques and decoration of pottery, as recent archaeological excavations in the region of the Persian Gulf have provided evidence of Hellenistic settlement in the area (SALLES, 1987), and the participation of these in the maritime network. Thus, the only true imports are the amphorae and sherds of *terra sigillata,* though graffiti marks very similar to those from Megalithic sites on the *terra sigillata* certainly raises several interesting possibilities. In the final analysis, the number of objects of Roman workmanship found in peninsular India is indeed small and cannot be used to substantiate the presence of Roman settlements in the peninsula.

The presence of *Yavana* settlements in south India as reflected in Sangam literature from the second century AD onwards should then be studied in the context of two larger issues : one, recent research on Roman coins found in India, especially those from peninsular India which indicate a later date for the import of coins than has hitherto been accepted ; and two, the gradual southward shift in the western Indian Ocean networks.

In the past, Roman coins found in India have been used to provide a chronological framework for Roman trade with the east. As the majority of the coins are those of Augustus (31 BC - AD 14) and Tiberius (AD 14-37), it had been argued by Sewell (1904) that trade began under Augustus, reached a peak under Nero (AD 54 - 68), declined until the time of Caracalla (AD 198 - 217) and then almost entirely ceased, but revived briefly in the fifth century. This framework has been repeated by later scholars to the extent that the chronology of sites in south India has been closely linked to it.

Recent research by MacDowall indicates that hoards found in India are very different from those found elsewhere in the Roman Empire and the coins used in the trade with India were specially selected for their metal content. These were exported from the Empire after major currency reforms which devalued the metal content. Hence MacDowall has concluded that most Roman silver *denarii* found in India issued by the Julio-Claudian emperors were almost certainly exported in the Flavian period, c. AD 70 to 100, and that the much more worn Republican *denarii* of the second-first centuries BC were exported under Trajan and Hadrian in c. 100 to 140 AD, after long circulation inside the Empire (MAC DOWALL, 1991 : 145-63). Similarly the gold *aurei* valued in India as bullion were also exported after a period of circulation inside the Empire, when they contained more gold than current issues.

But perhaps what is most significant and to which little attention has been paid so far is the distribution of Roman copper coins in India. These occur in India from the second half of the third century AD in Gujarat, but from the second half of the fourth century « the flood of late Roman bronze coins starts » and these have been found mainly in southern Tamilnadu in the districts of Madurai and Karur with a scatter in the Madras area (BERGHAUS, 1991 : 111). These small Roman copper coins reflect the pattern from Sri Lanka where thousands of such fourth and fifth century coins have been found (WALBURG, 1991 : 164). Equally significant is the fact that the copper coins from the Tamil coast have mint marks of Alexandria and Antioch, while coins from Sri Lanka have those from Constantinople as well. This southward shift in the maritime network and its implications for the nature of the trade needs to be analysed, especially in view of the diverse literary references to the *Yavanas* discussed in the paper.

It is significant that a fourth century inscription from Nagarjunakonda refers to a *yonaraja* or *yavanaraja* from Sanjayata or Sanjan on the Konkan coast who was invited by the Abhira ruler Vasusena on the occasion of the installation of a wooden image of Astabhujasvami or Visnu (*Epigraphia Indica*, XXXI : 197-203). The ethnic identity of the *yonaraja* is not clear, though by the time of the Silaharas, the term *Yavana* also included Arabs and other communities from west Asia.

Himanshu Prabha RAY
Centre for Historical Studies
Jawaharlal Nehru University

REFERENCES

BERGHAUS, P., 1991, « Roman Coins from India and their imitations », A.K. Jha, ed., *Coinage, Trade and Economy,* Nashik : 108-21.

DE PUMA, R.D., 1992, « The Roman Bronzes from Kolhapur », V. Begley & R.D. De Puma, eds., *Rome and India - The Ancient Sea Trade*, Oxford University Press, New Delhi : 82-112.

MACDOWALL, D. W., 1991, « Indian Imports of Roman Silver Coins », A.K. Jha, ed., *Coinage, Trade and Economy*, Nashik : 145-64.

RAY, H.P., 1994, *Winds of Change : Buddhism and the Maritime Links of Early South Asia*, Delhi.

RAY, H.P., *forthcoming*, « Ter : an early centre on the trans-peninsular route », A.K. Jha, ed., *MacDowall Felicitation Volume*, Nashik.

SALLES, J.-F., 1987, « The Arab-Persian Gulf under the Seleucids », A. Kuhrt & S. Sherwin-White, eds., *Hellenism in the East*, London : 75-184.

SEWELL, R., 1904, « Roman Coins found in India », *Journal of the Royal Asiatic Society* : 591-637.

A RESURVEY OF 'ROMAN' CONTACTS WITH THE EAST *

The general neglect of maritime studies of the Indian subcontinent is ironic, especially in view of the vast coastline of peninsular India, but equally intriguing is the almost unsurmountable influence of the colonial legacy on contemporary history writing. Maritime contacts are invariably studied as brief interventions by « foreign » societies, be it the Romans, the Arabs or the Europeans. Indian communities seem to be passive receivers in this vibrant transoceanic network, validating as it were the framework posited by Warmington in 1918 : « the moving force from first to last came from the West, the little-changing people of the East allowed the West to find them out » (p. 1).

The terminology adopted further confirms the similarities and the discussion focuses on colonies, the development of ports and more recently on the Roman empire at the hub of a world-system which sucked in peripheral regions of South Asia into its economy (WOLF, 1990 ; SIDEBOTHAM, 1992).

The objective of this paper is not to negate the importance of Roman trade, but to shift the focus to the indigenous maritime networks in the Indian Ocean at the beginning of the Christian era, and to evaluate Roman intervention within this context. There is also an urgent need to recognise that this indigenous system was not a reflection of the better documented European trading network of the modern period ; instead it functioned within different parameters and responded to its own internal mechanisms. These rhythms were conditioned by a variety of factors, significant among these being traditional boat-building and navigation techniques, as also the fact that maritime trade in the western Indian Ocean was by no means a luxury trade dominated by the demands of the elite, but was sustained by movements of subsistence goods and agricultural products. It was then a continuous process, no doubt marked by shifts and changes in

* *Acknowledgements*. An earlier version of this paper was presented at the Maison de l'Orient Méditerraneen, Lyon, in 1991, at the invitation of Dr. J.-F. Salles. I am grateful to him and his colleagues for this opportunity. I was also fortunate to have the benefit of the comments of Prof. A. Tchernia, who was kind enough to attend the seminar.

Athens, Aden, Arikamedu
New Delhi, 1994
H. P. RAY, p. 97-114

routes. These include the somewhat earlier sea-lanes through the Persian Gulf to India or the more direct route between the Red Sea and the west coast of the Indian subcontinent that developed from the beginning of the Christian era onwards. The relative importance of these routes varied over time depending on the political and economic configurations of the hinterland. Equally versatile have been the partners in these transoceanic ventures, and the Greeks, Egyptians, Arabs and Indians have all participated in this maritime network.

It is also seldom appreciated that external and internal frontiers were practically non-existent in antiquity, and in the Indian context transoceanic voyaging was often an extension of the internal trade networks. In contrast to the port cities of the modern period, in most cases, elite groups were based in centres away from the coast, and « ports » in antiquity were merely transit points for the transfer of commodities from the maritime to the overland network.

A survey of the ancient port sites of the Indian subcontinent shows that these owed their prosperity less to their geographical location and more to the resources of their hinterland. The vast Indian coastline boasts of few natural harbours, and a consistent practice has been to locate ports and market centres at the mouths of rivers some distance away from the coast for easy landfall and accessibility to the routes of the interior. Here a major difference between the rivers of the north with those of peninsular India has to be emphasized. Unlike the Ganga which has been a primary artery of inland communication till the beginning of the century, the rivers of peninsular India flow through undulating terrain and are navigable only for short distances generally within their deltaic regions.

Another characteristic feature of Indian seafaring was its emphasis on fair weather sailing. The crafts used for coastal and transoceanic voyages were hauled ashore for drying and repairs at the end of the sailing season, and as they drew little water, these could easily enter the estuaries and river mouths. Hence elaborate structures and harbour installations were not built, unlike the practice in the Graeco-Roman world. Secondary literature, nevertheless, is replete with references to early harbours and the identification of brick structures as wharfs. Excavations at Dharanikota led to the recovery of a brick-built structure identified as a wharf along the inner side of an earlier navigation channel (*IAR* 1962-63 : 1-2). Another brick wharf was uncovered at Rajbandar port, on the island of Elephanta (Rao, 1989 : 297). At Arikamedu, it has been suggested that the brick walls of the so-called warehouse served as a dock (Rao, 1970 : 95), while a somewhat later brick wharf was identified at Kaveripattinam on the river Kaveri (*IAR* 1962-63 : 13). This led Rao to conclude, somewhat erroneously, that « on almost all the seaports mentioned by the author of the *Periplus* and by Ptolemy, some kind of a dockyard for anchoring ships and wharfs for haulage of goods must have existed ». This singular preoccupation with the identification of place names mentioned in Greek texts and the need to detect early docks and wharfs has resulted in a total neglect of the causes that led to the growth and expansion of early coastal sites.

One of the texts that continues to form the foundation for a reconstruction of Rome's trade with the East is the first century AD *Periplus Maris Erythraei*. It has been argued elsewhere (RAY, 1994) that the *Periplus* is unquestionably an extraordinary compilation of information on commodities traded between the ports of the Red Sea and the Indian subcontinent, but it also marks a distinct break from earlier Greek writing. It belongs to a different genre of literature and represents not the evolution and expansion of Graeco-Roman interests in the Indian Ocean, but the codification of available knowledge for the benefit of Oriental Greek merchants and seafarers. It is interesting that though the *Periplus* refers to a variety of local water craft in use in the western Indian Ocean, nowhere does it mention Roman ships, or shipyards along the Red Sea where these could have been made. Archaeological surveys in Egypt indicate Roman military presence at several sites along the Red Sea and a network of roads across the desert linking these to centres on the Nile (SIDEBOTHAM, 1992). The primary reason for this network of roads, however, was not the promotion of trade, but the exploitation of the porphyr mines and quarries. The west coast of the Red Sea is an arid region and the available archaeological data indicate that settlement along the coast was seasonal. Given the sparse precipitation in the Eastern desert of Egypt and the scarcity of both timber and potable water, the west shoreline seems to be an implausible area for any large scale construction of ships. Perhaps one serious contender for this position may be the port of Clysma in the north. It is nevertheless clear that without further research, Roman ship-building capabilities in the Mediterranean cannot be transposed to the inhospitable coasts of the Red Sea.

A brief mention of the implications of the newly discovered Vienna papyrus may not be out of place here. Dating to the mid-second century AD, it contains the text of an agreement between two shippers, whereby one contracts to serve as an agent for a cargo belonging to the other and to oversee its transportation to Alexandria. The names of the merchants are lost, but the details of the cargo from Muziris which arrived in one of the Red Sea ports is interesting. It comprised of nard, ivory and textiles of the total value of 131 talents, which according to CASSON (1992 : 10) could have purchased almost 2,400 acres of Egypt's farmland. But relevant to our discussion is the fact that it shows the private control of maritime enterprise and the compact nature of the commodities involved. The total weight of the consignment was no more than 7190 pounds or three and a half tons (*ibid.* : 35). It is clear that merchants regularly bought space on sea-going vessels, but there is no mention of the nature of ships involved, and the assumption that these were Roman ships is not borne out by the evidence.

This raises the question of the nature of commodities involved in the maritime network of the western Indian Ocean. It has repeatedly been argued that the indigenous communities of the western Indian Ocean were involved in coastal trade involving subsistence goods and agricultural products, while the foreigners, be it the Romans, the Arabs or the Europeans monopolised transoceanic voyages in their larger, better equipped vessels and traded in the exotica of the East (JAIN, 1990 : 71 ; THAPAR, 1992 : 3).

This is indeed a curious argument as it totally ignores evidence of indigenous developments in seafaring from iconography, literary sources, and the evolution of indigenous traditions of boat-building and navigation in the Indian subcontinent. The details of sea-craft represented on Satavahana coins and in the paintings and reliefs of Ajanta and Aurangabad have been discussed elsewhere, as also the beginnings of an indigenous tradition of boat-building and navigation in the Indian Ocean (RAY, 1994a : chap. 6). Another dimension of the issue hinges on the supportive role of ideology to seafarers, *i.e.* Buddhism in the Early Historical period and Jainism in the early medieval period (*ibid.* : chap. 5).

This division of interests between coastal and transoceanic trade in the Indian Ocean basically stems from the stereotyped view of the fragile Indian boat-building capabilities as propounded by Hornell and followed by subsequent writers. It was argued for example, that little improvement or change seems to have taken place in the construction of boats of the Indian subcontinent prior to the coming of the Europeans. Thereafter rapid advances were made : iron nails were used in place of stitching ; and the square-sterned design was introduced in place of the sharp two-ended one previously characteristic of the Persian Gulf and Indian shipping (HORNELL, 1970 : 236). This view no doubt stems from the traditional approach to Indian shipping which states that « there appears to have been less of a transoceanic seafaring tradition among the inhabitants of the Indian subcontinent, and the bulk of the ship-building in that area was associated with the demands of coastal or river traffic » (MUCKELROY, 1978 : 136).

Contrary to these assertions, it is now accepted that a distinct boat-building tradition, termed the sewn-plank tradition, evolved in the Indian Ocean, which was different from that of the Mediterranean. Visitors to the region in antiquity were struck by the contrast, though in most cases they denegrated the stitched boats as being fragile. The Greek writer Onesikritos came to India with Alexander and sailed down to the mouth of the Indus. There he saw some vessels sailing to Sri Lanka and according to his description later quoted by Strabo : the craft he had seen sailed badly « owing to the wretched quality of their sails and the peculiarity of their structure » (MCCRINDLE, 1901 : 20). Pliny shared Onesikritos' opinion about the performance of these crafts, the only difference is that Pliny observed that they were suited to the particular characteristics of the sea that they had to navigate (*ibid.* : 103). The *Periplus* refers to several local vessels of the Indian coast, such as *trappaga*, *kotymba*, (sec. 44) *sangara* and *kolandiophonta* (sec. 60). *Trappaga* and *kotymba* are referred to as long ships, while *sangara* are described as very big dug-out canoes held together by a yoke, and *kolandiophonta* are large vessels that sail to Southeast Asia and the region of the Ganga.

One of the characteristic features of these vessels as described by early writers is that no nails were used to hold the planks together. According to Procopius, this was because of the belief that magnetic rocks in the sea would drag iron-fastened ships to destruction. The same explanation occurs again in later works, and Marco Polo attributes the absence of nails to the hardness of the wood used which would have split if nails were driven into it. Ethnographic studies indicate that the practice of stitching has continued into present times, because of the flexibility of the hulls thus constructed (McGRAIL & KENTLEY, 1985). Al-Idrisi refers to the fact that sewn hulls are pliant and so less easily broken than nailed ships if they run onto the coral reefs of the Red Sea or elsewhere. Similarly, on the Malabar and Coromandel coasts of India, sewn boats can ride ashore on the heavy surf and stand the shock of being landed on a sandy beach from a breaker. This emphasis on flexibility in the Indian Ocean tradition is in marked contrast to the western tradition, where the emphasis was on the rigidity of the hull and excessive flexibility was considered a weakness. Sewn hulls were versatile and inexpensive and could be rapidly constructed, nor is there any doubt about the seaworthiness of these vessels.

Another aspect of the debate is the use of pottery for historical reconstruction. In the past, the study of pottery has been dominated by two major concerns : first, to identify « foreign traits » in the pottery assemblage and to use these as indicators for the presence of foreign settlers, be they Roman (WHEELER, 1946) or the *yavana* (THAPAR, 1992) ; and second, to date the earliest occurrence of foreign pottery types for working out a chronology of maritime contacts (WHEELER, 1946 ; BEGLEY, 1992).

A critical evaluation of foreign pottery found at Arikamedu and other sites shows that apart from the amphorae and *terra sigillata* sherds, the bulk of the pottery from Early Historical sites was locally made, though in certain cases the decorative elements and techniques may have been borrowed. A discussion of the pottery has been dealt with elsewhere (RAY, 1993), but Whitehouse aptly sums up the debate thus : « The Roman finds from pre-Claudian Colchester in southern England are not wholly dissimilar from the Roman finds from Arikamedu (fragments from at least 13 amphorae, 26 Arretine vessels and 3 glass objects deposited in less than 40 years), and there is no reason to suppose that the population included a community of resident aliens » (WHITEHOUSE, 1990 : 490).

Thus, objects of foreign origin such as amphorae or ceramics do not indicate the presence of foreign traders in the subcontinent, but more significantly consumption centres of the local elite. A reanalysis of the « foreign objects » clearly shows that neither the hoard of bronze objects from Kolhapur, nor the finds of *terra sigillata* and amphorae from Arikamedu form a homogenous group of imports. The bronze objects from Kolhapur, for example, are a motley collection and include objects of local manufacture as well as those of the common Roman type dating between the first and third centuries AD, as also some earlier specimens. Indeed, De Puma concludes that they may have been gathered for remelting at the local foundry (De Puma, 1992 : 101).

The same diversity of fabric is true of the amphorae. Wheeler identified these from Arikamedu as belonging to the Mediterranean type and fabric used for transporting wine and oil, and sought corroboration of this from ancient Tamil texts which mention the *yavanas* importing wine into India (Wheeler, 1946 : 41-5). An examination of these sherds shows that they belong to a variety of fabrics. Nearly half of the double-handled fragments are Greek Koan amphorae, while others belong to the islands of Knidos and Rhodes including a few fragments of early Spanish garum amphorae dated between the first century BC and the first century AD (Will, 1992 :151-6).

Twenty-six sites in India have so far yielded amphorae fragments and sixteen of these are in Gujarat and Maharashtra, where many of these such as Nevasa, Bhokardan, Junnar, Paunar, etc. are inland centres. In contrast, amphorae fragments have been found at coastal sites in Tamilnadu, the largest number having been reported from Arikamedu. This variation in the distribution pattern between the two regions stems from the very diverse nature of inland networks, and this distinction shall be discussed later in the paper. It should nevertheless be reiterated that merely on the basis of the find-spots of amphorae, sites can no longer be categorised as Indo-Roman centres. Instead this distribution can only be explained in terms of the location of early urban centres.

The largest number of amphorae sherds have been reported from Arikamedu. Wheeler reported 116 sherds from his excavations, and though twice that number were found in the renewed excavations in 1990-91, these represent mainly body sherds. Even a basic reckoning of the few hundred amphorae sherds over a span of four centuries at Arikamedu would make it obvious that this cannot be interpreted as the flourishing wine trade that Wheeler made out. This trickle could have reached India either through the Greek settlements of the Gulf or through trade with the Red Sea. The *Periplus* may be quoted especially with reference to a market for wine in limited quantities at Barygaza and the Malabar coast (secs. 49, 56) — principally Italian, but also Laodicean and Arabian.

An appropriate question at this point would be : was wine-drinking an accepted social norm in ancient India which led the local elite to « import »wine ? The beginnings of the wine trade in India dates from the period of Hellenistic contacts. References in early Greek literature mention Indian cheese and wine in the region that is now eastern Afghanistan, and Strabo (11, 10, 1) praises the wines of Arachosia which were said to last for three generations in vessels not smeared with pitch. In the early centuries of the Christian era, Begram or Kapisa was famous for its wines, and the *Arthasastra* (II.25.24) in particular mentions the north-west as the region where the best wines originate. References in early Sanskrit literature indicate that wine-drinking had become an acceptable aspect of the elite culture of that period, and this is reflected in art as well. Drinking vessels have been found at Taxila and drinking scenes are frequently represented not only in the art of Gandhara, but also at the Buddhist sites of Sanghol and Mathura. Equally significant is the find of locally made storage vessels resembling the imported amphorae at Early Historical sites, including Tamluk and Chandraketugarh in the lower Ganga basin, and at Arikamedu. At Arikamedu these vessels occur throughout the occupation of the site, dating from the pre-Arretine layers onwards (WHEELER, 1946 : type 74, 75).

The distribution of distinctive pottery types in the Indian subcontinent can therefore be used only to demarcate internal communication networks, and this is evident from a comparison of the two ceramics : the *Red Polished Ware* (*map 1*) and the *Rouletted Ware* (*map 2*). While the former is concentrated in Gujarat and dispersed at sites in the Deccan and the Ganga valley, the latter spread through the coastal route along the eastern littoral of the subcontinent with two major river valleys, the Krishna and the Kaveri providing trans-peninsular communication.

It is significant that this pattern is reflected both in the *Periplus* as also in early inscriptional and literary sources. For example, the *Periplus* describes at some length the ports of the Gujarat and Konkan coasts of the Indian subcontinent and the commodities traded at each (sec. 41-57). In contrast, the east coast receives rather a summary treatment (sec. 58-63). Given this emphasis of the text, it is clear that the west coast was the focus of Roman trade with the east, and there is little evidence of circumnavigation of Sri Lanka till the fourth-fifth centuries AD. How then is the location of Arikamedu along the Tamil coast to be explained ? This can only be done in the context of the local networks within the Indian subcontinent.

By the second-first centuries BC, the core region of urbanisation in the Indian subcontinent had shifted westward from the middle Ganga valley, largely on account of the increasing importance of revenues from trade vis-a-vis agriculture to the early polities. In the north-west the Kusanas consolidated their rule and emerged as a dominant power by the beginning of the Christian era, with the major centres being Puskalavati and Mathura. Both Puskalavati and Mathura were strategically located to tap the profits from the overland trade with central Asia, Kusana access to the west coast being denied by the control of a large part of Gujarat by the Ksatrapas. Access to the maritime routes of the western Indian Ocean was dominated at this time by the ports of the Gujarat coast such as Bharuch and Sopara. The major advantage of these ports was access to an extensive hinterland through routes that connected to urban centres of the Ganga valley as also their location as outlets on the trans-peninsular highway across the Deccan plateau (RAY, 1986 : chap. 1). At the same time, Bharuch and Sopara participated in the coastal trade with settlements in the Gulf

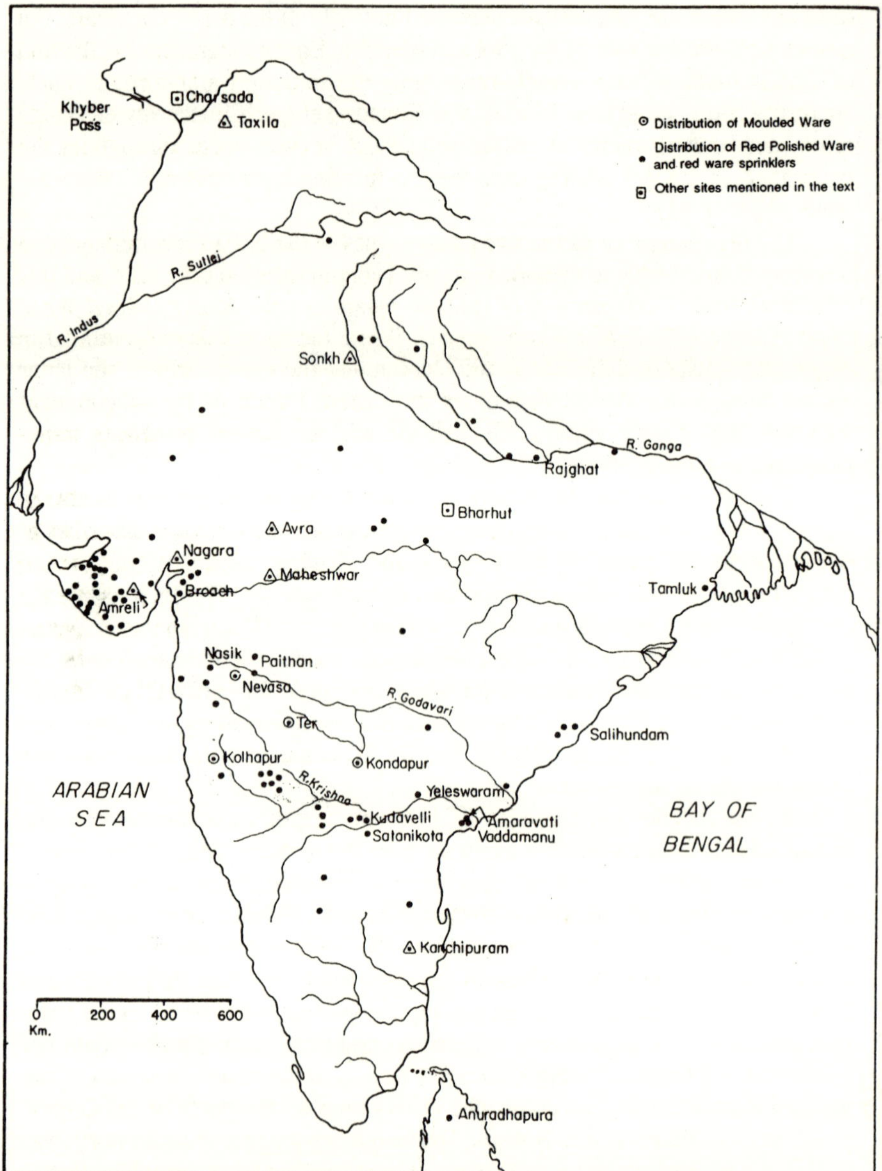

Map 1. — *The distribution of the* Moulded Ware *and the* Red Polished Ware *in Historical India* (H.P. Ray)

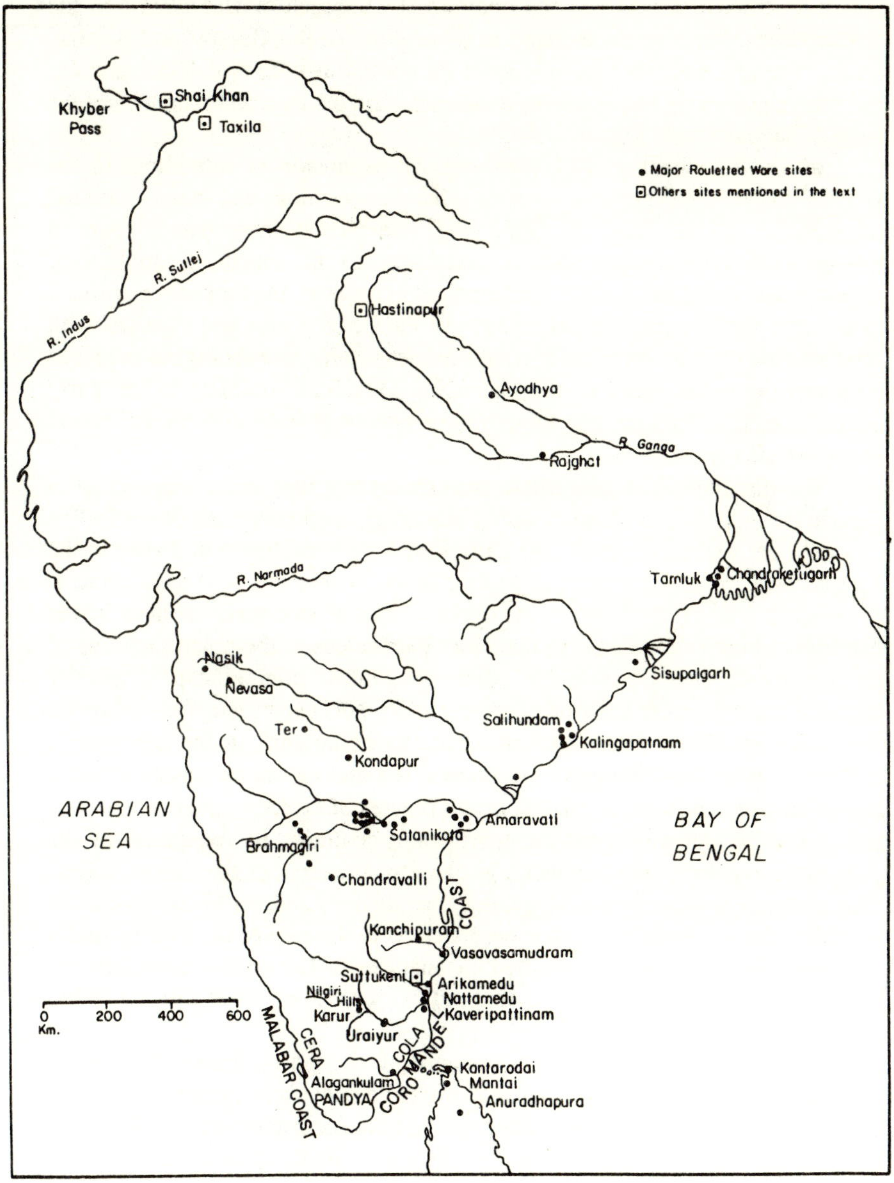

Map 2. — *Major* Rouletted Ware *sites in Historical India* (H.P. Ray)

as also those further south on the Malabar coast and Sri Lanka. This importance of Bharuch is no doubt reflected in the detailed account given in the *Periplus,* which describes (sec. 41-52) the approach to Bharuch or Barygaza and the commodities that were in demand at these ports of the Gujarat and Konkan coasts. The text then goes on to recount the conflict between the Ksatrapas and the Satavahanas who had established themselves in the Deccan for control of the trade of Bharuch (sec. 52).

By the first century BC, there was an expansion of settlement in the Deccan and the emergence of several urban centres along the major overland routes (RAY, 1986 : chap. 2). Under the Satavahanas there was a spurt in monumental architecture and as elsewhere in the north, a qualitative improvement in the methods of construction. In contrast, the far south continued to be controlled by the three chiefdoms of the Colas, Ceras and Pandyas with little evidence for the presence of a state infrastructure. Archaeological evidence indicates the continuance of the iron-using Megalithic tradition in the early centuries of the Christian era, though in certain areas there was transition and change much earlier.

The distribution of Megalithic sites shows that they are concentrated in peninsular India and Sri Lanka, with a scattering in other regions of the Indian subcontinent such as Kashmir, the cairn burials of Baluchistan and sites in the Kaimur and Vindhyan ranges of central India. Within this vast area, there is considerable diversity both in the types of burial structures as also in the material culture. It would seem that from the nucleus in the upland regions of the peninsula, around 1000 BC, these megalithic communities gradually expanded into the river basins and coastal areas. This expansion involved better adaptation to the environment and a corresponding shift in the subsistence pattern, from an exploitation of the mineral resources to an increasing reliance on agriculture. An external catalyst in this process of expansion and change was the increasing demand from the fourth-third centuries BC onwards for the mineral resources of the peninsula by the urban centres of the Ganga valley. This interaction between the Megalithic communities and the Mauryan state in the third-second centuries BC has been studied in the case of the Deccan and it has been shown how this resulted in changes in the social, political and economic fabric of the local communities (CHATTERJI, 1976 ; RAY, 1986 ; SENEVIRATNE, 1985).

In addition to the trading systems of the north, these Megalithic communities also participated in an extensive regional exchange network which included sites in Andhra, Tamil Nadu, the Malabar coast and northern Sri Lanka (SENEVIRATNE, 1985 : 166-7). Some of the items involved were shell, pearls, crystal, carnelian and so on. In addition to the land routes that linked the Megalithic sites, another major connection was coastal extending from the Malabar and Tamil coasts to northern Sri Lanka.

An apt example of the interface between the Megalithic exchange system and the northern coastal network is the site of Kodumanal. It is situated 125 kms from the coast on the river Noyyal, a tributary of the Kaveri system. The site is located in a region rich in semi-precious stones such as beryl, quartz and sapphire, on an ancient route connecting the Malabar coast via the Palghat pass with Karur, the major inland centre of the Ceras. Archaeological excavations at the site have provided evidence for two periods of occupation : Megalithic (250 BC - AD 100) ; and Early Historical (AD 100 - 250), with significant differences in the nature of economic activity between the two periods. In the earlier period, the emphasis was on exploiting the natural resources of the region such as iron ore deposits and semi-precious stones and in exchanging these with centres further north as also those inland. Period II was marked by agricultural activity and greater participation in the coastal networks with ports of the Gujarat coast (RAJAN 1990 : 93-100).

The results from Kodumanal are crucial for several reasons. For the first time they provide archaeological evidence for the interaction between the Megalithic and the Early Historical coastal networks on the Malabar coast, and the consequent social and economic changes in the far south from the beginning of the Christian era onwards. Secondly they have larger implications for a study of Roman trade, especially the local routes through which imports along the Malabar coast may have been channelised. A proper assessment of foreign objects found in south India is possible only in the context of local consumption centres, and the significance of these centres is linked to the emergence of a local elite rather than as colonies of foreign merchants. This is evident from a distribution of prestige items in south India, especially gold and silver jewellery. A discussion of these shall be taken up later, but first some details on the location of Kodumanal.

Kodumanal is situated on a major inland route linking the Palghat pass (*map 3*) with a prominent centre of the Cera chiefdom on the Kaveri river according to literary sources, viz. Karur. More than 150 Megalithic sites including twenty habitation-cum-burial sites have been found in the region comprising the districts of Coimbatore and Periyar. The site of Kodumanal is extensive with more than 150 burials spread over an area of 100 acres on the east and north-east sides of the habitation (RAJAN, 1990 : 99). Further east as far as the coast the tracts along the Kaveri are dotted with Megalithic sites and many of these continued till the beginning of the Christian era. In contrast to the river basin, the delta of the Kaveri was not attractive on account of the problems of water management in the region. Nevertheless, the Tamil coastal districts of Chingleput, South Arcot, Madurai, Thanjavur and Tirunelveli were settled during the Megalithic period. Details of these Megalithic sites need not be discussed here ; only one point should be emphasised and that is the emergence of major centres of consumption in the Kaveri basin and the Tamil coast around the beginning of the Christian era. This development was marked by a change in

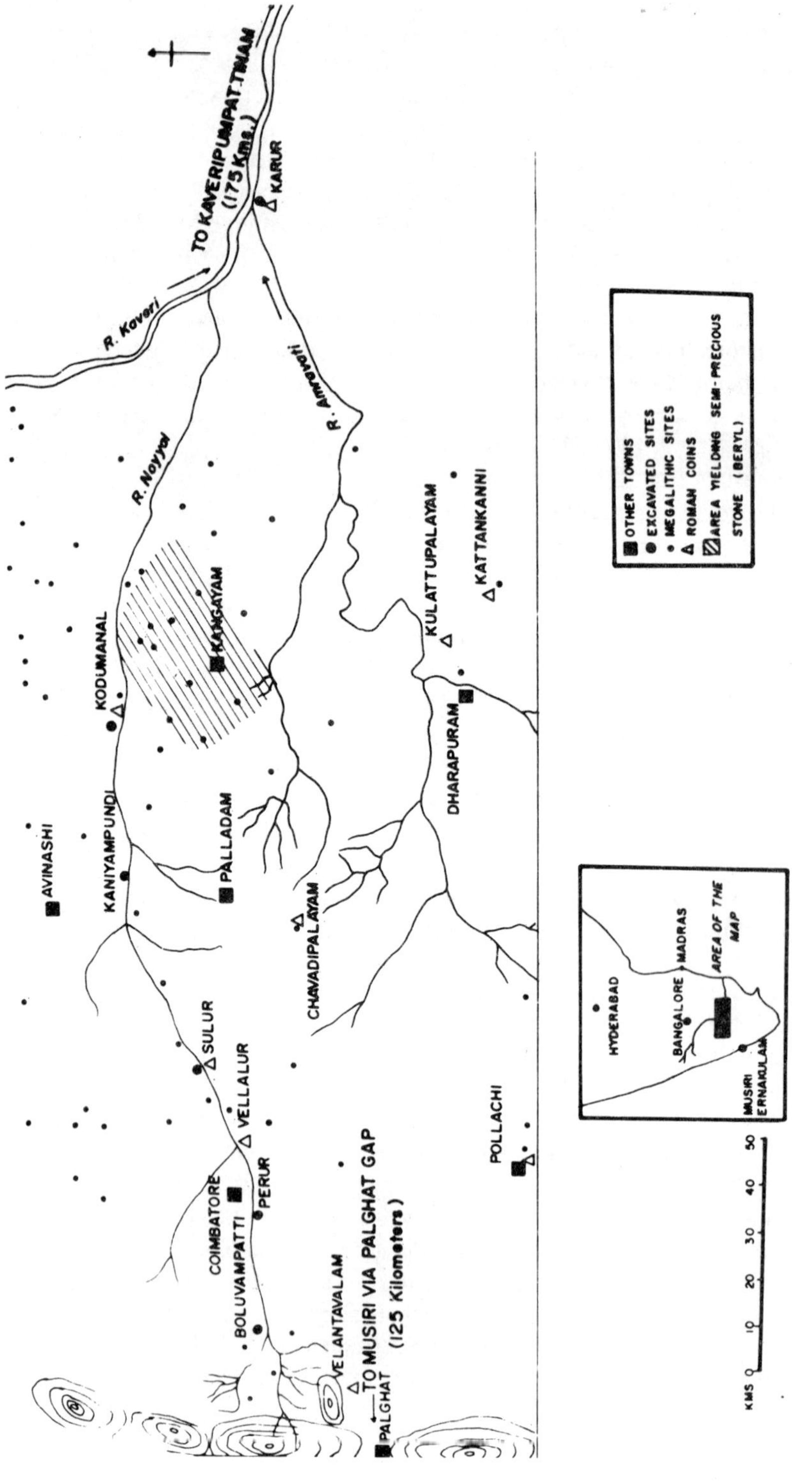

Map 3. — *The Nayyal and Amaravati valleys, South India* (H.P. Ray)

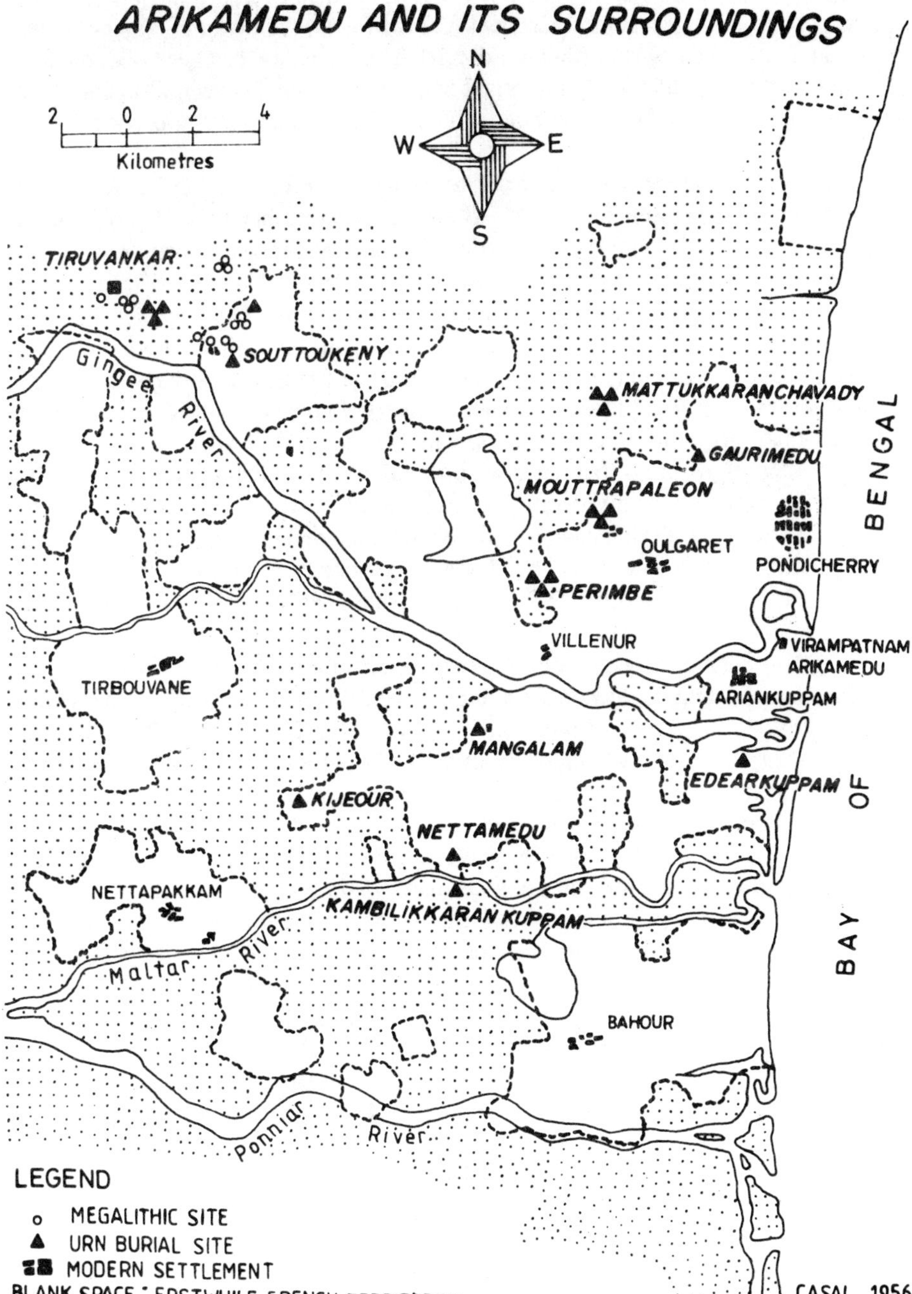

Map 4. — *Arikamedu and its surroundings* (H.P. Ray)

the material culture as indicated by the development of new pottery styles, the adoption of a script and the acceptance of a different religion, *i.e.* Jainism on the evidence of the caves in Madurai district. This transition has been documented at Kodumanal, but equally important is the relationship between Arikamedu on the Tamil coast and the Megalithic urn burial sites in its vicinity (*map 4* ; CASAL, 1949).

Further research is necessary to establish the connection between elite groups and Megalithic burial sites, as there is considerable intra-site diversity in the nature of grave-goods. Nevertheless certain status-markers such as jewellery made of precious metals is limited to a few sites, and what is significant is that many of these sites bear a close similarity to each other. Grave goods from the burials at Kodumanal included silver spiral bangles and rings, gold rings and beads and a large number of carnelian and agate beads. But perhaps the prized object was an animal figure (probably a tiger) of copper inlaid with alternating triangular pieces of carnelian and sapphire (RAJAN, 1990 : 100).

One of the areas that has been little researched is that of the Nilgiri Hills and its Megalithic grave complex, particularly in the context of the recent discoveries from Kodumanal. The finds from the graves are very significant and include a Roman gold coin found several years ago from a plundered grave, silver finger-rings, bronze vessels and lids, and a large number of beads. More relevant to our discussion are the gold and silver ornaments. Some of the jewellery such as tiny ear-rings made of octahedral gold beads, or ear-rings in the shape of stylized flowers are unique to the collection, but several other items are strongly suggestive of links with sites in coastal Tamil Nadu. These include a number of beads made up of small balls of gold luted together which bear a striking similarity to a necklace composed of such beads from the Megalithic site of Souttoukeny near Arikamedu (KNOX, 1985 : 526). Other examples of a common craftsmanship tradition include gold chains either made of pairs of circular links or of single links doubled back (*ibid.*).

The finds of gold objects in Megalithic burials are limited and known from a few sites only, the Nilgiri Hill sites and those of coastal Tamil Nadu being some of the richest. Another site where gold diadems were found from urn burials is the extensive site of Adichanallur in Tirunelveli district (REA, 1915). Equally significant are the jewellery hoards from Tamil Nadu. Nearly 200 of these are now in the Madras museum, though the details of their contents and chronological affiliation are not available. Some of these undoubtedly date to the early centuries of the Christian era, such as the gold jewellery hoard found in 1939 in the village of Vellalore in Coimbatore district, west of Kodumanal on the river Noyyal (DEVASAHAYAM, 1985). Together with the gold jewellery the hoard also yielded coins of Emperor Tiberius (*ibid.* : 53).

In the Indian subcontinent familiarity with Roman coins is evident from the widespread use of ornaments, referred to as bullae, and made in imitation of Roman coins. They are generally of clay, but occasionally in metal. A majority of the Roman coin hoards were, however, found in south India, their distribution being scattered and sparse elsewhere in the Indian subcontinent. In the north, the finds of Roman coins have been restricted to ritual deposits in Buddhist stupas and as stray finds in the Ganga plains and the Deccan.

In contrast, there are two main concentrations of Roman coins in peninsular India : the Coimbatore district of Tamil Nadu ; and along the Krishna river in Andhra Pradesh. These hoards mainly comprise of coins of the Julio-Claudian period and it is only the late Roman coppers of the fourth-fifth centuries AD that are found on the Coromandel coast (TURNER, 1989 : 5). This distribution of Roman coins in the Indian subcontinent is linked to the varying degrees of monetisation in the different regions of the country. Thus under the Kusanas and the Satavahanas, the north and the Deccan had a complex currency system, and as a result any Roman coins imported were exchanged « at some profit against the local currency » (*Periplus*, sec. 49). In contrast the ports of the Malabar coast offered a market for a « great amount of money » (*ibid.*, sec. 56), most of which was used for high value exchange on account of the low level of monetisation of the economy of south India.

It would be pertinent to question the importance of Kodumanal, in the maritime network, in view of its inland location 125 km from the coast. The explanation of this lies in the curious phenomenon of the Malabar coast termed as mud-banks. « It has been observed that marine deposits of fine sized particles of green and black mud have been found near certain ports between Pantalayini (25 kms north of Calicut) and Quilon (which are 300 kms distant from each other). During the monsoon these sediments spread themselves over the entire thickness of the water layer, forming a colloidal suspension that may be 7 kms long and 5 kms wide » (DELOCHE, 1983 : 443). These mud-banks provide mooring places to seafaring vessels where goods can be off-loaded, though the consumption centres would perhaps be located further inland.

A reflection of this practice is to be found in the *Periplus* which states that : « they [incoming ships] anchor in the open roads to take on their cargoes because the river has sandbanks and channels that are shoal. The kings themselves of both ports of trade (Muziris and Nelkynda) dwell in the interior » (sec. 55). The *Periplus* (sec. 60) is also explicit on another point, that the commodities imported along the Malabar coast were transported in local vessels to centres on the Tamil coast. The emergence of Arikamedu on the Tamil coast as an important centre in the Early Historical period is then linked to the mechanism of the earlier Megalithic exchange network.

In the final analysis, the Red Sea trade with India was, on the one hand, a continuation of the earlier circuit, though at the same time it supplemented the expansion and complexity of the maritime network. The *Periplus Maris Erythraei* was a remarkable text, not only for the details that it provided, but also as a new genre of literature that broke away from the earlier high-brow perceptions of the East prevalent from the time of Alexander in Greek literary works. The attempt should then be to piece together the different parts of the picture of the western Indian Ocean maritime network with the results from the different sectors en route, rather than to continue with the monolithic model of an over-arching Roman trading diaspora.

Himanshu Prabha RAY
Centre for Historical Studies
Jawaharlal Nehru University
New Delhi

BIBLIOGRAPHICAL REFERENCES

BEGLEY, V., 1986, « From Iron Age to Early Historical in South Indian Archaeology », J. Jacobson, ed., *Studies in the Archaeology of India and Pakistan*, Delhi : 297-320.

BEGLEY, V., 1992, « Ceramic Evidence for Pre-*Periplus* Trade on the Indian Coasts », V. Begley & R.D. De Puma, eds., *Rome and India - the Ancient Sea Trade*, Oxford University Press (Delhi) : 157-96.

CASAL, J.-M., 1949, *Fouilles de Virampatnam-Arikamedu*, Paris.

CASSON, L., 1989, *The Periplus Maris Erythraei*, Princeton University Press.

CASSON, L., 1992, « Ancient Naval Technology and the Route to India », V. Begley & R.D. De Puma, eds., *Rome and India...* : 8-11.

CHATTERJI, A., 1976, *Socio-Economic Conditions in Early Andhra, c. 200 BC - AD 300*, Doctoral thesis, Jawaharlal Nehru University.

DE PUMA, R. D., 1992, « The Roman Bronzes from Kolhapur », V. Begley & R.D. De Puma, eds., *Rome and India...* : 82-112.

DELOCHE, J., 1983, « Geographical considerations in the localisation of ancient sea-ports of India », *The Indian Economic and Social History Review*, 20, 4 : 439-48.

DEVASAHAYAM, N., 1985, « Roman Jewellery from Vellalore site during the Sangam period », *Lalit Kala*, 21 : 53.

HORNELL, J., 1970, *Water Transport*, Newton Abbot.

HUNTINGFORD, G.W.B., 1980, *The Periplus of the Erythraean Sea*, London.

JAIN, V.K., 1990, *Trade and Traders in Western India*, Delhi.

KNOX, J.R., 1985, « Jewellery from the Nilgiri Hills. A Model of Diversity », J. Schotsman & M. Taddei, eds., *South Asian Archaeology, 1983*, Naples : 523-33.

MCCRINDLE, J.W., 1901, *Ancient India as Described in Classical Literature*, Westminster.

MCGRAIL, S. & KENTLEY, E., 1985, *Sewn Plank Boats*, Oxford.

MUCKELROY, K., 1978, *Maritime Archaeology*, Cambridge.

RAJAN, K., 1990, « New Light on the Megalithic Culture of the Kongu region, Tamil Nadu », *Man and Environment*, 15, 1 : 93-102.

RAO, S.R., 1970, « Shipping in Ancient India », *India's Contribution to World Thought and Culture*, Madras: 83-107.

RAO, S.R., 1989, « Docks and Wharfs », Ghosh, A., ed, *An Encyclopaedia of Indian Archaeology*, Delhi : 297.

RAY, H.P., 1986, *Monastery and Guild : Commerce under the Satavahanas*, Oxford University Press, Delhi.

RAY, H.P., 1993, « East Coast Trade in Peninsular India, c. 200 BC AD 400 », A.J. Gail & G.J.R. Mevissen, eds., *South Asian Archaeology 1991*, Berlin : 573-84 .

RAY, H.P., 1994, « The Western Indian Ocean and the early maritime links of the Indian subcontinent », *The Indian Economic and Social History Review*, 31, 1.

RAY, H.P., 1994a, *The Winds of Change : Buddhism and the Maritime Links of Early South Asia*, Oxford University Press (Delhi).

REA, A., 1915, *Catalogue of Prehistoric Antiquities from Adichanallur and Perumbair*, Madras .

SENEVIRATNE, S., 1985, *Social Base of Early Buddhism in South-east India and Sri Lanka*, Doctoral dissertation, Jawaharlal Nehru University.

SIDEBOTHAM, S.E., 1986, *Roman Economic Policy in the Erythra Thalassa*, Leiden.

SIDEBOTHAM, S.E., 1992, « Ports of the Red Sea and the Arabia-India Trade », V. Begley & R.D. De Puma, eds., *Rome and India...* : 12-38.

THAPAR, R., 1992, « Black Gold : South Asia and the Roman Maritime Trade », *South Asia*, XV, 2 : 1-27.

TURNER, P.J., 1989, *Roman Coins from India*, London.

WARMINGTON, E.H., 1928, *The Commerce between the Roman Empire and India*, London.

WHEELER, R.E.M. Ghosh, A. & Krishna Deva, 1946, « Arikamedu : an Indo-Roman Trading Station on the East Coast of India », *Ancient India*, 2 : 17-124.

WHITEHOUSE, D., 1990, « *The Periplus Maris Erythraei* (review of Casson) », *Journal of Roman Archaeology*, 3 : 489-93.

WILL, E.L., 1992, « The Mediterranean Shipping Amphoras from Arikamedu », V. Begley & R.D. De Puma, eds., *Rome and India...* : 151-6.

WOLF, G., 1990, « World Systems Analysis and the Roman Empire », *Journal of Roman Archaeology*, 3 : 44-56.

THE PERIPLUS OF THE ERYTHRAEAN SEA AND THE ARAB-PERSIAN GULF *

The tentative issue of the present contribution is an attempt to clarify an obvious paradox : on the one hand, the Arab-Persian Gulf is totally absent from the most important historical source about trade between the West and India in the 1st cent. A.D., [1] the *Periplus Maris Erythraei*, and on the other hand, continuous archaeological exploration in the Gulf area since the fifties shows lavish evidence of a region which was well-populated and active as a major maritime trade lane at that time. Such a discrepancy of information will lead us to evaluate the true nature of the international trade through the Gulf and to question the identity of the merchants sailing in the Gulf as well as their relations with India.

---

* This paper was presented at the Madras International Seminar, « India and the Roman World between the 1st and 4th century A.D. », *Integral Study of the Silk Roads : Roads of Dialogue*, UNESCO, 19-24 December 1990. I express my sincere thanks to Prof. B.K. Thapar, INTACH, New Delhi, who kindly gave me permission to publish this paper before the final publication of the Madras Seminar. Apart from a couple of bibliographical references, the paper has not been revised since its final writing in the Summer 1991 and does not take into account recent publications such as *Rome and India. The Ancient Trade*, see A. TCHERNIA, *in this volume*.

1. It is not the place here to discuss again the date of the *Periplus* (see the important editions in the bibliographical references *s.v. Periplus*). SCHOFF : 15 suggests a date *ca* 60 A.D. ; HUNTINGFORD : 12 prefers a date between 95 and 135 A.D. ; CASSON concludes to the period 40-70 A.D. Several arguments point strongly to a Claudio-Neronian datation, and we can dismiss later dates without further discussion. Another question which is not going to be debated here is whether the *Periplus* was written after or before Pliny's *Natural History*, which seems to ignore it among its sources.

Athens, Aden, Arikamedu
New Delhi, 1994
J.-F. SALLES, p. 115-146

The historical background

An easy interpretation could be based on historical general views, a kind of *longue durée* explanation shortened to a few centuries. During the Achaemenid and Seleucid periods, trade between India and the West used to sail through the Arab-Persian Gulf, then cross the deserts of the Arabian peninsula by caravans such as the ones handled by the Gerrhaean middlemen, or reach the Levantine coast via the Euphrates and a northern trans-Syrian land route where the Gerrhaeans were present as well. [2] Meanwhile, the Red Sea was just being explored by the Ptolemies, [3] and most scholars agree that the Bab al-Mandab was not regularly crossed by westerners before the end of the 2nd cent. B.C. but exceptionally in 324 by Anaxacrites expedition, and perhaps on other rare occasions. [4] Then the adventure of Eudoxus of Cyzicus took place in the last decades of the 2nd century B.C. ; Strabo declines it as a true story, but the expedition is considered as an important step by modern scholars ; [5] besides the individual personality of Eudoxus and his disputes with the Lagid kings, the whole anecdote includes the « discovery » of the monsoon by Hippalus [6] — perhaps an Egyptian Greek pilot — and the actual opening of Egypt and the Red Sea to the Indian trade around 100 B.C., although commercial exchanges remained at a low level during the 1st century B.C. as stated by Strabo : « [...] and I learned that as many as one hundred and twenty vessels were sailing from Myos Hormos to India, whereas formerly, under the Ptolemies, only a very few ventured to undertake the voyage and to carry on traffic in Indian merchandise » (*Geo*, 2, 5, 12. ed. Loeb). [7]

---

2. SALLES 1987 ; ID. *in press*, « Achaemenid and Hellenistic trade » ; POTTS 1990, *The Arabian Gulf*, vol. II : 1-22.

3. Among various reasons which might have pushed the Ptolemies to extend their authority over the Red Sea, mention should be made of a possible interruption in the flow of transarabian caravans as a consequence of the Syrian Wars. See recently ROUGÉ 1988, and the ancient paper by TARN 1929.

4. In a huge bibliography on the subject, see ROUGÉ *supra* ; DESANGES 1978 ; HÖGEMANN 1985 (about Anaxicrates : 80-87) ; SALLES 1988.

5. The major work is THIEL 1966, *Eudoxus of Cyzicus*. More recently, see the references cited by A. TCHERNIA, *in this volume*, which deny the existence of Hippalus as a pilot.

6. By *discovery* we should understand a western revelation recorded in western sources ; it does not mean that the monsoon system was ignored by other sailors, and we will see below that it was probably used by Arab and Indian shipmen as early as the beginning of the 1st millennium B.C. See above n. 5.

7. See also *Geo*, 17, 1, 13 : « [...] not so many as twenty vessels would dare to traverse the Arabian Gulf far enough to get a peep outside the straits » (ed. Loeb). The Indian trade might have been operative as early as the mid-2nd cent. B.C. as evidenced by a maritime loan contract *SB* III 7169, generally interpreted (but not unanimously) as

At the same time, in the second half of the 2nd century B.C., the political situation dramatically changed in the Middle East. The Seleucid authority over Babylonia and the Gulf was challenged then ousted by the Parthians who progressively took over the area, more precisely the northern end of the Gulf maritime lane : the Characenian kingdom, whatever might have been its fluctuating relations with its Parthian suzerains, [8] became the new owner of the east-orientated and ancient *emporion* of the Shatt al-Arab [9] known as Spasinou Charax, and kept it at least up to the end of the 2nd century A.D. On the other hand, the troubled relations between Rome and the Parthians from Crassus to Trajan would have supposedly closed the commercial exchanges between these two areas of the ancient world. [10]

Consequently, when peace and security were restored in the Eastern Mediterranean by Augustus, booming thus the demand for « exotic » products [11], it was pure logic that the Red Sea should have become the « royal

---

referring to the Indian ocean (τὴν ἔξω θάλασσαν), HAUBEN 1985. Would it be a mere coincidence that the five contractors were military officers of the army and the navy at a precursory period when the travel to the East was hazardous and risky ?

8. The detailed history of the Characenian kingdom during the 2nd-1st cent. B.C. remains partly blurred, especially with reference to a supposed « imperialism » over the northern Gulf area (NODELMAN 1960) : for example, there is no evidence that the Arab city of Gerrha ever passed under Characenian control although we know of a Characenian governor in Bahrain in the 2nd cent. A.D. (POTTS 1990, *The Arabian Gulf* : 145-149). Unless new evidence is offered, we may assume that Gerrha should have persevered in its transarabian caravan activity throughout the 1st cent. B.C.-1st cent. A.D. independently of any Characenian interference. As often, deciphering the conclusions of political changes should be rather cautious.

9. After Nebuchadnezzar had founded the city of Teredon near Basrah (known as Diridotis by Arrian who adds that merchants used to bring frankincense and aromatics there), Darius founded the *emporion* of Aginis in the same region, also known as Ampe. Later, Alexander the Great built an Alexandria nearby, which became an Antiocheia and finally Spasinou Charax. Except for the latter, we know nothing about the exact location, history and destiny of these vanished cities clustered along the Shatt al-Arab : they were obviously intended to attract and control the convoys of loaded ships coming from the Gulf and further east, SALLES *in press*.

10. See, at the same time, the emergence of Palmyra as a major caravan-station in the 1st cent. A.D., during a period of Roman-Parthian hostility (TEIXIDOR 1984 : 8-14 ; GAWLIKOWSKI 1988) ; or the writing of the *Parthian Stations* by Isidore of Charax at the very end of the 1st cent. B.C., a sign that overland trade was not abandoned either despite the political instability on the borders.

11. SIDEBOTHAM 1986, insists on the non-luxiourous items which were traded from India to Egypt : « The literary evidence indicates that Roman imports from India [...] were luxuries. However, a number of Indian exports to the Roman world were necessities : plants or plant products [...], most of which served as condiments, food, clothing or for medicinal purpose. [...] ; we can conclude that this trade was not exclusively one in luxury commodities » (24).

route » of the Indian trade while the Arab-Persian Gulf vanished, thence being ignored by the Greek merchant of Berenike who wrote the *Periplus*.

Geographical notes in the *Periplus* (*Map 1*)

As attractive as it could be, this demonstration is oversimplifying and partly erroneous ; a complete shift of the trade patterns from the Arab-Persian Gulf to the Red Sea cannot be seriously argued, and we should try to account for the silences of the *Periplus*. Since it remains the unique text which provides us with scant information on the geography of the region, more specially of the Omani peninsula and the Straits of Ormuz, the first point to make clear is the degree of knowledge the author of the *Periplus* had of it, and how he treated the area in his works.

L. Casson points out that the description of the coast leading from the Masirah island (Sarapis in the *Periplus*), north of the Qamar Bay, to the Straits of Ormuz is « among the less satisfactory portions of the *Periplus* » (§ 34, 11, 21-23 : 176). In terms of actual distances and directions, the Masirah island lies at least 550 miles south-east of the Straits of Ormuz ; from Masirah, the coast runs northwards (NNE) up to the Ras al-Hadd, then frankly north-west from the Ras al-Hadd to Suhar, finally almost north to the Straits. However, the text of the *Periplus* is not as clear as our modern maps. Leaving the island of Masirah/Sarapis, one sails due north « in the vicinity of the entrance of the Persian Gulf » (§ 34) ; it would thus mean that the 550 miles distance is assimilated to a « neighbourhood », very unusual a statement when compared to the rest of the text where the distances are rightly estimated in most cases. Schoff and Huntingford prefer a translation suggesting a navigation « towards » the entrance of the Gulf, and both rightly stress that the term used in the paragraph is θάλασσα instead of κόλπος, which normally designates the Gulf elsewhere in the text. Could it be the accurate ancient name of the Gulf of Oman, sometimes called the Sea of Oman, which is different from the Persian Gulf ? In that case, we would be sailing up to the Ras al-Hadd in § 34, and not towards the mouth of the Gulf. On the other hand, one would wonder why the author of the *Periplus*, a merchant who was really concerned by information about sailing conditions, would not have recorded the Ras al-Hadd, one of the most visible seamarks along the Arabian coastal navigation.

Then comes a rather unorthodox description of the Kalaios Islands which could hardly refer to the modern Daymaniyat islands, as rightly stressed by Casson (176) ; however, since the information provided by the *Periplus* is extremely vague and partly erroneous, there is no reason to dismiss Schoff's suggestion of the name Kalaios being related to the name of the Islamic city of Kalhat, north of Sur (Schoff, Calaei Islands : 147). The text continues : « In the vicinity of the furthest tip of the Isles of Kalaios [...], a little further on is the mouth of the Persian Gulf... » ; actually, the distance is more than 200 miles

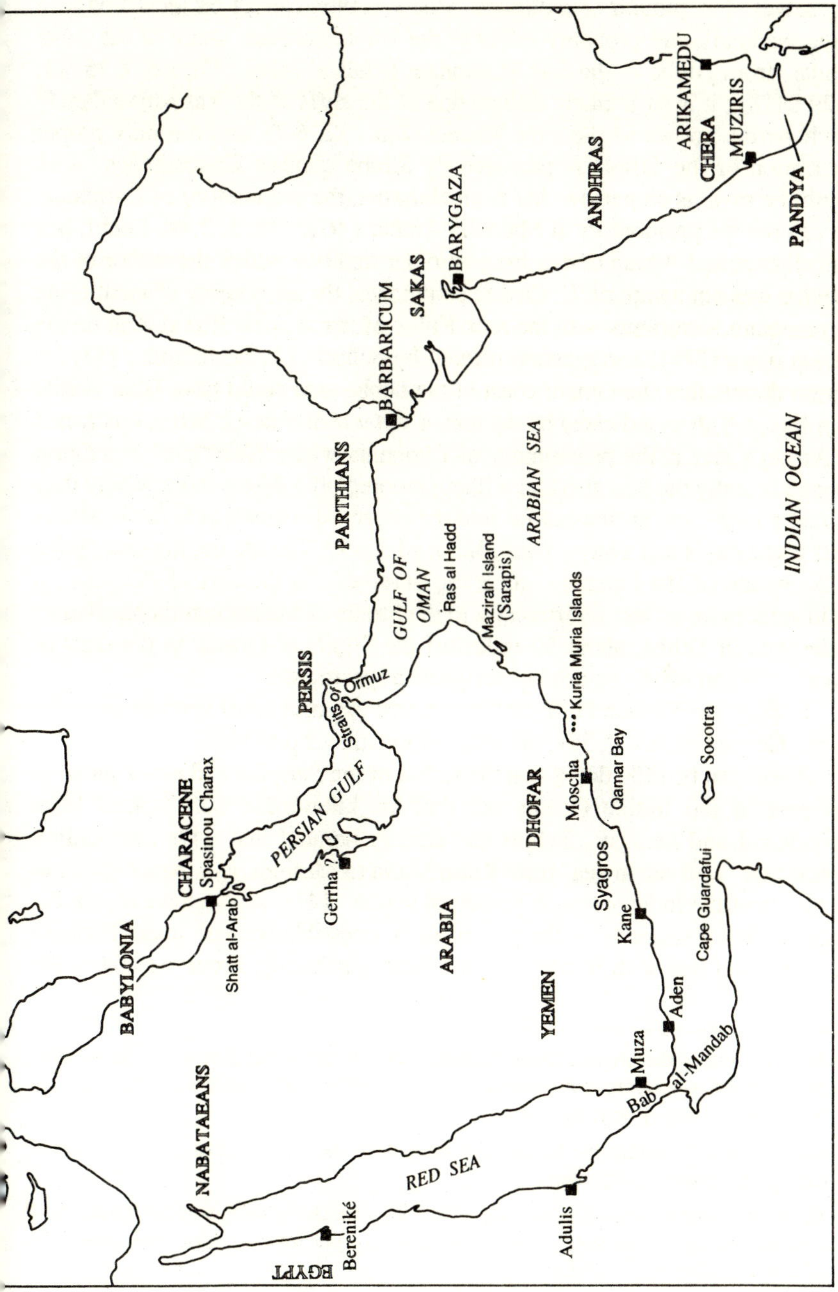

Map 1. — *The Indian Ocean at the time of the* Periplus of the Erythraean Sea (J.-F. Salles, V. Bernard, S. Raisson)

when considering the Ras Musandam itself, which is much more than « a little further on ».

The description of the *Periplus* rises several problems about the Straits themselves. The mound or mountain Asabô/Asabon cannot be identified as a single landmark and probably refers to the whole northern range of the Jabal Akhdar, from Dibba to the Ras Musandam (Rûûs al-Jubal : Casson, § 35, 11, 27-29 : 178) ; it is an unlikely designation of the cliffs of the Ras Musandam [12] which Arrian knows as the cape Maceta (*Ind.*, 32, 6-7), and the only proper description of the Straits is provided by Strabo quoting Eratosthenes : « its mouth, he says, is so narrow that from Harmozi, the promontory of Carmania, one can see the promontory at Macae in Arabia » (*Geo,* 13, 3, 2, ed. Loeb). But Eratosthenes and Arrian derive from an older tradition which the author of the *Periplus* was not aware of. L. Casson emphasizes the uncertainty of identifying the mountain Semiramis with the rock Kuh-e Mobarak, near Ras al-Kuh on the Persian coast (178), a suggestion offered by Schoff (*s.v.* Semiramis : 148) ; [13] Casson doubts that the Omani coast in the Dibba area could have been visible from Ras al-Kuh as indicated by the text, a fact which is nevertheless confirmed by Arrian's text if the promontory of Carmania where Nearchus' expedition stopped is really the Ras al-Kuh : « [they] moored off a desert shore, where they sighted a long cape jutting out far into the ocean ; it seemed as if the headland itself was a day's sail away » (*Ind.*, 32, 6, ed. Loeb). To sum up, the description of the mouth of the Persian Gulf is too unreliable in the text of *Periplus* ; it could refer more or less indifferently to the Straits of Musandam themselves or to the area of Dibba, about 50 miles off the Straits of Ormuz in the Gulf of Oman :.[14] it can hardly be used to designate a specific site.

Finally, the Persian Gulf itself is « a vast expanse [and] spreads up to the places deep within it » (§ 35) ; no more information is provided.

There can be little doubt that the author of the *Periplus* had never sailed in this part of the Indian Ocean and that his knowledge only comes from secondhand and hearsay : Schoff has already pointed that « his own sailing carried him 'well out at sea' from Kuria Maria to Masirah, and thence direct to the mouth of the Indus » (*s.v.* A barbarous region : 147), although the reason the modern scholar suggests — the area being inaccessible because under Parthian rule, that is at war with Rome — is not fully convincing. From the text of the

12. SCHOFF relates the ancient name Asabô/Asabon to the Jabal Sibi in the Musandam promontory (*s. v.* Asabon mountains : 148) ; HUNTINGFORD equates Asabon and Ras Musandam, without any argument.

13. HUNTINGFORD locates the Semiramis moutain in the Larak island, in the Straits of Ormuz, without any argument.

14. CASSON points that the width of the « Gulf » in the Dibba area is about 60 miles — corresponding to the 600 stades mentioned by the text — while the Straits at Musandam are only 30 miles wide.

Periplus, Masirah appears as the *ultima terra cognita* in Arabia. Later sources of Islamic period confirm the crucial position of Masirah ; when studying the Arab nautical texts by Ahmad bin Majid al-Nejdi and Suleyman bin Ahmed bin Suleyman al-Mehri in the XVth cent., H. Grosset-Grange describes the routes around Arabia and stresses the role of Masirah as a place of splitting navigation in the Sea of Oman ; one first reaches Fartak, then : « Là commence vraiment le faisceau des routes vers l'Inde. Mais pour contourner l'Arabie on va d'abord chercher la terre au Dhoufar, la région étant une "mine de Kaous toute l'année à l'exception de la période allant environ du 10 décembre au 20 janvier." De là on file grand train jusqu'à déborder les Khouria Maria (Suleyman fait passer en dedans), et on double Madraky à une vingtaine de miles nautiques ainsi que Maçira [...]. Enfin on court 24 heures ou moins, au long d'une côte franche, attentif désormais à ne pas manquer Hadd, point d'éclatement vers le Gouzerat, le Sind, ou pour continuer sur Mascat, Ormuz ou davantage ». [15] Beyond Masirah, the author of the *Periplus* departs from his normal practice : very few distances or sailing times between places, harbours, roadsteads, anchorages, prominent landmarks, etc., are recorded and no information is provided for any journey from the western end of the Straits of the Persian Gulf to the port of Apologos in the Shatt al-Arab (on this port, see *infra*). The descriptions of the cited sites remain vague, the imports and exports of Apologos are not listed in this section of the text, and the harbours of the Persian Gulf are ignored : the merchant of the *Periplus* never entered the Arab-Persian Gulf and did not travel that leg of the Indian Ocean trade.

L. Casson warrants the looseness of these geographical descriptions by the lack of interest of the author of the *Periplus* in these sectors because they had no commercial value for him ; the suggestion is not supported by any argument — and cannot be, indeed — and leads us to evaluate the actual wealth of the Gulf area.

The archaeological evidence (*Map 2*) [16]

A major improvement in our knowledge of the Omani peninsula was the tangible evidence of how much it was opened to eastern influences and men, a phenomenon fully achieved in the Harappan period (late 3rd/early 2nd mill.

15. GOSSET-GRANGE 1977, 9e partie : 27.

16. This paper cannot give a full account of the relations between the Indian continent and the Gulf area (including Oman) as shown by the most recent archaeological finds ; the very short survey which is presented below will provide an opportunity to update a few bibliographical references. It will not be repeated under each section that a comprehensive study and bibliography of the sites are to be found in POTTS 1990, *The Arabian Gulf*, vol. II.

B.C.),[17] when Indian items and cultural features were scattered on both sides of the peninsula and in the oases of the interior as well ; the interactions between coastal communities around the Sea of Oman, from the Ras al-Hadd — and even further west — to Gwadar, Pasni, the Karachi area and further on to the Bombay region, have never ceased from the proto-historic times to the Roman period and, indeed, later.[18] For the period of the *Periplus*, the following evidence can be summarized from the Ras al-Hadd[19] to the Shatt al-Arab.

Oman peninsula, Sea of Oman

1. Nothing datable to the Roman period is recorded by the French-Italian project at *Ras al-Hadd*. A survey carried out by M. Kervran on the Islamic site at *Kalhat* did not yield any pre-islamic evidence.

2. In the interior, several cemeteries of the *Samad* culture were dated from 300 B.C. to 700 A.D. by the German archaeologists : few finds can support scant evidence of contact with the east.[20]

3. *Muscat* might be the harbour that Ptolemy names κρυπτὸς λιμήν and is reputed to have been founded by Himyarite traders ; no archaeological evidence can support this tradition.[21]

4. Surveys and regular excavations have been carried out in the region of *Suhar* : a 1st century B.C. (?) - 1st cent. A.D. settlement is clearly attested. However, the interpretations are quite different : « Finally, since the SH11 site appears to have been occupied at last at the very last centuries B.C., this settlement by the coast may well have been the port of Omana, or associated in trade with that port » is the conclusion of the *Harvard Archaeological Survey* in

17. On Harappan finds in Oman, CLEUZIOU 1986, with references to previous works ; new Harappan discoveries are disclosed by AL-TAKRITI 1989, and CLEUZIOU 1989a. See also the discussion by CLEUZIOU 1989b. New information on the early second millennium B.C. is being provided by the German mission at Ras al-Khaimah. A well-stratified site from the third millennium to the Iron Age with Harappan connections, near Umm al-Qaiwayn (U.A.E.), was published by POTTS, 1990, *Tell Abraq*, and POTTS 1991, *Tell Abraq-1990*. A re-evaluation of the Harappan trade from an Indian point of view was recently proposed by CHAKRABARTI 1990.

18. On the emergence of coastal prehistoric communities around the Sea of Oman and the interactions between Arabia and Baluchistan, Pakistan and India, see TOSI 1986a and 1986b. For the Hellenistic period, for example, LONGO 1987.

19. Further south, see the unpublished thesis by AL-SHANFARI, Director of the Department of Antiquities of the Sultanate of Oman, on an archaeological exploration of the Masirah island : « Hellenistic finds » were reputed numerous. A re-examination of « Hellenistic » (= Late Iron Age) items from Khor Rori (including *Terra Sigillata* and/or *Indian Red Polished* wares) was proposed by YULE & KAZENWADEL, *Materialen* (see abbreviations), and YULE & KERVRAN, 1993.

20. See YULE & KAZENWADEL, *Materialen*, and YULE & KERVRAN, 1993, among the latest reports.

21. COSTA 1989 : 99.

1973 ; on the other hand, emphasizing that SH11 is located more than 1 mile inland and that the coast cannot have progressed so far since the historical times, Kervran concludes : « Il me paraît peu probable que SH11 ait pu être le site d'une ville hellénistique importante ». [22] In her soundings inside the fortress of Suhar, Kervran reports Mesopotamian-like glazed potteries and so-called *Indian Red Polished* wares in the deepest levels of the site, which nevertheless became important in the Sassanian period only. [23]

Oman peninsula, Gulf side

5. At *Bidya*, about halfway between Fujairah and Dibba, « Hellenistic » burials re-used 2nd millennium built-graves ; [24] a green-glazed high-footed kylix with thumb-handles was uncovered and a pillar-moulded glass bowl as well, together with a small glass flask. [25] All this material can be dated to the 1st century A.D. and is most probably imported, especially the pillar-moulded bowl which might originate in Alexandria or in Italy ; the small flask likely comes from eastern Mediterranean workshops (Syria ? Phoenicia ?). More is expected from the survey and excavations carried out by a Swiss mission in the Emirate of Fujairah.

6. The site of *ed-Dur*, near Umm al-Qaiwayn in the United Arab Emirates, appears as a major place of the eastern part of the Gulf and should be labelled as an *emporion*, despite the qualifications sometimes expressed. [26] The architectural remains include temples, public buildings and a large number of subterranean built-tombs, sometimes of a very elaborated architecture ; the « city » itself remains unknown and might have been built of light and perishable material : reeds, wood, *pisé*, mudbrick, etc., as it was usually done in « urban » compounds of the region just before the recent modernization. On the

22. KERVRAN 1984 : 285-286.

23. KERVRAN and HIEBERT 1991, and *Materialen.*

24. Although inadequate, the term « Hellenistic » has been in use for several decades among archaeologists working in the Gulf area ; it refers to a long period from *ca* 300 B.C. to *ca* 300 A.D. ; it is still commonly used, with all the necessary qualifications. The term *Late Iron Age* for the period 300 B.C.-700 A.D. is confusing.

25. AL-TAKRITI 1989 : 106-107, pl. 75 & 97 for the kylix (the parallels suggested by al-Takriti are not fully convincing) ; 108 and pl. 82 for the glass vessels. The pillar-moulded glass bowl finds very close parallels at ed-Dur, *infra*, and in Bahrain (DURING-CASPERS 1980 fig. 6a and pl. XXV-XXVI : similar finds are reported at Arikamedu in India) ; the flask can be compared to a similar one in Bahrain, BOUCHARLAT & SALLES 1989 : n° 201 : 115, a common fabric of the « Early Imperial Period » in the Levant.

26. The site has been excavated by an international team from 1987 to 1990. Several preliminary reports were published : BOUCHARLAT *et alii* 1988 ; BOUCHARLAT *et alii* 1989, where previous bibliography can be found ; HAERINCK *et al.* 1991 ; HAERINCK *et al.* 1992 ; HAERINCK 1992, and *Materialen.*

other hand, the environmental components do not preclude the living feasability of a large community. [27] The archaeological finds are overnumerous and diversified (pottery, glass vessels, stone vases, carved ivory, beads, metal objects, etc.) and the imports obvious : *Eastern Sigillata* pottery, *Indian Red Polished* ware (?), Roman and Syrian glassware, Characenian coins, a coin from Tiberius, Latin graffiti, bronze objects, etc. [28] The local culture exhibits many foreign influences : the glazed pottery is inspired by Mesopotamian and Northern Gulf models, a painted ware is related to contemporary productions in the Baluchistan, the local bronze coinage copies « degenerated » Alexander types, and several architectural features, alabaster vessels and decorated bronze bowls point to a South Arabian inspiration. Such an intermixture of imports and foreign influences together with the local components is probably the best clue to support the view of an *emporion* widely opened to inter-regional and international trade. [29]

7. About 30 miles inland is the site of *Mleiha*, in a large agricultural plain on the western piedmont of the Omani range. [30] A « Hellenistic » level was uncovered which yielded Rhodian amphora handles among the imports, and a rich local culture. The 1st century A.D. level is closely related to the material culture of ed-Dur, and the historical-economical relationship between the two sites should be an issue for further research.

8. Scattered finds datable to the 1st cent. B.C./1st cent. A.D. are occasionally mentioned in the United Arab Emirates and a review of these discoveries is needed.

Qatar and Bahrain

9. « Hellenistic » green glazed pottery was found in *Qatar*, but the context remains uncertain.

10. The archaeology of the *Bahrain Islands* has been presented in several contributions since the pioneering works of the Danish expedition in the fifties,

---

27. As a regional example, it should be stressed that the community settled in Kuwait-City in the XVIII-XIXth centuries used to get its fresh water, vegetables, etc. from as far as Jahra to the north, sometimes from the island of Failaka, and even by boats from the Shatt al-Arab in the early XXth century, that is far away from the city itself.

28. Several of these objects have been published in the preliminary reports mentioned above. See also a brief summary and historical interpretation in BOUCHARLAT 1989a : 216-217. The local coinage was studied by SALLES 1980, and POTTS 1988b, « Arabia and Characene » ; see now POTTS 1991, *The Pre-Islamic coinage.*, and *Supplement to The Pre-Islamic coinage*, 1994.

29. On the interpretation of the *emporion* in the Roman period with special references to the *Periplus*, see A. BRESSON, 1993.

30. Preliminary report in BOUCHARLAT 1989b, and summary in ID. 1989a ; see recently BOUCHARLAT & MOUTON 1991, and ID, *Materialen.*

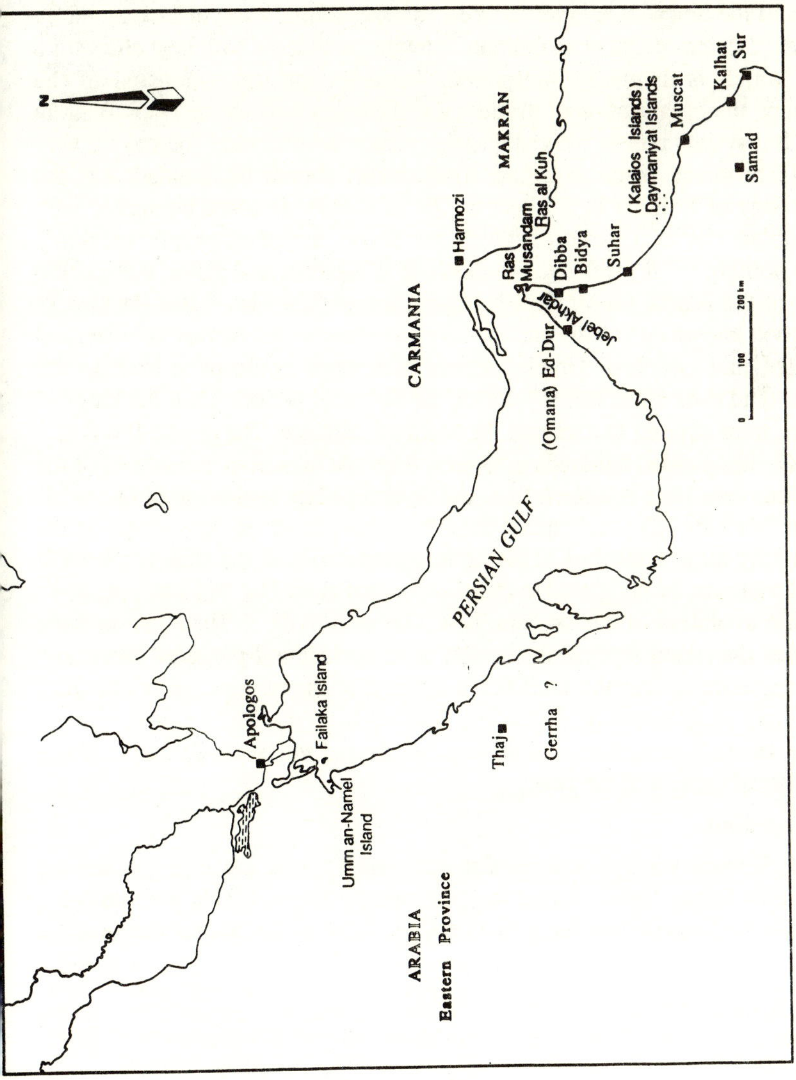

Map 2. — *Archaeological sites of the Arab-Persian Gulf*
(J.-F. Salles, V. Bernard, S. Raisson)

leading to preliminary reviews of evidence in the early eighties and synthesis in the nineties. [31] The period from 300 to 100 B.C. is well-documented in the « City V » level at Qal'at al-Bahrain, the main site of the island, and in a few cemeteries of the interior, with evidence of contacts both with the East (Iran, India) and the Seleucid area to the West (Mesopotamia, coast of Levant, etc.) ; recent excavation at Qal'at al-Bahrain [32] might provide us with new clues for a period which is diversely interpreted. Actually, the true extension of the settlement, the organization of the city, and the exact function of Tylos-Bahrain in the Gulf system remain blurred questions since the historical sources are very limited ; however, some awkward comparisons should be avoided, *e.g.* the archaeology of Bahrain as a whole or Qal'at al-Bahrain alone compared with the Arabian city of Gerrha of which we know, archaeologically speaking, strictly nothing : [33] it would lead to unjustified balances and distort the specific history of the island. I have already argued somewhere else [34] that the Greeks had a good knowledge of the archipelago according to the literary sources, and suggested that Greek or Greek-partners merchants could have traded with Bahrain (and even lived there ?) during the Seleucid period, when the kings of Seleucia were striving to maintain the Mauryan alliance. The period 100 B.C. - 200 A.D. has yielded hundreds of objects from the numerous cemeteries of the island, but very little is known from the contemporary settlement at Qal'at al-Bahrain (see note 32) ; the imports datable to this period are very scarce on the site, slightly more numerous in the various cemeteries of the island : the main cultural traits can be compared to those uncovered at ed-Dur, but Bahrain shows a specific evolution in the 1st cent. B.-C.-1st cent. A.D. [35] There can be little doubt that the island enjoyed the wealth of its agricultural products, pearls and other productions, and the facilities it offered to the navigation in the Gulf, landing and fresh watering : excluding Bahrain from the interregional network of trade would be nonsense, and the true function of the island definitely lies in the historical context of the area.

Eastern Arabia

11. Several surveys and regular excavations took place in the eastern province of Saudi Arabia during the past twenty years ; beside the numerous reports in the Saudian journal of archaeology *Atlal*, an essential archaeological

---

31. BOUCHARLAT & SALLES 1981 ; SALLES 1984a ; a brief chronology of the ceramic evidence is presented in *Materialen.* See also POTTS 1990, T*he Arabian Gulf*, vol. II : 102-153.

32. New excavations are being carried out by P. Lombard on the site of Qal'at al-Bahrain since 1988, see *Materialen.*

33. *E.g.* BOUCHARLAT & SALLES 1981 : 75 ; BOUCHARLAT 1986 : 443-444.

34. SALLES, *in press*, « Achaemenid and Hellenistic trade ». ID. 1992b.

35. HERLING & SALLES, « Hellenistic cemeteries in Bahrain », in *Materialen.*

and historical synthesis on the region was presented in 1984 and fulfilled by reports on the site of Thaj. [36] The fabulous city of Gerrha which Strabo, Pliny and Ptolemy knew of, remains unidentified yet, [37] but several indications point to a large amount of disposable wealth in the « Hellenistic » eastern province ; the true imports [38] probably reflect the role of the province as a major trading place on the east-west route in the Hellenistic period (see above, *The Historical background*), a fact which is emphasized by the enormity of the remains at Thaj (especially the city-wall), the richness of the Dhahran gold hoards [39] and the abundance of indigenous silver and bronze monetary issues. [40] In spite of the discrepancy between the archaeological results and the well-established wealth of the province (ancient sources, exceptional archaeological finds), one can assume that Eastern Arabia enjoyed a prominent rank in the Gulf system at the time of the *Periplus*.

Failaka (Kuwait)

12. The main phase of occupation on *Failaka Island*, off Kuwait, is the Seleucid period, *ca* 300 - 150 B.C., and it was demonstrated that the history of the site is to be related with the growth and decline of the Seleucid power. [41] However, a late 1st cent. B.C./1st cent. A.D. re-occupation was evidenced by the Danish expedition, [42] although its chronological and historical interpretation is still debated. [43] As far as we can understand, close relations have existed between Failaka and the kingdom of Characene from *ca* 50 B.C. to *ca* 50 A.D. (100 A.D ?) ; the discovery of Characenian coins and pottery in other islands off Kuwait (Akkaz, Umm an-Namel) would incline us to see the area as a stage of the trade heading to Spasinou Charax, perhaps a tenure of the Characenian/Mesene kingdom. Incidentally, a fragment of definitely Indian black ware (but not *Northern Black Polished Ware*) was found in the deepest levels of the Hellenistic fortress F5 (*ca* 300 B.C.) during the 1989 excavation :

36. POTTS 1983 and 1984 ; reports on Thaj in *Atlal* 1984 and *Atlal* 1985. See now POTTS 1990, *The Arabian Gulf*, vol. II : 23-102.

37. A recent attempt was proposed by LOMBARD 1988, with previous bibliography.

38. For example, black-glazed Attic pottery, Rhodian amphora handles, etc. ; see POTTS 1984, and SALLES 1987 : 82-84. Updated statements on Thaj and 'Ayn Jawan chronology and finds can be found in *Materialen*.

39. POTTS 1989 : 56-65.

40. A thorough study of the coins found in Eastern Arabia is presented by POTTS, 1991, *The Pre-Islamic Coinage*, and *Supplement*.

41. SALLES 1987 ; CALLOT 1989 and 1991. See also the reports on recent excavation on Failaka, *Failaka. Fouilles Françaises 1983* (I) ; *1984-1985* (II) ; *1986-1988* (III), and *Materialen*. On the Seleucid coinage on Failaka, CALLOT 1993.

42. HANNESTAD 1983 : 78.

43. SALLES 1990b ; ID., 1993.

we are not able to suggest anything else than a souvenir brought back by one of the soldiers who took part in Alexander's expeditions to India and/or Nearchus' return.

This very brief review of the archaeological evidence from Failaka to Muscat — not to speak of the Iranian coast which is still hardly known [44] — demonstrates a rather dense settlement pattern of the Arabian coast of the Gulf and a great activity often related to regional or international trade. [45] The author of the *Periplus* could not ignore the region because it was an *empty quarter*, and other explanations should be proposed.

The segmentation of the routes of the *Periplus*

A careful investigation of the *Periplus* clearly shows a segmentation of the sailing routes from Myos Hormos to Muziris and a multiplicity of the stages and agents of the trade ; although there is no true indication of cabotage and unloading/reloading of the goods in the details of the text, it is unlikely that a cargo of western products shipped at Myos Hormos would have reached Muziris on the same boat at the end of a straight voyage, and vice-versa — direct shipments did certainly exist, but the argument here is that they were not a rule. Several examples of such segments in the Indian Ocean routes can be found in the *Periplus*. When studying the trade patterns on the East African coast and the approximate knowledge the author of the *Periplus* had of this section, Frezouls [46] underlines that the coast beyond the Cape of Aromates (Cape Guardafui) was inaccessible to the Greeks : « [it] is under the rule of the governor of Mapharitis, since by some ancient right it is subject to the kingdom of Arabia as first constituted. The merchants of Muza [...] send out to it merchant craft that they staff mostly with Arab skippers and agents, who, through continual intercourse and intermarriage, are familiar with the area and its language » (§ 16, transl. Casson). The text clearly indicates a monopoly of Muza's trade beyond Cape Guardafui, thence « forbidden » or at least closed to non-Arab merchants and sailors (Egyptian, Greek, Roman or whoever). [47] It

44. See a review of the evidence in BOUCHARLAT & SALLES 1981 : 65-72.

45. The distinction being between trade inside the Gulf (= regional) and exchanges with countries outside the Gulf, to the east (Iran, India, etc.), or to the west, from Mesopotamia to the eastern Mediterranean (= international).

46. FREZOULS 1984 : 311.

47. It does not mean, indeed, that one does not find Roman objects in the Horn of Africa, as evidenced by glass vessels for example (see STERN 1985 ; recently, DESANGES 1992) ; they would have been cargoed by Arab sailors, from Muza or Adulis since the latter is reputed for its exportation of glass (*Per.* § 6), but the presence of Roman

seems obvious that this specific section of the Indian Ocean trade, Muza-Rhapta-Muza, was an outgrowth of the main route from Alexandria to India, a firmly autonomous and non-Greek segment.

Several other segments existing along the major route had purely local functions, for example in southern Arabia : Muza-Adulis, Muza-Socotra, Kane-Moscha, Kane-Sarapis, Socotra-Syagros, etc., [48] probably managed by Arab agents and sailors ; others were transoceanic : Kane-India, [49] East Africa-India, where Indian sailors were apparently more numerous. Casson argues in the same direction and details other external routes, *e.g.* from India to Ceylon and Malaysia, or between India's west and east coasts, etc., his major example being the Arab-Persian Gulf : « The merchants of Roman Egypt must have been indifferent to [the trade of the Persian Gulf], for the author carries his readers right past the mouth of the gulf» (19), clearly indicating that this section was a tributary of the main route. However, Casson's argumentation concerning the ramifications along the main route is not fully convincing. Assuming that the Roman merchants were not interested in the trade of the subsidiary areas, Casson stresses that the author of the *Periplus* intended to give a total picture of the Indian Ocean trade in order to leave the opportunity to any Roman skipper to visit these « side »-countries : « If one happened to leave India with space still left in his hold, presumably he could, if he chose, fill it with cargo of this cheaper nature to be dropped off en route home » (19). The term cheaper would definitely appear as an exaggeration since the different degrees in quality which the *Periplus* mentions on several occasion do not correspond to any division between the main route and its subsidiaries, such as « first choice » on the first one and « sub-quality » on the second. On the other hand, the accurate analysis proposed by Casson on « *Barter and Purchase* » (29-31) cannot fit with his previous suggestion of « filling the cargo on the way back » : a merchant who would have spent all his money by purchasing goods in India could hardly buy anything more on his return trip unless he wasted his capital, *i.e.* his Indian goods ; the alternative being that the segmentation of the trade and the routes would bring the Roman merchant to meet agents and shipments coming from outside the main route.

The reason why these ramifications and subsidiaries of the main route were badly known by the Roman merchants, and thence cursorily described in the *Periplus*, might be that they were held by non-Greek agents and sailors and rather tightly closed to « non-authorized persons ». An indication of this seems to be the so-called « secrets of navigation » expressed for example by the fabulous tales recorded from the time of Herodotus down to the centuries of

---

objects would not be an indication of Roman traders. The same opinion will be developed below about the Arab-Persian Gulf area.

48. SALLES 1988 : 96-97.

49. *Per.* § 32. On this route, see CASSON 1980 : 33.

Sindbad the Sailor [50], which were intended to keep intruders and newcomers away from its own area of navigation and trade : « It is reasonable to suppose that the Arabs made a concerted effort — perhaps involving various forms of intimidation — to keep the Greeks out the Indian Ocean and to guard their trade secrets ; only in this way could they maintain their monopoly over this lucrative trade ». [51] The case of the Arab-Persian Gulf appears as a good opportunity to approach the question.

A first point to be examined is the political situation. The *Periplus* clearly states that Persia began beyond Moscha *limen*, somewhere near the Kuria Muria islands, including then a large part of the Dhofar and the whole coast of Oman. This cannot be a surprise since the Oman peninsula has been Persian for centuries, *e.g.* during the Achaemenid period. [52] When Schoff assumes that Oman has recently been conquered by the Parthian empire at the time of the *Periplus* (127 and 147), it would mean that another power had ruled over Oman in the preceding centuries, a hypothesis which is not confirmed by any historical source. Following most of the classical sources, we better assume that the Omani area never ceased being « Persian » from the mid-first millennium B.C. onwards, whatever could have been the actual autonomy of the local rulers or *shaykhs*. According to the text of the *Periplus*, the Persian domination extended from the Dhofar to the Shatt al-Arab, where Apologos is reputed, paraleipsis, to be a Persian harbour since Omana is designated as « another port of the Persis » (§ 36) ; the Arabian coast of the Gulf would thus have been under Persian control, a theory which is confirmed by 2nd cent. A.D. sources. [53] The eastern boundary of Persia/Persis remains rather vague, and perhaps includes the whole coast of Makran up to the Indo-Parthian kingdom of the *Parsidae*. [54] The Gulf is then wholly Persian, a fact which elucidates the mention of the *Periplus* according which Apologos and Omana used to trade with Arabia : the text of this section does not designate the Arabian coast of the Gulf which is definitely

---

50. Her. III, 107 : the theme of the winged snakes protecting rare products is common in the stories of Sindbad, such as some other themes already known by Herodotus : these are terrifying legends probably continuously retailed in order to « protect » a specific area.

51. VAN BEEK 1958 : 147 and note 41.

52. SALLES 1990 : 114-115 ; POTTS 1990, *The Arabian Gulf*, vol. I : 393-400.

53. POTTS, *in press*, « The Parthian presence ».

54. SCHOFF considers *Parsidae* as a corruption of Persis and refers to Carmania in this section of the *Periplus* (161) ; CASSON considers that the Makran coast belongs to Persis and ends on the boundary of the *Parsidae* kingdom (§ 37, 12, 14-16 : 182). Both commentators agree on the river Putali as the limit of Persis. When sailing back from the mouths of the Indus, Nearchus found Greek-speaking pilots as far east as Gedrosia and reaches a friendly country in Carmania, *e.g.* SALLES 1988 : 86-87.

Persian, but the south Arabian coast starting near Moscha and stretching westwards.

The strict definition of the term « Persian » remains debatable, whether it is a generic name for Parthian or it reveals the actual power of the more or less independent Persis province of the empire. However, more information was recently presented which may point to a close relation between the two extremities of the Arabian coast of the Gulf, Mesene and Oman. [55] A passage from Pliny refers to « the country as far as Charax [...] inhabited by the Omani » (*N.H.*, VI, 145, ed. Loeb), suggesting the presence of Omani people in the kingdom of Characene in the early 1st cent. A.D. ; at a very close date, Isidore of Charax knows of Goaesus, king of the Omani, emphasizing the specific relation between these two regions in the late 1st cent. B.C. Later on, the legends of some of the coins issued by the king Meredat designate him as « *Omanophilos* » or « *King of the Omani* » (141/142 A.D.) ; the same king appointed a governor in Bahrain in 131 A.D. Potts suggests that Meredat might have annexed the Bahrain islands and the kingdom of Oman, promoting himself in 142 as « a kind of 'emperor' of the Arabian coast of the Gulf », [56] an ambition which provoked a strong reaction against the Mesene kingdom by the Parthian king Vologases IV in 152 A.D. Indeed, there are still several blanks in this incomplete history, but the available evidence — texts, coins and archaeological finds [57] — demonstrate a great concern of the Characene/Mesene kingdom in the affairs of the Arabian coast of the Gulf, from Failaka to Oman, in the 1st and 2nd centuries A.D. and perhaps earlier. Whether the Persian authority over the Gulf recorded in the *Periplus* should be explicited as a Characenian control or not, remains a working hypothesis ; but there is no conclusive objection why the « trade-unit » Apologos-Omana defined by the *Periplus* (*infra*) could not rely on a political unity.

Apologos, near Spasinou Charax, [58] was an ἐμπόριον νόμιμον according to the definition proposed by Rougé : « L'*emporion nomimon* est l'*emporion* d'un état plus ou moins organisé dont le souverain veille à la sauvegarde du commerce moyennant des dons obligatoires qui ne peuvent être considérés comme les taxes que l'on prélèverait *ad valorem* sur des objets de commerce transitant par un port marchand » ; Rougé points another specificity of the

55. The following development is borrowed from POTTS 1988.

56. POTTS, *op. cit.* : 155.

57. See the suggestion that the so-called *BI-Ware* group of pottery could be of Characenian origin, SALLES 1990 : 327-329.

58. SCHOFF and CASSON relate the name Apologos with the port of Ubullah, known as a Persian place in the sources related to the Nestorian history, VI-VIIth cent. A.D. Al-Ubullah (Obollah) is mentioned on several occasions in the sources referring to the pre-Islamic « Arab Wars » ; it became the port of Basra in medieval times.

emporion nomimon : « la sécurité est assurée ».[59] It would mean that beside the economic or fiscal common tax (*ad valorem* on the products in transit), probably imposed by the administrators of the market-place, a « political tax » would have existed, imposed by the king in exchange of the security of foreign cargoes and merchants : despite the silence of the texts, such a situation could well have been existing at Apologos, where both the Characenian merchants and king would have profited together from the long-distance trade. As for him, Casson argues that « neither king nor gifts are mentioned in connection with Apologos » and defines the *emporion nomimon* as « one whose ruler insisted that all trade pass through his hands or those of his agents, where there was no free bazaar but only an authorized office of trade » (276 and note 24), emphasizing the monopoly imposed by the political authority ; however, the commentator seems to underestimate the vicinity of the capital of the kingdom, Spasinou Charax, and its relation with the trading centre. Whatever the exact legal status of the harbour at Apologos might have been, there is not a single hint for the view sometimes expressed that the *emporion nomimon* might have accepted some special arrangements with Rome : as they were politically absent from the Gulf, the Romans were legally absent from Apologos.[60]

Omana, another port of Persis, is simply described as an ἐμπόριον, that is a place where goods were exchanged. The term does not connote any indication on the size of the site — *emporia* could have been immense areas such as Alexandria or rather small ones if one considers the seven *emporia* spread out along the East African coast —, on the presence or absence of any anchorage or mooring facilities, on the buildings or docks which might have existed or not, on the administrative status, etc. Such a distinction is important to stress since, when looking for the actual location of Omana along the shores of the Gulf, one should refuse the theory that the *emporion* has to be a large archaeological site, or that an *emporion* cannot have existed here or there because there is no archaeological site of importance : there is very little chance that Omana had resembled Alexandria or Antioch, and it would rather match the size and archaeological « status » of the Indian harbours, Muziris, Arikamedu, etc.[61] « Where should Omana be located ? » has been debated for a very long time and we do not intend to review this point here again.[62] If a location in the vicinity of Suhar can be dismissed without too long a discussion, the alternative between

59. ROUGÉ1987 : 409. On the *emporion*, see BRESSON, 1993.

60. Where the Palmyrenian merchants most probably had a privileged status.

61. Indeed, the fortunate combination of an important archaeological site where the archaeological finds attest important exchanges, and of the textual indications about the location of Omana could help in identifying the *emporion*.

62. Various argumentations and bibliographical references are summarized in SALLES 1980 : 102-105, and POTTS 1985 : 86. See now POTTS, *The Arabian Gulf*, vol. II : 305-317.

the coast of Carmania [63] and a location inside the Arab-Persian Gulf is still a matter of scholarly discussion. The main objection which I have opposed in 1980 to the temptation of locating Omana at ed-Dur was the length of the sailing trip from the Straits of Ormuz to Omana, six days being apparently too long ; Potts replies that this trip can even take eight days. [64] Since the reconciliation of Pliny's and the *Periplus'* arguments lead to a likely location of the *emporion* inside the Arab-Persian Gulf, a fact which the text of the *Periplus* cannot dispute, the archaeological and historical arguments in favor of a location at et-Dur appear strongly convincing as they have been brillantly demonstrated by Potts. [65]

The maritime route Apologos-Omana described in the *Periplus* appears thus as a trade-« unit », where mutual exchanges between the two *emporia* accept a single tributary : a direct navigation brought frankincense from Kane to Omana which exported sewn boats to Arabia — most likely south Arabia as mentioned above (*Per.* § 36). The lists of imports and exports of the two trading centres are not differentiated, and any goods which went to, or came out from one of them were to be found in the other ; nothing exterior is added, which means also that the products originating in the Gulf which were assigned to exportation had to be collected in one of these two *emporia* : before being places of international trade, Apologos and Omana played the role of regional *ports of trade* in Polanyi's acceptation. [66]

---

63. Chah Bahar or Tiz according to CASSON (180, *s.v.* § 36, 12 : 3-4), who even suggests Gwadar or Pasni if the sailing distance (six runs) is reckoned from the Persian side of the Straits, that is Kuh-e Mobarak.

64. SALLES 1980 : 104 ; POTTS 1988 : 154-155 and 166, note 110 ; POTTS 1990, *The Arabian Gulf*, vol. II : 309.

65. A qualification could be made : if Omana is actually ed-Dur, there is no indication of any further stage on the trip to Barbaricum/Karachi, which should thus have completely taken place in the open sea. Modern information on the traditional navigation in this region points to the same route : the sailing trip from the Straits of Ormuz to India does not stop at any stage and keeps the open sea up to its final destination (MICHEA 1955). The same author describes the area of Ras al-Khaimah as a gathering place where ships used to spend some time waiting for their departure to India : « Vers la fin de septembre ou le début d'octobre, on voit aux approches du détroit d'Ormuz des voiles qu'il serait vain de vouloir compter. Ce sont les flottes qui descendent des ports du Golfe Persique et se rendent au détroit où elles se groupent en attendant le début de la mousson. Les bateaux mouillent une ancre sur des petits fonds au voisinage d'un pauvre point d'eau... Quand viendra le vent ?... Enfin, un jour l'agitation gagne la flotte. Les antennes sont hissées, les voiles tombent et se gonflent. A l'horizon, on ne voit déjà plus que les triangles des voiles des premiers partis... ».

66. A suggestion which, consequently, curtails the role of Gerrha and Qal'at al-Bahrain in the 1st century A.D., as possibly indicated by the archaeological evidence.

The final destination of the Apologos-Omana route and its trade was Barygaza in the Gulf of Cambay. [67] The question whether ships to and from the Gulf used to stage at Barbaricum at the mouths of the Indus or not, is not elucidated by the text of the *Periplus* : it is most likely since the harbour was one of the heads of the western trade from the Red Sea. No technical need for an intermediate landing between Omana and Barygaza is recorded in our sources on the traditional navigation along this route (see above, note 64), but unless Barbaricum was a « protected » or « forbidden » place — there is no mention of a legal status in the *Periplus* —, there should be no reason why the Gulf ships could not have stopped there in order to negociate or supply their cargoes.

A final comment on these routes in the Sea of Oman should be underlined : the text of the *Periplus* mentions that Apologos and Omana used to export to Barygaza and Arabia. We have seen that Arabia certainly means south Arabia ; taking into consideration the different segments of routes we have already defined, this precise mention might indicate a route *to* Arabia *via* Barygaza : we would find here another « trade-unit » Barygaza-Arabia (= southern Arabia) which may appear as strong as the Apologos-Omana segment. [68]

However, the true picture which emerges from the *Periplus* is a three-stage sailing route : Apologos-Omana-Barygaza. We can consider it as a more or less steady and invariable route and trade-unit, with the same ships and agents working regularly along. At a first glance, no Roman ships would have used this route, since no exports from the Egyptian ports of the Red Sea ever reached directly Omana or Apologos according to the text of the *Periplus* ; the shipmen of the Apologos-Omana-Barygaza leg of the Indian Ocean trade would have been Indians, more probably Arabs or Persians, the Arabs being specifically in charge of the Kane-Omana route (see *infra*).

---

67. The epigraphical evidence recorded by CASSON (21, note 19, citing MATTHEWS, *JRS* 1984) comes from Palmyra and is dated to the middle of the 2nd cent. A.D. : two inscriptions honor the benefactors or managers of maritime expeditions to Scythia, a common name of the mouths of the Indus already found in the *Periplus* (§ 38) : they sailed from the Gulf (Charax ? the city is not mentioned although it was the terminus of most of the caravans from Palmyra ; Apologos ?) to most probably Barbaricum although the name is not cited ; there is no mention of a destination further east. See also SEYRIG 1941, and SEYRIG 1946 : 203-207.

68. This tributary route is first mentioned when the text of *Periplus* describes the activity of Kane on the South Arabian coast : « It also carries on trade with the ports across the water — Barygaza, Skythia, Omana — and with its neighbour, Persis » (§ 27) : Omana is for frankincense, *supra*, and the relation Kane-Barbaricum confirms that the latter was a stage on the route Omana-Barygaza (see *infra*).

The circulation of goods and the agents of trade

The lists of goods travelling along the Apologos-Omana-Barygaza segment of the Indian Ocean trade do not rise any difficult problems. The Gulf area used to import wood : « teakwood, and beams, saplings, and logs of sissoo and ebony » (§ 36, transl. Casson) ; this is no surprise since wood has been imported in the region since the 3rd millennium at least, and still is. Part of these beams might have been intended for the building market of Babylonia, Susiana and Mesopotamia, which lacked wood for its palaces, temples and houses, common or « exotic » woods : the palace of Darius included teak and other woods from the Sind. [69] Wood was used as well for shipbuilding in the Gulf itself, certainly in large quantities as it still is ; although the shipbuilding tradition in the Gulf is very old — see the Dilmun merchants in the 3rd millennium —, the region cannot provide the raw material which was brought from Oman, southern Iran, Baluchistan and above all, India. These imports of heavy freight required « big vessels » as noticed by the *Periplus* (§ 36). Copper was brought from Barygaza to the Gulf as well, a fact which has puzzled the commentators : after he has emphasized that, despite being a copper-producing country, India imported western copper through Barygaza, Casson concludes that « our information about Indian copper is contradictory » (29). As for him, Schoff argues that the western copper imported to Barygaza was re-shipped to Omana and Apologos ; it might fit with the processes to be described in the conclusion of the present paper. Besides these explicit mentions of imported goods which deal with raw materials only, we must assume other perishable products such as grain, rice, oil and slaves exported from India to Socotra or Moscha *limen* and mentioned in the *Periplus* (§ 31, § 32), and probably several other ones which were not accounted for a notice. Such imports did not leave any archaeological trace as expected, unless we accept that a special type of pottery found in the Gulf at ed-Dur, Bahrain, etc., and in south Arabia, the *Black Ware,* [70] represents actual Indian containers.

Apologos and Omana exported regional products : the pearls of the Gulf, reputed inferior in quality to the Indian ones ; the dates [71] and their wine, for it is unlikely that the wine exported from Apologos could have come from local

---

69. *E.g.* SALLES 1990a : 127, with references.

70. See a suggestion that this type of pottery could be of Indian origin, SALLES 1984b : 247.

71. There is no reason — except for the proposed location of Omana — to suggest that the dates of Apologos-Omana could have come from the Dashtiari Plain, in the Persian Baluchistan, as pointed by CASSON, § 36, 12 : 10-12 : 182 ; there is strong evidence that dates were a speciality of southern Iraq, east Arabia and Bahrain since the period of the Dilmun dates. About date-wine, see SCHOFF : 157.

vineyards ; and native clothing. The purple cloth [72] might have originated in Babylonia, well-known for its manufactures of garments. According to Schoff, trade in gold and slaves was an ancient tradition among the Arabs. Apparently, the lists of exports do not record the goods which were carried down to Charax by the Palmyrenian caravans which, actually, are not explicitely known. Finally, another paradox emerges from this brief survey of the goods traded along the Gulf-India route : beside the problematical copper, there is no mention of any western product. The *Periplus* describes the Apologos-Barygaza « trade-unit » as an almost entirely autonomous segment in the Indian Ocean trade, without any Roman interference ; however, as scarce as they are, there are western imports in the archaeological sites of the Gulf, and the question of how, *i.e.* through which way, they did reach these sites is the next step of the discussion.

Let us try to trace the itinerary of a Roman pillar-moulded glass bowl found in Bahrain, at ed-Dur or Bidya : whether it was manufactured in Italy or in Alexandria does not really matter since it had to come from the west and reach the Gulf through one of its ports, Apologos or Omana. An arrival through Apologos would mean that the glass bowl had first sailed to Antioch or any port of Syria, then reached Palmyra by the means of a caravan ; from this desert *emporion,* [73] it had continued its way by caravan again and by stream-navigation on the Euphrates down to Spasinou [74] from where it was re-exported again to Bahrain, ed-Dur or Bidya — and perhaps further east since similar bowls have reputedly been found at Arikamedu. Such a trip is certainly feasible, although it asserts its own limits for goods like glassware, and there is no serious reason to turn down the possibility that the pillar-moulded glass bowls at Bahrain or ed-Dur had come through Babylonia and Mesene/Charax. However, as just mentioned above, the goods of the Palmyrenian caravans are not listed among the exports of Apologos, and further research will have to scrutinize the tangible remains of this trade route through each of its stages, since our present knowledge of it is only based on a few textual sources.

An arrival through Omana should be considered along the two proposed locations for this *emporion*. If it is a port of Carmania (location 1), the Roman glass bowl would thus have been re-exported from Carmania to the Gulf, having first sailed along the Red Sea from Berenike or Myos Hormos, then along the Arabian coast to Masirah island, finally in the open sea to Omana in Carmania from where it was sent into the Gulf ; [75] incidently, it should be reminded that glassware is not listed by the *Periplus* among the imports at Omana (§ 36). Such

72. SCHOFF translates « purple dye » as HUNTINGFORD does, without any reference to cloth. *Murex* is present in the waters of the Gulf, but it should be reminded that producing purple dye requires enormous quantities of shells.

73. The expression is discussed by TEIXIDOR 1984.

74. For the route from Palmyra to Spasinou, see GAWLIKOWSKI 1988.

75. The Arabian section of this sailing route has been described above, see note 15.

a trip would have been rather complex, and although it did not leave any trace in the texts or archaeological remains, it should not be denied *a priori* : in the context of international trade, zigzag patterns are always more elaborated than a straight line advocate would think. If Omana is located inside the Gulf, at ed-Dur for example (location 2), the merchant cargoing the Roman glass bowl would have had to circumnavigate the Arabian peninsula, from Alexandria to the Ras Musandam and ed-Dur, Bidya being probably one of his stages. I have tried to demonstrate elsewhere [76] that the circumnavigation of Arabia was *not* a trade route and if it ever existed, remained individual and extraordinary an adventure ; in one way, the author of the *Periplus* comforts this view when he ignores the Gulf of Oman and the Persian Gulf sections of the Indian Ocean navigation.

The problem can be submitted in another way : through which maritime lanes did the Roman traders, suspected to call at the Persian Gulf ports as mentioned by Pliny, use to sail ? « Homna and Attana, towns said by our traders to be now the most frequented ports of the Persian Gulf » (Pliny, *N.H.*, 32, 149, ed. Loeb). Actually, the *negotiatores* quoted by Pliny do not claim that they have visited these ports themselves, and the illegible description of this region proposed by Pliny and his sources would tend to prove the contrary ; [77] in the same way, the author of the *Periplus* records his poor knowledge of this area from secondhand information only. Later on, in the 2nd cent. A.D., Trajan's expedition in Characene in 116 resulted from strictly political ambitions, Attembelos' homage to the old emperor giving way to a system of « client-state » ; [78] no source claims it was planned to open the Persian Gulf to the Roman merchants. Actually, there is not a single serious piece of textual evidence that Roman traders used to call physically at the ports of the Persian Gulf in the 1st cent A.D., and everything that was said above tends to prove they did not ; the western knowledge of the Arab-Persian Gulf comes from hearsay and secondhand information, not from Roman, Greek or Alexandrian sailors in its waters. [79] However, since true Roman objects have been found in

---

76. SALLES 1988.

77. See an attempt of clarification by POTTS 1990, *The Arabian Gulf*, vol. II : 303-313; and my comments in a review of Potts' book, SALLES 1992a : 204-213

78. ANGELI BERTINELLI 1976 : 17.

79. Back to the problem of the sources. SCHOFF : 15, argues that Pliny has used the *Periplus* among his sources without citing it : « His index would omit an obscure sea-captain, just as his text omits him, referring merely to 'information in which reliance can be placed' » ; if so, Pliny would have used by secondhand a secondhand information. Without dealing with the question of the *Periplus ante* or *post* Pliny, we should emphasize that Pliny never used anything else than secondhand information, often reliable and sometimes fanciful, which, in the present case, does not specify the physical presence of Roman traders in the Gulf and only echoes that Homna and

excavations on sites of the Gulf, somebody must have carried them there : who and where from will be the last issue of this paper.

The classical sources which provide us with a western description of the Indian Ocean trade hardly mention the Indian merchants : an early reference is the Indian pilot that Eudoxus of Cyzicus took back with him, and the *Periplus* relates that Indians were sailing to Moscha *limen* (§ 32, although they are not clearly cited), to Socotra (§ 30) and eventually to east Africa. Casson quotes references of Indians who visited Alexandria (34 and note 53), not to speak about the Indian embassies to Augustus (*ibid.* : 38). A preliminary interpretation of the Indian sources should be followed on, [80] but they do not give much information about Indian sailing in the Indian Ocean and not at all about Indians in the Arab-Persian Gulf : the sailing and trading traditions of ancient India is a topic needing urgent investigation. In the Arab-Persian Gulf, to the exception of the Palmyrenian expeditions to the mouths of the Indus, the merchants and sailors were almost certainly Arab and/or Persians [81] like their Dilmunite ancestors, and it may appear a truism to assert that the Apologos-Barygaza segment of the Indian Ocean trade was handled by Arabs and Persians.

I would suggest that the western goods which were found in the archaeological sites of the Gulf had been carried along the non-Roman segment Apologos-Barygaza of the Indian Ocean trading routes ; they had first reached the north India harbours on Roman ships, from Alexandria through the Red Sea and the Indian Ocean navigation, and were then cargoed from Barygaza and Barbaricum to the Gulf by Arabo-Persian merchants and sailors. The fact that Barygaza was one of the major *emporia* in the whole system of the Indian trade cannot be questioned : the harbour is cited twenty-eight times in the *Periplus* (Casson : 22-23 and 271-277). It was noted above that the western copper exported to the Gulf was brought to Barygaza first ; on this large market, the traders or sailors could have taken Roman pottery, other western items or even *Indian Red Polished* wares at the same time, in order to fill their cargoes and sell such valuable objects in their home country. On their stage to Barbaricum, they could have got Alexandrine (or Italian) glassware such as the pillar-moulded bowl previously used as a footmark ; the Indus harbour was known for its imports of Roman glassware (§ 9). [82] Actually, Barygaza as the prominent

---

Attana were active ports. I must confess that using this passage to assert the presence of Roman merchants in the Gulf was clearly an overstatement : SALLES 1980 : 105.

80. SCHLINGLOFF 1982, bibliography in note 13 : 72-73.

81. A recurrent characteristic of the regional settlement since « immemorial times » is that Arabs and Persians are settled indifferently on both shores of the Gulf, without any strict division based upon their « national » origin.

82. See the interrogations by SEYRIG 1946 : 205-206, discussing the trade of Palmyrenian caravans : among the goods carried by the caravans, « on voudrait pouvoir citer aussi les verreries, pour lesquelles les Phéniciens avaient tant de réputation, et sans doute le transport de ces objets par caravanes est-il possible malgré leur fragilité. Mais la

harbour of the region and Barbaricum as well, were centres of re-distribution of oriental and western goods, *i.e.* places where, for example, a Roman merchandise ceased to be economically Roman and became anything else, even though it kept its cultural essence from Rome or Alexandria. Is it a mere coincidence if the single Roman coin found at ed-Dur is from Tiberius, the coinage *par excellence* of the Roman-Indian exchanges ? [83] One would suspect it was brought back from India by a merchant of the Apologos-Barygaza segment, as a souvenir (?) without any commercial purpose.

Several qualifications should be objected to the theory of Barygaza being a major centre of re-distribution for western goods. [84] The first one is the lack of archaeological evidence in the area of ancient Barygaza (Broach), although very little has been actually excavated there ; would the site have been that important in the international network of the 1st-2nd cent. A.D., one would expect to find large amounts of western objects, which did not happen. [85] However, it should be stressed that the *emporia* were transit places where goods were exchanged, without any storage function ; they operated as markets, not as « industrial areas ». Another problem to make clear is the role of the hinterland of Barygaza ; there can be no doubt that the *emporion* was fed by Indian and foreign products from the interior, and the overland trade should not be underestimated, even with distant countries (Gandhara, Afghanistan, Iran, Central Asia, etc.) ; the re-distribution of the goods from overseas was most probably intermingled with the exportation of the products which had reached Barygaza from inland. Finally, we should not focus the interpretation on Barygaza alone and we need to extend it to the northern Deccan as well, which played a prominent role in the commercial relations of India with the west as early as the Hellenistic period, and in the diffusion of western products (and influences ?) towards the rest of the continent, the Ganga valley, the Bengal, Orissa and Andhra, and even the Tamil coast to the south. [86]

---

précieuse série de verres peints et modelés [...] à Bégram en Afghanistan (où il ne me paraît pas douteux qu'elle soit montée de Barbaricum ou de Barygaza) comprend certaines pièces d'un caractère trop indiscutablement alexandrin pour que l'on puisse s'aventurer dans une hypothèse syrienne ».

83. See POTTS 1990, *The Arabian Gulf*, vol. II : 292-293, who cites « a great number of gold coins minted by Tiberius Cesar [...] discovered at Sohar in 1601 ».

84. I am much grateful and indebted to Dr Himanshu Prabha Ray for her critical comments and definite suggestions on these problems as seen from the Indian side.

85. The same objection should be made about Apologos, Omana, Kane, etc., that is most of the *emporia* mentioned by the *Periplus*.

86. See RAY, 1986, *Monastery and Guild*, and more recently, *ead.* « The western Indian Ocean and the early maritime links of the Indian subcontinent », *The Indian Economic and Social History Review*, 31/1 [1994] : 65-88 ; and, in press : *Winds of Change. Buddhism and the Early Maritime Links of South Asia*, Oxford University Press, Delhi.

*

To sum up, nothing we know from the *Periplus* and other sources about the organisation of long-distance trade in the Gulf, pertains to any Roman presence in the area, and there is no true evidence that this route was participating in the flow of exchanges between the west and the east, namely Alexandria and India. Two inscriptions mention Palmyrenian expeditions from Charax to the Indus valley in the 2nd century A.D., and we may assume that these trips were not exceptional if not frequent ; however, these straight navigations without references in textual sources and economic information from Palmyra itself look somehow « aside » of the general activity, as if the Palmyrenians had a kind of autonomy inside a wider system more or less foreign to them. The true nature of the international trade in the Gulf area as clearly evidenced by archaeological finds at ed-Dur, Bahrain and other places can be described as Arabo-Indian exchanges, even though Roman items were sometimes carried from the Indian markets along this local and independent channel ; in one way, the Arab-Persian Gulf was fed with western products by India.

Jean-François SALLES
Institut F. Courby, UMR 9969
CNRS, Lyon

Bibliographical references

Abbreviations

AAE : *Arabian Archaeology and Epigraphy*, Copenhagen.

AMB I : *L'Arabie et ses mers bordières. I. Itinéraires et voisinages* (Séminaires 1985-1986), sous la dir. de J.-F. Salles, Travaux de la Maison de l'Orient n° 16, Lyon, 1988.

ANRW : *Aufstieg und Niedergang der römischen Welt*, W. de Gruyter, Berlin-New York.

AOMIM : *Arabie orientale, Mésopotamie et Iran méridional de l'âge du Fer au début de l'époque islamique*, sous la dir. de R. Boucharlat & J.-F. Salles, Éditions Recherche sur les Civilisations, mémoire n° 37, Paris, 1984.

API : *L'Arabie préislamique et son environnement culturel* (Actes du Colloque de Strasbourg, 24-27 juin 1987), éd. T. Fahd, CRPOGA, Université des Sciences Humaines de Strasbourg, Leiden (Brill), 1989.

Arabia Antiqua : *Arabia Antiqua. Hellenistic centres around Arabia*, ed. by A. Invernizzi & J.-F. Salles, Serie Orientale Roma LXX, 2, Ismeo, Roma, 1993.

Araby the Blest : *Araby the Blest. Studies in Arabian Archaeology*, D.T. Potts ed., The Carsten Niebuhr Institute of Ancient Near Eastern Studies Publications 7, Copenhagen, 1988.

BTA : *Bahrain through the Ages. The Archaeology*, Shaykha Haya A. Al-Khalifa & Michael Rice Eds., KPI, London 1986.

Golf Archäologie : *Golf Archäologie. Mesopotamien, Iran, Kuwait, Bahrain, Vereinigte Arabische Emirate und Oman*, her. von K. Schippmann, A. Herling & J.-F. Salles, Verlag Marie L. Leidorf, Buch am Erlbach, 1991.

Materialen : *Materialen zur Archäologie der Seleukiden-und Partherzeit im südlichen Babylonien und im Golfgebiet*, hrsg. von U. Finkbeiner, DAI, Abteilung Baghdad, E. Wasmuth Verlag Tübingen, 1993.

PSAS : *Proceedings of the Seminar for Arabian Studies*, London.

References

ANGELI BERTINELLI (M. G.), 1976, « I Romani oltre l'Eufrate nel II secolo d.C. (le province di Assiria, di Mesopotamia e di Osroene) », *ANRW II*, 9-1 : 3-45.

BOUCHARLAT (R.), 1986, « Some notes about Qal'at al-Bahrain during the Hellenistic period », *BTA* : 435-444.

BOUCHARLAT (R.), 1989a, « Entre la Méditerranée et l'Inde. Établissements du Golfe Persique à l'époque gréco-romaine », *RA* (Bulletin de la SFAC, XXI, 1987-1988) : 214-220.

BOUCHARLAT (R.), 1989b, « Documents arabes provenant des sites 'hellénistiques' de la Péninsule d'Oman », *API* : 109-126.

BOUCHARLAT (R.), HAERINCK (E.), PHILLIPS (C. S.) & POTTS (D. T.), 1988, « Archaeological reconnaissance at ed-Dur, Umm al-Qaiwayn, U.A.E. », *Akkadica* 58 : 1-26.

BOUCHARLAT (R.), HAERINCK (E.), LECOMTE (O.), POTTS (D. T.) & STEVENS (K.G.), 1989, « The European Expedition to ed-Dur, Umm al-Qaiwayn (U.A.E.). An interim report on the 1987 and 1988 seasons », *Mesopotamia*, XXIV : 5-72.

BOUCHARLAT (R.) & MOUTON (M.), 1991, « Cultural change in the Oman peninsula during the late 1st mill. B.C. as seen from Mleiha, Sharjah Emirate (UAE) », *PSAS* 21 : 23-34.

BOUCHARLAT (R.) & MOUTON (M.), 1993, « Importations occidentales et influence de l'hellénisme dans la péninsule d'Oman », Arabia Antiqua : 275-289.

BOUCHARLAT (R.) & SALLES (J.-F.), 1981, « The history and archaeology of the Gulf from the 5th century B.C. to the 7th century A.D. : a review of evidence », *PSAS*, 11 : 65-94.

BOUCHARLAT (R.) & SALLES (J.-F.), 1989, « The Tylos Period », *Bahrain National Museum Archaeological Collections. I. A Selection of pre-Islamic antiquities from excavations 1954-1975*, P. Lombard and M. Kervran eds., Ministry of Information, Bahrain : 83-134.

BOWERSOCK (G. W.), 1988, review of SIDEBOTHAM, *Roman Economic Policy..., The Classical Review* : 101-103.

BRESSON (A.), 1993, « Les cités grecques et leurs *emporia* », *L'emporion*, textes réunis par A. Bresson et P. Rouillard, Centre Pierre Paris, De Boccard, Paris : 163-226.

CALLOT (O.), 1989, « Failaka à l'époque hellénistique », *API* : 127-144.

CALLOT (O.), 1991, « La forteresse hellénistique de Failaka », *Golf Archäologie* : 121-132.

CALLOT (O.), 1993, « Failaka-Ikaros sous Antiochos III : étude numismatique », *Arabia Antiqua* : 257-274.

CASSON (L.), 1980, « Rome's trade with the East : the sea-voyage to Africa and India », *Transactions of the American Philological Society Association*, 110 : 21-36.

CASSON (L.), 1986, « P. Vindob G40822 and the shipping of goods from India », *Bulletin of the American Society of Papyrologists*, 23, 3-4 : 73-79.

CHAKRABARTI (D. P.), 1990, *The External Trade of the Indus Civilization*, Munshiram Manoharlal, New Delhi.

CLEUZIOU (S.), 1986, « Dilmun and Makkan during the third and early second millennia B.C. », *BTA* : 143-156.

CLEUZIOU (S.), 1989a, « Excavations at Hili 8 : a preliminary report on the 4th to 7th campaigns », *Archaeology in the United Arab Emirates*, V, Department of Antiquities and Tourism, Al-Ain : 89-100.

CLEUZIOU (S.), 1989b, « The chronology of protohistoric Oman as seen from Hili », *Oman Studies. Papers on the archaeology and history of Oman*, ed. by P. M. Costa and M. Tosi, Serie Orientale Roma LXIII, Roma : 47-78.

COSTA (P. M.), 1989, « Historical interpretation of the territory of Muscat », *Oman Studies. Papers on the archaeology and history of Oman*, edited by P. M. Costa and M. Tosi, Serie Orientale Roma LXIII, Roma : 97-118.

DESANGES (J.), 1978, *Recherches sur l'activité des Méditerranéens aux confins de l'Afrique*, École Française de Rome.

DESANGES (J.), 1992, « Le fonds Révoil du Musée de l'Homme », *REA*, 94/1-2 (Colloque de la SOPHAU, Nantes-Angers, 24-26 mai 1991) : 99-105.

DURING-CASPERS (E. C. L.), 1980, *The Bahrain Tumuli. An illustrated catalogue of two important collections*, Nederlands Historich-Archaeologisch Instituut te Istanbul, XLVII.

Failaka. Fouilles Françaises 1983, sous la dir. de J.-F. Salles, Travaux de la Maison de l'Orient n° 9, Lyon, 1984.

Failaka. Fouilles Françaises 1984-1985, sous la dir. d'Y. Calvet & J.-F. Salles, Travaux de la Maison de l'Orient n° 12, Lyon, 1986.

Failaka. Fouilles Françaises 1986-1988, sous la dir. d'Y. Calvet & J. Gachet, Travaux de la Maison de l'Orient n° 18, Lyon, 1990.

FRÉZOULS (E.), 1984, « Quelques enseignements du *Périple de la Mer Érythrée* », *Ktema* n° 9, Strasbourg : 305-325.

GAWLIKOWSKI (M.), 1988, « Le commerce de Palmyre sur terre et sur eau », *AMB I* : 163-172.

GOSSET-GRANGE (H. M.) Capitaine, 1977, « La navigation arabe en Océan indien au moment des grandes découvertes », *Jeune Marine* (twelve articles starting in n° 16, Feb. 1977).

HAERINCK (E.), 1992, « Excavations at ed-Dur (Umm al-Qaiwain, U.A.E.). Preliminary report on the Fourth Belgian Season (1990) », *AAE*, 3, 3 : 190-208.

HAERINCK (E.), METDEPENNINGHEN (C) & STEVENS (K.G.), 1991, « Excavations at ed-Dur. Preliminary report of the second Belgian season (1988) », *AAE*, 2, 1 : 31-60.

HAERINCK (E.), METDEPENNINGHEN (C) & STEVENS (K.G.), 1992, « Excavations at ed-Dur. Preliminary report of the third Belgian season (1989) », *AAE*, 3, 1 : 44-60.

HANNESTAD (L.), 1983, *Ikaros. The Hellenistic Settlements. 2. The Hellenistic Pottery*, Jutland Archaeological Society Publications, XVI : 2, Copenhagen.

HARRAUER (H.) und SIJPESTEIJN (P. J.), 1986, « Ein neues Dokument zu Roms Indienhandel. P. Vindob. G40822 », *Anzeiger der Österreichischen Akademie der Wissenschaften*, phil.-hist. Kl. 122 (1985) : 124-155.

HAUBEN (H.), 1985, « Ceux qui naviguent sur la Mer Extérieure (*SB* III 7169) », *Zeitschrift für Papyrologie und Epigraphik*, 85 : 135-136.

HÖGEMANN (P.), 1985, *Alexander der Grosse und Arabien*, Zetemata. Monographien zur klassischen Altertumswissenschaft, C.H. Beck, München.

KERVRAN (M.), 1984, « A la recherche de Suhar : état de la question », *AOMIM* : 285-298.

KERVRAN (M.) & HIEBERT (F.), 1991, « Sohar pré-islamique. Note stratigraphique », *Golf Archäologie* : 337-348.

LOMBARD (P.), 1988, « The Salt Mine Site and the 'Hasaean' Period in Northeastern Arabia », *Araby the Blest* : 117-135.

LONGO (O.), 1987, « A trip among Fish Eaters », *Newsletter of Baluchistan Studies*, n° 4, Napoli & Roma : 11-18.

MICHEA (H.), Capitaine, 1955, « Sous voiles à travers l'Océan Indien », *Mer Outre-Mer*, n° 64.

NODELMAN (S. A.), 1960, « A preliminary History of Characene », *Berytus*, XII-2 : 83-112.

Parthian Stations, by Isidore of Charax, *An account of the overland trade route between the Levant and India in the 1st century B.C.*, translation and commentary by W. H. SCHOFF, Ares Publishers, Chicago 1914, reprint 1976.

(The) Periplus of the Erythraean Sea, Travel and trade in the Indian Ocean by a merchant of the first century, translated from the Greek and annotated by W. H. SCHOFF, Logmans, Green and Co, New York 1912 ; Oriental Books Reprint Corporation, New Delhi, 1974.

(The) Periplus of the Erythraean Sea by an unknown author, with some extracts from Agatharkhides 'On the Erythraean Sea', translated and edited by G. W. B. HUNTINGFORD, The Hakluyt Society, London, 1980.

(The) Periplus Maris Erythraei, text with introduction, translation and commentary by L. CASSON, Princeton University Press, 1989.

POTTS (D.T.), 1983, « Thaj in the light of recent research », *Atlal*, 7 : 86-101.

POTTS (D.T.), 1984, « Northeastern Arabia in the Later Pre-Islamic Era », *AOMIM* : 85-144.

POTTS (D.T.), 1985, « From Qadê to Mazûn. Four notes on Oman, c. 700 BC to 700 A.D. », *The Journal of Oman Studies*, 8, 1 : 81-95.

POTTS (D.T.), 1988, « Arabia and the Kingdom of Characene », *Araby the Blest* : 137-167.

POTTS (D.T.), 1989, *Miscellanea Hasaitica*, The Carsten Niebuhr Institute Publications 9, Copenhagen.

POTTS (D.T.), 1990, *The Arabian Gulf in Antiquity*, 2 vol., Clarendon Press, Oxford.

POTTS (D.T.), 1990, *A Prehistoric Mound in the Emirate of Umm al-Qaiwayn, U.A.E. Excavations at Tell Abraq in 1989*, Munksgaard.

POTTS (D.T.), 1991, *Further excavations at Tell Abraq. The 1990 Season*, Munksgaard.

POTTS (D.T.), 1991, *The Pre-Islamic coinage of Eastern Arabia*, The Carsten Niebuhr Institute of Ancient Near Eastern Studies Publications (CNI) 14, Copenhagen. 1994, *Supplement to The Pre-Islamic coinage of Eastern Arabia*, CNI 16, Copenhagen.

POTTS (D.T.), in press, « The Parthian Presence in the Arabian Gulf », *The Indian Ocean in Antiquity*, British Museum Symposium 1988, J. Reade ed., British Museum.

RAY (H. P.), 1986, *Monastery and Guild. Commerce under the Satavahanas*, Oxford University Press, New Delhi.

ROUGÉ (J.), 1987, « '*Emporion nomimon*'. Recherches sur la terminologie du *Périple de la Mer Érythrée*» , *Index. Quaderni camerti di studi romanistici*, 15. *Hommages à Gérard Boulvert*, Napoli : 405-411.

ROUGÉ (J.), 1988, « La navigation en mer Érythrée dans l'Antiquité », *AMB I* : 59-74.

SALLES (J.-F.), 1980, « Monnaies d'Arabie orientale : éléments pour l'histoire des Émirats Arabes Unis à l'époque historique », *PSAS* : 97-109.

SALLES (J.-F.), 1984a, « Bahrain 'hellénistique' : données et problèmes », *AOMIM* : 151-163.

SALLES (J.-F.), 1984b, « Céramiques de surface à ed-Dour, Émirats Arabes Unis », *AOMIM* : 241-270.

SALLES (J.-F.), 1987, « The Arab-Persian Gulf under the Seleucids », *Hellenism in the East*, A. Kuhrt & S. Sherwin-White eds., Duckworth, London : 75-109.

SALLES (J.-F.), 1988, « La circumnavigation de l'Arabie dans l'Antiquité classique », *AMB I* : 75-102.

SALLES (J.-F.), 1989, « Les échanges commerciaux et culturels dans le Golfe arabo-persique au 1er millénaire av. J.-C. Réflexions sur Makkan et Meluhha », *API* : 67-96.

SALLES (J.-F.), 1990a, « Les Achéménides dans le Golfe arabo-persique », *Achaemenid History. IV. Centre and periphery,* Heleen Sancisi-Weerdenburg & Amélie Kuhrt eds., Nederlands Instituut voor het Nabije Oosten Leiden : 111-130.

SALLES (J.-F.), 1990b, « Questioning the BI-Ware », *Failaka. Fouilles Françaises 1986-1986* : 303-334.

SALLES (J.-F.), 1992a, « L'Arabie sans Alexandre », review of D.T. POTTS, *The Arabian Gulf in Antiquity*, vol. II, *Topoi*, 2 : 201-235.

SALLES (J.-F.), 1992b, « Découvertes du Golfe arabo-persique aux époques grecque et romaine », *REA*, 94/1-2 (Colloque de la SOPHAU, Nantes-Angers, 24-26 mai 1991) : 79-97.

SALLES (J.-F.), 1993, « Hellénisme et traditions orientales à Failaka », *Arabia Antiqua* : 223-256.

SALLES (J.-F.), in press, « Achaemenid and Hellenistic trade in the Indian Ocean », *The Indian Ocean in Antiquity*, British Museum Symposium 1988, J. Reade ed., British Museum.

SCHLINGLOFF (D.), 1982, « Indische Seefahrt in römischer Zeit », *Zur geschichtlichen Bedeutung der frühen Seefahrt*, Her. von Hermann Müller-Karpe, Verlag C.H. Beck, München : 51-85.

SEYRIG (H.), 1941, « Inscription relative au commerce maritime de Palmyre » *Annuaire de l'Institut de philologie et d'histoire,* 4 (*Mélanges Cumont*) : 397-402 = *Scripta Varia*, 1985 : 259-264.

SEYRIG (H.), 1946, « Rapports de Palmyre avec la Mésène, la Susiane et les Indes », *Antiquités Syriennes, III*, Geuthner, Paris : 196-205.

SIDEBOTHAM (S.), 1986, *Roman Policy in the Erythra Thalassa 30 B.C. - A.D. 217*, Mnemosyne Suppl. 91, Brill.

STERN (E. M.), 1987, « Early Roman glass from Heis on the North Somali coast », *Annales du 10e Congrès de l'Association internationale pour l'histoire du verre*, Madrid-Ségovie/23-28 septembre 1985, Amsterdam.

AL-TAKRITI (W. Y.), 1989, « The excavations at Bidya, Fujairah : the 3rd and 2nd millennia cultures », *Archaeology in the United Arab Emirates*, V, Department of Antiquities and Tourism, Al-Ain, UAE, 101-114.

TARN (W. W.) 1929, « Ptolemy II and Arabia », *The Journal of Egyptian Archaeology*, XV, 9-25.

TEIXIDOR (J.), 1984, *Un port romain du désert. Palmyre et son commerce d'Auguste à Caracalla*, Semitica XXXIV, Librairie A. Maisonneuve, Paris.

THIEL (J. H.), 1966, *Eudoxus of Cyzicus. A chapter in the history of the sea route to India and the route round the Cape in ancient times*, Groningen.

TOSI (M.), 1986a, « The emerging picture of Prehistoric Arabia », *Annual Review of Anthropology*, 15, 461-490.

TOSI (M.), 1986b, « Early maritime cultures of the Arabian Gulf and the Indian Ocean », *Bahrain through the Ages. The Archaeology*, Shaykha Haya A. Al-Khalifa & Michael Rice Eds., KPI, London, 94-107.

VAN BEEK (G. W.), 1958, « Frankincense and myrrh in ancient South Arabia », *Journal of the American Oriental Society*, 78, 141-151.

YULE (P.) & KERVRAN (M.), 1993, « More than Samad in Oman : Iron Age pottery from Suhar and Khor Rori », *AAE*, 4/2, 69-106.

Maps 1 & 2 : Vincent BERNARD and Sonia RAISSON.

ROME AND INDIA
ARCHAEOLOGY ALONE ? *

Rome and India, The Ancient Sea Trade, V. BEGLEY, R.D. DE PUMA eds., The University of Wisconsin Press, 1991, 248 p.

The 88th annual meeting of the Archaeological Institute of America took place at San Antonio, Texas, from the 27th to the 30th of December, 1986. Section IV of this meeting was devoted to a colloquium on *Rome and India : The Sea Trade* which brought together American archaeologists and some of their Indian colleagues. Abstracts of the papers were published in three pages of the *AJA*, 91/2 (1987), 291-294. The papers — revised, enlarged and updated till 1989 by their authors — have been published in the above mentioned volume in their unabridged form. An Introduction (which could well serve as a review of the book) by Vimala Begley highlights the salient features of each paper and examines the issues each one throws up. This volume also incorporates an article by E. Marianne Stern on glass, and, in conclusion, two articles by K. Warner Slane and D. Whitehouse which take a critical look at the preceding contributions. The book has been edited with care and taste ; it contains several illustrations, legible maps, a geographical index and a general index. The arrangement of the articles provides the book with unity and substance at least in the field of ceramics.

The meeting chose to concentrate on archaeology : most of the contributors examined archaeological material in India of Western origin, or supposedly of Western origin, or influenced by the West. Only two contributions which come after Vimala Begley's Introduction have a somewhat different orientation. With respect to navigation in the Indian Ocean, Lionel Casson (*Ancient Naval Technology and the Route to India,* 8-11) once again takes up a theme he had dealt with previously in an article published in 1980 as well as in his edition of the *Periplus of the Erythraean Sea*, 290-291. As shown by Pliny and the *Periplus*, the date of departure from Egypt of the ships bound for the Indian

---

* Translation into English : Miss Poonam PURI And Mrs Huguette SALLES.

Athens, Aden, Arikamedu
New Delhi, 1994
A. TCHERNIA, p. 147-156.

shores is calculated on the basis of their arrival there in September or early October, when the monsoon abates, and landing is not too dangerous a business. The crossing however, used to be undertaken in windy weather and heavy seas : the size and building techniques of Roman ships enabled them to brave the weather whereas the Arabs only sailed at the time of the NE monsoon (a point debated by D. Whitehouse, 216).

In a paper which, except for a few paragraphs, takes up a text already published in 1986 in the *Münstersche Beiträge z. antiken Handelsgeschichte*, V, 2, 16-36, and which subsequently appeared in 1989 in *L'Arabie pré-islamique et son environnement historique et culturel* (T. Fahd ed., Strasbourg, 195-223), S.E. Sidebotham summarizes or updates several themes developed in his work of 1986. Among the Red Sea ports, Myos Hormos was decidedly not located at Abu Sha'ar as it was made out to be since the 19th century. The excavations undertaken by the author in 1987 tend to confirm doubts expressed over the last few years (among others by M. Reddé and J.-C. Golvin, « Du Nil à la Mer Rouge », *Karthago*, 21, 1987, 5-64 - see 61-63). The fort dates back to the 5th-7th century and there are no traces of a harbour. Myos Hormos was situated perhaps further north in the region of Zeit Bay : one Bedouin told the author that ancient vestiges could be seen there. However, this would only serve to heighten the discrepancies regarding the distance as given in the *Periplus*, 1, between Berenice and Myos Hormos, which is only 1800 stadia, whereas there are 2300 between Berenice and Abu Sha'ar. The author devotes the second half of his paper to trade, without going against the line of argument he defended in 1986, *i.e.* an imperial policy which aimed deliberately and systematically at developing trade with the Orient. Several reviewers, particularly G. Bowersock (*CR*, 38, 1988, 101-104), and L. Casson in his edition of the *Periplus* (35-39) have, however, pointed out the flaws of such a categorical stand. There is no denying the passion of the Roman elite at the beginning of Augustus' rule for India with its fabled countries, its pepper and its pearls. Augustus boasted that he had received ambassadors from that country, and commercial relations must have been accompanied by political relations. However, this does not constitute an economic policy, and Egyptian infrastructure can be mainly explained by the presence of state-owned mines and quarries located not too far from the shores of the Red Sea. In order to prove the Emperor's involvement in Oriental trade, the author proceeds to onomastic comparisons which, to my mind, seem somewhat venturesome. Claudius granted Roman citizenship generously, especially in the East, and there is no reason to believe that all the *Ti. Claudii* listed in the archives of Nicanor and elsewhere, were imperial freedmen. The connection made between the *Ti. Claudius Epaphroditus* of the ostraka Petrie 290 and the well known freedman of Nero is hardly plausible. Nor for that matter does the connection between *Anicetus* of the ostraka 237-239 and the *Anicetus* charged with killing Agrippina seem to hold. In parenthesis, we would like to add that the inscription on the plaster stopper of the amphora fig. 2, 16 and 2, 17 reads *Ti(beri) Cl[a]ud[i C]allisti*. All this obviously does not detract in any way from the wealth of information that S.E. Sidebotham provides in very few pages about the ports of departure of the Indian Ocean trade.

After these two articles, we get into the heart of the subject, with texts that are entirely archaeological in nature. S.B. Deo (*Roman trade : Recent Archaeological Discoveries in Western India*, 39-45) and K.V. Raman (*Further Evidence of Roman Trade from Coastal Sites in Tamil Nadu*, 125-133) have defined their subject geographically. The former provides us with a general overview of the material which in some cases is examined in greater detail in subsequent papers ; he allows the reader to find his bearings and is the only author to present the recent numismatic evidence, as well as an interesting table on the clay *bullae* copied from Roman coins and often found in the Deccan and in northern India. P. J. Turner's book, *Roman coins in India*, London, 1989, came out too late for it to be quoted. K.V. Raman deals with three newly explored sites on the Tamil Nadu coast, where some fragments of Roman amphoras have been found. Arretine ware remains limited to Arikamedu. But one can find traces of glass bead manufacturing in these ports and the author concludes his text with an invaluable account of the products likely to be of export interest to the three kingdoms dealt with in his study : Pandya Nadu, Cola-Nadu and Tondai Nadu.

The rest of the contributions are arranged on the basis of the material studied. R. D. De Puma (82-112) discusses bronzes and Marianne Stern glass (113-124). The former takes up the publication of Roman statuettes and bronze objects found in 1945 at Kolhapur in Maharashtra ; these are the only discoveries of their kind made in India. The most famous is a Poseidon statuette, with his hand resting on his knee, one of the many replicas of a lost original of Lysippus. The Kolhapur copy is most likely Hellenistic ; however, the possibility of ascribing it to the Early Imperial era should not be excluded. The author redistributes the other objects according to whether they were made indigenously or in the West, in Campania in the first century A.D. to be specific. It is worthwhile mentioning here two Dr.2-4 amphora fragments, also found at Kolhapur, and published by H.D. Sankalia (*JRAS*, 1957, 207-208, quoted by S.B. Deo) ; on this occasion, he has put forward the hypothesis that the bronzes had been hidden at the time of a violent destruction of which there are archaeological traces, and which must have occurred when the Andhra domination was coming to its end. He puts these events at the first century A.D. R. D. De Puma prefers to subscribe to the hypothesis that these were metal reserves.

After an introduction in which she reminds us what the *Periplus* says on glass exports to India, E. Marianne Stern (*Early Roman Export Glass in India*, 113-124) contributes to our understanding of the discovery of glass in India. Though the manufacturing of glass beads was significant, it does not seem as if India produced glass vases, which thus must have been imported from the West.

The author had no opportunity to personally examine the Paithan, Ter and Nevasa discoveries, and talks about them on the basis of old publications. But she has examined the Arikamedu finds at the Pondicherry Museum, where she found an « enormous quantity of glass » — worked, rough or manufacturing scrap. She provides us with important preliminary indications about them, and points out in particular two fragments belonging to rare, precious vases. The article ends with a comparative overview of the manufacturing techniques of glass beads in Arikamedu that P. Francis Jr. has since described in detail (« Beadmaking at Arikamedu and beyond », *World Archaeology*, 23, 1, 1991, 28-43). One can find the same information, but in greater detail and with a colour plate in an article quoted n. 37 as to be published : « Early Exports Beyond the Empire », in *Roman Glass, Two centuries of Art and Invention*, M. Newby, K. Painter eds., London, 1991, 141-154.

About half the volume deals with ceramics and amphoras ; these are actually the materials on which most work is being done. This collection begins with a negative but decisive contribution. After having examined the *Red Polished Ware* — ceramics of the 1st cent. B.C. frequently found in Gujarat — on ninety sites and having published the material of twelve with a great deal of precision, Nancy Pinto Orton (46-81) can state with authority that such ceramics had not been influenced by Western crockery.

With his usual competence and accuracy, Howard Comfort resumes the study of the *sigillata* pottery from Arikamedu, with special reference to the stamps. He was able to study five (of which one, RVFIO, was unpublished), and he indicates somewhat briefly four others, also unpublished, in the Pondicherry Museum. All the pottery dates back between 10 and 20/25 A.D., with one exception : the *Attius* stamp which couldn't be later than 10 B.C. H. Comfort actually brings data in favour of Tiberian dates (a sherd is decorated with appliqué relief, and four stamps of the Pondicherry Museum are *in planta pedis*) that L. Ohlenroth (« Zur Datierung des Funde von Arikamedu », *Germania*, 1952, 389-392, which curiously enough has not been quoted by the author but by E. Marianne Stern, n. 41) did not know of when he observed, like H. Comfort, the absence of Haltern Service I vases, and assigned the Arikamedu *sigillata* to the last few years of the occupation of this military camp [Haltern] which was considered to have been abandoned in 16 A.D. ; this date was later revised to 9 A.D. H. Comfort considers that the *sigillata* was intended for the use of the Romans settled there, which raises the problem of the graffiti on the pottery, many examples of which have been published by Wheeler. They are for the most part in the Brahmi script, but there is also a beautiful Greek *kappa*, and the amphoras, as I shall mention later, seem to confirm such a presence. It can be seen however, given the chronological concentration of most of the finds and the absence of the later forms of Arretine ware (K.W. Slane nonetheless points out that n° 23 of Wheeler belongs to the Goudineau 39b form, which he dates from 20/25 onwards), that the period in question was indeed very brief : less than twenty years. In such circumstances, Wheeler's idea that the disappearance of Roman ceramics at Arikamedu was due to a general curtailment of exports, not a lull in local demand, seems to be invalidated.

It is unfortunate that E. Lyding Will was not able to provide such an indepth study of the amphoras : work is still going on and her text provides only a general outline. What is noteworthy is the mention of types which Wheeler had not published : some fragments of Betic amphoras, either for *garum* (Dr. 7 and 8) or for olive oil (Dr.20), and Dr.6 amphoras (which are not Istrian oil amphoras but northern Italian wine amphoras). The author could also have mentioned two handle attachments, the fragment of a rim and a base which belong to Tripolitan oil amphoras. They can be seen in the Pondicherry Museum. Other fragments have yet to be identified. After these additions to Wheeler's table, and even if, as E. Lyding Will has rightly pointed out, wine amphoras seem to be in a majority, the diversity of amphora fragments at Arikamedu is indeed surprising : most of the main Mediterranean types at the beginning of 1st cent. A.D. are represented there. The presence of *garum* and olive oil amphoras, products much less likely to interest Indians, can only be explained, to my mind, by the settling of Greek and Roman merchants on the site.

Vimala Begely, in a much more ambitious and indepth article, analyzes the characteristics of two ceramic types : *moldmade ware*, for the most part vases decorated in relief found in Gujarat and Maharashtra, and *rouletted ware*, decorated with incised circles on their floor, whose distribution is centered in Tamil Nadu and to which the author has already devoted many a study. Neither of the two has been imported, but in both cases, the decoration would let us think of Western influences. The long petals on the *moldmade ware* bowls are reminiscent of the Megarian bowls or their metal predecessors, and the incised decorations of the *rouletted ware* remind us of black glazed Hellenistic ware, the *Eastern sigillata A*, or, in the Western Mediterranean region, of the Campanian and Arretine ceramics. There is no previous record of such decoration in India, and one is quite happy to go along with the author when she says the resemblances are not accidental. But, as always in such cases, determining chronological coincidences (there is a hiatus of half a century between the Megarian bowls and the appearance of the *moldmade ware* in India), the patterns of diffusion (imported models have not been found and the inference is that they have to be assumed : K.V. Slane considers the *Eastern sigillata* to be the best bet), and the exact prototypes are decidedly more difficult to establish. In grappling with all these problems, the author has collected a sizeable amount of data, and provides a detailed discussion on the typology, the chronology and the distribution of these ceramics as well as of some others. K.W. Slane, thanks to her excellent understanding of ceramics in the Eastern Mediterranean, discusses several points concerning Arretine ceramics (which I persist in calling so because it has come to be used as such and everyone understands what it means, knowing full well that a large part was not manufactured in Arezzo), amphoras and *rouletted ware*; I have taken and shall continue to take into account several of her observations.

J. Carswell's article (197-203) on the excavations which he supervised at the harbour of Mantai on the northern coast of Sri Lanka occupies a special place in this volume. The author emphasizes the importance of a site inhabited uninterruptedly from the middle of the first millennium B.C. to the 10th cent. A.D., which has « the potential for providing detailed evidence of one of the largest urban complexes in South Asia ». He merely indicates with a great deal of circumspection the existence of material testifying to trade with the Roman Empire. R. Silva and J. Bouzek, in a brief note entitled « Mantai — a second Arikamedu ? », published in *Antiquity*, 225, March 1985, 46-7 and quoted by K.W. Slane (n. 18), had spoken of Arretine ware and *Eastern sigillata B*.

Finally, we will have to go along with D. Whitehouse's final remarks : no, the Romans were not the sole trade operators in the Indian Ocean ; the Arabs and the Indians themselves played a considerable part, but as the sources available are not as rich, we tend to speak more of the former. We can only proceed on the basis of what we have, and in this field we have to wait for archaeology to show us the way. Yes, we must not forget the archaeological finds in the Persian Gulf : H.P. Ray and J.-F. Salles deal with these in an article entitled « A Resurvey of the so-called Roman Trade with the East », which is yet to be published ; finally, yes, the main reason for trade was then as later on the unbelievable wealth and taste for luxury of the Roman elite.

Though all the articles do not display the same degree of originality or depth of research, and the authors are sometimes repetitive when in trying to introduce their data, they refer to a well known general framework, the book which I have just reviewed is undoubtedly rich in new evidence and approaches in respect to several categories of material, and represents a significant advance on several accounts. Its ambitious title and emphasis on archaeological data as sources of economic history does however pose certain problems. The first being that the word « trade » has to be defined more clearly. When one reads on p. 151 that India « must have been a substantial market for the Greeks and the Romans », one begins to dread historical misinterpretation : Western merchants were not going to sell anything to India, they were on the lookout for silk, nard, pepper, pearls and beryls that they sold back at a hundred times the price, as Pliny states, to their wealthy fellow citizens. India was never thought of as an outlet for wine and ceramics of the Roman Empire. Bartering wine offered even more favourable terms than bartering *denarii,* and that is all. This was not happening within the framework of a vast international market. One is happy to find on the last page of the volume D. Whitehouse reminding us that « at any given moment, the pattern of trade depended on at least two variables, the political relations of the customer and those of the supplier », which thereby questions for example the statement on p. 113, where the author undoubtedly got carried away by archaeological enthusiasm : « During the reign of Emperor Augustus, the Indian trade became an extension and a branch of the trade in the Mediterranean and was to remain so through the Middle Ages ». Let us move on to the supposed continuity, to strongly state that trade with India had nothing to do with domestic trade in the Mediterranean. For several obvious reasons, and because the reading of the *Periplus* clearly points to the control exercised by the kingdoms of North and Central India on western trade at Barake, Barygaza and Kalliana, C.R. Whittaker, in a review of Lionel Casson's publication (*Times Literary Supplement* 4530, 26 January - 1st February 1990, 95) put things in perspective with the explanation that it was the world of Polanyi's « Port of Trade ». When Casson (1989, p. 274-276) reviews the debate over the meaning of the term ἐμπόριον νόμιμον : « legally authorised markets », or « where the merchants are protected by law » or further still (and this is Casson's interpretation), « where the sovereign exercises a monopoly », one realizes that these three characteristics are precisely those of a « Port of Trade », that they combine rather than exclude all three. It is hardly surprising then that Augustus received the embassy of Indian kings, a political guarantee and sanction for Roman merchants, which could according to the times and the region undergo fluctuations that did not have anything to do with the economic order. This was true for Kalliena (*Periplus, 52*), and Federico De Romanis, p. 174-183 of the article I am going to quote later, suggested a reconstruction of events involving pirates, the Cheras and the Pandyas which led Western merchants to show a preference for the ports of the Pandyas over Muziris towards the middle of the 1st cent. A.D. ; and a century later, a Chera king to cast the Yavanas in chains and seize their goods. The shortcomings of the sources compel us in most cases to do so, but in all thoroughness it is not logical to treat India as a unique entity with respect to its relations with the merchants and its way of carrying out trade. A look in the *Periplus* at the lists of products exported from Barake and Barygaza on the one hand, and from the ports in the south on the other is sufficient. In the former, practically all the products came from the Himalayan slopes, or in the case of silk, from further afield ; in the latter, exported goods with the exception of silk came locally. The different regions did not undertake the same kind of activity, the former being merchant kingdoms which benefited from their intermediary situation, whereas the latter were first and foremost producers. Nor did they choose in the same way the goods to be traded, as the Roman coins clearly indicate. As for the problem of traffic between the kingdoms themselves, this remains for the most part to be studied. For this reason, the conclusion of Vimala Begley, who has shown separate ceramic distribution patterns for Western India (*moldmade ware*) and the South-East (*rouletted ware*), as well as their stylistic and technical independence is exemplary. This is a worthwhile avenue for future research, particularly should one add ceramological and numismatic data, taking into account political and social history as H.P. Ray has done in her *Monastery and Guild* (Oxford, 1986) and as V. Begley herself underscores : « An unknown factor, and one which may have been instrumental in determining the trade patterns of the extreme south, is the relationship between the southern kingdoms ».

I have often quoted the *Periplus*, and I have just spoken of coins. The authors have also often referred to these, though more to the former than to the latter. But the editors regret in the preface, and quite rightly so, that they were unable to include any numismatic contribution, and no specialist was asked to provide an overview of the literary sources. The question to ask is whether in the case of such a subject archaeology can be isolated from other research materials ; furthermore what are the inferences to be drawn thereafter.

Within a diffusionist framework, from which it does seem difficult to move out, the contributions dealing with influences tend to attach importance to commercial imports. But this is not the only option and there is no general rule to say that imitation proves trade. In the article I have just quoted, H.P. Ray and J.-F. Salles bring out the importance of contacts between India and the countries of the Persian Gulf, where one could learn decorating the floor of the vases with incised strias at local potters imitating Hellenistic ceramics. The second type of inference is quantitative. What do the objects carefully studied in this volume really prove, if we rely exclusively on such records ? S. B. Deo is realistic when he says (p. 43) : « There is very little concrete archaeological evidence of Roman imports in western India ». With the exception of Arikamedu, this seems to hold good for India as a whole. E. Lyding Will writes (p. 151) that Mediterranean amphoras have been found on several sites in India and develops the idea of a « substantial market » ; but on what exactly is this idea based ? Towards the end of 1990, Olivier Guillaume and I managed, after a preliminary study of the main publications, to identify 29 sites in India where the discovery of Western amphora fragments had been indicated. It does seem as if the list is fairly complete, as the list given by S. B. Deo in his article for Gujarat and Maharashtra mentions only one additional site. With the exception of Arikamedu, only one site provided more than some fragment : 31 at Nevasa. Elsewhere, when figures are given, they range from 1 to 5. E. Lyding Will indicates (fig. 9, 4 and n. 11) the first and only stamp of Latin amphora found in India (read *[M] Livi Caustr(i)*, see especially H. M. Cotton and J. Geiger, *Masada II*, Jerusalem, 1989, n° 948). This is insignificant in relation to all that can be found inside the Roman Empire. Obviously, the number of excavations has been few, and extrapolation is based on the idea that there are several Arikamedus buried under the Indian ground. But this can be done because there are on the one hand the texts — the *Periplus*, Strabo, Pliny and Tamil poems —, and on the other hand the 7000 Roman coins found in India. Without these sources, the archaeology of pottery sherds can only have curiosity value.

Several contributors include among their concerns the need to fix a date for when the trade under study began. A 2nd cent. B.C. date is mentioned on the basis of the neck of an amphora (fig. 9, 1) ; its convex shoulder is uncommon, and for me this neck remains undatable. The undoubtedly more reliable account of two Greek stamps, probably from Cnidus, photographs of which are provided by K.W. Slane (fig. 12, 3 and 4), points to the beginning of the 1st cent. B.C. This is not much. We shall have to await the study of Hellenistic coins found in India. In 1978 (p. 663) M. G. Raschke wrote (wrongly so : see Sidebotham, 1986, p. 17) « the absence of Ptolemaic coins in India has long been noted » ; Peter Berghaus has recently given us very different indications. One of the most ancient coin found in India is a silver coin of the 3rd cent. B.C. struck at Cyzicus in Mysia. Ptolemaic coins, especially in bronze, are not uncommon in Western India, and small Hellenistic bronzes from Asia Minor were found at Karur and Madurai (« Roman coins from India and their imitations », in *Coinage, Trade and Economy, 3rd Int. Colloquium*, Amal Kumar Jha ed., Nashik, 1991, 108 ; and « Zu den römischen Fundmunze aus Indien », *Revue Suisse de Numismatique*, 1992, 234). When and how did these bronze coins come ? Could they have been used for trade and if not, what were they doing there ? It is not possible to reflect upon the two stamps from Cnidus without asking these questions. And we would do well to remember that the best *terminus ante quem* for the relations between Alexandria and India is given by Greek epigraphy which attests the existence of a ἐπιστράτηγος τῆς ʼΕρυθρᾶς καὶ ʼΙνδικῆς θαλάσσης, at the latest in 62 B.C., perhaps in 74/73 (see A. Bernand, *Les inscriptions grecques de Philae*, I, Paris, 1969, n° 52 and 53 ; and L. Mooren, « The Date of SB V 8036 and the development of the Ptolemaic maritime Trade with India », *Ancient Society*, 3, 1972, 127-133).

For these reasons, I would in conclusion like to take the liberty to make a case against separation, in our field of interest here, between archaeology, numismatics, philology and history. The most significant breakthroughs have not come from the field of archaeology in the last few years. Though none of the contributors had the opportunity to mention Santo Mazzarino, we may also note with satisfaction that the name « Hippalus » and the « invention of the monsoon » have never been mentioned. This is red letter day : at last history has cast away this absurd sentence, just as one stroke of the pen of the great Italian historian has cast away the hardy Captain Hippalus in whom Wheeler saw « one of the greatest names in the history of navigation ». For those who have not yet had the pleasure of reading it, let us recall Santo Mazzarino's posthumous article : « Sul nome del vento *hipalus* ('ippalo') in Plinio », in *Helikon*, 22/27, 1982/1987, VII-XIV. The great Italian historian has shown that, in book VI, 100 of the *Natural History*, it was not legitimate to correct, as has been done since the time of Hardouin (1741), the text of the manuscripts with *hipalum* or *hypilum* to *hippalum*. The wind in question is a wind ὕφαλος, one that rises from the sea like the auster and the aquilon (*NH*, II, 128 : *ille infernus ex imo maris spirat, hic summo*), a phenomenon subscribed to till the 17th century, *e.g.* by R. Bohun in his treatise entitled *A Discourse Concerning the Origine and*

Properties of Wind, Oxford, 1671, p. 10. The myth of the pilot Hippalus was created on the basis of this adjective. Should one care to read in the same and following volumes of this journal the articles of his pupil Federico De Romanis (« Roma e i Notia dell'India, ricerche sui rapporti tra Roma e l'India dravidica dal 30 a.C. all'età Flavia », *ibid.*, 143-210 ; « Romanukharattha e Taprobane : sui rapporti Roma-Ceylon nel I sec. d.C. », *Helikon*, 28, 1988, 5-88), it becomes clear how the history of relations between the West and India can be enriched through the study of epigraphy and the Latin, Greek and Tamil texts, when such an inquiry is undertaken by a historian who has trained under a great master and is extraordinarily gifted for philology. May we one day be able to find and dig out another Arikamedu and unveil what remains of Barygaza and Muziris ! In the meantime, as we wait patiently for this distant future, we look forward much more eagerly to a future publication of the thesis which this young scholar defended at San Marin, entitled *Cassia, Cinnamomo, ossidiana. Mediterraneo ed* ΕΡΥΘΡΑ ΘΑΛΑΣΣΑ *da Neco ad Augusto.*

A. TCHERNIA
EHESS, Marseille.

Abbreviations quoted in the text

L. CASSON (1989), *The Periplus Maris Erythraei,* Text with Introduction, translation and commentary, Princeton.

M.G. RASCHKE (1978), « New Studies in Roman Commerce with the East », *ANRW*, 9, 2, p. 604-1361,

S.E. SIDEBOTHAM (1986), *Roman Economic Policy in the Erythra Thalassa*, Leyde.

R.E.M. WHEELER, A. GHOSH, K. DEVA (1946), « Arikamedu : An Indo-Roman Trading Station on the East Coast of India », *Ancient India*, 2, p. 17-124.

PALLADIUS' BRAHMANS *

Among the Greek texts which discuss the sages of India, Palladius' *Account on the Life of the Brahmans* stands out for its composite nature. Yet this is the only text in which the Brahmans have been dealt with independently, without any attempt to place them in a larger ethnographical, novelistic or philosophical context. That however does not make it a more reliable source on the Indian sages of Antiquity ; indeed, it has long been proved that Palladius handled his material on Indian reality from a Western point of view, working in elements taken from other texts dealing with India. Accordingly, his portrayal of the Brahmans is partly true and partly shaped by his philosophical stance.

Palladius was a bishop in Bithynia and Galatia at the start of the 5th century. He was also the author of *Lausiac History*, a description of the life of the first Egyptian monks, and of the famous *Dialogue on the life of St. John Chrysostom*. He was particularly interested in monasticism and its relationship with Hellenism, and compared pagan asceticism with monastic asceticism.

It was in this frame of mind that Palladius wrote his *Life of the Brahmans*. His account took the form of a letter addressed to a high dignitary of the Roman Empire.[1] The composite nature of the letter shows that Palladius did not limit himself merely to the scientific truths of geographers.

The letter is divided into two parts ; the first part is a description of India and the Brahmans, the second a lesson in wisdom. The Brahmans, an Indian people who are custodians of wisdom, provide the link.

In the first part of the letter, Palladius' information on India is not completely reliable. He himself confessed his inability to verify its authenticity first hand. The torrid heat kept him from venturing beyond the « limits of India », that is a promontory on the Somalian coast where an Indian settlement

* Translation into English : Miss Poonam PURI.

1. Probably Lausus, the emperor's chamberlain to whom *Lausiac History* was dedicated.

Athens, Aden, Arikamedu
New Delhi, 1994
C. MUCKENSTURM-POULLE, p. 157-166

had been established.[2] Palladius merely recorded the information provided to him by a Theban jurist who had been kept prisoner for a long time in North-West India. The jurist was on his way to Taprobane, or Ceylon, when the Bisads, a people thought to be similar to the inhabitants of the Bay of Bengal, captured him.[3] During the six years he spent in captivity, he acquired the language of his jailers and learnt much about the peoples of India. Thus though Palladius' information is second hand, his source seems to be fairly reliable.

The second half of Palladius' letter is more problematic. First, Palladius claims to have borrowed his lesson in wisdom from Arrian, from whom he was to quote.[4] Now from the point of view of vocabulary, style and composition, the text said to be Arrian's differs so greatly from the works of Arrian that it cannot possibly be attributed to him. Hence it would appear that Palladius errs when he claims Arrian to be the author of this treatise. It is equally clear that Palladius himself was not the author. There is an earlier text in a second century papyrus[5] quite similar to the one cited by Palladius, though the differences in the two versions are not ascribable to the latter. The lesson in wisdom is therefore not an original work but goes back to an intertextual tradition. At best, Palladius must have adapted it.

As far as its structure is concerned, the second part of Palladius' letter consists of a number of poorly connected sequences. The treatise begins with a monologue delivered by the master of the Brahmans, Dandamis, who compares Alexander's career to the passage of the sun.[6] Next, Alexander addresses a prayer to wisdom, asking for help to meet the Brahmans.[7] Then, the Brahmans describe their way of life to Alexander, condemn the behavior of the Indian sage Calanos, and advise the Macedonian king to meet Dandamis.[8] As Alexander is unable to find him, he sends « one of his friends », Onesicratos,[9] who invites Dandamis to

---

2. The meaning of the expression τὰ ἄκρα Ἰνδικῆς becomes clear thanks to Pliny (IV, 175) who tells us about the existence of a « *promunturium Indorum* » on the Somalian coast : R. DELBRUECK, « Südasiatische Seefahrt im Altertum"» *Bonner Jahrbücher*, 155/156 (1955-56) : 49.

3. For the identification of the Bisads, J. DESANGES, « D'Axoum à l'Assam : le voyage du *Scholasticus* de Thèbes », *Historia*, 18 (1969) : 632.

4. Pall., I, 15. We have quoted Palladius' text as it appears in Wilhem BERGHOFF's edition, *Palladius, De Gentibus Indiae et Bragmanibus, Beiträge zur klassischen Philologie*, 24, Meisenheim, 1967.

5. P. Genev. inv. 271, published by V. MARTIN, in *Museum Helveticum*, 16, n° 2 (1959) : 77-95, and 116-136.

6. II, 1.

7. II, 2.

8. II, 3-12.

9. This is a corruption of Onesicritus, historian entrusted by Alexander to talk with the Brahmans. See Strabo, *Geographica* and Plutarch, *Life of Alexander*, 65.

come and see Alexander, but the master of the Brahmans declines to do so.[10] Yet, at the beginning of paragraph 19, Alexander is seen in the presence of Dandamis and enters into a long dialogue with him. The sage asks the conqueror to give up battle; Alexander prefers to follow his destiny but acknowledges the wisdom of Dandamis and offers him gifts which the sage does not accept. Finally, even after Alexander has left,[11] Dandamis continues to tell him what to do, criticizing the dissolute ways and taste for luxury of the West.

This second part of Palladius' letter, intended as a lesson in wisdom, is in reality a series of monologues and dialogues clumsily held together by a narrative framework. The inconsistencies in the two parts of the letter as well as in the various sequences of the second part, and the fact that the second half is centered on the Brahmans prove that Palladius' ethnographical presentation was actually a ploy to introduce a moral precept. Besides, the extremely heterogeneous nature of the « lesson in wisdom » shows that it was made up from a number of earlier philosophical texts relating to the Brahmans and the material was later reworked to suit Palladius' purpose. So, instead of a clear picture of the life and thought of the Brahmans, what we have is a hotchpotch of themes.

Nevertheless, we can glean something about the Brahmans, for the letter does provide us with some ethnographical information. Of course, the extent to which one can rely on it is debatable, as we are dealing with second hand information which tends to be vague and contradictory, whether it has to do with the identity, the localization or the way of life of the Brahmans.

In the first part of his letter, Palladius defines the Brahmans, in accordance with what he was told by the Theban jurist, as an *ethnos*.[12] In Greek, *ethnos* usually means a group, a body of people acting together, of the same nature or profession. Thus, Xenophon speaks of a ἔθνος ῥαψῳδῶν, corporation of rhapsodists,[13] and Plato of a ἔθνος δημιουργικόν, a class of artisans.[14] As such, *ethnos* is a good equivalent for the notion of caste. However, the word does not take into consideration the fact that one is Brahman because one is the son of a Brahman, an idea better translated by the word Porphyrius used, γένος.[15]

One cannot of one's free will become a member of this *ethnos*. Nor has it anything to do with kinship or belonging to the same region. A Brahman is a Brahman because of divine decision and individual predestination.[16] Palladius

10. II, 13-18.

11. II, 40.

12. I, 11.

13. *Symposium* III, 6.

14. *Gorgias* 455b.

15. *De Abstinentia*, IV, 17.

16. I, 11.

does not make the distinction, as did Porphyrius, between the Brahmans, a caste of hereditary priests, and the Samans, men chosen among those who wished to know of divine things.[17]

In the second part of the letter, Palladius defines the identity of the Brahmans chiefly in relation to their way of life and with reference to two models, Calanos and Dandamis. The latter, « superior to all men »,[18] is a master of wisdom who respects God, loves his fellow men, does not care for gold, foregoes pleasures and possesses all the virtues that Arrian and Plutarch had attributed to him, namely freedom and gentleness.[19] On the other hand, Calanos is a traitor who, out of greed and stupidity, went over to the Greek camp.[20] For the Brahmans, Dandamis is a model for what to do and Calanos for what not to do.

The region ascribed to the Brahmans is as vague as their definition. In the first part of his letter, Palladius, basing himself on the account of the Theban Scholasticos, asserts that the Brahmans lived « at the borders of India and Serica, along the Ganges ».[21] Now Palladius had never seen the Ganges, but he tried to cover up his ignorance by taking recourse to literary tradition both Biblical and profane. He claimed that the Ganges was none other than the Phison river « of which it is said in the Scriptures that it sprung from paradise ».[22] Perhaps the idea of comparing a Biblical name with a profane one came to Palladius from Flavius Josephus' *Antiquitates Judaicae* : « The Phison, which means abundance, flows towards India into the sea. The Greeks call it the Ganges ».[23]

By taking up this parallel, Palladius is suggesting that the land of the Brahmans is similar to paradise. A paradise clearly demarcated from the territory of other men or for that matter even from the wives of the Brahmans, for Palladius states that whereas the Brahmans lived on the oceanic bank of the Ganges, their wives remained on the Indian bank. The separation between the two is all the more pronounced as the river is difficult to cross : in its waters lives a ferocious sea monster, the odontotyrannos, a kind of amphibious elephant capable of swallowing a man ; on its banks are huge dragons, ants and scorpions of the kind described by Herodotus and Ctesias of Cnidus in their Indian bestiaries.

---

17. *De Abstinentia*, IV, 17.

18. II, 32.

19. Arrian, *Anabasis*, VII, 2, 2-4, and Plutarch, *Life of Alexander*, 65, 3.

20. I, 4 and II, 11.

21. I, 1.

22. I, 1.

23. *A.J.*, I, 38. See M. ALEXANDRE, « Le site du paradis » : 187- 224, in *Peuples et pays mythiques*, Paris, 1988, *Actes du Ve colloque du Centre de Recherches Mythologiques*, ed. by François Jouan and Bernard Deforge.

However, in the second part of Palladius' letter we find no reference to the Ganges. The Brahmans speak of another river, the Tiberoboam, whose water is as sweet as honey. There is no attempt to locate the river. The Brahmans live nearby; in a luxurious forest where fruit is in abundance, reminiscent of the country of the Oxydrakai in *The Romance History of Alexander* (Pseudo-Kallisthenes).[24] Palladius appears to have been guided more by literary tradition than reality in his localization of the Brahmans.

Be it the banks of the Ganges or the Tiberoboam, the Brahmans lived in a state of nature. Palladius was struck by the complete absence of the means of production and comfort among them. « They have no quadrupeds, no tillage, no iron, no house, no fire, no bread, no wine, no clothes, nothing tending to increase their production or contribute to their pleasure ».[25] The Brahmans thus renounced wealth and material goods in antiquity. They knew nothing of agriculture, the main source of subsistence, nor of craftsmanship, however rudimentary. They chose to live in poverty. Their rejection of material civilization went as far as denying themselves all comfort, and their poverty turns into asceticism. The fact that they wore no clothes suggests that their asceticism and refusal of civilized life brought them closer to animality. They admired the vigor of wild beasts who lived on grass alone.[26]

The Brahmans lived in harmony with nature, caring little for social or economic organisation. Their asceticism was based on nature's philosophy. By rejecting the material goods men so cherished, they came closer to nature into which they hoped to merge. Their philosophy brings out three aspects of asceticism : frugality, nudity and chastity.

The Brahmans believed strongly in frugality ; they wanted to tamper as little as possible with nature which they revered above all other things. Consuming or even transforming worldly goods was seen as a blasphemous assault on creation. However so as not to die of starvation, they accepted vegetarianism, for gathering fruit and vegetables did not mean killing the plant. The restrictions on food were in no way incidental ; by living on fruit and vegetables alone, the Brahmans hoped to partake of plant life. Their frugality was thus based on both their respect for nature and their desire to be absorbed in it.

They viewed nature not as a mere model but as a mother. Dandamis drank from the pure spring water as if he were sucking at his mother's breast.[27] In this

---

24. *Romance History of Alexander*, III, 5, 4.

25. I, 11.

26. « Bulls, horses and does live on the plants that grow on the shores, drink water and dwell in the mountains. That is why they have considerable vigor and solid muscles », II, 45.

27. « Dandamis rested near a spring which he sucked like the pure breast of mother earth », II, 13.

immediate contact with creation, the Brahmans were seeking to rediscover primeval harmony. Coming closer to nature through food conferred upon men, worthy of such asceticism, wisdom to which ordinary mortals could not hope to aspire. Calanos, by going over to the Greek camp, rejected wisdom. « It was not enough for Calanos to drink the water of the Tiberoboam and eat things made of milk, the stuff of which forms minds worthy of God ».[28] The expression « water of wisdom » shows clearly that nature is by its very essence sacred ; the Brahmans' respect for nature lay on this bedrock. It is interesting to note that apart from vegetables, they were ready to consume animal products which did not result in the killing of the animal just as fruit gathering did not lead to loss of plant life.[29] By taking fruit, vegetables, water and milk products, the Brahmans reconciled their need for food with their deep respect for nature that brought them closer to the sacred.

Just as their food, instead of separating them from nature, drew them closer to it, so their clothing and shelter were part of their asceticism. The Brahmans went naked ; no veil separated them from creation. They lived as they were born,[30] refusing man made clothes that separated men from other elements of creation like animals or plants. Though living in a state of nudity was not easy, it served to toughen body and soul without going against nature's way. As they said : « Real courage is to fight with one's naked body against the vagaries of the elements ».[31] The fact that the Brahmans went naked does not mean they enjoyed suffering ; nor did they think of it as a means to attain higher goals like the ennoblement of the soul. Suffering for them was accepting their condition as natural beings : « Not one of us walks on burning coals or inflicts pain upon himself to tire out his body ».[32]

Nature, which had given animals and even plants the means to protect themselves against inclement weather, had not left man unprotected. So it would have been an act of impiety on the part of the Brahmans to wear clothes in order to safeguard themselves from the rigors of mother nature.

The Brahmans owned neither clothing nor shelter. Walls and roofs would only cut them off from the world and prevent them from gazing upon the vault of heaven.[33] Such an argument was particularly appealing to a Greek steeped in a philosophy that held the cosmos to an absolute order which men were required to imitate. Like their frugality or nudity, the Brahmans' rejection of shelter was not

---

28. II, 4.

29. See II, 24 : « I do not eat meat like a lion ; the meat of other living beings does not rot in me ; I have not become the graveyard of animal carcasses ».

30. « I am wrapped in the coat I had when my mother brought me into the world », II, 38.

31. II, 6.

32. I, 4.

33. II, 7.

a search for suffering. If they preferred to sleep on a bed of leaves, it was because nature permitted it. However in the period between the *Romance History of Alexander*, written before, and Palladius' letter, their attitude towards shelter seems to have changed somewhat. In the *Romance History of Alexander*, the Brahmans, making a few concessions to their comfort, built huts for themselves.[34] In Palladius' letter their asceticism was taken to extremes : neither sheet, nor roof was allowed to separate them from mother nature.[35] From this, one may infer that perhaps Palladius was not speaking of the same Brahmans. The ones he described could well have been a more austere sect of the same caste.

However a more likely explanation for the differences in description is that the two texts did not share the same literary aims. Whereas the *Romance History of Alexander* used the exotic in an attempt to please the reader, Palladius' letter with its portrayal of asceticism was intended to edify the public. As neither Palladius nor the author of Pseudo-Kallisthenes ever came to India, their description of the country was governed more by their literary ambitions or by what they had been able to gather from their sources. The fact remains that Brahman asceticism involved rejecting both clothing and shelter.

Marital relations were treated in a more specific way. In the first part of his letter Palladius states that the Brahmans lived on one side of the Ganges and their wives on the other : « The men live close to the oceanic bank of the Ganges. The wives live on the other side, on the Indian bank. The men cross the river in July and August to meet their wives [...]. And after living with their wives for forty days, they cross back again ».[36] Thus the Brahmans broke their self-imposed continence only twice a year. Palladius explains that this happened during the best period for marital union. Here again, the Brahmans followed the path of nature and gave in to their sexual desires only when nature favored it. The intention was not to maximize fertility but to subdue desire. Geographical separation helped the Brahmans maintain their continence.

Thus birth control came about naturally. « Nonetheless, after a woman has brought into the world two children, the husband no longer crosses the river to meet his wife. Leaving behind an heir, the Brahmans practiced continence for the rest of their lives ». The Brahmans limited themselves to two children so as to carry on the race without multiplying it. Their thinking was that in keeping the same numbers they were acting in consonance with nature ; multiplying the race would be going against the natural order. Low fertility and chastity were based on a philosophy of the universe which placed obedience and respect to the laws of nature above pleasure. The special case of sterility showed that there was no point in forcing nature. « On the other hand, if a woman happens to be sterile,

34. See the *Romance History of Alexander* (Pseudo-Kallisthenes), III, 4, 5.

35. II, 24 : « For me, sai· Dandamis, the sky is a roof, the earth a bed... ».

36. I, 13.

her husband crosses the river for five years to meet her. If she still cannot conceive, he no longer goes near her ». Five years was thought to be a reasonable period to determine whether a woman was sterile or not. The only possible outcome of these unions was the identical reproduction of what existed. There was no individual satisfaction as the individual was merely a part of the whole. The species did not increase as it could not exceed the place ascribed to it in the whole. Palladius concluded : « That is why there is no overpopulation in this caste ; life is difficult in this region and there is a natural continence ».

Brahmanic asceticism is part of a larger and more consistent philosophy than Palladius' simple description would have us believe. Its basic premise is respect for nature from which the Brahmans did not wish to be cut off in any way. Physically, clothing and shelter would separate them from nature. Morally, food which required killing living creatures would go against nature's way. Socially, the growth of the species or economic prosperity would destroy nature. Palladius may have well chosen those aspects of the Brahmanical way of life which best suited his purpose, however his underlying philosophy is consistent if not realistic.

Indeed, Palladius' portrayal of the Brahmans may be seen as a moral evaluation of the pagan Graeco-Roman world of which the person to whom his letter was addressed was unquestionably a part.

Though placed in an Indian setting, Dandamis' diatribe as reported by Palladius dwells on the general religious and philosophical themes of renunciation and temperance. It is worthwhile noting however that Dandamis did not provide any clear philosophical system to justify his thinking. He merely listed all the shortcomings of the Western lifestyle in contrast to the life of the Brahmans. He spoke chiefly of three things : personal hygiene, moderation of passion and elevation of the soul. The Western pagan model did not meet any of these three requirements.

Now all this is not exclusive to Brahmanical philosophy. Many others have emphasized these prerequisites : the Cynics, the Stoics, the Epicureans and finally, the Christians. Among the various ideas expressed in the melting pot of Dandamis' diatribe, Christianity was thrown into relief, if only by virtue of the role played by the author of *Life of the Brahmans*. Two elements lead us to the conclusion that Palladius recomposed this diatribe from a Christian perspective. First, Dandamis refers to[37] the catching of wild animals for circus games : they will eat men and be eaten by men. Nevertheless, man had to be respected, « he who was in the image of the divine nature which all men share and which was created by the hand of God ». The cannibalism of the men who ate the wild beasts of the arena was an argument the Christians used each time the pagans accused them of cannibalism.[38] The Christian denigrators of such bloody

37. II, 47.

38. See for example Tertullian, *Apologetic,* IX, 11.

performances commended respect for man, in the name of his divine filiation, as is the case with Palladius' Dandamis. Besides, the notion of God as the Creator, though not an exclusively Christian one, nevertheless sets apart Christianity; the same can be said about the idea of awaiting a divine judgment after death expressed by Dandamis.[39]

The other element, pointing to the fact that Dandamis' diatribe has borrowed from several philosophies, is specifically Christian, namely the criticism of the Epicureans, Stoics and Peripatetics : « What can one say about Epicureans, men who smear themselves with perfumed oil, saunter nonchalantly in delicate ladies wear and pollute the air with artificial fragrances ? About Stoic philosophers who care too much for money ? Or about Peripatetic philosophers ? But all are great and praiseworthy in your land ! ».[40] Dandamis makes no mention of the Cynics, the Neo-Platonists or the Pythagoreans. It is very likely that Palladius wished, through the intermediary of the master of the Brahmans, to spare them, as they did not renounce Dandamis' thinking.

Dandamis attacked only the pagan philosophers, not their philosophy. Some Christians had no qualms about Christianizing pagan ideas while proclaiming their upholders to be unworthy. Dandamis' discourse was adapted by Palladius with a view to effect a Christian taking over of pagan ideas. This was done through the « prism » of Brahmanical philosophy. That Brahmanical religion and uncorrupted pagan philosophy lead to Christianity does seem to be the meaning of Palladius' letter.

In particular, the kind of renunciation extolled by Dandamis comes from the monastic ideal of Palladius' time. Like Dandamis, the monks of the Egyptian desert fasted to the extent of vegetarianism, abstained from liquor and sex, contrasting the purity of their withdrawal to life in society which was inevitably corrupted. Like Dandamis, they too, out of charity, held out their way of life as a model : « Taking pity on you, we shall help you by not sharing your ideas. Indeed, we abhor arrogance and love mankind as a whole. We are the masters who defend the truth and show the path of justice to those who wish to do good in this life ».[41] Pagan philosophies, Brahmanical thinking and monasticism all share the ascetic ideal. But the idea that the ultimate aim is the contemplative preservation of truth and proselytism by example is very Christian. Palladius makes Brahmans and, more generally, uncorrupted followers of pagan philosophies, the precursors of monks.

The Gnostic influence can also be seen in the philosophy Palladius attributes to Dandamis. The Roman Hippolytus[42] had already described the philosophy of the Brahmans as a gnosis : he had come to know of it from a

39. II, 17.

40. II, 53.

41. II, 55.

42. *Philosophoumena*, I, 24.

Brahmanical discourse, once again taken up by Palladius. Though the latter removed from his account openly Gnostic themes, references can be found especially in Alexander's opening prayer to wisdom. The Gnostics honoured wisdom greatly and, like Alexander in his prayer, they held it to be the creator of nature, the mother of Pronoia.[43] Thus the Brahmans' respect for nature takes on a new colouring. It was their desire to communicate with divine nature that drew them closer to it : nature gave to them the wisdom from which it came.

Similarly, the idea of an elitist progression towards this wisdom through voluntary deprivation is a Gnostic one : all philosophies, be they Christian or pagan, lead to wisdom the moment they advocate renunciation, higher knowledge and nature worship. Influenced by the Gnostics, Palladius tried to fuse various ideas, including the ones he was supposed to defend as a bishop, into a heterogeneous whole. It appears that the *Life of the Brahmans* was intended to be an ambiguous text from the philosophical point of view.

Palladius' Brahmans are not real Brahmans. Their philosophy is too composite, their life too similar to that of the monks. Nonetheless, the fact remains that Palladius took the Indian sages as models and examined their philosophy for his moral opus, *Life of the Brahmans*. Here was a Westerner using India not for the exotic but to evaluate the lifestyle and philosophy of his own universe. The East gave to the West many models of asceticism. The *Life of the Brahmans* was a great success during all of the Middle Ages, especially with the monks, for it showed the extent to which the renunciation to the world and the quest for saintliness could go.

Claire MUCKENSTURM-POULLE
University of Besançon

43. See B. BERG, « Dandamis : an early Christian portrait of Indian asceticism », *Classica et Mediaevalia*, 31 (1970) : 279.

INDIAN BOAT BUILDING TRADITIONS
THE ETHNOLOGICAL EVIDENCE

It has been commonly assumed that since the economy of India in the past has been largely self-sufficient, there was no overwhelming reason for the country to develop a strong maritime tradition. However, as early as the Ṛgvedic period, there are references which point to a knowledge of the sea and the practice of navigation.[1] Some of the rites and superstitions observed by a group of fishermen in the Sundarbans, Bengal, could perhaps relate to earlier practices as well. While at one level, the rites pertain to propitiation of the forces of nature, at another, the symbolism is more complex. On the day the keel is laid the caste priest of the owner performs the worship of *bir*, hero/deity. After the boat is ready, the same rite is repeated. Married women, symbolic of fertility, smear the stern and prow with *galai*, vermillion, and mustard oil. The boat is greeted with *baran dala*, winnowing fan, containing various cereals, a lighted oil lamp, water and *kusha* grass. The presiding deity of the boat is Kastha Devi. There is a notion that the helmsman, *majhi*, should lead an austere life on the boat to earn the blessings of Devi. Devi also provides various indications in dreams but these have to be correctly interpreted. The time for sailing is fixed by the caste priest according to the almanac with the proviso that mornings of Tuesday and Wednesday are always permissible. Before setting out *puja* is performed to Śani and Satya Narayan while the caste priest performs that to the Goddess Ganga. At the boat, Ganga, Kali, Ban Devi, Kastha Devi and Gaji, a Muslim *pir* may be invoked. Different fishing grounds have different presiding

---

1. The Ṛgveda has been dated by P.V. Kane to B.C. 4000 (KANE, 1941). The term *samudra* used in the Ṛgveda, could refer to the aerial ocean in the sky, or to the actual sea. The term *arnava* was used for the nether ocean on the lower hemisphere. The *samudra* from which the sun, Bhujju, was rescued, related to the former. The similes used, however, showed that people had the knowledge of the sea. F. Max MULLER, 1964, I : 117.15 ; V : 59.2 ; VIII : 45.9. The greatness of Vasiṣṭha was compared to the unfathomed depth of the ocean. Soma was said to swell like the sea, B.R. SHARMA, 1952-53 : 180, 189.

Athens, Aden, Arikamedu
New Delhi, 1994
L. VARADARAJAN, p. 167-192

deities who have to be appeased.[2] There is thus a sufficient record of the presence of an early tradition of seafaring, but in the absence of material remains any attempt to reconstruct boat building technology has to place reliance on the vibrancy of craft tradition both in terms of techniques, processes, tools and implements as well as that of hereditary skills transmitted across generations. The task of identifying the constituents of a tradition which existed at a remote period of time in India is facilitated by the existence of a wide data base of ethnological evidence which lends itself to selective usage. The criteria for selection can be rationally explained as material artefacts and a living craft tradition are both subject to an inner logic which shapes the nature of innovation accepted and the norms which guide selectivity in obsolescence. This topic will not be taken up here as it involves aspects of a wide ranging methodological enquiry beyond the scope of the present exercise.

By virtue of its physical location India has played an important role in serving as an entrepôt between two sectors : Mediterranean Europe, East Africa and the Gulf region on the one hand, and Southeast Asia and China on the other. As a result of this exposure a range of technologies can be identified along the shores of the Indian subcontinent. Since the emphasis of this survey is on the boat rather than all categories of seagoing crafts, the catamaran will not be taken up for analysis.

The Indo-Gangetic estuaries and Peninsula India have abutted onto three sets of maritime tradition — the coir sewn tradition of the Arabian sea inclusive of the East African Coast, the *jong* tradition of Southeast Asia impinging on Bengal and, perhaps, Orissa, and, connected with the *jong* tradition, is the aspect of the Austronesian/Indonesian tradition of outrigger boats and constructional devices such as the lashed lug. These three constituents could be stated to form the basis of boat building techniques in India and also in the Indian Ocean. The three traditions have not been mutually exclusive. The regimen of winds and currents and the struggle for survival in the face of natural adversities has ensured a considerable degree of mutual borrowing and adaptation of technologies among the component maritime groups. Among those adaptations and innovations, mention may be made of constructional usages of Byzantium

2. RAY CHAUDHURI, 1980 : 114-118, 120. Bandevi is the presiding deity of poisonous snakes, tigers and other wild animals which live in the Sundarbans. Fishermen appeased Bandevi as they had to get firewood from the jungle, *ibid.* : 123. In northeast coastal Andhra Pradesh, comprising East Godaveri, Visakhapatnam and Srikakulam districts, apart from Hindu deities, the majority of whom are female, Muslim saints such as Madina Sahib of Calingapatnam and his brother, Naguru Meera Sahib of Madras, are worshipped by the fisherfolk. Both the Muslim saints are said to have come from Arabia, M. SURYANARAYANA, 1977 : 106-116, 124. For Islamic attitudes to the sea, see *Pakistan Navy Staff College Review* (Pakistan Navy Staff College, Sharea Faisal, P.O Box 2029, Karachi), Sayyid Q. FATIMI, « Maritime Imagery in Shah Latif's Mystic Poetry » : 85-97.

(skeleton first) (BASS & DOORNINCK, 1982 : 311) and the Mediterranean (nails, *e.g.* FATIMI, 1990 : 14). Unlike other areas of artisanal activity such as textile manufacture in which similar technologies could emerge in different centres independently of each other, bench marks of boat technology appear to bear a much stronger diffusionist orientation. However, within the geographical spread of a particular technology, there appears to be a wide range of region specific variation.

The first of the major traditions to be taken up for discussion is the Austronesian one. The reason why Austronesian/Indonesian boat usages have an immediate bearing on Indian boat building technology is because some explanation has to be identified for the cleavage which has been found to exist between the boat building practices followed in the islands of Lakshadweep, excluding Minicoy, and the Maldives. In the first group, plank joinery approximates the coir sewn tradition of the Arabian sea ; in the latter, however, continuous sewing is notable by its absence. In its place planks are edge to edge joined by means of adze prepared pegs (*Fig. 1*). The curve of the hull is ensured by paring of planks rather than by selection of naturally curving tree trunks, usage of moulds and bending of planks through firing. To ensure maximum fitting between strake edges, planks are meticulously shaved during the course of construction. Luting by means of placement of coconut husk horizontally between planks is undertaken before two horizontally facing planks are pegged together (*Figs. 2, 3*). In the hull area near the mast head, however, a series of protuberances are to be found. At present these play no functional role, but they can be explained as vestigial lugs (*Fig. 4* ; see MANGUIN, 1988 : 6-10 ; VARADARAJAN, 1988 : 5-7). This suggests a diffusion of the lashed lug technique associated with Indonesia and described by G.A. Horridge (HORRIDGE, 1982) and P.Y. Manguin (MANGUIN, 1985).

P.Y. Manguin, in tracing the evolution of the Southeast Asian *jong*, bases his argument on archaeological material dated respectively to the period between the third and eight centuries A.D. and thirteenth to fifteenth centuries A.D. All dated pre-fourteenth century ship structures found in archaeological contexts in Southeast Asia belong to one specific technical tradition. The components of the ship are held together by vegetal stitches or lashings made from the fibre of sugar palm, *Arenga Pinnata*, the *tali ijuk* of the Malay/Indonesia and *cabo negro* of the Filipinos. This method has survived into the contemporary period in a variety of forms scattered over most of the region from Hai-nan and Vietnam to the Philippines and eastern Indonesia. This area has well known Austronesian connotations. The stitching, unlike the Arabian Sea prototype, is discontinuous. From his analysis of a boat dated between *ca* A.D. 233-353 found on the Pontian river on the east coast of the Malay Peninsula, P.Y. Manguin states that on each side of the adjacent planks at regular intervals inboard two sets of lugs with openings are carved (MANGUIN, 1985b : 334, fig. 20, 9A). On each side of the carved lugs, two holes are pierced. The fibre used in sewing is passed through the respective holes and the lug and fastened securely. Manguin speculates that following contemporary Indonesian practices, the ties were held fast by some sort of wedge driven into the loop and caulking was undertaken to make the joints watertight. In the Butian find from Mindanao, Philippines, dated between *ca* A.D. 210-430, P.Y. Manguin notes that all the characteristics pertaining to lashed lug craft as described by G.A. Horridge are to be found (MANGUIN, 1985b : 333-335 ; *id.*, 1989 : 201-210). In this method planks are bound together both by means of fibre lashings held in place by being passed through the hollowed out lugs carved at regular intervals along adjacent planks, as also by pegs interspersed along horizontal facings of adjoining planks. Thwarts, and/or discontinuous ribbing were additional structural devices inserted according to the size of the boat and lashed in the same way through the lugs to provide additional strength to the hull. The engineering principle involved was that the compression forces between the planks had to be overcome before the seams could begin to come apart (HORRIDGE, 1982 : 1-3, fig. 2). The importance of the Pontian find is that it shows the progressive adoption of dowelling (MANGUIN, 1989 : 212). The Minicoy and Maldives plank joinery could be linked with a later development of the same tradition when dowels replace the lashed lug. For small boats the thwarts would provide sufficient strengthening.

Apart from the case of the lashed lug tradition, Austronesian as distinct from Austro-Asiatic [3] influences are also indicated by the dispersion of outrigger crafts along the southern coasts of India as recorded by J. Hornell (HORNELL, 1923 : 151-152, 160-167) and J. Deloche (DELOCHE, 1980 : 185, 191). The northernmost point for the dispersion of the outrigger was Bombay on the West coast. The ubiquitous presence of the craft on the Konkan coast (*Figs. 5, 6*) and extending further into Manlagore in Kerala caused J. Hornell to refer to this factor as the « Indonesian influence » (HORNELL, 1946 : 195, 210). In the Gulf of Manar, the outrigger is recorded at Kilakarai while in the Palk Strait the boomed float is replaced by a balance board. This is a long plank laid athwart the gunwhales of the craft. When necessary one to three crew members load themselves on to this plank on the weather side to secure the desired counter balance. Beyond Adirampattanam and Muthupet the outrigger disappears (HORNELL, 1923 : 160-165 ; also 1946a : 260-263). The South Indian arena of the

3. The Austroasiatic family comprises about 150 languages. It is made up of two branches — Munda and Mon-Khmer. The Munda family, divided into ten languages and two branches, the Northern and Southern, is spoken in Northeast India. The most important languages are Santali and Mundari. Mon-Khmer languages are spoken throughout much of Southeast Asia, mainly in Laos, Vietnam, Kampuchea, Thailand, Burma, the Malay Peninsula, Meghalaya (Khasi) and the Nicobar Islands. This group is divided into three branches, Northern (which includes Khasi), Eastern (which includes Khmer) and Southern (which includes the Nicobari group). RUHLEN, 1987 : 148-149, 151, 15 ; BELLWOOD, 1985 : 2-3. For historical perspectives see BELLWOOD, 1985 : 162, 268 ; *id.*, 1989 : 6, 25, 26.

outrigger forms part of a larger belt extending in the sector from East Africa and Madagascar to Śri Lanka. Further to the east, from its focal point in Indonesia, the tradition has spread to Micronesia, Polynesia and Melanesia. [4] S.Q. Fatimi refers to an Arab boat, the *kalaya*, plural *khaluya*, built on the island of Bahrain. It had an outrigger and was referred to by Tarafa bin al-Abd, died *ca* A.D. 564, and al-Muraqqish al-Akbar, died *ca* A.D. 550. By the time of al-Farazdaq, died A.D. 728, it had become obsolete. (FATIMI, 1990 : 27-32, 37). Although in present times outrigger boats play a limited role in the Indian Ocean, it was not so in an earlier period. Moreover, as an indicator in boat typology this model cannot be overlooked.

The question may be asked as to what is meant by the term Austronesian and how this influence became so pervasive in a maritime environment. The problem is controversial but certain contours are perceptible. According to P. Bellwood linguistic dispersal was accompanied by actual physical settlement. Leaving this aspect aside, the fact that the dispersal of the language is also accompanied by the prevalence of certain maritime modes such as the outrigger and the lashed lug cannot be controverted [5].

In present times the Austronesian family of languages is distributed from Madagascar in the west to Eastern Island in the east. All Austronesian languages are derived from one common ancestral language — Proto-Austronesian. This has been located in Taiwan *ca* B.C. 3000. It had moved into Luzon in the Philippines and Proto-Austronesian split into the Formosan and Malayo-Polynesian sub-groups. *Ca* B.C. 2500 there was further expansion into south Philippines, Borneo, and, through the Moluccas, into Timor. The movement into Oceania started *ca* B.C. 1500. P. Bellwood, deriving his conclusions from the linguistic work of R. Blust, divides this dispersal into three channels : the central Malayo-Polynesian Austronesian which led through the Moluccas and Lesser Sunda ; the eastern Malayo-Polynesian and Oceanic Austronesian which could be traced via Halmahera, north coastal New Guinea into Oceania, and the western Malayo-Polynesian Austronesian which, for the purposes of this article, is the most germane. This sub-group expanded through the Philippines to Sulawesi, Borneo, Java and then doubled back to Sumatra, Malaya and Vietnam. During the early centuries of the Christian era it reached Madagascar. [6] H.P. Ray has traced a long distance trade network dated to the early centuries of the

4. HORNELL, 1943 : 91-100 ; *id.*, 1943a : 40-53 ; *id.*, 1944 : 3-17, 170-184 ; KENTLEY & GUNARATNE, 1987 : 41.

5. HORNELL, 1943 : 91 ; KENT, 1979 : 97 ; MANGUIN, 1985 : 327, 336-340. See also DORAN, 1981.

6. ADELEAR, 1989 : 26 ; BELLWOOD, 1984-85 : 108, 11-113 ; *id.*, 1985 : 2, 3 and map, 122, 232-233 ; *id.*, 1987 : 207-208, 210. For historical perspectives see CHANG, GRACE & SOLHEIM II, 1964 : 359-406. SOLHEIM II, 1991, presents a somewhat different sequence from that presented by Bellwood.

Christian era which includes sites in Malaysia which concerned itself with the distribution of Malaysian tin and gold (RAY, 1990 : 20).

Since the emphasis of this article is on boat tradition, the complexities and intricacies of Austronesian dispersion from the linguistic angle is not relevant (SEBOEK, 1971). However, Austronesian journeying by sea to Madagascar [7] is very germane to the question of the peg fastened tradition of Minicoy and the Maldives.

After an examination of the meteorological and hydrographical factors involved, G. Donque has outlined three possible routes, all feasible to a greater or lesser degree according to the season, linking Indonesia to Madagascar. (DONQUE, 1965 : 52-59). J. Poirier dates the initial arrival of Indonesians to Madagascar between the third and sixth century A.D. [8] The second phase is dated between the third and sixth centuries A.D. P. Vérin places the first arrival

7. It would, perhaps, be useful at this point to bring together dispersed references to the presence of Southeast Asians both in the Arabian Sea sector and in the South China Sea/Indonesian Archipelago from the turn of the Christian era to *ca* 12th century A.D. The term used for this group varies according to whether the sources are Chinese or Arabic, but both sets of references clearly point to the same group, that is, the one identified by P. Bellwood as western Malayo-Polynesian Austronesian. From the opening years of the Christian era to *ca* A.D 750, Chinese records make references to a group initially called *Man-i* (Barbarian), the appellation being changed to *Kun Lun* in the Tang period, A.D. 620-907. The *Kun Lun* are said to dominate the trade of the Southern Seas. They possessed large ships which the Chinese called *K'un Lun Po.* The homeland of the *K'un Lun* comprised Java, Sumatra, Borneo, Champa and Cambodia. Coming to another source we find the Roman geographer Pliny, referring to the carriers involved in the cinnamon trade as the *Troglodytes.* The *Troglodytes* journeyed over a vast expanse of sea with their trade commodity which they brought to South Arabia. The source for the best cinnamon at this time was the region around North Vietnam. Supplies were brought to South China from where they were distributed. It is important to remember that at this period the Chinese did not engage in long voyages towards the south. The *Troglodytes* could well be the *Man-i* of the Chinese. Turning to the Arab Sea sector in the 10th century we find the Arabs referring to the Indonesians in East Africa and Madagascar as *Wak-Wak,* while the Chinese used the term *Kouen Louen luseng-k'i.* This group came in search of commodities such as ivory, tortoise-shell, panther skin, ambergris and *Zanj* slaves, all in demand in their own country and China. In 1240 Ibn al-Wardi refers to the trade in iron ore from the country around Sofala. This was highly prized in India and served the needs of Indian wootz manufacture. The *Kun Lun* may have played a role in this area as well, which would provide added reason for traces of their presence in South India (the outriggers), and in the Maldives (the boat building tradition). VARADARAJAN, 1983 : 349 ; *id.*, 1987 : 92 n° 12, 98-99 and n° 37, 38 ; CHITTICK, 1977 : 220 ; NAINE, 1984 : 654 ; DEVISSE, 1985 : 61, 67-69 ; MANGUIN, 1980 : 274-276 ; *id.*, 1989 : 211.

8. POIRIER, 1979 : 55 ; VÉRIN, 1975 : 46. For a summary of the discussion on Indonesian mouvements and Madagascar, see VARADARAJAN, 1987 : 98-88 and n° 37, 39.

at the sixth century A.D. [9] For the initial voyages Vérin prefers to identify as the route the passage along which outriggers are to be found, following the southern contours of India and then veering off towards the East African coast. [10] During the second phase the route passed through, on the one hand, Śri Lanka, South India, the Maldives and Lakshadweep and on the other, the northeast or northwest coast of Madagascar. Indonesian presence along such an alignment would provide a very plausible backdrop to the evidence of the pegged boat building tradition in Minicoy and the Maldives. It needs to be stated, in this context, that Minicoy and Maldives possess a much stronger seafaring tradition than the remaining portion of Lakshadweep, [11] and even today, memories of past linkages with Indonesia persist in the Maldives.

If a process of diffusion is associated with the spread of outrigger crafts and the technique of lashed lug joinery, could the same process have been at work with regard to the coir sewn craft of the Arabian Sea littoral ? The kind of joinery which is depicted on the boat in the Miracle Panel, East Gate Front, South Pillar, Sanchi, Stupa 1, dated to the first century B.C. could be identified with the non-padded face of a coir stitched hull (*Figs. 7, 8*). J. Deloche, however, prefers an identification with *vadhera* [12] plank joinery (DELOCHE, 1978 : 11-16). In this context it is of interest to see the close parallel in plank joinery in visual terms between the boat depicted in the Sanchi stupa (*Fig. 7*) and that found in the Dahshur wooden funerary boat dated to the reign of Sesostris III, B.C. 1836-1818, at the Egyptian Museum, Cairo (*Fig. 9*). [13]

If an identification with coir stitching is accepted, its origin could be traced back to at least the first century B.C. However, West coast plank joinery is

---

9. POIRIER, 1979 : 54-55 ; VÉRIN, 1975 : 46.

10. R. Kent states that the outrigger is confined in Africa to the Comoro Islands, Madagascar and the shores of East Africa on the side opposite to Madagascar stretching from Porto Amalia to Mombasa in Mozambique, KENT, 1979 : 97.

11. VÉRIN, 1975a : 179. The adze is the favoured instrument in boat construction both in Minicoy and Maldives. Vérin remarks that the stone or metal adze is commonly encountered in Austronesian cultures, *ibid.* : 183. Unfortunately the Indonesian element has not been studied as a component in Maldivian culture. See GEIGER, 1919, reprint 1986. In the case of Lakshadweep, a Polynesian (for which the word Indonesian should be substituted) origin has been postulated by N. Muthukkoya (MUTHUKKOYA, 1986), but the hypotheses of the author have to be scientifically tested. The comment on the vibrancy of seafaring tradition in Minicoy and the Maldives *vis-à-vis* the other portions of Lakshadweep is based on field work on the islands undertaken by this author.

12. J. Hornell has used the term Tongue- and Groove-Seam (HORNELL, 1930), but boat builders in Billimora use the term *vadhera* to describe the same method of plank joining.

13. See GREENHILL, 1976 : 109-110. For further details relating to the Dahshur boat joinery see JENKINS, 1980 : 124-125.

divided into two sets of techniques. In the case of the Konkan and Kerala Pattamar, one or other technique is practiced according to the size of the boat. [14] The first technique is that of coir stitching while the second may be defined as *vadhera*. The practice of coir stitching stretched from the East African coast and along the West Asian coast to the coast of western India. Thereafter it skipped the Cape Cormorin area and picked up the thread one again near Karikal reaching its point of termination near Puri, Orissa on the coast of the sub-continent. It spread its tentacles into Lakshadweep as well. Under such circumstances, until a very detailed study has been undertaken, it would be very difficult to pin point possible centres of origin or trace channels of diffusion. Admiral Paris has defined the second technique as « très ancienne et tout à fait indienne » (very ancient and totally Indian), but then goes on to add that the same method is also utilised by the Arabs (PARIS, 1843 : 18). J. Deloche has stated that the *vadhera* system was practiced in the area extending from the entrance to the Persian Gulf to the neighbourhood of Calicut.

The term *vadhera* is used by Gujarati boat builders to refer to the type of joinery still practiced in Billimora. Writing in the 19th century Admiral Paris confirmed a description of *vadhera* provided by the Dutch traveller, Stavorinus in the eighteenth century. [15] Planks are rabbeted and then meticulously planed (*Figs. 10, 11*). Luting then takes place the material used being an initial coating of a kind of glue on which layers of cotton wool are aligned (*Figs. 12-14*). At distances of 1.5 metres four holes in sets of two in vertical alignment are bored along the two edge joined planks. Sewing now takes place in a discontinuous manner each double set of stitches being held taught by the insertion of a wedge of wood on one surface in course of sewing. The holes are then plugged. Finally long iron nails are driven through the planks and ribs, the projecting inner ends being beaten down to serve as clamps, HORNELL, 1923 : 145 (*Figs. 15, 16*).

The usage of nails in a traditional constructional technique does not need to cause surprise but the impetus for this probably came to India through Islam. Despite Indian mastery in metallurgy, the avoidance of nails as a constructional device appears to have formed part of a cultural reflex. The Arab Caliphate had access through the East Mediterranean to the Mediterranean nailed boat building tradition. Al Hajjaj (A.D. 661-714) is credited with the introduction of tarred and nailed ships into the Indian Ocean. The Umayyad poet, al-Farazdaq (A.D. 728) refers to ships « fastened by iron clamps ». That such boats were not uncommon is attested by the trade in scrap iron obtained from the dismantling of nailed ships which had developed in Basra. Although the texts quoted by Fatimi refer

---

14. Eyde records *ca* 1834 that the larger Pattamar were nailed (*vadhera* joinery) while those of 60 tons and less were coir sewn, EYDE 1843 : 10. The identification between *vadhera* and *pattamar* joinery is based on technical details provided by Paris (*ibid.* : 18), WILSON, 1909 : 13-14, and POUJADE, 1948 : 18, fig. 15, and 19.

15. For the description of Stavorinus see VARADARAJAN, forthcoming : 17-20.

also to caulking, in view of the slurring over of technical detail which is a common feature of this category of source material, for the purposes of this article, the important aspect is that of references to nails and clamps. [16] P.Y. Manguin refers to a number of Portuguese 16th century sources, which refer to the usage of nails in Gujarat and the west coast of the Deccan, and which also appear to refer to the *vadhera* technique. [17] The choice of the use of iron nails or treenails was a conscious one made by the Indian boat users and had nothing to do with the availability or otherwise of iron. Indeed, India has an ancient and well attested tradition of iron smelting and it was from this country that the earliest items in wootz, Indian steel, were prepared and exported. [18]. For the makers of Damascus steel, to forge the iron spikes used in *vadhera* plank joinery so that these became « tough and flexible », as noted by Stavorinus (VARADARAJAN, forthcoming : 18), would have posed no problem.

With regard to coir sewing, two procedures are adopted. Planks are not rabbeted but are flush laid. Some kind of luting substance may be used, an adhesive paste or putty and some vegetal matter or even cloth. Wooden pegs may be selectively used for spot strengthening. Holes are bored along the jointed planks (*Fig. 17*). Thereafter the sewing operation starts. Two workers have to ply the needle, one inboard and the other outboard. (*Figs. 18, 19*). As the needle is pulled in and out (*Fig. 20*), padding material can be laid in strips either inboard or outboard or on both surfaces (*Fig. 21*). This is kept in place by the stitches and the sticky nature of the padding. In Lakshadweep it comprises a gum like substance, *pantham* (remarkably similar to the material noted by seventeenth century European observers and used for the same purpose) and coir. [19] This padding process can be approximated but not identified with caulking as the padding is not pushed between planks but is couched on the lines of plank joining to improve water proofing capacity. In his description of the sewing of east coast Masulas, referred to by Europeans as *chelinque*, E. Kentley illustrates two methods. The second is the one which has the largest geographical spread in the sewn craft area taken in its entirety, but the first predominates in the purely Masula tradition. In the first method the padding is

---

16. VARADARAJAN, forthcoming : 37, n° 48 ; FATIMI, 1974 : 149-155 ; *id*., 1978 : 45.

17. MANGUIN, 1985a : 10-11. Since the sources also refer to sewing, Manguin leaves open the question as to wether the Portuguese sources are, in fact, referring to the *vadhera* technique. Since the choice of sewing or opting for the *vadhera* technique appeared to depend on size, there is no contradiction in the Portuguese sources, and therefore, no reason to be sceptical about their validity.

18. Indian wootz has a tradition extending back 2000 years. When the Roman Emperor Diocletian, A.D. 284-305, established an arms manufacturing unit at Damascus, the imported steel was referred to as Seric (Chinese). This was because, being an item in long distance trade, the Romans were ignorant about the real place of origin of wootz, see YATER, 1982 : 3 ; ID., 1983 : 3.

19. See ARUNACHALAM, 1990 : 205.

laid only on one surface. In the second, padding is secured both inboard and outboard along the plank seams. Admiral Paris, in describing the one surface layering of the Calicut *manji* describes a further refinement which is to be noted in Lakshadweep also. In this case the padding is laid inboard. To protect the stitching outboard which appears as a series of repeats of two parallel lines, each stitching is recessed into a groove which is etched into the planks. This protects the coir from outside forces. This is also the practice in Lakshadweep (*Fig. 22*).

In the Masula tradition, where the padding is laid only on one side, the stitching on the obverse side would show itself in the sets of two parallel lines as has been stated above. However, where both sides are padded, the procedure of sewing follows a different order and while on one side there would be a series of crosses, on the other there would be a series of verticals connected by diagonals. [20] The description by Prins of the method sewing of the Mtepe in Lamu approximates work practices documented by this author in the island of Andrott in Lakshadweep in 1989. According to Prins, « sewing was done with three strands of coir rope, roughly three-quarters of an inch thick, tapered and twinned together, with a slip of palm leaf acting as a needle ». In the actual process of sewing, two men worked together, one sitting inside and one standing outside. The one sitting inside passed the needle, the man outside pulling the rope through and twisting it with a forked stick which was used as a lever to stretch the rope tight. (*Fig. 23*). The first man meanwhile hammered the caulking to flatten it. The caulking consisted of loose coir fibre hammered into the seam ; on top of this was placed a packing of thick paste made of pounded mangrove bark ; over this a layer of crushed strips of coconut husk was to be found and finally, on top of all this, a layer of crushed and dried stems of doam palm leaves was laid. All these components are sewn into position whenever two planks are stitched together. As soon as the rope was tightened enough, the man inside knocked in a peg to wedge the tightened rope (*Fig. 24*). He used the same peg in succession, always wedging the rope in, where the other man had tighened it. As had also been noted by Hornell at an earlier date, successive lengths of six feet were sewn in this manner. On completion wedges were driven into each hole from the inside, any protuberance being planed down (*Fig. 25*). Variations existed but these are not described in greater detail. [21] Contrary to the views expressed by European travellers of the early colonial period, coir sewn boats are not weak and clumsy contrivances built by Asiatics and Africans

20. KENTLEY, 1985 : 311-312 ; PARIS, 1843 : 20 ; DELOCHE, 1980 : 183. Cf. KENTLEY & GUNARATHNE, 1987 : 39-40 ; HORNELL, 1943a : 43 ; *id.*, 1943 : 173-175.

21. PRINS, 1982 : 94-98 ; HORNELL, 1941 : 61. Deloche points out that the majority of coir sewn vessels on the west coast on India have padding inboard. However, there are two iconographic depictions of boats in the Goa Museum, dated respectively to the 13th and the 15th centuries, which appear to have the padding outboard, see DELOCHE, 1987 : 168, figs. 8, 10.

because of a pitiful lack of access to iron nails. The boats were built in conformity to functional requirements and were well adjusted to surmount the stresses and strains of known hydrographical and meteorological conditions. Since the practice was that of fair weather sailings, the ships lent themselves to being dragged ashore during the times of monsoonal closure of ports for cleaning, refitting and repairs. There appears to have been a lesser preoccupation with the aspect of ballasting than European ships. It was not a level of inferior technology which dictated the construction of such boats, but culturally selective solutions evolved in response to specific needs. [22] Indeed, when Admiral Paris was exposed to the west coast Patamar he was moved to remark, « nous trouvâmes encore preuve que le meilleur navire est réellement celui que le pays a produit, et que les habitants manœuvrent » (we again found proof that, basically, the best ship is that which is produced by the country itself and which the natives themselves manœuvre). (PARIS, 1843 : 17).

On the East coast a major tradition is represented by the Masula tradition. The Masula was called *pataku* in Tamil, *padava* in Telugu. [23] According to G. Bouchon and L.F. Thomaz this was a small galley utilised for commerce as also in naval warfare. [24] This author has argued elsewhere that the *masula* may well hold the key for identifying the possible form of the south Indian ship (VARADARAJAN, forthcoming : 21). The early Europeans made frequent references to another small craft, the *sampan*, used essentially as a small carrier. The agent of the French East India Company, François Martin, reported the activities of such a boat on March 1674 : the owner was a local Muslim potentate. In view of the number of such boats owned by Indians it cannot have been exotic to these shores. An indigenous variant may have been developed on the eastern shores of the Bay of Bengal from a Chinese or Southeast Asian prototype. [25] In present

22. T. Severin makes an interesting observation in this connection. Circumstances dictated the choice of *aini*, *Artocarpus hirsuta*, for the building of the boom Sohar, which was to duplicate voyages made by the Arab ships from Sohar to China in the 8th-12th centuries. *Aini* has been disfavoured in modern times because of its lime content which caused nail sickness, and from its tendency to split when nailed. If this wood was used for sewn ships, the high lime content would in fact, become an advantage as it would discourage infestation by woodworms. The range of woods from which a choice could be made thus became larger (SEVERIN, 1985 : 280).

23. DELOCHE, 1980 : 183 n° 5. This is not to be confused with the *padava* of Gujarat, *ibid.*, 191, n° 9.

24. However, even though the origin of the Malaysian word *perahu* may be Sanskrit, as is stated by Bouchon & Thomaz, the *masula* bears no ethnological relationship to the Indonesian *prahu*. See BOUCHON & THOMAZ, 1988 : 423, *perau*, *q.v.* For the Indonesian *prahu*, see HORRIDGE, 1981.

25. See VARADARAJAN, 1981 : 340. Cf. BOUCHON & THOMAZ, 1988 : 420-421, *champana*, *q. v.* According to the two authors, this was a small boat which could hold from five to thirty persons.

times, a vessel by this name exists in the Chittagong area of Bangladesh (JANSEN *et al.*, 1989 : 72). In view of early 16th century Portuguese references to the presence of the *jong* on the East Coast (BOUCHON & THOMAZ, 1988 : 467, « Navires Asiatiques, Jonques », *q. v.*) this Southeast Asian boat, itself a product of a hybrid tradition, appears to have been a constituent in the boat tradition of the Bay of Bengal. [26] Another dimension of which nothing is known, is the nature of the ship in which the elephant trade was carried between the East coast and Siam and Sri Lanka. A Thai document dated A.D. 1815 refers to three ships belonging to one, Sanghranaiken Sresthi of Porto Novo, sent to Siam for the purchase of elephants. While there are some descriptive details about the Thai ship involved in this trade, nothing is mentioned about the Indian craft (WRIGHT : 8, 11, 17, 40 n. 9). The 10th-11th century boat depicted in an Orissan sculpture with an elephant on board at the Indian Museum, Calcutta, is not sufficiently clear to warrant being used as evidence for boat typology (VARADARAJAN, forthcoming : fig 10b and 42, 106). We find, therefore that the East coast of India, unlike the West coast, provides scanty ethnological evidence of what, undoubtedly, must have once existed as a great tradition of maritime venture. It is to be hoped that the new evidence which is emerging on the trade of Bengal with the *Kun Lun* countries in the period second century B.C. to about fourth century A.D. will clear the mist, even if in a limited manner. [27]

In conclusion, it may be stated that if the method of plank joinery is taken as a parameter in boat technology, innovative impact of the post-European period appears to be minimal. The impetus may have been felt in areas such as changes in the form of the hull, nature of rigging and navigational instrumentation. In view of the evidence which has surfaced with regard to the existence of skeleton first construction in the Mediterranean Sea region dated to the 10th century A.D. and associated with Islam (DARMOUL, 1985 : 156-158), the introduction of this practice could have predated the 15th century. The usage of moulds (BASCH, 1972 : 34-39) and templets, however, may well have been work practices grafted onto Indian tradition during this period. However, ethnological tradition shows that the usage of these has been marginal in the past. The contours of sailing crafts defined in terms of plank joinery which have survived the introduction of steam power have a remarkable contiguity in tradition with past usages.

Finally, on the basis of raw material available and extant ethnological evidence, it could be stated that India had an identifiable tradition of seafaring of its own. There were plentiful sources of local woods to cater the needs of ship building. Mangrove wood made the sturdiest dowels, while *vela madhu*, *Terminalia tomentosum*, and *aini*, *Autocarpus hirsuta*, were preferred for the

---

26. For the southeast Asian *jong*, see MANGUIN 1985 : 16-19. In present day Bangladesh, the *jong* is listed as a riverine boat, JANSEN *et al.*, 1989 : 76-77.

27. MUKHERJEE, 1990 : 33-35.

keel. Teak, *Tectona grandis*, lent itself to the fashioning of planks, keels, stem and stern posts. Ribs were made from jackfruit, *Autocarpus intergrifolia*, while masts were fashioned from pun, *Calophyllum tomentosum.* The lateen gaff, requiring considerable flexibility, could be made from *pali, Palaquum ellipticum* (CLEMENSHA, 1943 : 122.) Field experience has confirmed that usages recorded in 1943 are valid into present times. Lakshadweep and the Maldives provided the best quality coir. Although the date of the first peopling of these islands remains unknown, C. Maloney argues for a date of the 1st to 2nd centuries B.C. for the Maldives (MALONEY, 1980 : 48-75.). These factors reinforce the case for the existence of a viable Indian maritime tradition. If seafaring traditions serve the needs of well developed commercial entreprise they can no longer remain insular. This appears to have been the reality in India, and since Arab codification has been so well projected through the works of Ibn Majid, it becomes difficult to isolate the Indian elements in the amalgam. In the absence of a strong ethnographic base on the east coast, the task of projecting an earlier tradition becomes that much more difficult. However, there is enough evidence to warrant a great deal more concerted work being done to fill in the gaps and present a more meaningful and cogent picture of Indian seafaring tradition.

Lotika VARADARAJAN
National Institute of Science Technology
and Development Studies, New Delhi

Bibliographical References

Abbreviation : Mouvements = *Mouvements de population dans l'Océan Indien*, Actes du Quatrième Congrès de l'Association Historique Internationale de l'Océan Indien et du Quatorzième Colloque de la Commission Internationale d'Histoire Maritime, tenu à Saint-Denis-de-la-Réunion du 4 au 9 septembre, 1972, Paris, 1979.

ADELAAR (K.A.), 1989, « Les langues austronésiennes et la place du malagasy dans leur ensemble », *Archipel*, 38 : 25-52.

ARUNACHALAM (B.), 1990, *Indigenous Traditions of Indian Navigation. Lakshadweep and Minicoy*. I. *Navigational Practices and Boat Building*, CSIR - NISTADS Project, Bombay, unpublished.

BASCH (L.), 1972, « Ancient wrecks and the archaeology of ships », *The International Journal of Nautical Archaeology and Underwater Exploration*, I, 1.

BASS (G.F.) & VAN DOORNINCK Jr (F.H.), 1982, *Yassi Adda*. I. *A Seventh Century Byzantine Shipwreck*, Texas.

BELLWOOD (P.), 1984-85, « A Hypothesis for Austronesian Origins », *Asian Perspectives*, 26, Pt. 1 : 107-117.

BELLWOOD (P.), 1985, *Pre-history of the Indo-Malayan Archipelago*, Academic Press.

BELLWOOD (P.), 1987, « The pre-history of Island South-east Asia. A multidisciplinary review of recent research », *Journal of World Prehistory*, I, 2 : 171-224.

BELLWOOD (P.), 1989, « Cultural and biological differentiation in peninsular Malaysia : the last 10,000 years », paper prepared for the *Second International Conference on Malay Civilization*, Kuala Lampur, 16-20 August 1989 : 1-45, unpublished.

BOUCHON (G.) & THOMAZ (L.F.) eds, 1988, *Voyage dans les Deltas du Gange et l'Irraouaddy. Relation Portugaise Anonyme (1521)*, Paris.

CHANG (K.C.), GRACE (G.W.), & SOLHEIM II (W.G.) eds., 1964, « Prehistoric and Early Historic culture horizons & traditions in South China », *Current Anthropology* 5, 5 : 359-406.

CHITTICK (H.N.), 1977, « The East Coast, Madagascar and the Indian Ocean », R. Oliver ed., *The Cambridge History of Africa*, 3, Cambridge.

CLAMENSHA (W.W.), 1943, « The Early Arab thalassocracy », *Journal of the Polynesian Society*, 52, 3 : 110-131.

DARMOUL (A.), 1985, « Les épaves sarrasines. Contribution à l'étude des techniques de constructions navales musulmanes et Méditerranéennes », M. Balley et L. Ladjimi Sebai, *L'Homme Méditerranéen et la Mer*, Tunis : 152-165.

DELOCHE (J.), 1978, « Techniques anciennes de constructions navales en Inde : le problème de la liaison des bordages (sources et méthode) », Paper presented at the *VIth European Conference on Modern South Asian Studies*, Paris. (This paper has been published but access has been limited to an earlier unpublished manuscript).

DELOCHE (J.), 1980, *La circulation en Inde avant la révolution des transports. II. La voie d'eau*, Paris.

DELOCHE (J.), 1987, « Études sur la circulation en Inde. VII. Konkan Warships of the XIth-XVth centuries as represented on Memorial Stones », *Bulletin de l'École Française d'Extrême-Orient*, LXXXVI, Paris : 165-184.

DEVISSE (J.), 1985, « Réflexion d'un Africaniste sur l'histoire du fer dans l'océan Indien », *Bulletin de l'Académie Malgache*, N.S. LXIII, 1-2 : 61-69.

DONQUE (G.), 1965, « Le contexte océanique des anciennes migrations : vents courants dans l'océan Indien », *Taloha*, 1 : 42-59.

DORAN (E.), 1981, *Wangka. Austronesian Canoe Origins*, Texas.

EYDE (J.), 1834, « Description of the various classes of vessels constructed and employed by the Natives of the Coasts of Coromandel, Malabar and the Island of Ceylon for their coasting Navigation », *Journal of the Royal Asiatic Society of Great Britain and Ireland*, 1 : 1-14, 14 plates.

FATIMI (S.Q.), 1974, « Hajjaj's reforms in the art of ship building in the Indian Ocean », *Oriental College Magazine*, Centenary Number, Lahore : 146-156.

FATIMI (S.Q.), 1978, « In search of a methodology for the history of Muslim navigation in the Indian Ocean », *The Islamic Quarterly*, XX, XXI, XXII, 1-2 : 40-51.

FATIMI (S.Q.), 1990, « Arab hulls and sails », paper presented at International Seminar ; *Integral Study of Silk Roads, Road of Dialogue, Al-Sind and Arab Seafaring Culture, Commerce and Urbanisation*, Pakistan, 27 November - 3 December : 1-63 (unpublished).

GEIGER (W.), 1919 (1986), *Maldivian Linguistic Studies*, trans. : J.C. Willis, ed. : H.C.P. Bell, *Journal of the Ceylon Branch of the Royal Asiatic Society*, XXVII, (extra number), Colombo, reprint Male.

GREENHILL (B.), 1976, *Archaeology of the Boat*, London.

HORNELL (J.), 1930, « The origins and ethnological significance of Indian boat designs », *Memoirs of the Asiatic Society of Bengal*, VII (1918-1923), Calcutta.

HORNELL (J.), 1930, « The tongue and groove seam of Gujarati boat builders », *Mariners Mirror* : 309-312.

HORNELL (J.), 1941, « The sea-going Mtepe and Dau of the Lamu Archipelago », *Mariners Mirror* : 54-68.

HORNELL (J.), 1943, « Outrigger devices : distribution and origin », *The Journal of the Polynesian Society*, 52 : 91-100.

HORNELL (J.), 1943a, « The fishing and coastal craft of Ceylon », *Mariners Mirror* : 40-53.

HORNELL (J.), 1944, « The outrigger canoes of Madagascar, East Africa and the Comoro Islands », *Mariners Mirror*, 3-17 : 172-185.

HORNELL (J.), 1946, « The sailing craft of Western India », *Mariners Mirror*, 32 : 195-217.

HORNELL (J.), 1946a, *Water transport, origins and early evolution*, Cambridge.

HORRIDGE (G.A.), 1981, *The Prahu, traditional sailing boat of Indonesia*, Oxford University Press.

HORRIDGE (G.A.), 1982, *The lashed-lug boat of the Eastern Archipelagoes, the Alcina Ms. and the Lomblen whaling boats*, Maritime Monographs and Reports n° 54, National Maritime Museum, London.

JANSEN (E.G.), DOLMAN (A.J.), JERVE (A.M.) & RAHMAN (N.), 1989, *The Country Boats of Bangladesh*, Dhaka.

JENKINS (N.), 1980, *The Boat Beneath the Pyramid*, London.

KANE (P.V.), 1941, *History of the Dharmaśāstra*, II, Part 2, Poona.

KENT (R.R.), 1979, « The possibilities of Indonesian colonies in Africa with special reference to Madagascar », *Mouvements* : 93-105.

KENTLEY (E.), 1985, « Some Aspects of the Masula Surf Boat », S. McGrail & E. Kentley eds., *Sewn Plank Boats*, National Maritime Museum, Greenwich, Archaeological Series n° 10, Oxford : 303-317.

KENTLEY (E.), GUNARATNE (R.), 1987, « The Madel Paruwa — A Sewn Boat with Chine Strakes », *The International Journal of Nautical Archaeology and Underwater Exploration*, 16, 1 : 35-48.

MALONEY (C.), 1980, *People of the Maldive Islands*, Madras.

MANGUIN (P.Y.), 1985, « The southeast Asian ship : an historical approach », *Journal of Southeast Asian Studies*, XI, 2 : 266-276.

MANGUIN (P.Y.), 1985a, « Late medieval Asian shipbuilding in the Indian Ocean. A reappraisal », *Moyen Orient et Océan Indien, XVIe - XIXe s.*, 2 : 21-30.

MANGUIN (P.Y.), 1985b, « Sewn plank craft of South East Asia. A preliminary survey », S. McGrail & E. Kentley eds., *Sewn Plank Boats*, National Maritime Museum, Greenwich, Archaeological Series n° 10, Oxford : 319-343.

MANGUIN (P.Y.), 1988, « Summary report on a survey of traditional shipyards in the Maldives, 22-29 March 1988 », *Workshop on Maritime History of India*, NISTADS, New Delhi, 25-26 June (unpublished).

MANGUIN (P.Y.), 1989, « The sewn-plank and lashed-lug craft of early South-East Asia », *Proceedings, Pertemuan Hmiah Arkeologi*, V, Yogyakarta 4-7 Juli 1989, 1, Regional Studies, Jakarta : 200-220.

MUKHERJEE (B.N.), 1990, « Kharoshti and Kharoshti-Brahmi Inscriptions in West Bengal (India) », *Indian Museum Bulletin*, XXV.

MUTHUKKOYA (N.), 1986, *Lakshadweepu Nootandukalilude* (Malayalam), Kottayam.

MULLER (F.M.), *Vedic Hymns*, Part-I, first edition Oxford University Press 1891, reprint Oxford University Press, Delhi, 1964.

NAINE (D.T.), 1984, *General History of Africa*. IV. *Africa from the Twelth to Sixteenth Century*, Paris.

PARIS (F.E.), 1843, *Essai sur la construction navale des peuples extra-européens. Collection des navires et pirogues construits par les habitants de l'Asie, de la Malaisie, du Grand Océan et de l'Amérique*, Paris.

POIRIER (J.), 1979, « Problèmes de la mise en place des couches ethniques et des couches culturelles à Madagascar », *Mouvements* : 51-59.

POUJADE (J.), 1948, *La Machoua de Versova*, Documents d'Ethnographie Navale, Fascicule 4, Paris.

PRINS (A.J.H.), 1982, « The Mtepe of Lamu, Mombasa and the Zanzibar Sea », *Paideuma*, 28, J. De V. Allen ed., *From Zanj to Zanzibar, Studies in History, Trade and Society on the Eastern Coast of Africa in Honour of James Kirkman on the Occasion of his Seventy-fifth Birthday*, Wiesbaden : 85-100.

RAY (H.P.), 1990, « Seafaring in the Bay of Bengal in the early centuries A.D. », *Studies in History*, 6, 1, n.s. : 1-14.

RAY CHAUDHURI (B.), 1980, *The Moon and the Net. A Study of A Transient of Fishermen at Jambudwip*, Calcutta.

RUHLEN (M.) ed., 1987, *A Guide to World Languages*. I. *Classification*, Stanford, California.

SHARMA (B.R.), 1952-53, « The concept of Ocean in the Vedas », *Journal of the Oriental Institute*, II.

SEBEOK (T.A.) ed., 1971, *Current Trends in Linguistics*, n° 8, The Hague, Paris.

SEVERIN (T.), 1985, « Constructing the Omani Boom », S. McGrail & E. Kentley eds. *Sewn Plank Boats*, National Maritime Museum Greenwich, Archaeological Series n° 10, Oxford : 279-302.

SOLHEIM II (W.G.), 1991, « The Nusantao and Prehistoric Contacts among the people of Southeast Asia, South China, Korea and Japan », *12th Congress of the International Association of Historians of Asia*, Hong Kong.

SURYANARAYANA (M.S.), 1977, *Marine Fisherfolk of North-East Coastal Andhra Pradesh*, Calcutta.

VARADARAJAN (L.), 1981, trans., annotated of *India of the 17th Century. Memoirs of François Martin (1670-1694)*, I, Part 1 : *1670-1674*, New Delhi.

VARADARAJAN (L.), 1983, « Indian Textiles and Early Trade Routes of the Orient », B. Dutta ed., *Aruna Bharti*, Professor A.N. Jani Felicitation Volume, Essays in Contemporary Indological Research, Baroda : 343-356.

VARADARAJAN (L.), 1987, « Commodity Structure and Indian Participation in the Trade of the Southern Seas, circa Ninth to Thirteenth Centuries », S. Chandra ed., *The Indian Ocean, Explorations in History, Commerce and Politics*, New Delhi : 90-108.

VARADARAJAN (L.), 1988, Report, ITIN Project — Lakshadweep and Maldives, *Workshop on Maritime History of India*, NISTADS, New Delhi, 25-26 June (unpublished).

VARADARAJAN (L.), forthcoming, « Sailing Craft of India », to appear in M.C. Joshi ed., *B.K. Thapar Felicitation Volume*.

VÉRIN (P.), 1975, « Austronesian Contributions to the Culture of Madagascar. Some Archaeological Problems », H.N. Chittick & R.I. Rotberg eds., *East Africa and the Orient*, New York, London : 164-191.

VÉRIN (P.), 1975a, *Les échelles anciennes du commerce sur les côtes nord de Madagascar*, I. Thèse présentée devant l'Université de Lille III.

WILSON (N.J.F.), 1909, *The Native Craft. A General Description of the Native Craft Visiting Bombay Harbour and Particulars as to Their Registry, Measurement and Lighting*, Bombay.

WRIGHT (M.), « Siamese Monks visit to Lanka in the early 19th Century », trans., from "Cotmaihet Ruang Somanathut Pai Lanka Thaswip", in Prince Damarong's *Ruang Praditthan Phra Song Sayamwong Nai Lankathavip*, Department of Religious Affairs, Bangkok, 1960, *Indica*, forthcoming.

YATER (W.), 1982, « The Legendary Steel of Damascus », Part-1, *The Anvils Ring*, Spring : 3-7.

YATER (W.) 1983, « The Legendary Steel of Damascus », Part-II, *The Anvils Ring*, Summer : 3-13.

FIGURES

1. Sharpening of pegs.
2. Shaping of planks.
3. Placement of planks.

Figures 1-3 were photographed at Odivala Attiri, Village Bada, Minicoy. Boat Owner : Haji Veerika Gothi ; Carpenter : Mohammed Efarathige.

4. Disused *Mas doni*, boat used in tuna fishing, Mafushi, Maldives. Note vestigial lugs.
5. Single outrigger, Aguada Beech, Goa. Indonesian outriggers have narrower hulls.
6. *Idem.*
7. Detail from Miracle Panel, East Gate, front, South Pillar. Sanchi Stupa I. 1st Century B.C.
8. Stem of disused *otam*, local boat type, belonging to Pattakal family Andrott. Out board, coir sewn hull.
9. Dahshur wooden boat, ca B.C. 2000. Courtesy Egyptian Museum, Cairo.
10. Rabbet joint as practiced at Billimora, Gujarat.
11. Two plank edges are brought together.
12. Luting with cotton wool.
13. Upper plank being brought down in alignment with lower plank.
14. Finished strakes. Ribs being placed in position in shell construction.

Figures 12-14 depict vadhera *joinery. Photographed at Narsibhai Morarji boat building yard, Billimora, Gujarat.*

15. Discontinuous sewing and nailing in *vadhera* joinery. From PARIS, 1843, fig. 10 : 6.
16. Joinery in single outrigger, Aguada Beach, Goa. Note similarity with fig. 15, above.
17. Kondalam, a Lakshadweep boat type, under construction at Amini, Lakshadweep. Cloth and *pandham* has been placed between planks ; holes have then been bored for sewing.
18. Needle made from spine of coco-nut leaf. Note progressive increase in ply of coir.
19. Sewing in operation, Kunhi Ahmad, boat builder, Chetlat, Lakshadweep.

20. Needle being pulled in and out in course of sewing.
21. Padding and coir being placed along joins in stakes.
22. Recessing of sewing.
23. Operation of sewing — mainte-nance of tautness in rope.
24. Wedgeing with peg.
25. Finishing operations inboard to outboard.

Figures 20-25 photographed in workplace of Kunhi Ahmad, Boat builder, Chetlat, Lakshadweep.

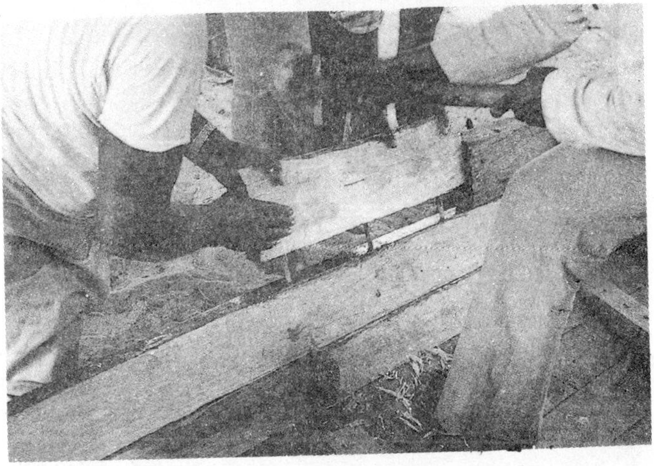

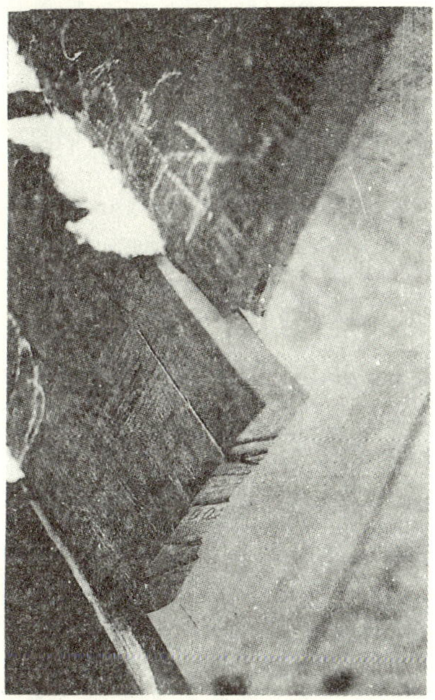

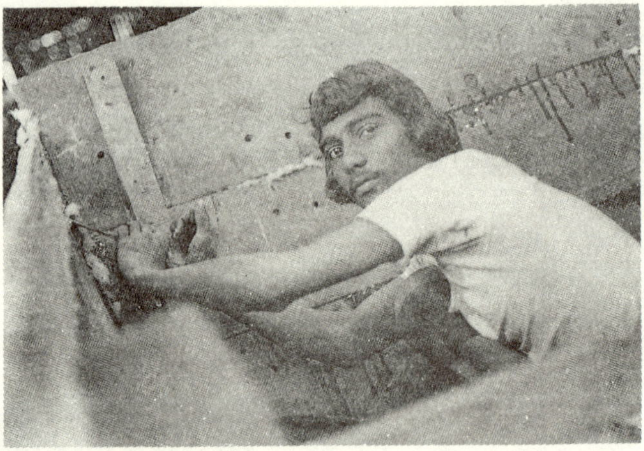

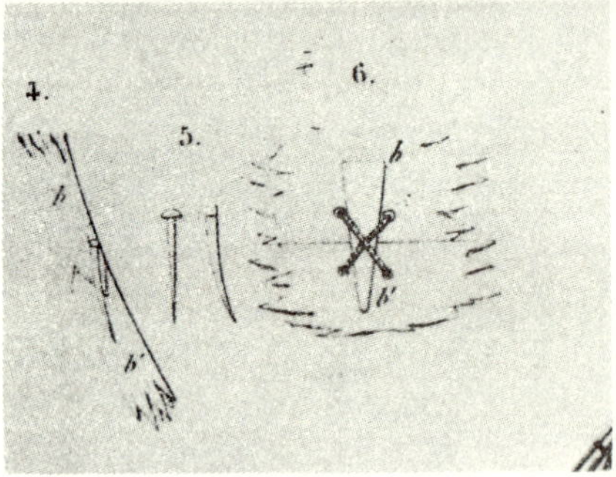
4.
5.
6.

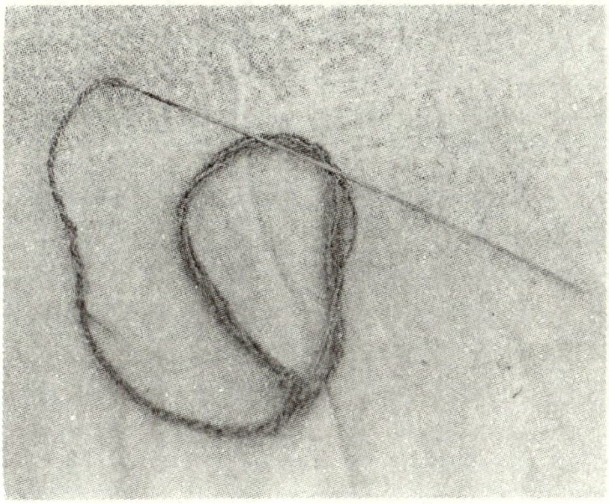

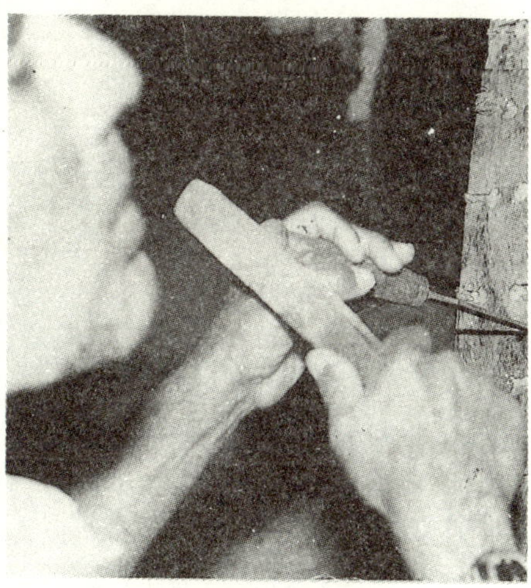

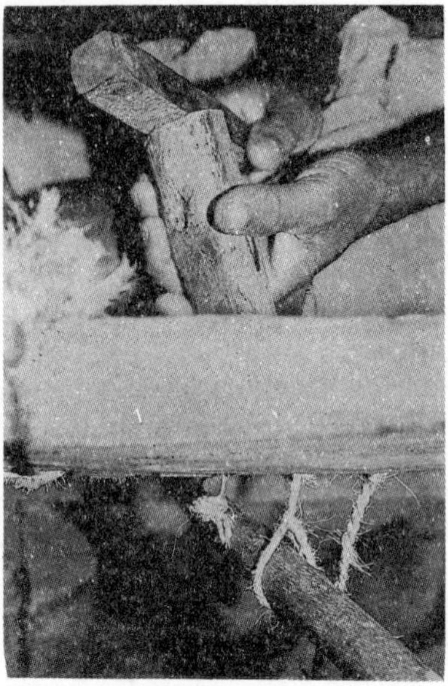

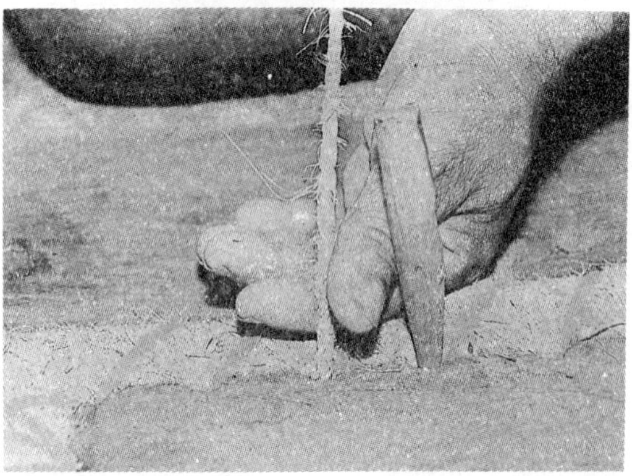

MONUMENTS OF SOCOTRA

The history of exploration

The first archaeological survey of Socotra was carried out in 1897 by Theodore Bent, who wrote about the existence of ancient relics on the island. [1] The next researcher to merit mention was P.L. Shinnie, a participant in the Oxford expedition of 1956. [2] A more notable contribution to the study of the Socotran archaeological monuments was made by D.B. Doe, who visited the island in 1967. [3]

P. Shinnie arrived at the following conclusion : « The results of the survey of Socotra were not spectacular. Expectation of finding remains of Classical antiquity were not fulfilled and, though it is not impossible that further investigation might find them, it will not be on the bare limestone plains of the north, where there is virtually no accumulation of soil. It must be assumed that those early traders, from whom the author of the *Periplus* got his information, spent little time on the island. We can well imagine that they came, as do the modern traders from South Arabia and India, for a few days only at a time, perhaps pulled their boats up on the beach, replenished their supplies of food and water and passed on to India or up the Red Sea leaving little behind them ». [4] Now it is clear that the Oxford expedition overlooked the most interesting objects, but then, P. Shinnie was virtually the pioneer of the archeological exploration of Socotra.

---

1. J. T. and Mrs BENT, *Southern Arabia*, London, 1900.
2. P.L. SHINNIE, « Socotra », *Antiquity*, XXXIV (1960), London, p. 100-110.
3. D.B. DOE, *Socotra. An Archaeological Reconnaissance in 1967*, Miami, 1970. Now, see also D.B. DOE, *Socotra. Island of Tranquillity*, London, 1992.
4. SHINNIE, « Socotra », *op. cit.*, p. 108.

Athens, Aden, Arikamedu
New Delhi, 1994
V.V. NAUMKIN & A.V. SEDOV, p. 193-250

The expedition gave particular attention to the study of remains of churches, defence installations, and dwelling houses. A study was made of the ruins of forts in the Feragey valley, around the village of Suq.

During his journeys to the mountains to take blood samples from the bedouins, Dr. N. Orr, a member of the expedition staff, came accross a row of houses which the inhabitants called « ancient » or « European ». P. Shinnie cites his description of these ruins discovered around Kishin, in Mahadum (south-western Haggier), on a limestone plateau near Zerih, in Adhein, and under mound Shelale. [5] He also compares the old structures with the new houses : « Present bedu houses have wooden beam — old houses have roofs supported on huge flat stones, some up to 6 ft. long, resting on a central pillar and radiating to the walls which sometimes slope in to meet them. One stone overhangs the other in a primitive attempt at vaulting. Round the walls raised beds. Doors often screened by small well of stone. Small sheep pen adjoining. Used for cows nowadays ». [6]

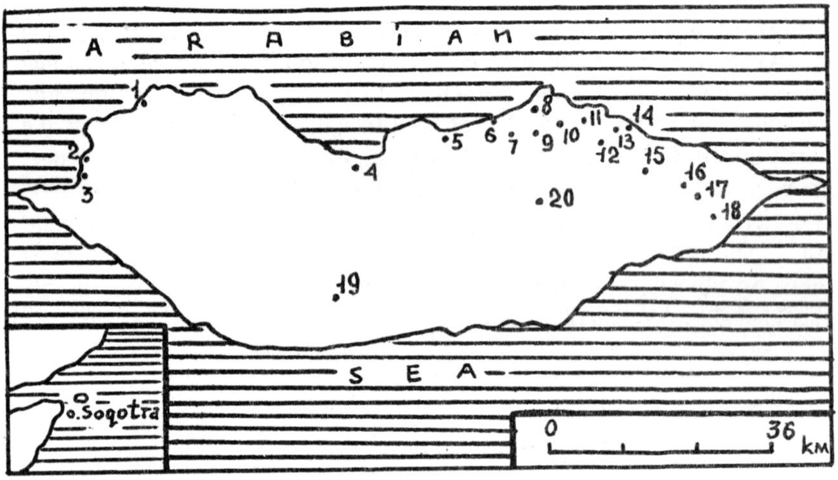

Figure 1. Monuments of the Socotran island.
1. Qallansiya. 2-3. Simar Qar. 4. Eriosh. 5. Qadhub and Haybak Pass. 6. Hadibo. 7. Tsinifiroh. 8. Suq. 9. Hajrya. 10. Feragey. 11. Möbrhim. 12. Lower Rökib. 13. Mathöbo. 14. Gyuzuf. 15. Shibhon. 16. Rakuf. 17. Hohabay Shzain. 18. Qalisan. 19. Dihub. 20. Hasin.

5. SHINNIE, « Socotra », *op. cit.*, p. 106-107.

6. SHINNIE, « Socotra », *op. cit.*, p. 107.

In his survey of the island D.B. Doe could rely on Shinnie's data. Doe's most considerable achievement was to register and describe all objects he had seen, although he had not discovered everything by far. Doe carefully surveyed the Suq area. He wrote that the island's best anchorages seemed to confirm the existence of objects of man's early stay on Socotra in Qallansiya (Ghubbat-Qallansiya) and Suq (Ghubbat-Hadibo and Bandar-Delisha). The advantage of Suq is that its anchorages lie on both sides of Ras-Haulaf, which offers certain protection both from the easterly and from the westerly winds. Suq itself lies in the centre, which facilitates internal communications.

In Suq and around the nearby lagoon Doe found fragments of ceramics similar to those discovered on the eastern African coast dating from the 10th-17th centuries. [7] As a result of his archaeological survey of the island, Doe generalised the data on all pre-17th century structures, identifying the following structural types :

« 1. Stone circles of large uncut stones and boulders.

2. Cave dwellings and protective walling to the exterior to give additional protection. This practice appears to have continued to the present day although caves were used from earliest times.

3. Terraces with boundaries of boulders and the use of protective boulders at defence points on narrow hill tracks.

4. Farmstead units of individual farmsteads of irregular planned walls constructed of masonry roughly coursed with vertical stone door jambs. The use of columns for roof timbers and paved floors. Usually small walled paddocks are attached. The stone-cell structures, of habitation units associated with farmsteads. These also have door-jambs and floor paving.

5. Farmstead using roughly squared masonry walling laid dry. These with preconceived plans, with columns symmetrically placed in groups of four or six. The use of vertical stones as jambs to openings and flat paving slabs.

6. Boundary walling. This great work of producing walls of rough boulders created by stone cleared areas which in turn formed boundary alignments enclosing areas of private ownership.

7. Walls of buildings and habitation areas which seem unconnected with the farmstead and boundary wall scheme. Probably belonging to goat herdsmen, and, on the coast, to fishermen and divers for oysters. These are to be found near the coast, on sites such as Simar Qar and the buildings at Suq. The walls are constructed of vertically-placed flat slabs as well as flat bedded stones at corners and wall junctions. At Suq the flat slab walls have a rough infill with cross stones to act as headers.

---

7. DOE, *Socotra*, p. 151.

8. Walls of masonry, again roughly-coursed and uncut but laid in a lime mortar made from burning of shells and blocks of limestone. Green and blue-glazed (Islamic monochrome) imported pottery has been found near walling of this type.

9. The use of lime plastered floors, found principally in the buildings at Suq.

10. Walls of roughly-coursed masonry laid in lime mortar but also plastered on the exterior, a type which includes the Mosques at Hadibo and Qallansiya and buildings to the present time ». [8]

Doe's classification is based on purely formal signs of relics and can be regarded as the result of a preliminary stage in the study of Socotra's archaeological monuments.

Basically, the planned systematic study of Socotra's archaeological relics was initiated by a group of the joint Russian (former Soviet)-Yemeni expedition, although the results of the research carried out by P. Shinnie and D. Doe were an invaluable help. At the first stage it was decided to give main attention to the island's eastern area, because according to our preliminary observations, remains of the oldest structures, overlooked by the British scholars, lay exactly there. Suffice is to refer to the dolmen-shaped structures first discovered by Naumkin during his first visit to the island in 1974. Investigations were carried out in 1983, 1984, 1985, 1987 and 1989 field seasons, when the joint Russian-Yemeni expedition started his work in South Yemen. The subsequent research was extended to the island's central and western parts (*Fig. 1*).

Pre-Islamic monuments

Neolithic (?) workshop

Apparently, one of the oldest known archaeological relics of the island is located not far from the modern village of Rakuf. Remains of a workshop (?) which had manufactured flint tools were registered here. It is the only place on the island's eastern plateau were there are outcrops of flint which form a crust on the plateau's sloping limestone slabs. Items made of flint have been found on an area of approximately 400 x 400 m. A total of 125 objects were collected, which can be classed as follows (*Fig 2-4*) :

Adze with transverse concave blade	1
Scraper	4
Scraper-shaped tool	6
Hollowed tool	8

8. DOE, *Socotra*, p. 151-152.

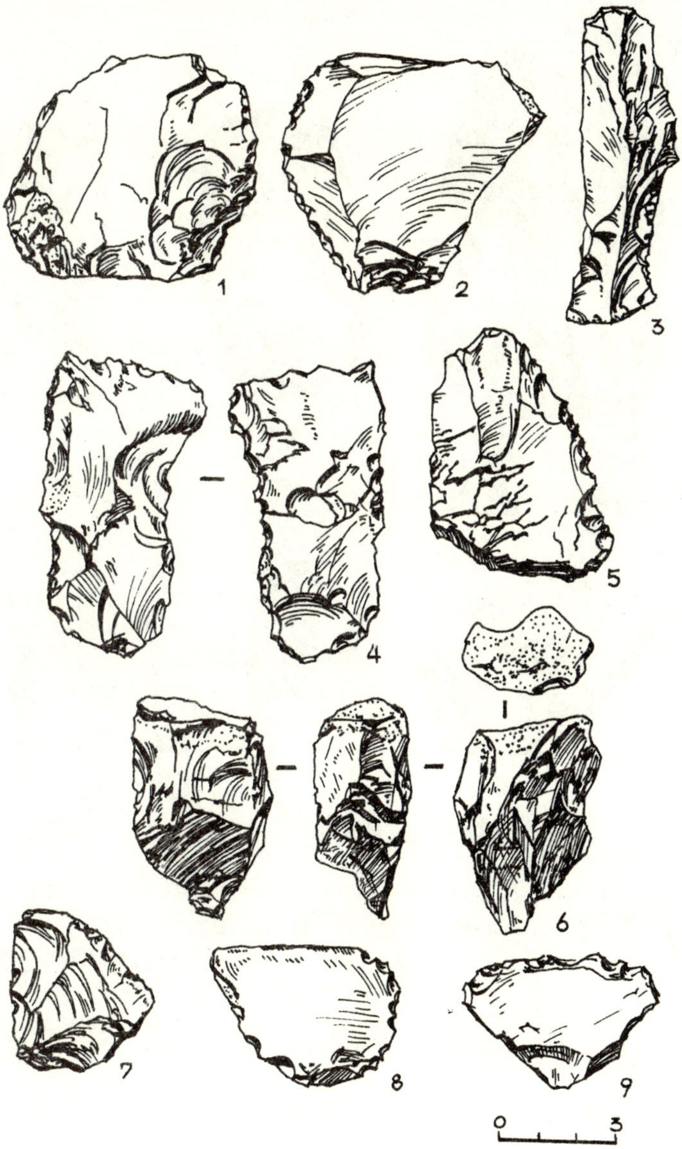

Figure 2. Rakuf workshop. Flint tools.

1, 9 : retouched chips. 2, 5, 7, 8 : retouched flakes. 3, 4 : hollowed tools. 6 : core.

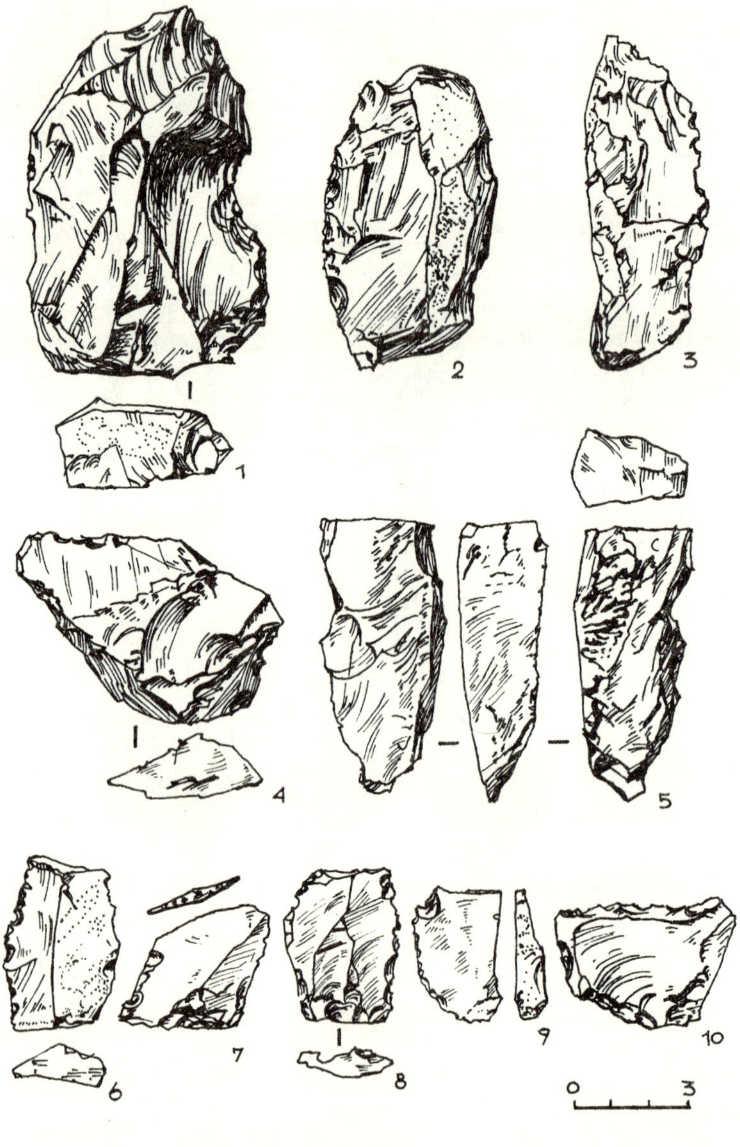

Figure 3. Rakuf workshop. Flint tools.

1 : hollowed tool. **2** : retouched chip. **3** : flake with traces of wear. **4, 9, 10** : retouched flakes. **5** : core-shaped fragment. **6, 8** : retouched blades. **7** : blade with traces of wear.

Point	7
Microblade	1
Retouched blade	2
Blade with traces of wear	1
Pointed blade	1
Burin on corner of flake	1
Burin of flake	1
Retouched flake (with somewhat worn edge)	8
Retouched chip (with somewhat worn edge)	4
Flake with traces of wear	23
Flake	21
Core	1
Core-shaped fragments	14
Fragments	21

The collection, most probably, reflects « historical times », possibly offering an idea about the material culture of the early islanders.

Cemeteries and settlements

Right there, close to **Rakuf**, lies the aforementioned small cemetery with extremely specific dolmen-shaped grave structures, unique on Socotra. The cemetery consists of approximately ten burial structures. However, only one has remained intact (*Photo 3*). It is rectangular in plan, stretching north to south. Its size is 1.92 x 2.64 m, and 0.7-1 m high. Its eastern and western sides and its northern butt-end walls are made up of three or four courses of horizontally laid, crudely processed slabs, the cracks between them being carefully filled with small stones. Its southern butt-end wall is built of two small, vertically dug in slabs, divided by a rectangular hole measuring 0.54 x 0.8 m. The structure is covered with a massive stone slab 1.92 x 2.64 m and 0.17-0.22 m thick. It is painstakingly smoothed over by the horizontal level (the northern wall is somewhat lower than the southern). The cemetery's other structures are destroyed. However, judging by the remains, they were structures resembling the described in shape but different in size ; apparently, the only difference was the side walls consisting not of horizontally laid slabs, but vertically dug in ones. For instance, yet another structure, now destroyed, rectangular in plan and stretching north to south, measured 2.5 x 3.08 m and was almost 1 m high. The

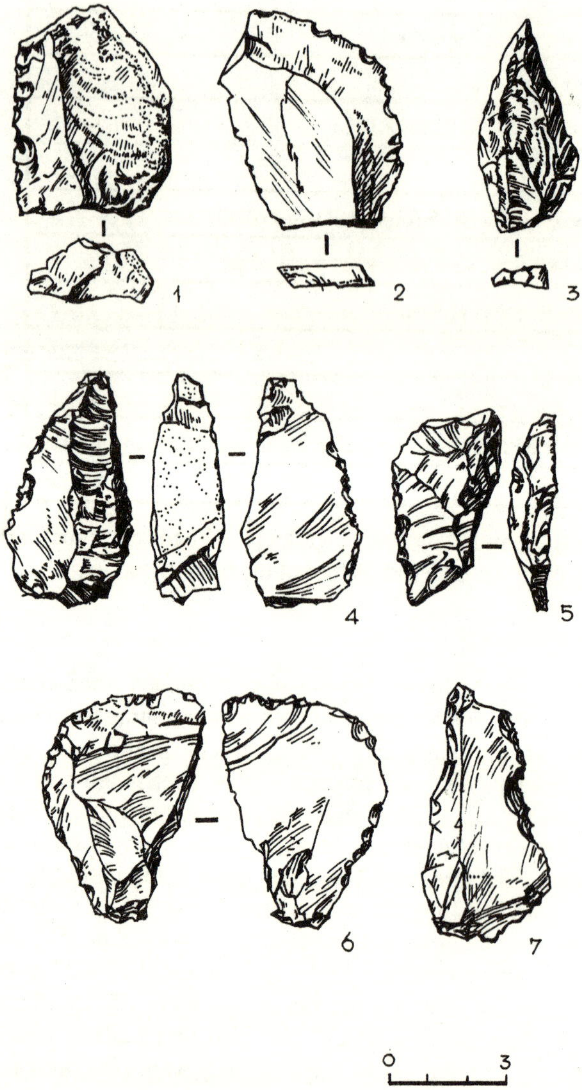

Figure 4. Rakuf workshop. Flint tools.
1, 4 : scraper-shaped tools. 2 : flake with traces of wear. 3 : pointed blade. 5 : scraper.
6 : retouched flake. 7 : hollowed tool.

entrance was also located in the southern wall, and the area around the structure was paved with stones.

Trial excavations (five small destroyed structures were unearthed) showed that pit-structures, dug out about one meter deep from the surface ground, were built of roughly dressed slabs, rectangular burial chambers of the « stone-cist » or « stone-case » types, with covers made of meticulously fitted slabs.

Grave 1. It is located in the central part of the cemetery, approximately 40 m north-east of a structure in a good state of preservation. The grave structure, rectangular in plan, is orientated west to east and destroyed. Two large slabs, measuring respectively 2.1 x 1 x 0.15 m and 2.15 x 0.98 x 0.12 m have survived. They formed the long side walls of the structure. The northern butt-end wall had fallen inside the structure. Its reconstructed overall dimension is 2.15 x 1.25 m, and 0.9 m high — the covering slabs and the butt-end walls have not survived (*Fig. 5*). The burial chamber is rectangular in plan, measuring 0.58 x 1.69 m and 0.45 m high, orientated west to east. Its walls are made of flat limestone slabs standing vertically along the pit walls of the grave. The cover is made up of three flat slabs measuring 0.72 x 0.68 x 0.1 m, 0.75 x 1 m and 0.76 x 0.6 x 0.1 m. The covering slabs are topped with a layer of loose dark earth 10 cm thick.

The burial chamber up to a height of about 0.35 m was found literally clogged up with crania and bones of human skeletons, occuring haphazardly in several layers. Nine crania (two at the western butt-end chamber wall, one at the middle of the southern wall, two in the central part of the chamber, three in the eastern part, and yet another at the northern wall), many long bones of arms and legs (all broken off), fragments of three lower jaws, and several fragments of pelvic bones were found. There is a complete absence of vertebrae, ribs, hand and foot phalanges, heel-bones, clavicles, and shoulder-blades. A small section along the burial chamber's eastern wall, measuring 0.57 x 0.1 m, turned out to be free of burials.

Finds (*Fig. 6*). In the middle of the burial chamber's eastern part, on top of the burial layer, over one of the crania was discovered a ball-shaped vessel with a tall narrow neck and a slightly flattened bottom (1). The vessel is of red clay, handmade, with a burnished red slip on the outer surface (vertical burnishing in the upper part and horizontal burnishing in the lower part and on the bottom). In the chamber's western part, close to one of the crania was a hollow little bone tube, a knife handle decorated with three stripes of grooves (2). A big fragment of a similar tube adorned with rows of through holes was found in the chamber's western part, also near the cranium (6). In the same part two small fragments of the end parts of iron knives (3, 4) were discovered amidst a mass of tubular bones. In the middle of the chamber, at its northern wall, a bronze pin with a slightly thickened knurled head (5) lay amidst a mass of bones.

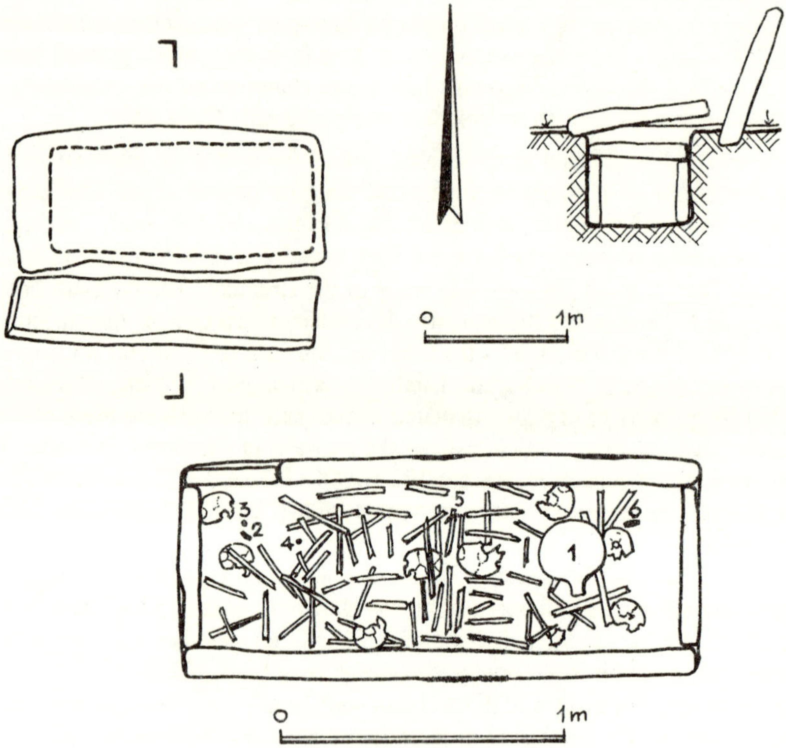

Figure 5. Rakuf cemetery, grave 1. Plans and section.
1 : pottery vessel. 2, 6 : bone tubes. 3, 4 : fragments of the iron knives. 5 : bronze pin.

Grave 2. It is located 12 m east of Grave 1. The grave structure has not survived. The covering slabs of the burial chamber's north-eastern part were visible on the modern surface (*Fig. 7*).

The burial chamber has a complex profiling. Its long side is orientated north-east to south-west. It consists of two parts. Originally, a pit rectangular in plan, measuring 1.45 x 2.15 m was dug to a depth of 0.35 m. Then, from a step 0.30-0.35 m wide at each of the four pit walls, the diggers deepened the pit by a further 0.4 m. The lower part of the pit measures 0.75 x 1.58 m. Its horizontal bottom is lined with eight flat slabstones, 5-6 cm thick. On the step made of flat slabstones a « stone-case » was built, three courses of slabs in height. The slabs measure 0.3/0.33 x 0.4/0.9 x 0.07/0.08 m. Judging by the remains, the case was covered with four, flat slabstones, measuring 1.45 x 0.35/0.65 x 0.1 m.

The pit's filling was loose dark loess. The burial chamber having been completely looted, no remains of the burial have been discovered. In the pit's

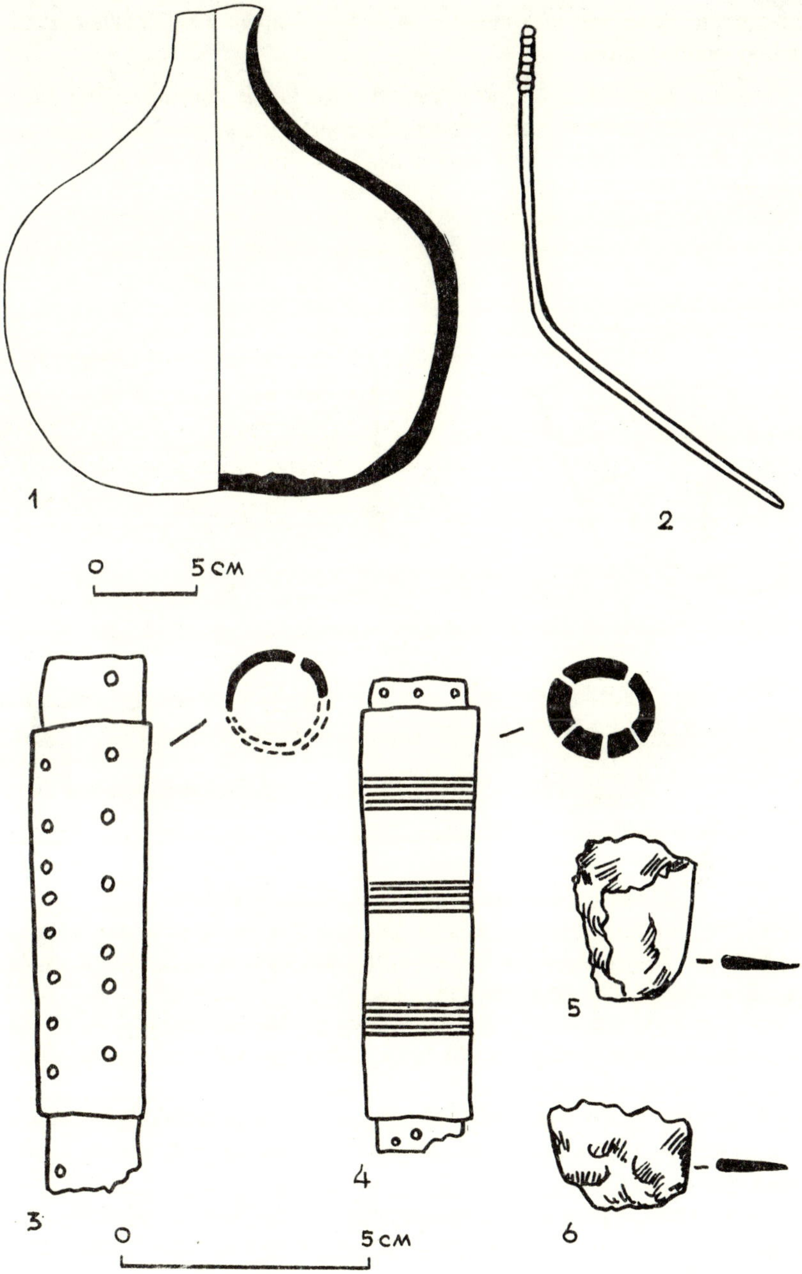

Figure 6. Rakuf cemetery, grave 1. Finds.

1 : pottery vessel. **2** : bronze pin. **3, 4** : bone tubes. **5, 6** : fragments of the iron knives.

north-eastern corner two inexpressive small fragments of a handmade ceramic vessel lay on the bottom.

Grave 3. Located in the north-eastern part of the cemetery. The grave structure is rectangular in plan, orientated north to south, and fully destroyed —before the excavation, there was a heap of ruined slabstones and their fragments.

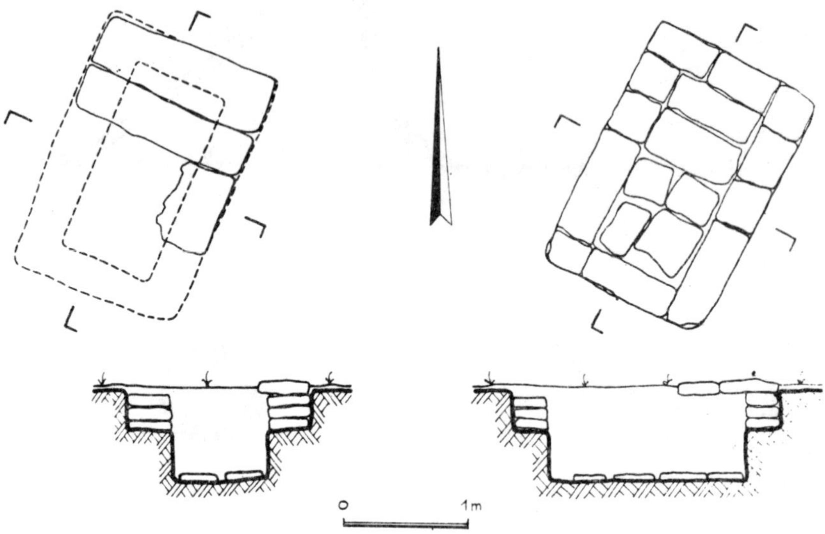

Figure 7. Rakuf cemetery, grave 2. Plans and section.

One slab, measuring 2.2 x 0.9 x 0.2 m, must have been the cover of the grave structure. In the same place lay fragments of the slabs of the burial chamber. The latter was a grave pit, rectangular in plan, measuring 1 x 2 m and 0.6 m deep, orientated north to south, with walls lined with vertical, flat slabs. The chamber's internal dimension is 0.75 x 0.8 m.

The burial was intensely disturbed : scattered fragments of long bones and ribs were found in the chamber's bottom and cranial fragments in its south-eastern corner.

Finds. A fragment of a handmade ceramic vessel (1) and a fragment of the bone handle of a knife (2) were found amidst bone fragments in the burial chamber's northern part.

Grave 4. Located 0.5 m west of Grave 2. Before the excavations the grave structure was a heap of ruins of what in plan had been a rectangular structure of large slabs, measuring 2/2.05 x 0.75/0.8 x 0.15/0.2 m. The two long walls of the structure and apparently one covering slab survived, as well as fragments of the structure's short butt-end walls and smashed slabs of the burial chamber's cover. The latter is of the traditional type. Viewed from the top, it is a rectangular grave pit, orientated north-north-east to south-south-west, measuring 0.85 x 1.9 m and 0.65 m deep. The walls are lined with vertical flat slabs, 10-15 cm thick. The chamber's internal dimension is 0.75 x 1.8 m.

The burial was intensively disturbed : only small scattered fragments of long bones, ribs and cranium were discovered on the « cist »'s bottom. No finds came the author's way.

Grave 5. Located in the north-western part of the cemetery, near Grave 3. Before the excavation, the grave structure was a heap of ruins of what in plan had been a rectangular structure orientated north to south. Two large slabs of the structure's cover survived. The size of the grave structure under reconstruction is 1.4 x 2.2 m and its height is 0.7-0.8 m.

Seen from the top, the burial chamber is a grave pit, measuring 1.3 x 2.1 m and 0.9 m deep. It contains a structure of the « stone-case » type. The bottom is laid with large slabstones about 15 cm thick and 40/42 cm wide, placed flatwide in seven rows. The chamber's cover has not survived. The chamber's internal dimension is 0.9 x 1.65 m, and it is almost 0.85 high.

The burial has not survived. It must have been completely looted. The chamber's filling is thickly compressed dense loess including fragments of cover slabs. In the south-western corner in the chamber's filling, 15 cm from its bottom, bits of charcoal were unearthed. No finds were discovered.

Thus, of the excavated five graves, four apparently contained single burials ; in all probability, remains of nine people originally buried elsewhere had been reburied in the fifth one. Regrettably, the obtained material does not permit the dating of the excavated burials with any degree of assurance. The bone material delivered to Moscow was found to be unfit for collagenous analysis. The extremely scant grave furniture yield no reliable references for dating either. Both the shape and the technique of manufacture of a ceramic vessel found in Grave 1 is sharply different from the pottery products found in other Socotran relics. This apparently suggests the imported origin of the vessel. The bronze pin from the same burial must be of the same origin. The knives' bone handles are similar to an ivory artefact found by P. Shinnie in a cave burial near Kishin. [9]

The graves of the Rakuf cemetery are sharply different from the graves explored in other parts of Socotra (see below). Similar dolmen-shaped structures occur among the monuments of the south of the Arabian peninsula [10], as well as

9. SHINNIE, « Socotra », *op. cit.*, p. 106, fig. 5.

10. Slightly similar burial (?) structures were recorded in the wādi Sirr, Inner Hadhramawt. W. DOSTAL, « Zur megalithfrage in Südarabien », in *Festschrift für*

in the south of the Indian subcontinent. [11] Structurally similar burial chambers are explored in cemeteries located in the Arab Gulf area [12] and in Oman. [13]

These data seem to favour the dating of the Rakuf cemetery from the second half of the first millennium B.C. [14]

In all probability, the graffiti discovered in the **Eriosh** area on the eastern coast of the island go back to the same period.

According to Doe, Eriosh is made up of three slightly concave, oval areas of limestone outcrops about 90 m long. They form a cohesive horizontal level stretching east to west. The graffiti occur only in the central area, on the northern side of which remains of a rather low wall are traced. « Many graffiti and pecked drawings are on the flat surface of the stone, including drawings of outlines of feet, purely geometric shapes and animal and human forms. There are also some graffiti which bear a resemblance to the characters of early South Arabian inscriptions of the mainland with Ethiopic characteristics, and an affinity with the characters found north of Dhufar and described by Bertram Thomas as Arabia Felix. Recording the graffiti photographically is difficult as the shallow pecking produces little cast shadow. After heavy rain during April the whole surface was covered with a thin layer of mud which had to be scraped. Part of the site was under about 6 in. of water and camels and goats were being watered there, possibly showing the use of the place by the goatherds in ancient times when the graffiti were made ». [15]

One hundred and eighty metres south-west of the inscription area lie ruins of structures also inspected by Doe. He failed to discover anything which would have helped him to date them, even approximately. The archaeologist noted that

---

Werner Caskel zum 70. Geburtstag, hrsg. Erwin Gräf, Leiden, 1968, s. 53-61, did not mention dolmen-shaped structures of the Rakuf cemetery.

11. See for example, J.R. McIntosh, « The megalith builders of South India. A historical survey », *South Asian Archaeology, 1979,* Berlin, 1981, p. 459-468.

12. P. Lombard et J.-F. Salles, *La nécropole de Janussan (Bahrain),* Travaux de la Maison de l'Orient 6, Lyon, 1984.

13. B.Vogt, « 1st mill. B.C. graves and burial customs in the Samad area (Oman) », in *Arabie Orientale, Mésopotamie et Iran Méridional,* ed. by R. Boucharlat et J.-F. Salles, Éditions Recherche sur les Civilisations 37, Paris, 1984, p. 271-284.

14. We can also compare the pottery vessel from grave n° 1 of the Rakuf cemetery with the vessels from Samad culture graves (Oman), dated between the 4th and 1st centuries B.C. (Vogt, *op. cit.*, p. 277, fig. 1, 3, 6, 7). Radiocarbon date of charcoal from grave n° 5 (Rakuf) chamber's filling is 1230 ± 140 BP or 720 ± 140 A.D. (sample Le-4317) ; the analysis was made in the Laboratory of the Institute of Material Culture Russian Academy of Sciences, St Petersburg. In all probability this date testifies that grave 5 was looted at the beginning of the VIIIth century A.D.

15. Doe, *Socotra*, p. 5-6.

the masonry was more perfect than in modern houses and that these structures were rectangular in plan. [16]

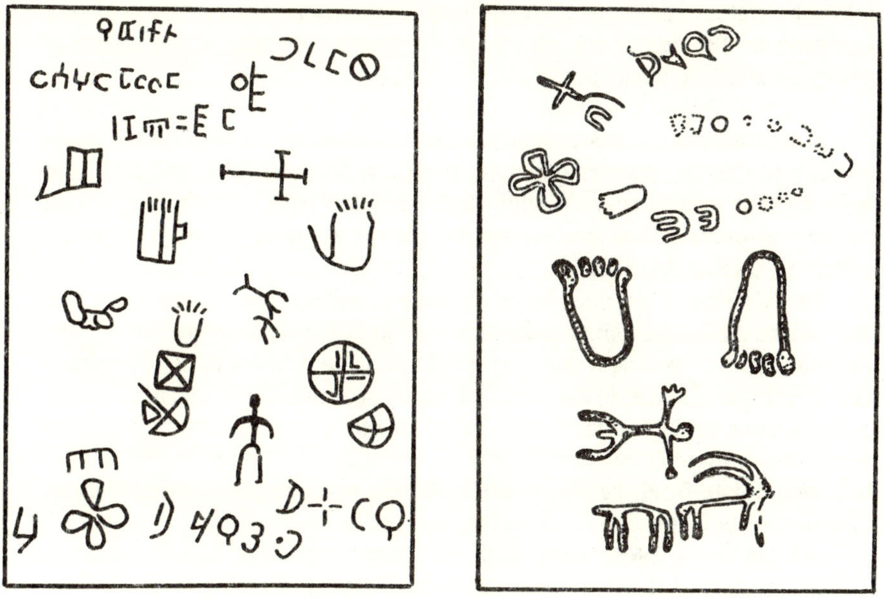

Figure 8. Eriosh graffiti.

Other ruins were inspected about 1.2 km south of the slabs with the graffiti, probably remains of a deserted village. Further south and east of Eriosh, isolated crumbled huts, round in plan, are registered. Round stone foundations, 4.5 m in diameter, with monolithic pillars in the centre, which supported rafters, were discovered on the top of a mound in Ras-Karma. Between this mound and the shore lie more ruins, which local inhabitants say have remained from ancient people. [17]

Thus, the survey of the territory around Eriosh has failed to help dating, even approximately, the graffiti and the remains of the nearby settlements. The graffiti and the drawings themselves were surveyed in detail by the authors

16. Most probably, T. Bent took exactly these structures for churches in 1897.

17. DOE, *Socotra*, p. 6.

(*Fig. 8*). It is safe to say that they were pecked in a limestone slab. Attemps to identify characters resembling South Arabian epigraphic writing were in vain. Possibly, their creators only imitated this writing, since they saw it but did not use it, being speakers of Socotri and not of South Arabian. The graffiti must have born a magic character. This can be said with assurance about the depictions of human feet : what is known as footprints hacked out in stone occur in various parts of the globe. The depiction of a goat or sheep, which was deified in South Arabia, also bore a clearly sacral character. Among the drawings registered by the author special mention is merited by one which seems to portray a camel and a man hunting it. [18]

A separate item in Doe's classification is « *boundary walling* » and « *walls of rough boulders* », registered in many places on Socotra. Thus, practically the entire eastern area is covered with these boundary walls stretching across a distance of many kilometres. A similar picture is observed in the island's western part, around Qallansiya.

The function of the stone boundary walls is not quite clear. Doe wrote that they « formed boundary alignments enclosing areas of private ownership ». [19] In his book, this scholar states that they are dividing the walls of plots of land and farms for growing incense, aloe and *Dragon* tree (cinnabar). [20] Apparently, such an explanation of these structures — as boundaries which in Antiquity divided plantations of fragrant trees and of aloe — seems closer to the truth. In this case they should date from the period when Socotra was a major supplier of aloe, frankincense and cinnabar, *i.e.* from the early centuries of our era.

In many points of the island both the Russian expedition and the missions of P. Shinnie and D. Doe discovered and explored remains of ancient *settlements* and *farmsteads* as well as *cemeteries* located in direct proximity to them and apparently connected with them. For instance, the ruins of a big settlement, fortified along its perimeter with a defence wall with towers (?), were discovered by Doe on a high plateau in the **Dihub** locality in the south-western part of the island. The settlement consisted of not less than twelve structures, some of them having retained roofs of slabstones. Doe noted that, in the opinion of local people, these were pre-Islamic structures. [21]

One of the most interesting monuments of the island's western part was what Doe called **Simar Qar**. Here, south of Cape Ras Badu, there are two

18. Depictions of a camel as a hunting object occur among the rock drawings discovered by archaeologists in Saudi Arabia, see E. ANATI, « The Rock Engravings of Danthami Wells in Central Arabia », *Bolletine del Centro Commune di Studi Preistorici*, 5 (1970), Roma, p. 196.

19. DOE, *Socotra*, p. 152.

20. D.B. DOE, *Monuments of South Arabia*, Falcon-Oleander, 1983, p. 19.

21. DOE, *Socotra*, p. 5.

groups of structures, one of which (settlement B) was discovered by Captain S.B. Haines as early as 1835. Settlement A is made up of many structures rectangular in plan whose walls are made of large, roughly coursed stones without use of mortar. Just south of this settlement a relatively low stone platform was discovered and, next to it, a stone « altar » shaped as a big stone block with two round hollows on its upper surface. One of the block's sides is decorated with a geometric ornemental design « which appears to portray an abbreviated inscription in early South Arabian ». [22]

The most complete study of the ancient farmsteads and cemeteries was made in the central and eastern parts of the island. In the locality called **Lower Rökib** the authors inspected remains of a large settlement. A substantial feature of the ruins of this settlement's structures is the impressive size of their stones. Attention is attracted by what is left of the fairly vast premises whose cover rested on two or four big stone supports. The ruins of similar premises with similar monolithic columns were inspected by Doe in the **Hohabay Shzain** locality and in the **Sshui** wādi. [23] East and south-east of the settlement there are remains of a necropolis. Judging by the grave structures, these are structural types common to Socotra (see further). However, they, too, stand out for the larger stones used for their internal arrangement.

Around the village of **Hasin**, on a small cape formed by the confluence of two wadis, Hasin and Makalhim, a cemetery formed of three isolated groups was located. About 80-100 m north-west of it, ruins of a structure have been discovered, possibly a farmstead : small stretches of the stone masonry of the wall foundations have survived. The ruins have been intensely disturbed : a modern house with outbuildings stands on them, material from the older structure having been used to set it up. It seems impossible to precise the designation and character of the original structure unless special research is carried out. One can only *a priori* assume the existence on this site of an ancient farmstead, apparently, contemporary to the cemetery.

The cemetery area measures approximately 80 x 100 m. Group Hasin-I consists of nine graves, three of them forming a chain stretching north-east to south-west, the remaining six graves forming a compact cluster. Group Hasin-II lies 30 m west, includes six graves, in two successive chains of three graves in each, stretching north to south. Another grave (Hasin III) was found 15 m to the south-east of the first group. Seven graves have been unearthed in the cemetery : three in the first and second groups, and an isolated large tomb (Hasin III).

Grave I, 1. The extreme north-eastern in the chain. The grave structure was a ring-shaped fence made of one row of stones, oval-shaped in plan, measuring 0.98 x 1.3 m, and stretching in a north-east to south-west orientation. The grave pit, measuring 0.4 x 0.7 m and 0.6 m in depth, has the shape of a rectangle with

22. DOE, *Socotra*, p. 1-2.

23. DOE, *Socotra*, p. 1, 91.

rounded corners stretching west to east. The walls are inclined, narrowing in the upper part — the pit showing a pear-shaped cross-section. The burial chamber is of the so-called « stone-case » type : its walls are composed of uncoursed stones, the upper rows being laid with a « lap » inside. The resulting dome-shaped structure is covered with three horizontally lying flat stones.

The grave was intensely disturbed. Fragments of long bones were found on the chamber's bottom, in its western part, and fragments of a jaw and teeth of a child's skeleton in the central part. Bones of a goat (?) were found to occur haphazardly with the former bones. No furniture was discovered.

Grave I, 2. Located south-west of Grave I, 1. Its fence is of irregular shape, close to oval in plan (one side is straight) measuring 1.06 x 1.85 m and stretching east-north-east to west-south-west. The grave pit, measuring 0.71 x 1.28 m and about 1 m deep, has the shape of a rectangle stretching west to east. The walls are inclined, narrowing in the upper part. The burial chamber is of the « stone-case » type. The walls of the structure are carefully lined with uncoursed stone in one row, the upper rows having an inside « lap ». The resulting dome-shaped structure is covered with four undressed, flat slabs : the cracks between them are meticulously filled with small pebbles.

On the bottom of the burial chamber, bones of three skeletons were discovered, strongly shifted from their original position and damaged. Two crania of adult skeletons and remains of a child's cranium lie in the eastern part, ribs and vertebrae in the middle area, and long bones of a leg in the western part. Judging by the bone arrangement, at any rate, one of the corpses lay stretched on his back, head eastwards. No furniture was found.

Grave I, 3. Located south-west of Grave I, 2. Its fence is oval in plan, measuring 1.6 x 2.8 m and stretching east-north-west to west-south-east. The grave pit is rectangular in plan with rounded corners, measuring 0.6 x 1.1 m and about 0.7 m deep. The burial chamber is of the « stone-case » type, its cover being heavily destroyed (caved in). The filling of the chamber was loose ground. The burial has not survived, and no furniture was unearthed.

Grave II, 1. The extreme northern grave in a chain of three graves. The external fence of the grave is oval in plan, measuring 1.76 x 3.35 m, and is orientated east-north-east to west-south-west. The internal fence is rectangular in plan, stretching in the same direction and measuring 0.97 x 2 m. The grave pit is rectangular in plan, measuring 0.5 x 1.7 m and 1.05 m deep, and stretching west to east. The burial chamber is of the « stone-case » type, its walls lined with stone masonry in one row. The chamber is covered with four, horizontally laid uncoursed slabstones, the cracks between them being filled with small stones and coated with clay. On the bottom of the chamber, a single skeleton was lying, stretching on his back, head westwards and facing south. No furniture was found.

Grave II, 2. The extreme northern burial in the chain. The external ring-shaped fence, oval in plan, is partly destroyed. It measures 2.3 x 2.8 m and its long side forms a line orientated east-north-east to west-south-west. The internal fence is rectangular in plan, measures 1 x 2 m, and forms a line orientated east-north-east to west-south-west (*Fig. 9*).

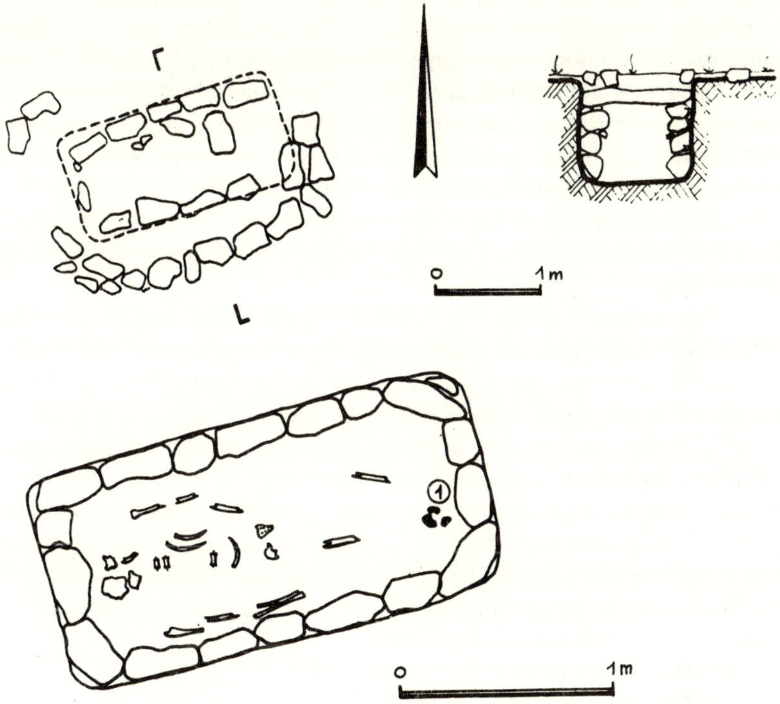

Figure 9. Hasin cemetery, grave II, 2. Plans and section. 1 : pottery vessel.

The grave pit is rectangular in plan with rounded corners ; it measures 1.05 x 2.1 m, and 0.98 m in depth. The burial chamber is of the « stone-case » type, the walls being carefully lined with one row of stones at the height of the third/fourth course. The masonry's upper rows are laid with an inside « lap ». The structure is covered with three large slabstones. The burial chamber is 0.7 m high, its internal dimension being 0.75 x 1.75 m.

A single burial was lying on the bottom of the chamber, in a poor state of preservation. Judging by the remains (fragments of the cranium, lower jaw, long bones of arms and legs, vertebrae, several ribs, and fragments of the pelvic bones), the corpse laid stretching on his back, head pointing to the west-soutwest. At his feet, at the eastern wall of the chamber, remains of a crashed ceramic vessel were found (1) (*Fig. 13* : 3).

Grave II, 3. This grave, the next in the same chain, lies south of Grave II, 2. Its external ring-shaped fence has survived only in the north-western part. It measures 1.8 x 2.6 m and is orientated north/ east-south-west.

The grave measures 0.85 x 1.05 m (the survived part) and its long side is orientated north-east to south-west (*Fig. 10*). The grave pit is rectangular in plan with rounded corners, measuring 0.88 x 1.8 m and 1.1 m deep. The burial chamber is of the « stone-case » type ; the walls, forming one row, are very carefully lined with a stone masonry, three to four courses high. The cracks are stopped up with small stones and stone chips. The masonry's upper rows are laid with an inside « lap ». The structure is covered with four large, flat stones. The chamber is 0.65 m high, its internal dimension being 0.65 x 1.6 m. On top of the chamber cover, the grave pit is poured over with a layer of compactly tamped earth with stone chips, 0.2-0.25 m thick, into which the stones of the internal fence were dug.

On the chamber's bottom a disturbed single burial laid on his back, stretching head south-west and facing south. The authors discovered no finds.

Grave III, 1. The grave structure has not survived : the grave was discovered by local people, who, as they were digging a well, came across the cover of a burial chamber at a depth of about one metre. The grave pit is rectangular in plan with rounded corners, measuring 1.8 x 4.3 m, about 2.5 m deep, and orientated west to east. The burial chamber is of the « stone-case » type. The walls are meticulously lined with one row of stones. The upper rows are laid with an inside « lap ». The chamber is covered with flat slabstones, the cracks between them being filled with small pebbles. The chamber's internal dimension is 1.6 x 4 m, and it is 1.4 m high.

The burial on the chamber's bottom was single (?) and heavily disturbed : a cranium was discovered at the middle of the pit's northern wall and a heap of bones at the opposite, on the southern side.

Six vessels (1-6) were found in the grave. One was in the western part of the pit, amidst the stones of the collapsed masonry of the western wall ; two other vessels stood near the cranium and the heap of bones, and three vessels formed a row along the wall in the north-eastern corner of the pit.

In a few more points of the island's eastern part, where now lie the villages of Ma'abid, Mathöbo, and Karya, remains of farmsteads or settlements with cemeteries around them were found.

Remains of the ancient farmstead at **Möbrhim** are an intensely destroyed square of structures (only the wall foundations have survived) around a square yard measuring 15 x 15 m. The structures must have been separate premises measuring 7 x 7 m and 5 x 7 m located right next to each other, with entrances from the yard. Now the farmstead is almost fully destroyed by a modern house built in the southern part of the ruins and by livestock structures, partly put up of building material from the ancient structure.

To the north-east the farmstead is adjoined by a çemetery occupying an area of 15 x 25 m. In ancient times it was fenced off : along the edge of the cemetery, on its eastern, southern and partly northern sides, the foundation of a fence is traced, marked by one row of stones. The cemetery itself is made up of

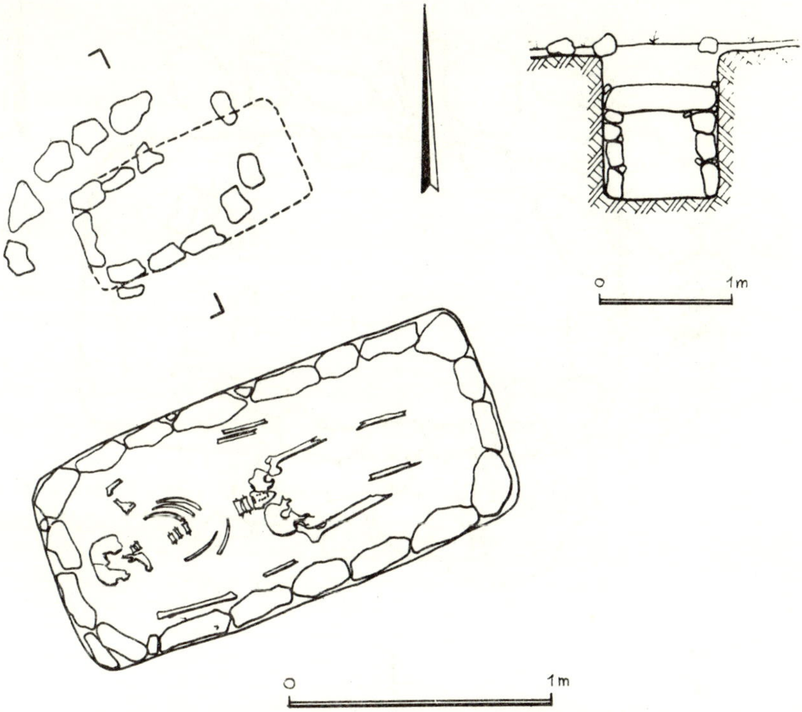

Figure 10. Hasin cemetery, grave II, 3. Plans and section.

several groups of graves stretching in five chains running north to south — each consists of four to six graves. In addition to this, on the northern and southern sides, the fenced area of the cemetery is adjoined by groups of two to four graves. Thus, the cemetery numbers 35-40 graves, rectangular in plan, stretching west to east (with minor occasional deviation north). Several of the graves are also enclosed with external oval fences. A grave found to be looted was excavated in the cemetery's western part.

Grave I. The grave structure was made up of two fences : external, shaped as a ring, oval in plan and formed by one or two rows of stones (the eastern part has not survived), measuring 2.8 x 3.2 m (extant part) and 0.3-0.45 m wide ; and internal, rectangular in plan and built of stones dug in along the perimeter of the grave pit (destroyed in the eastern part), measuring 1.7 x 2.2 m (extant part). The fences stretch west to east. The grave pit is rectangular with rounded corners, measuring 1.5/1.7 x 3 m (narrowing in the western part) and 1 m deep.

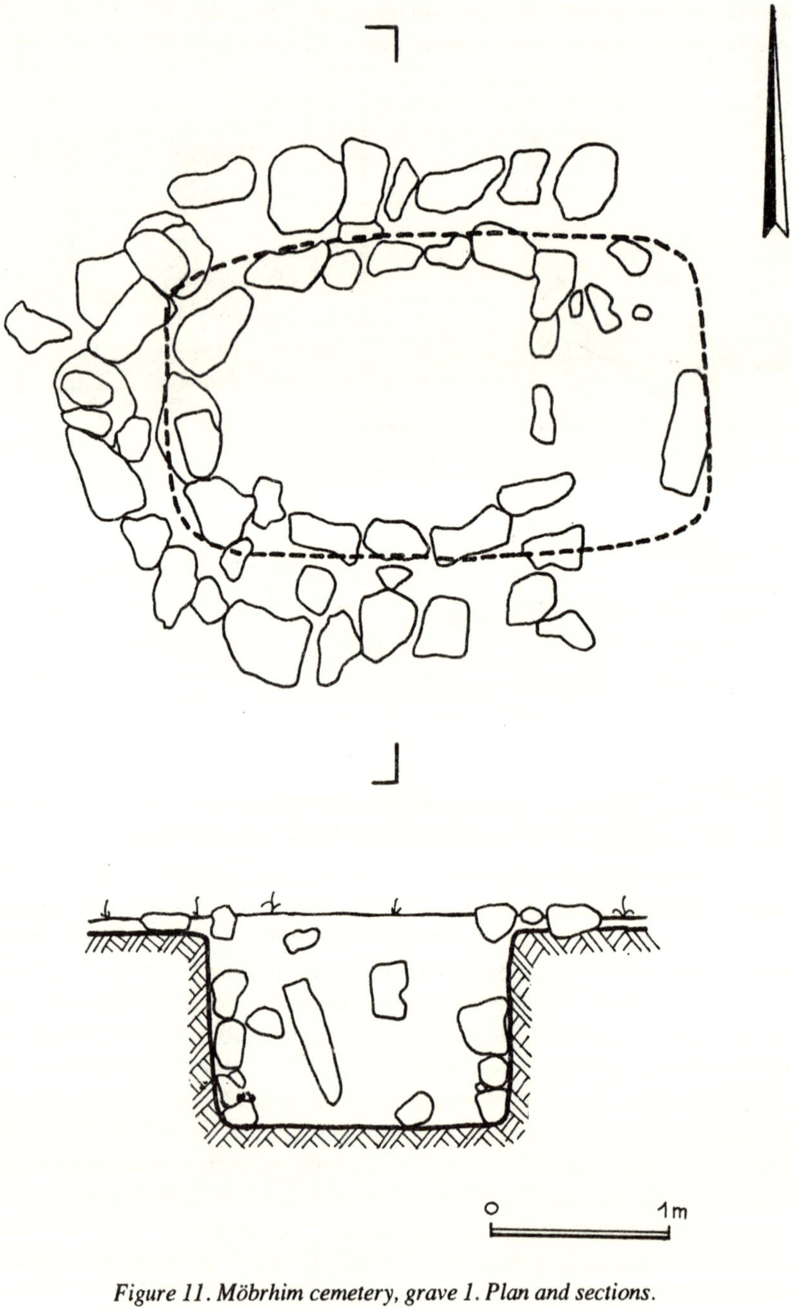

Figure 11. Möbrhim cemetery, grave 1. Plan and sections.

The burial chamber, of the « stone-case » type, is intensely destroyed, especially in the eastern part. The walls are made up of uncoursed stones, the cracks between them are filled with small stones. The chamber is 0.7/0.8 m high (three to four courses). The covering stones are absent : one has caved into the pit, the others lie south of the grave on the modern surface. The chamber has a loose filling with a certain number of stones — apparently, remains of the fence, walls, and cover of the chamber which fell inside at the looting (*Fig. 11*).

The burial was fully destroyed. Several fragments of ceramic vessels — apparently, the remains of the grave furniture — were found amidst the covering stones thrown south of the grave (*Fig. 13* : 4, 6, 8).

The settlement and cemetery of **Mathöbo** lie on both sides of the bed of the Mahzulalö wādi. The haphazardly located foundations of approximately ten stone structures have survived. They occupy an area of about 40 x 50 m on the eastern bank of the wādi, and of 15 x 20 m on the western side. Judging by the remains, an individual structure was a small house of a room or two, measuring 6 x 8 and 8 x 12 m and surrounded with a stone fence. The walls of the structure are built of uncoursed stones put together without the use of mortar. Some of the ruins have survived to a height of 1-1.5 m.

A relatively small cemetery of about forty graves falls into three compact groups, 15-20 m north of the settlement. The biggest group is composed of 25-30 graves. South of it, in direct proximity to the ruins of the structures, lies a group of three or four burials. Another group lies on the opposite bank of the wādi, south-east of the former. It consists of five or six graves backed out in a rocky bluff of the wādi bed. The flat stones of the grave structure's cover are bare, and in almost all the burials a stone or two are twisted out of the cover.

The graves in the first and biggest group of the cemetery form several chains of three or four graves (some chains contain eight), stretching north to south. The grave structures are fences rectangular in plan, made of dug-in long stones 0.25-0.3 m high, and filled with small stone-chips and earth. The fences surround areas of 1.5/1.8 x 2.2/2.7 m, running west to east, some of them with a slight deflection northwards. Individual fences are lined with what in plan are round heaps of stones up to 2.8 m in diameter. Several big fences are adjoined by small rectangular ones (0.8 x 1.4 m), stretching in the same direction.

In the first group of the cemetery, in the western part, an isolated grave was unearthed.

Grave I. The grave structure is a stone fence, rectangular in plan, made of one row of stones dug in along the grave pit perimeter. It measures 1.04 x 2.02 m and is orientated west to east. Inside the fence is a thick layer of small stonechips with a bit of earth (*Fig. 12*).

The grave pit is rectangular with rounded corners, measuring 1.04 x 2.02 m and 0.9 m deep. The burial chamber is of the « stone-case » type. The walls are

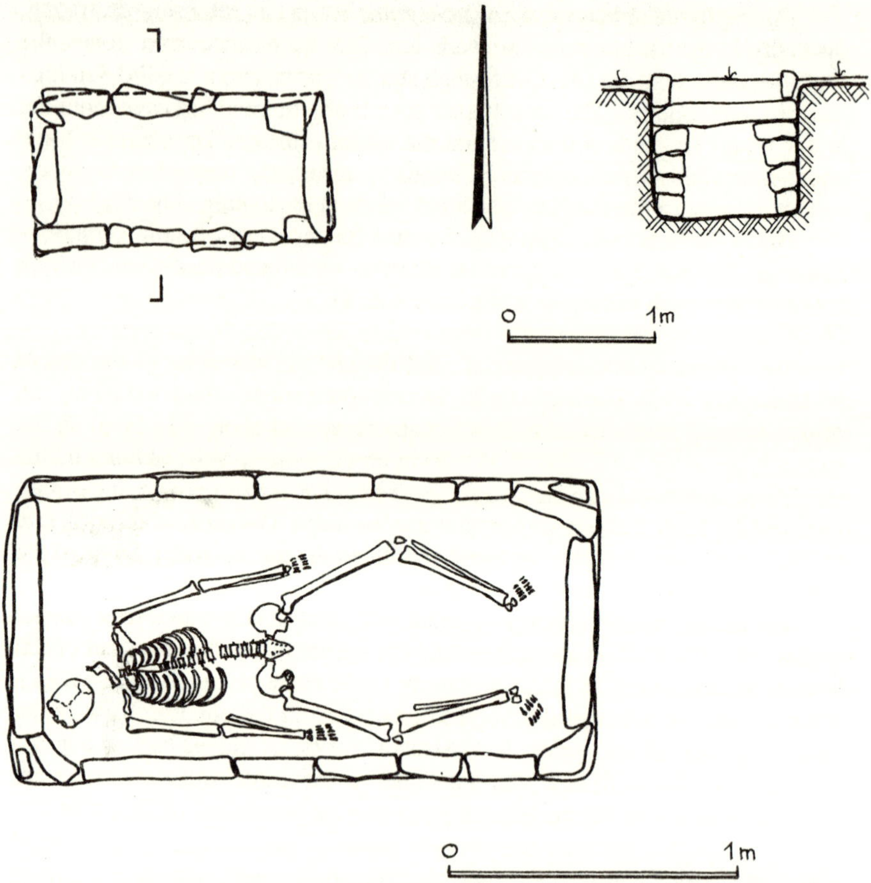

Figure 12. Mathöbo cemetery, grave 1. Plans and section.

made of carefully fitted, roughly coursed slabstones, rectangular in size. The height of the walls of the chamber consist of four courses (0.65 m), every next course being laid with a certain overhang over the previous — to reduce the space necessary for covering. The north-eastern, south-eastern, and south-western corners of the chamber are rounded with stones placed aslant. The chamber is covered with four massive, flat slabstones, measuring 1 x 0.60 x 0.20 m, 0.95 x 0.50 x 0. 20 m, 0.98 x 0.48 x 0.18 m and 1 x 0.52 x 0.20 m, the cracks between them being meticulously filled with small stones and pebbles. The pit above the chamber's cover, 0.15 m deep, is filled with compactly tamped earth with a small amount of stone-chips. It is exactly into this filling by the pit's contour that the fence stones were dug, whose additional supports are the slabs of the chamber's cover. The chamber's internal dimension is 0.85 x 1.8 m.

A single burial was lying on the bottom of the chamber, stretched on his back, head pointing to the west (the cranium, first lying on the back of the neck, must have rolled off into the chamber's south western corner).

The skeleton is in the anatomical order, hand stretched along the body and legs bent at the knees and spread apart — what is known as the horse-rider's posture (they must have been lifted). No finds were discovered.

Remains of yet another farmstead and a cemetery around it have been discovered in the **Gyuzuf** locality, one kilometre south of the modern village of Karya (in the eastern part of the island). The ruins of the farmstead lie on a comparatively low hill on the slope of the wādi Karya. Regrettably, as in many other cases, the structures are almost fully destroyed by modern building schemes. However, one can trace a common wall, Π shaped in plan and built with uncoursed stones, which should have fenced a yard opened in the direction of the wādi bed. Remains of four or five intensely ruined structures are grouped along the fence. The ruins of other structures are registered west of the fence.

The cemetery, also partly destroyed, lies south-east of the remains of the farmstead. The graves were marked on the surface by rectangular stone fences orientated west to east, with deflections north to south. The fences measure 0.8-1 x 1.7-2.1 m.

In the southern part of the cemetery, in direct proximity to one of the fences, two ceramic vessels were discovered right under the turf, one dug in bottom up, the other lip up (*Fig. 13* : 1, 2). These are possible remains of a funeral feast. A half-ruined grave was excavated in the central part of the cemetery.

Grave I. The grave structure is a stone fence, rectangular in plan, built of one row of stones dug in along the grave pit perimeter. The pit measures 1.2 x 1.9 m and is orientated west to east. Inside the fence lies a thick layer of stone-chips. The grave pit is rectangular in plan, and measures 1.2 x 1.9 m, 0.8 m in depth. The burial chamber is of the « stone case » type. The walls are built of roughly coursed slabs. The chamber's cover is formed by four large slabstones. Its internal dimension is 0.5-0.75 x 1.9 m (the western part is narrower), and it is 0.65 m high.

The burial on the bottom of chamber was intensely disturbed (perhaps looted). Judging by the arrangement of the ribs and long bones of arms and legs, the corpse laid stretched on his back, head pointed to the east. Goat bones (?) were found in the same place. The furniture did not survive. However, small fragments of ceramics were discovered in the layer of sinters on the bottom of the chamber — apparently, remains of the grave furniture smashed by the looters (*Fig. 13* : 5, 7, 9).

A cemetery akin to the described burial structures and ceremony was studied on a hill 20 m. south-east of the modern village of **Shibhon**. The graves unearthed here were found by local people as they were mining building stone on the hill. One grave was almost fully destroyed, another partly, and the items of the grave furniture discovered in them were found scattered on the surface.

Four graves were excavated in the cemetery. The grave structures barely survived. However, the remains show that there were fences, each made of one row of stones.

Grave I. It is the extreme western grave in a group of four. On the surface it must have been marked with a stone fence, individual stretches of which have survived. The grave pit, rectangular in plan and measuring 0.8 x 1.85 m and 1.2 m in depth, is orientated west to east. The burial chamber is of the « stone-case » type, its walls built of uncoursed stones. The floor is paved with small pebbles. The chamber is covered with large, flat slabstones. Its internal dimension is 0.6 x 1.65 m, and it is 0.8 m high.

A burial was found on the bottom of the chamber, and a skeleton was lying stretched on his back, head pointing to the west, possibly a child ? No furniture was unearthed.

Grave 2. Located west of Grave 1. The grave structure has not survived (local inhabitants have cleared the surface of the grave pit's stone cover). The grave pit is rectangular in plan, measuring 0.9 x 1.85 m and 1.1 m in depth. The burial chamber is of the « stone-case » type, its walls built of uncoursed stones. Its bottom is paved with small pebbles, and it is covered with large slabstones. Its internal dimension is 0.65 x 1.7 m, and it is 0.9 m high.

Remains of a collective burial of several people, adults and children, were found in a layer of sinters on the bottom of the chamber. Next to them laid the grave furniture : fragments of a ceramic vessel (1), iron knives (3, 4) and beads (2) — in the western part of the chamber — , bronze ear-rings (5), and iron rings (6, 7) — or buckles fastening the knives to the belt ?

Grave 3. Located three metres south-west of Grave 2. Almost fully destroyed : only the lower part of the grave pit with remains of a stone burial chamber has survived.

The layer of sinters on the bottom of the chamber was found to contain a single (?) burial, head pointing to the west. The grave furniture included a fragment of a glazed ceramic bowl (1) — in the western part of the chamber — , iron knives and fragments of iron (2-5) (remains of a wooden sheath survived on one of the knives), an iron ring — or buckle — (6), and beads (7).

Grave 4. Located two metres south of Grave 2. It is heavily ruined : stones of the burial chamber's cover had been extracted, and the upper part of the chamber is damaged. The grave pit is rectangular in plan with intensely rounded corners ; it measures 2.1 x 2.8 m, and 1.8 m in depth, and stretches west to east. The burial chamber is of the « stone-case » type ; its walls are lined with uncoursed stones, the upper rows having an inside « lap ». The resulting dome-shaped structure must have been covered with horizontally laid slabs.

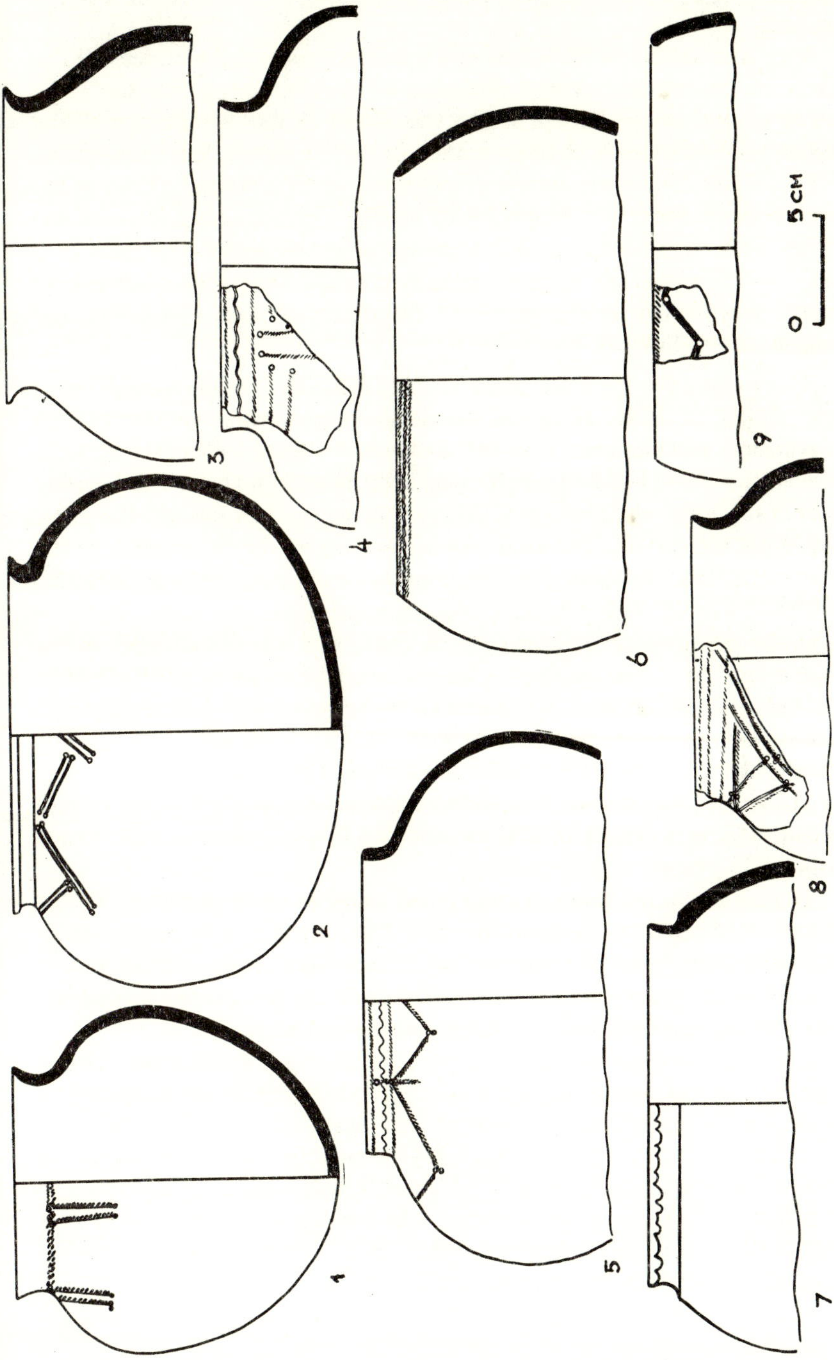

Figure 13. Pottery from different Socotrian cemeteries.
1, 2, 5, 7, 9 : Gyuzuf cemetery. **3** : Hasin cemetery, grave II, 2.
4, 6, 8 : Möbrhim cemetery, grave 1.

In the western part, the bottom of the chamber is paved with small pebbles (by 0.4 m). Fragments of iron knives were found in the filling of the upper part of the chamber (1-2). The chamber's internal dimension is 1.9 x 2.6 m, and it is 1.5 m high.

A layer of sinters on the bottom of the chamber contained what seems to be remains of two burials, with a profusion of accompanying furniture. The cranium of one of the buried bodies was found in the eastern part of the chamber, and fragments of another cranium and pelvic bones were discovered in its western part. The grave furniture was made up of a ceramic (1) — in the centre of the chamber — , fragments of another ceramic vessel (2) — at the northern wall —, iron knives (3, 4), pieces of rotten wood —remains of a sheath ? — (5), a flat cake made of specially prepared Dragon tree resin (6), an intensely fragmented bronze vessel (7), fragments of glass vessels (8), and fragments of metal rods (9-10).

A rich collective tomb was discovered at **Qallansiya**, on the western coast, in the winter of 1989. Here, on the north-eastern fringe of the village, approximately one kilometre from the seashore, in a place called Qadera, local people, as they were building a well, came upon an ancient grave. The covering system of the burial was discovered 0.5 m below the modern surface. The grave structure did not survive. The local people extracted one of the covering stones and penetrated into the burial chamber, from which they removed a considerable part of the grave furniture, thus disturbing the burial itself.

Under the massive slabstones of the cover was a burial chamber of the « stone case » type, boat-shaped in plan. Its internal dimension is 1.0 x 2.55 m and 1.2 m in height. Its walls are lined with big boulders, four to five courses in height, the stones of the masonry's upper courses successively overhanging inside the chamber. The thus considerably narrowed space is covered with four large slabs. The long side of the chamber stretches east to west. In the eastern butt-end wall, at a height of 0.85 m from the floor, is made a little niche, measuring 35 x 52 cm and 20 cm deep.

The burials in the chamber were found to be intensely disturbed. By the time they were inspected by the authors they had formed a fairly thick (over 20 cm) homogenous layer of complete and broken bones, ribs, vertebrae, and crania, lining the entire chamber floor. Most probably, the burial assumed this aspect after the penetration of the local people into the grave.

According to witness stories, the grave furniture laid in the wider, eastern part of the chamber — *i.e.*, judging by analogy with burials in other cemeteries, at the feet of the buried bodies ; during an additional inspection, the authors also discovered several objects here. A total of 12 glass vessels (7 complete and 5 in fragments), 8 ceramic glazed vessels, 6 handmade little vessels, an iron knife, an iron dagger, stone beads, a bronze mirror, a little ring, and a cup fragment were revealed. On one of the glazed cups three letters of what is an unidentified writing, so far, are made in brown paint (*Fig. 14-16*).

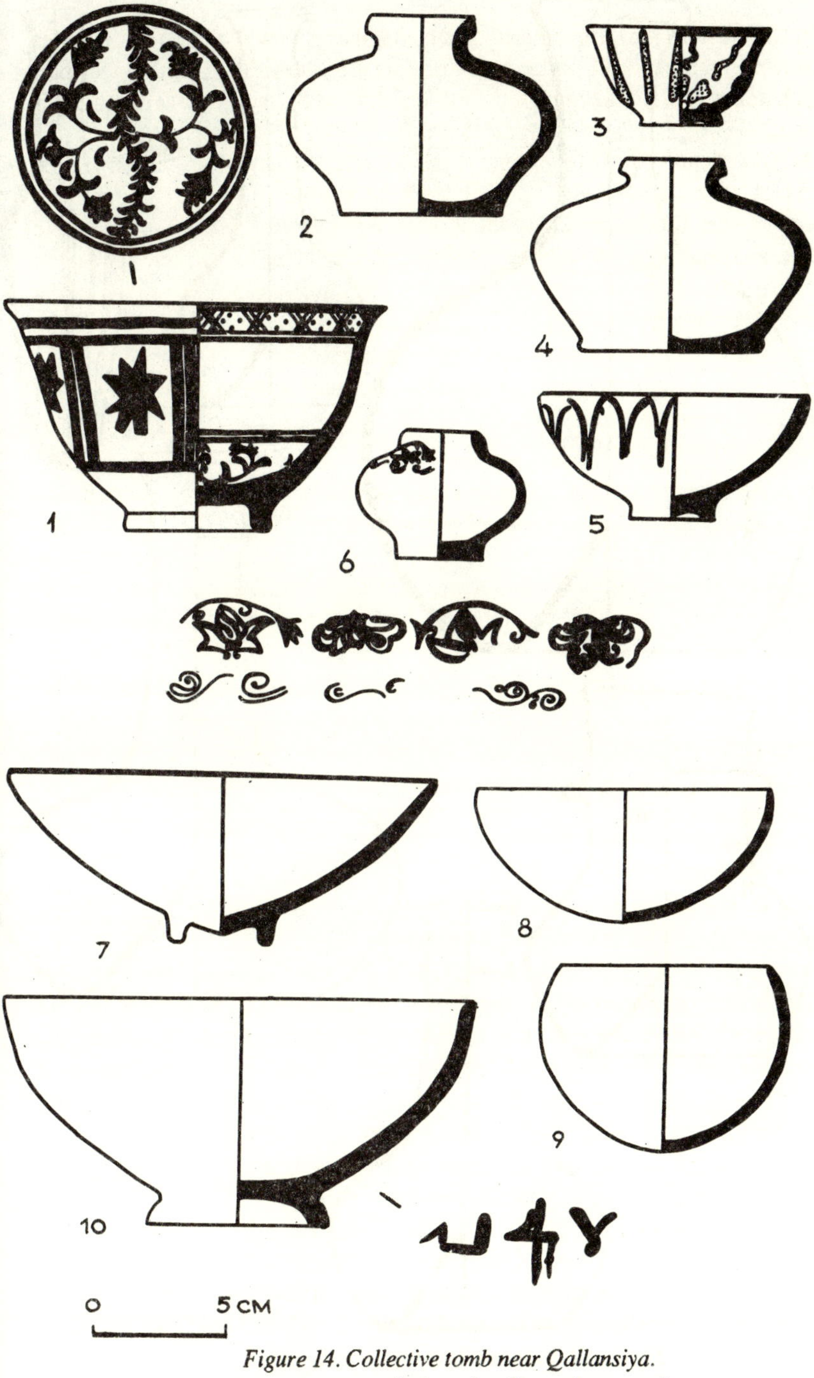

Figure 14. Collective tomb near Qallansiya.
1-10 : pottery vessels (**8, 9** : locally made pottery).

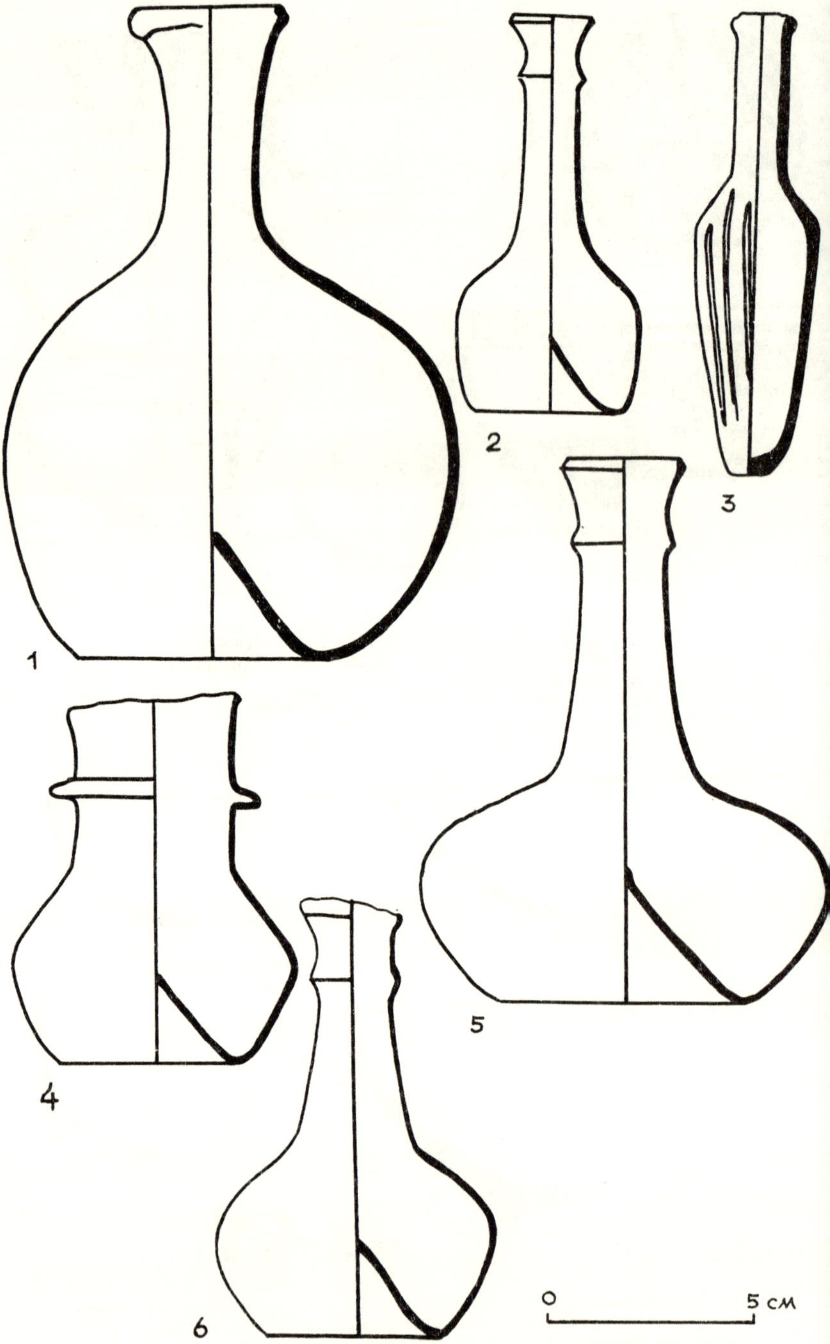

Figure 15. Collective tomb near Qallansiya.
1-6 : glass vessels.

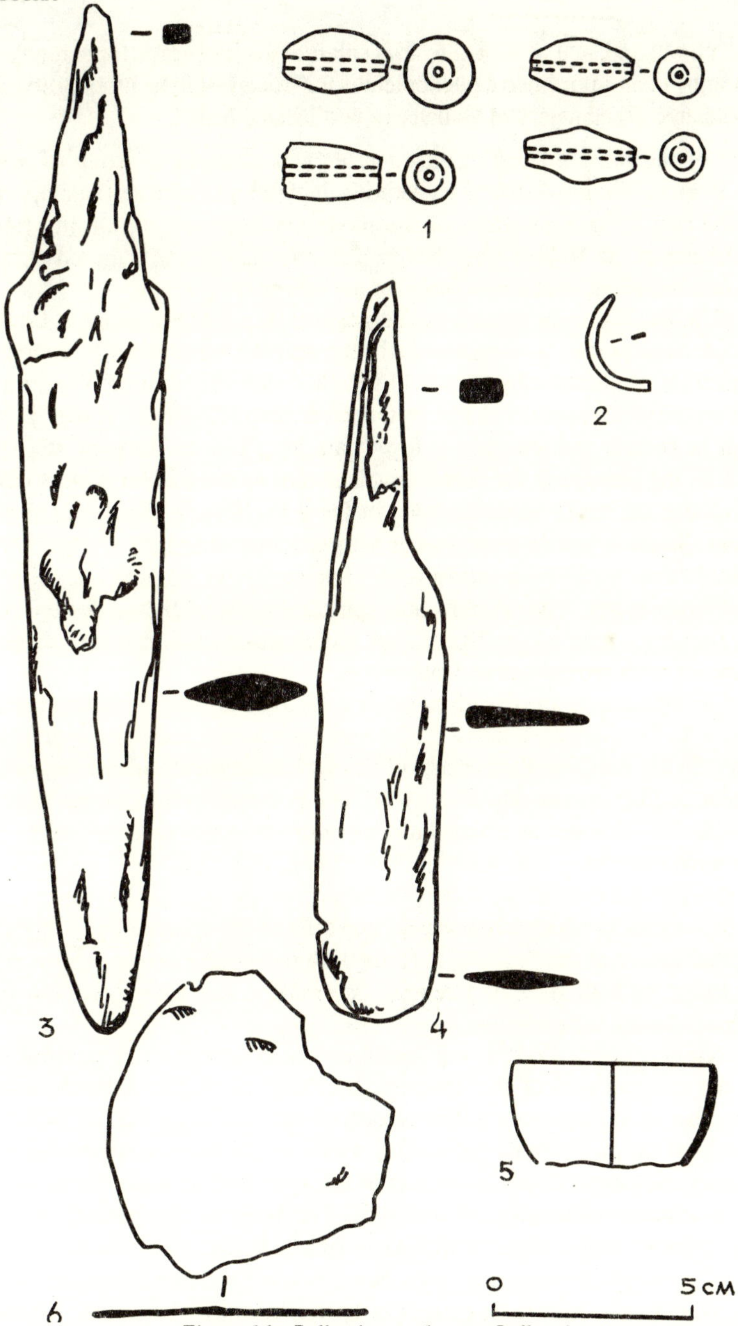

Figure 16. Collective tomb near Qallansiya.

1 : stone beads ; **2** : fragment of bronze ring ; **3** : iron dagger ; **4** : iron knive ; **5** : fragment of bronze cup ; **6** : fragment of bronze mirror.

Such an abundance of furniture in a small collective grave (apparently, a family tomb) is an unorthodox phenomenon for Socotra. In all probability, an old, pre-Islamic (?) cemetery of Qallansiya was located here.

One of the most interesting discoveries was made by a group of joint Russian (former Soviet)-Yemeni Expedition in 1985. A large settlement was discovered two kilometres south of the modern village of Suq, on the right (eastern) bank of the **Hajrya** wādi bed, which stretches towards the coast and empties into the sea at the eastern fringe of the village (*Fig. 17*).

In plan, the site is an irregular quadrangle (100 x 130 m), its sides facing the four cardinal points. It is surrounded by a defence wall, about two metres wide, made up of undressed stones held together with clay mortar. The extant height is negligible, about 0.2-0.3 m, but, according to informants, it was 0.7 to 1 m high at certain sections just a few years ago. Due to its poor state of preservation the passage in the defence wall cannot be traced. But it must have been located at the north-western corner of the wall. Here, in the corner of the settlement, stood what in plan was a semi-circular structure — the stone foundations of its walls have survived — , five metres in diameter, possibly a corner defence tower. The western and southern walls of the settlement are straight, forming a right angle. The eastern and northern walls have an irregular configuration, with projections and curvatures.

The settlement is clearly divided into two parts : the western one is occupied with dwelling structures, the eastern with a vast cemetery within the town wall. In the south-western corner of the settlement stands a large building, rectangular in plan, measuring 20 x 30 m. The preserved walls are up to two metres high. The structure is isolated and separated from the other buildings by 10-12 m wide « streets ». The walls of the building, 1 to 1.3 m thick, are built of roughly dressed stones held together with mortar ; on the outside they had a clay coating 3-7 cm thick, which has survived in places on the external western wall. The internal layout of the building is formed by rectangular rooms, apparently seven, located on both sides of a central « corridor », and a large room in the eastern part, closing the « corridor ».

A sounding carried out at the south-eastern corner made it possible to explore the external wall of the structure. It is built of roughly dressed stones stuck together with clay mortar. The preserved part of the wall is 1.7 m high, and is erected on an artificial pavement, which might have strengthened the small natural elevation. In the lower part of the wall, 0.65 m above the ground, there is a window measuring 30 x 60 cm. The heap on the outside of the building's cleared wall consists of the stones of a collapsed wall masonry and a loess loam compressed into a very thick mass. A small ceramic collection came from the sounding —mostly fragments of typical Socotran handmade, round-bottomed vessels, and fragments of non-Socotran glazed vessels as well as body sherds of large wheel-made storage jars.

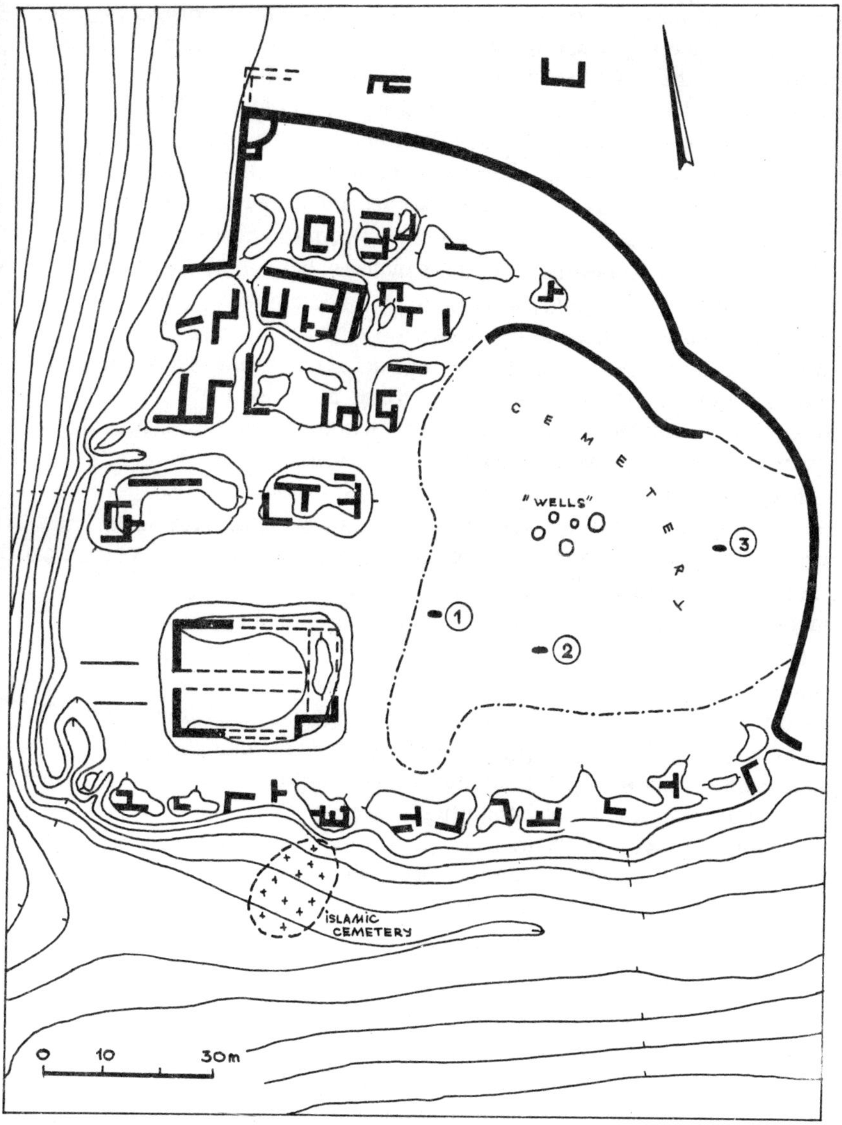

Figure 17. Hajrya settlement. Sketch plan.

The north-western corner of the settlement— a compact mass of stone-structures — directly adjoins a section of the western defence wall, being separated from the northern wall and a building standing apart in the south-western corner of the settlement by streets only 7 to 10 m wide. The overall dimension of the mass of stone-structures is 60 x 70 m. Three « streets » about 5 to 7 m wide running west to east, and « lanes » 1 to 1.5 m wide and perpendicular to the « streets » divide the mass of stones into ten or eleven large housing blocks (10-15 x 30-40 m). The internal layout of each block is formed by several rectangular rooms 6 x 8 and 8 x 10 m each. The preserved height of the structure walls is 0.5-0.7 m. They are built of roughly dressed stones bound together with clay mortar. A row of houses rectangular in plan (5 x 6 and 4 x 8 m) adjoining each other is traced along the southern fringe of the settlement.

In the ruins of one of the dwelling structures, the north-eastern corner of one of the houses was cleared out close to the middle of the western fringe of the settlement. The entrance to the house, 1.3 m wide, lay here. The walls are built of roughly dressed stones bound together with mortar. Their preserved height is about 1 m from the floor. The floor, made of clay, is compactly tamped. Several fragments of characteristic Socotran ceramics, charcoal, and fragments of iron knives were found in the house filling and on the floor.

The eastern part of the settlement is a vast cemetery, its most westerly graves coming right up to the buildings. The grave structures are stone fences rectangular in plan (1-1.1 x 2.2 x 2.4 m), stretching west to east with occasional deflection northwards. As a rule, they form chains of three or four graves (sometimes eight to twelve) running north to south. In individual cases, one can register either fences adjoining each other, or fences paired by additional common rectangular or oval ring-shaped stone heaps. Here and there occur isolated fences, some of them with external rectangular or oval stone heaps. The graves occupying the eastern part of the cemetery are somewhat different as regards the aspect of their grave structures. These are relatively small (1.3-1.6 x 0.4-0.7 m) fences, close to oval and usually stretching north-east to south-west, east-north-east to west-south-west, or (few) west to east. In most cases they display a haphazard location relative to each other, only some of them forming chains of two or three graves in each. Three graves were excavated in various parts of the necropolis, which are described below.

Grave 1. Located in the south-western part of the cemetery, in direct proximity to an isolated structure. The grave structure is a fence of one course of stones, rectangular in size and dug along the contour of the grave pit — the south-western side of the fence has not survived. The fence covers an area of 1 x 2.5 m ; it is 0.1 m high, and its long side is orientated north-east to south-west (*Fig. 18*). The grave pit is rectangular in plan with rounded corners, measuring 0.98 x 2.52 m and 0.95 m in depth, its long side stretching north-east to south-west. The burial chamber is of the « stone-case » type. Its walls are lined with specially matched, small undressed stone-blocks of rectangular cross section, in four courses, 0.52 m high. The cracks between the blocks are filled with small stones. The chamber's internal dimension is 0.7 x 2.52 m. The cover of the chamber is made of five large, flat slabstones measuring 1 x 0.45 x 0.25 m and 0.96 x 0.37 x 0.15 m.

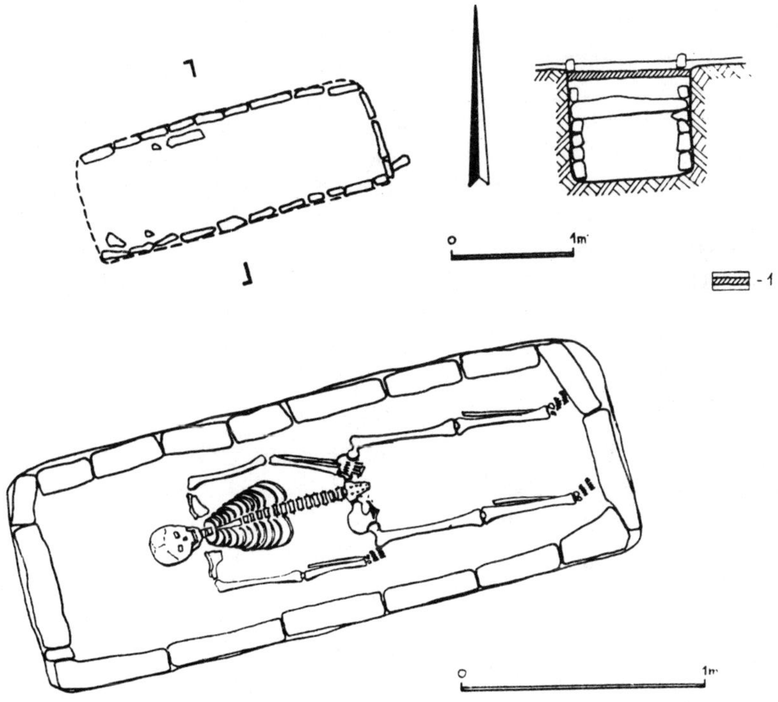

Figure 18. Hajrya cemetery, grave 1. Plans and section.
1 : layer of clay mortar.

On top of the covering slabs was arranged another, lower fence of stones stretching along the pit's contour. Then the grave pit was thickly filled with tamped earth and stonechips — a layer 0.15-0.18 m thick — , and at the level of the ancient surface, above this filling, the pit was heaped with a layer of clay mortar 5-6 cm thick. It was exactly on this mortar that stones of the upper fence, coming out, were placed. The space within the fence was filled with a thin layer of thickly tamped earth with stonechips.

The bottom of the burial chamber was also poured over with a layer of clay mortar 2-3 cm thick. The corpse must have been laid in the still liquid clay mortar. The burial is single, the body stretching on the back, head pointing to the south-west and face upwards. The skeleton is in the anatomical order, the legs and right arm outstretched, the left arm bent at the elbow, its hands resting on the pubis. No furniture was found.

Grave 2. Located in the southern part of the cemetery, approximately 16 m east of Grave 1. The grave structure is a fence rectangular in plan, formed by one course of stones — the south-western corner being destroyed. The fence encloses an area of 1.3 x 2.05 m, its long side orientated west to east. The grave pit is rectangular in plan with rounded corners and a narrowed eastern part. It measures 0.8 x 1.95 m ; it is 1.05 m deep, and its long side stretches west to east. The burial chamber is of the « stone-case » type, boat-shaped in plan, narrowing in the eastern part ; the walls are built of dressed stones to a height of 3-4 courses (0.55 m), and the cracks are stopped up with small stones. The chamber's internal dimension is 0.6 x 1.7 m. The cover of the chamber consists of four, large slabstones, the cracks between them are filled with small pebbles. On top of the covering slabs up to the modern surface was found a thick filling of small pebbles mixed with sand and whiting — the fill is 0.3 m thick.

The bottom of the burial chamber is covered with a layer of sand mixed with pounded reddish stone. The burial is single, the body stretching on the back, head pointing to the west. Both arms are bent, the right hand lying on the pelvic bones, the left on the belly. The anatomical order of the skeletal bones is partly disturbed. No furniture was excavated.

Grave 3. Located in the eastern part of the cemetery. The grave structure is a fence of one course of stones having the shape of an elongated oval in plan. It measures 0.8-1 x 2.1 m, its long side orientated north-west to south-east. The grave pit is an elongated oval in plan, measuring 0.8 x 2.1 m, 1.8 m in depth, orientated north-west to south-east. The pit walls are vertical. The burial chamber is of the « stone-case » type, its walls lined with undressed stones to a height of 5-6 courses (0.7 m), the cracks being filled with small stones. The chamber's internal dimension is 0.6 x 1.9 m. The cover consists of four, large slabstones, the cracks between tehm are stopped up with small stones. On top of the burial chamber's covering slabs, the grave pit is poured over with a layer of well-tamped sand with pebbles, 0.85 m thick.

The burial is single, the body lying on his back, outstretched, head pointing to the south-east ; the cranium is almost fully destroyed. No furniture was discovered.

The central part of the townsite area, occupied with the cemetery, is free of graves. Five ring-shaped structures built of stones of varying diameters ranging from 2 to 7 m lie here — probaby remains of filled wells or water-reservoirs.

The material revealed on the townsite in 1985 and 1987 suggests preliminary conclusions as to when this site existed. Numerous fragments of Socotran-looking vessels were discovered both on the surface of the settlement and in the small cleanings in the ruins of its structures. These are fragments of handmade, round-bottomed or flat-bottomed vessels having a thin carved ornament frequently smutted on the outside which indicates their use as kitchen ustensils, small hemispherical bowls which must have served as drinking vessels, etc. The vessels are manufactured without the use of a pottery's wheel and their surface is meticulously scraped with shells. The shape, the ornamentation and the mode of manufacture of these vessels suggest the traditional vessels of the modern Socotrans (*Fig. 19* : 2-11 ; *fig. 20* : 10).

Together with this pottery were found sherds of an entirely different aspect. These are fragments of large, light-clay bowls whose surface was covered with green glaze of varying shades, running the gamut from light-turquoise to dark-green, as well as fragments of red-clay wares whose external surface was coated with dark-brown slip. All these vessels were manufactured on a potter's wheel (*Fig. 20* : 4, 11-15). Most of this pottery dates from around the 10th-13th centuries, having parallels in the material of contemporary monuments in the Arabian Peninsula and the Arab Gulf area. This date is also confirmed by the result of the radiocarbon analysis of a charcoal sample taken from the filling of one of the houses set amidst the ruined structures at the western fringe of the settlement : 1190 ± 140 A.D. [24]

However, in addition to the enumerated pottery, that of a much earlier period was discovered on the surface of the settlement : fragments of the handle of a massive Roman amphora (*Fig. 19* : 1), fragments of high-quality red slipped bowls and jars, made in all probability in the Mediterranean region in the early centuries A.D. (*Fig. 20* : 4, 5, 8). Furthermore, in the same place, fragments of vessels of *black and grey ware* were found, possibly of Indian or Arab Gulf origin, as well as fragments of thick-walled, handmade vessels similar to those discovered in the strata of the 1st-4th centuries A.D. in ancient sites of the wādi Hadramawt (*Fig. 20* : 1-3, 9). Some pottery fragments have direct parallels in the material excavated at Qana, in the strata of the 3rd-4th centuries A.D. (*Fig. 20* : 6, 7) [25]

Thus, the preliminary analysis of the material allows two basic conclusions : (1) the settlement of Hajrya emerged most probably in the early centuries of our era ; these must have been the « remains of Classical antiquity [...] on the bare limestone plains of the north » of the island which P. Shinnie failed to discover ; and (2), life on this settlement must have ended in the 12th-13th centuries A.D.

The graves discovered and studied on Socotra, in the ground cemeteries of Hasin, Shibhon, Mathöbo and Möbrhim, on the Hajrya settlement etc., go back to the pre-Islamic epoch of Socotran history. This is evidenced by the burial site

---

24. Sample Le-4318. The analysis was made in the Laboratory of the Institute of the History of Material Culture, Russian Academy of Sciences.

25. Excavations of the well-known ancient Hadramawtian port of Qana, around the modern village of Bir-Ali, have been carried out by the joint Russian (former Soviet)-Yemeni Expedition since 1985.

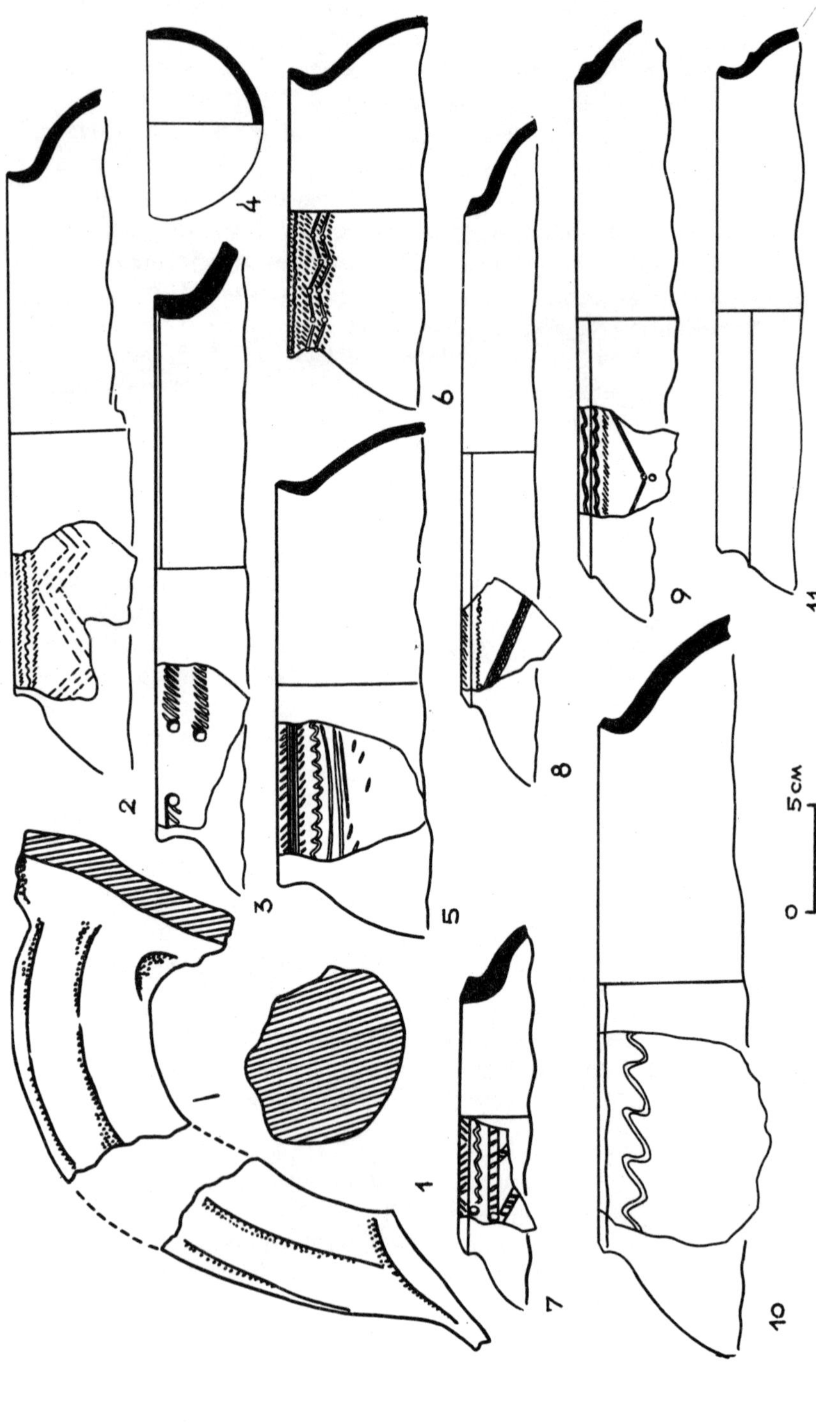

Figure 19. Hajrya settlement. Pottery finds from the surface.
1 : fragments of the amphora handle ; 2-11 : locally made pottery.

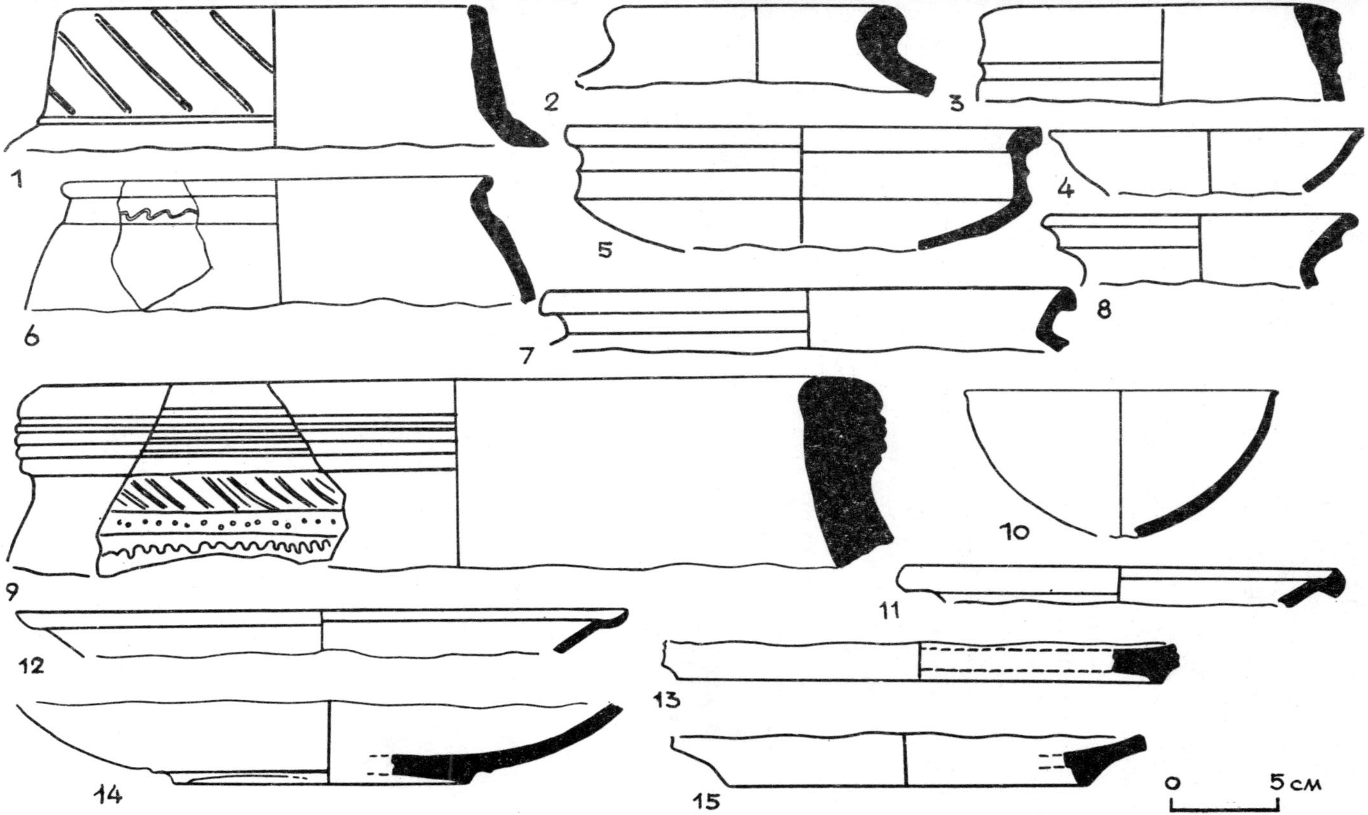

Figure 20. Hajrya settlement. Pottery finds from the surface.
1-9, 11-15 : imported pottery (**11-15** : glazed pottery) ; **10** : locally made pottery.

itself (posture and orientation of the bodies, presence of collective burials as well as animal bones in the graves), the design of the burial structures (stone chamber with a flat cover), and the presence of grave furniture. The exact dating of each of the cemeteries studied by the authors and of the ruins of dwelling structures next to them is an extremely difficult problem. At this stage, the authors can only suggest hypotheses as to the general chronological limits of all these monuments.

The collagenous analysis of the bone material taken from the graves in the Shibhon cemetery has yielded a wide scope for determining the absolute age of the burials : from 790 to 1110 BP. : in other words, the burials may go back to the period between 840 and 1160 A.D. [26] The ceramic vessels from the collective tomb near Qallansiya should date around the 12th-13th centuries —possibly up to the 14th century. Such a preliminary conclusion should be made both for the ceramic vessels with blue and light-green glaze, which probably have been made in Zabid (Yemen) or in some centres of southern Iran, and for the vessels which came to Socotra from Southern China and other countries of South-East Asia. [27]

The graves excavated in the cemetery of the Hajrya settlement, both in terms of the burial rite and of the grave structure design, are akin to the grave unearthed in the other cemeteries : Hasin, Gyuzuf, Mathöbo, Möbrhim, etc. The presumptive chronological limits of the existence of the settlement and, consequently, of its necropolis are from the early centuries A.D. to the 12th-13th centuries. It is quite probable that all explored cemeteries date from the same period, possibly up to the 14th century. It is essential to note that, by the 12th-13th centuries which are the suggested date of the existence of these cemeteries, the island had not yet been exposed to Islam, which would have involved, in the first place, the emergence of graves with Islamic types of burial customs.

The ground structures of the modern Islamic graves show a clear connection with the traditions of the pre-Islamic Socotran burials. On the north-east, the ancient Möbrhim cemetery is adjoined by a modern Islamic cemetery, about 80-100 graves. Their structures are small fences, subrectangular or elongated-oval in plan, measuring 0.4-0.6 x 1.2-1.6 m. The long sides of the fences stretch north-east-south-west, north-north-east/ south-south-west, and (few) north/ south. Within the fence, along its central axis, stand two or three vertically dug-in stones. Some of these stones have had a crude anthropomorphous (?) shape imparted to them. According to informants, inhabitants of the nearby villages are not buried in this cemetery. It is used as a burial ground only by bedouins from the mountains or from elsewhere, who

---

26. The analysis was made by Dr. L.D. Sulerzhitsky in the Laboratory of Absolute Age and Isotope Geochemistry of the Geological Institute of the Russian Academy of Sciences.

27. I would like to thank my colleague B. Lyonnet, CNRS, Paris, for her assistance.

come to the palm plantations in the neighbouring wadis. South of the Hajrya settlement and outside it, there is also a small cluster of about ten Islamic graves. These are small stone fences, oval or rectangular in plan, stretching north to south. The fences are frequently surrounded by another ring of stones, oval in plan — one of these fences is even surrounded by two rings. Within a fence, along its long central axis, one or two stones are usually dug in, whose upper parts frequently have anthropomorphous outlines imparted to them. The fences measure 0.5-0.7 x 1.2-1.45 m, and the external rings enclose an area of 1.3-1.6 x 1.9-2.1 m.

Thus, the Islamic modern cemeteries bear close external resemblance to the ancient ones. However, the burial ground structure has a different shape of the fence — near-oval ones prevail — , size — they are smaller, some considerably smaller —, orientation — the ancient graves predominantly stretch west to east with minor deflections northwards — , and the presence of dug-in stones within the fence.

The study of the objects of material culture obtained in the excavations of graves in ground cemeteries, just as the comparative study of the grave themselves, suggest some preliminary cultural-historical conclusions. Apparently, the similarity of the types of grave studied in various cemeteries, not infrequently far-off by fairly long distances — virtually, the authors saw a unique principle of cemetery organisation all over the explored area, a similar type of grave structure, and a cohesive burial rite with, however, minor specific local features — points to the cultural and ethnic unity of the ancient Socotrans who have left these cemeteries behind them, or, at any rate, of the people of that part of the island where such cemeteries are known to exist and were studied. Among the objects of grave furniture, alongside clearly imported items such as stone and glass beads,[28] glass vessels, a bronze vessel and ear-rings of bronze, and glazed ceramic vessels, there are locally made objects. Above all, this applies to handmade, round-bottomed ceramic vessels and wide-bladed iron knives found in the graves of the Shibhon, Hasin, and Möbrhim cemeteries and in a grave near Qallansiya. Perfectly identical items are manufactured on the island to this day, and modern Socotrans use them in their everyday life. Possibly, this indicates a certain cultural continuity between the ancient and the modern islanders.

Interesting comments are made by local participants in the excavations concerning certain objects of the grave furniture. For instance, according to informants, modern Socotrans traditionally manufacture small clay pots such as those discovered in the Hasin cemetery burial, specially for the remembrance of dead children — one pot for each dead child — which is practised during the

28. Amongst the finds from the graves of the Shibhon cemetery, there are etched beads of Indian carnelian, beads made of jade, coral, amber, amethyst, agate, translucent white crystal, selenit or « tiger's eye », and opaque blue glass.

Moslem festival of sacrificial offering (*id al adha*). On the festival's first day water is poured into them, and they are drunk from. Then the pots are smashed and thrown out. Muhammed Mubarak Ali of Hasin says : « Perhaps in the past they were put into graves with children, or adults' graves whose children had died, so remembrance is all that has remained of this custom ». The modern Socotrans have no custom of putting any furniture into the grave. However, if a lonely person whose property nobody can inherit dies in a tribe, the tribe does not take his property but buries it with him (except for the livestock).

The hafts of the iron knives found in the graves did not survive. They should have been made either of organic materials, which have not been preserved in the ground, or were so valuable for the fellow-tribesmen of the defunct person that they were removed from the knife. Modern Socotrans make such hafts from goat horns, softening them over the flame of a hearth. One of the excavated knives, having an elongated triangular blade, was compared by a participant in the excavations with a modern knife for cutting dates and removing their pits. Another knife, with a leaf-shaped blade, evoked analogies with a circumcision ritual knife. Indeed, modern Socotrans use for this operation knives of a kindred shape, whose blades are made sharp on one edge, with hafts made of horn.

Interesting statements were made by informants about the protective functions of necklaces and individual beads. White bead necklaces made of big stones were worn around the neck to ensure the drying of ulcers on the head (they are now rarely worn, mostly by old people). Beads are believed to heal purulent ulcers, a frequent disease on Socotra. A necklace of coloured beads was worn as an amulet, believed to keep off the *diasar* fly, whose bite, according to Socotran beliefs, may cause illness and even death. Informants said that mountaineers had put on their children's hands and above the elbows string bracelets with small beads in them. A string of big oval beads was put around the belt ; a bead was placed on the back to keep off low back pains.

The presence of domestic animals (goat) bones in the graves together with human remains appears to be almost incredible to modern Socotrans. At any rate, now and as far back as anybody can remember, such cases are unknown.

In addition to burials in ground cemeteries, burials of another type were discovered on Socotra : *collective graves in natural caves.* On a « burial mound » east of the village of **Suq** described by B. Doe, on a hillside, there were ruins of certain structures which the scholar thought were ancient structures of the town of Suq. Lower down the hill, he registered no less than four caves, the opening of which were protected with stone or brick walls. The caves were found to contain collective burials, which were in a very poor state of preservation, all the bones being scattered and broken. No furniture was discovered. [29] A similar cave, not far from **Kishin**, was also visited by P. Shinnie. [30]

In 1984, V.V. Naumkin and V.S. Shinkarenko discovered burials of this type approximately two kilometres south-east of the village of **Shaab**, over a wādi on the slope of Mt. Bagbaga. Here, at a height of about 100 m from the foot, there is a large dome-shaped cave of natural origin, 2.3-3 m high and about 4 m in diameter. It had an oval mouth located on the mountain's south-western side ; once it had been closed with stones fastened with clay. Not so long ago, this wall had been breached by playing children. Parts of the skeletons of about ten people and goat bones were heaped haphazardly inside. Further, a few more burial grounds were discovered 30 m south-east on the mountainside. The openings of three small caves were found on the north-eastern side of the mountain, the protective stone masonry of which had also been breached. The bones from the collective tombs on the slope of Mt. Bagbaga were turned over to the Laboratory of Absolute Age and Isotope Geochemistry of the Geological Institute of the Russian Academy of Sciences, where Dr. L.D. Sulerzhitsky made their collagenous analysis. His absolute dating was 1.300 BP. : thus, these burials date from approximately 650 A.D.

Similar collective cave tombs were inspected at **Haybak Pass**, near the village of Qadhub, in the central part of the island's northern coast, and south of Qallansiya, at **Cape Ras-Badu**.

In spite of the results of the collagenous analysis and dating, the problem of the date of the cave burials cannot be regarded as fully resolved. According to informants, Socotra's mountaineers occasionally used to bury their dead in natural caves until recently, blocking their openings with stones. As a rule, this was done during droughts and epidemics, when people had no strength left to dig graves. At the same time, medieval authors said that Socotrans buried their dead in caves. D.B. Doe believed that caves had served for the reburials of the remains of people initially buried in individual graves elsewhere. [31]

Relics of Mahri colonization and Portuguese conquest

A special group is formed by relics connected with the Mahri colonization of the island in the 15th-16th centuries and the brief Portuguese conquest of Socotra at the very dawn of the 16th century. Landing on the island in January 1507, the Portuguese had to take a powerfully strengthened fort built by the Mahri Arabs at the village of Suq by storm. The extant ruins of the **fortress on**

29. DOE, *Socotra*, p. 46-47.

30. SHINNIE, « Socotra », p. 106.

31. DOE, *Socotra*, p. 48.

Mt. Hawari, east of the village, accurately correspond to the description of the storm detailed in the chronicles.

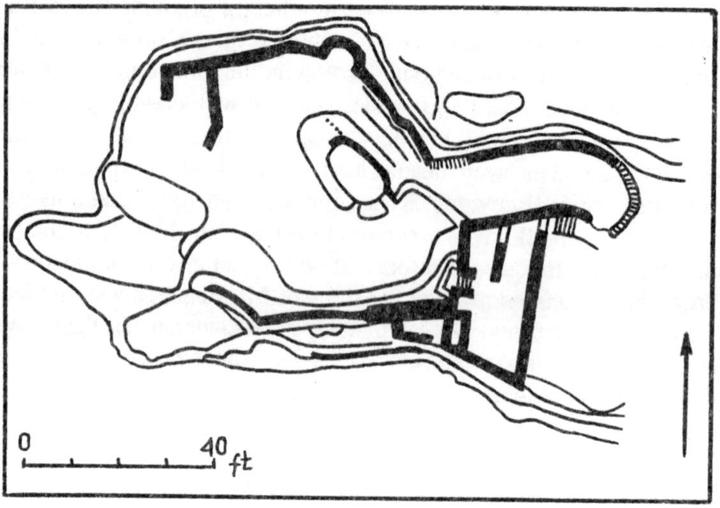

Figure 21. Fortress on Mt. Hawari. Sketch plan.

The fortress lies on the top of a mountain overlooking Suq from the east. The climb was from the north, from the direction of the lagoon. In the climb's upper part Doe registered remains of some fortification, which might have protected the entrance to the fortress. The defence walls of the fortress, built of roughly dressed stones held together with cement, followed the configuration of a natural area on the mountain-top. In the northern part, a semi-circular bastion was built facing the sea. Inside the fortress there was a big reservoir for water, oval in plan. The south-eastern corner of the fortress is occupied with what in plan is a trapeziform platform, with two stepped ramps inside and outside the fortress. It measures approximately 5.2 x 11.6 m. [32] In all probability, the tower in which the fort's last defenders took refuge was located exactly here (*Fig. 21*).

D.B. Doe believed that the fortress on Mt. Hawari was a « Portuguese construction ». However, he offered no argument for his statement. Portuguese chronicles say that the conquerors restored this fort, captured from the Arabs, giving it the name of St. Michael and using it for the needs of the garrison left on Socotra. The Mahris who, several years later, regained their rule on the island, according to all indications, not only continued to use the fortress but also erected new strongholds.

---

32. DOE, *Socotra*, p. 46.

Less than 50 m south of the modern fringe of Suq the ruins of another fort, « the lower fort », were inspected by D.B. Doe and P. Shinnie. It is almost fully destroyed, but its layout can be restored with sufficient assurance. It is a rectangular structure, measuring approximately 20.35 x 25.15 m with four round towers about 4.5 m in diameter at each of the structure's corners. Inside, the fort had premises where P. Shinnie conducted exploratory excavations. The glazed ceramics were yielded there, which the scholar said to go back to the 16th-17th centuries. [33] D.B. Doe has compared the layout of the fort with towers at the corners with a similar layout of fortresses known in the Hadhramawt. Referring to the work by R.B. Serjeant, he defined such a structure as « Yafi », connecting its building with the Mahri occupation of Socotra, and concluding that it was built after 1541. [34]

Indeed, the « yafi » fortresses are square or rectangular in plan ; in the corners of the rectangle or square formed by the walls rise battlement-topped circular towers. The people of the Yafi area [35] who built these stongholds called them *ḥiṣn bi-ma'ā-ṣirig*, or a fortress with towers. Such structures have survived to this day around Yafi and in the Hadhramaut. A remarkable sample of this style is the palace of the Sultan al-Qathiri in Seyun, the biggest city of the wādi Hadhramawt.

On the southern fringe of Suq there are remains of another small fortress. The structure is rectangular in plan, with a round tower having a diameter exceeding 3.5 m in the north-eastern corner. North of these ruins lie remains of yet another rectangular structure, measuring approximately 12 x 23 m. In Doe's opinion, one of these structures could have been an Arab fort stormed by the Portuguese in 1507. [36]

Not far from Hadibo, on **Mt. Hasun**, most scholars (T. Bent, P. Shinnie and D.B. Doe) inspected the remains of a fort in a good state of preservation (*Fig. 22*) ; it measures about 15 x 18 m. In the centre of the area surrounded by a powerful defence wall lies a tank for water, measuring approximately 6.7 x 8 m and no less than 1.5 m deep. The fort occupies an important strategic position on the northern coastal plain of the island around what is now the village of Hadibo. All scholars agree that it was built during the Mahri occupation. [37]

---

33. SHINNIE, « Socotra », p. 105.

34. DOE, *Socotra*, p. 46-47.

35. Yafi is the highland area of Yemen. The tribes which lived there are known from the ancient times by their martial spirit and strength. Up to now, there are a lot of high watching towers in the Yafi mountains, which were erected near almost every dwelling.

36. DOE, Socotra, p. 47.

37. DOE, *Socotra*, p. 41-42 ; SHINNIE, « Socotra », p. 103-104.

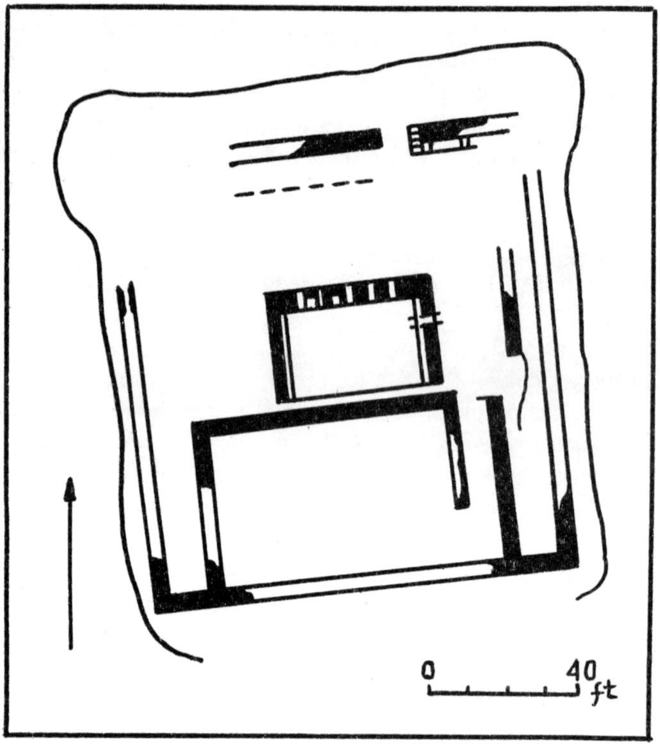

Figure 22. Fort on Mt. Hasun. Sketch plan.

In the **Feragey** Valley, south of the Haggier, T. Bent discovered the remains of another fort in 1897 (*Fig. 23*). Next to it seemed to lie the ruins of a village. According to the description of P. Shinnie, this fort which stood in the narrowest part of the valley viewed from above, was triangular in plan, with rectangular towers in its two corners. Remains of small rooms were discovered along one of the walls, inside the fort, and at another wall, a well was found. In Shinnie's opinion, the fortress was built by the Mahris for control of the Socotran bedouins — possibly during the restoration of their control of the island after the withdrawal of the Portuguese in the 16th century.[38] The fortress might have totally controlled the main road leading from the south of Socotra area to the north ; it stood at the very heart of the aboriginal territory and should have been an ideal base for further Mahri advance inside the island or for punitive raids.

38. SHINNIE, « Socotra », p. 107.

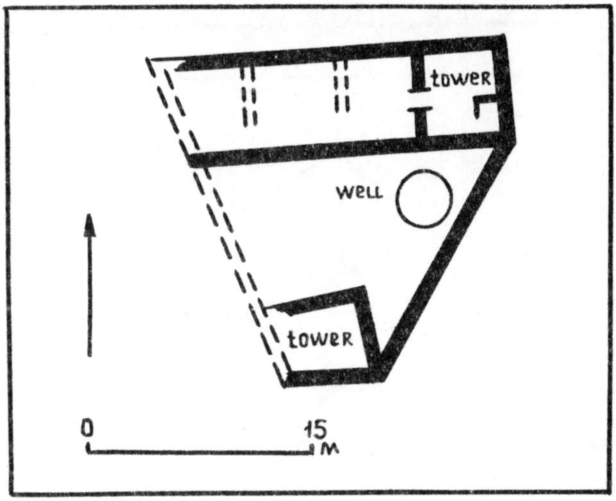

Figure 23. Fort in the Feragey Valley. Sketch plan.

Christian monuments

Where now is the village of Suq, P. Shinnie and D.B. Doe explored remains of a large building which both decided had been a church. It is known that the day after their successive landing on the island the Portuguese served a mass in a mosque located not far from the fort they had taken by storm. They converted the mosque into a church, calling it the Church of Our Lady of Victory. Presumably, it was exactly its ruins that were excavated in 1956 and 1967.[39]

Judging by the publication of D.B. Doe, the excavated structure had an overall dimension of about 12.2 x 15.2 m, its long side being orientated north-west to south-east (*Fig. 24*). The greater part of the cement floor, with nine bases of columns forming three rows, and a section of the north-eastern wall of the structure about 0.8 m thick, are in a good state of preservation. Another row of columns, the fourth and most easterly one, was found to be fully destroyed : thus, the roof of the building should have been resting on twelve columns. The bases of the columns show cross-sections of various shapes : square, eight-pointed star, octagon, and cross-shaped — square with chosen wedge in the corners. The drums of the columns are lost : they might have been made of wood. However, in 1987, the authors were able to see round drums of

39. True, the layout of the excavated building published by P. Shinnie and D.B. Doe does not coincide either in size or in wall orientation. Cf. SHINNIE, « Socotra », fig. 3, and DOE, *Socotra*, fig. 26.

combined-stone columns among the ruins of the church, about 40 cm in diameter with a central hollow for fastening with each other.

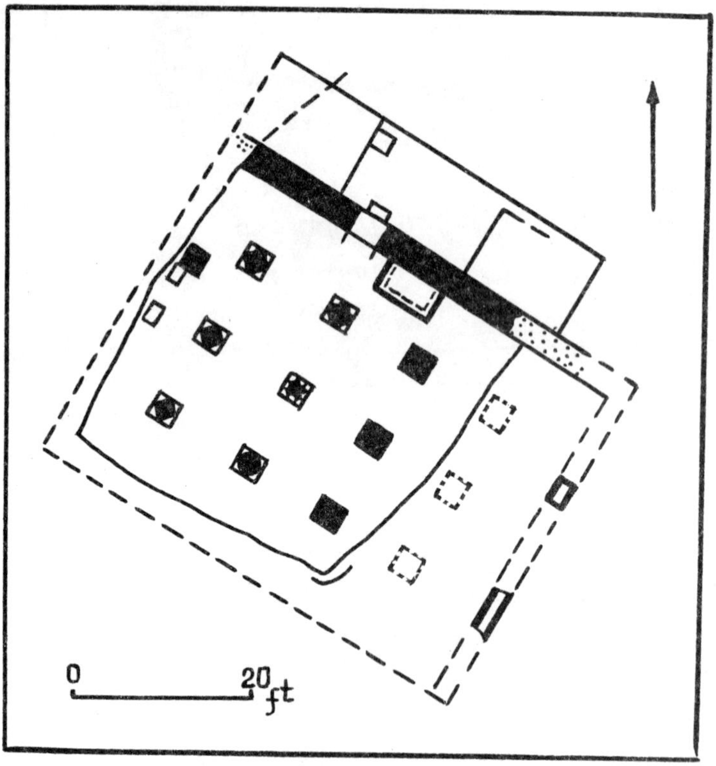

Figure 24. The church at Suq. General plan.

At approximately the middle of the northern wall of the structure, a comparatively low pedestal was annexed, the surface of which had a cement coating ; D.B. Doe called it « table » or « bench ». It measures 0.9 x 1.9 m, and it might probably be the remains of an altar (?). A passage about 1.5 m wide, with a stone threshold, was also arranged in the same wall. The passage led to an open platform measuring about 2.9 x 4.6 m, the surface of which also had a cement coating. North-west and south-east of the entrance, two symmetrical elevations approximately 30 cm high were found. Such structures, as correctly observed by D.B. Doe, frequently occur in modern houses in Hadibo. They are also known to exist on the mainland, for instance, in the ancient and modern villages of the wādi Hadhramaut, for example at the site of Raybun and the village of Meshhed. D.B. Doe assumes that this might have been the exact location of a small open belfry. [40]

Another, lower level below the floor of the building was also excavated. It was precisely in this level that remains of two fragments of pilasters (about three-fourth) were discovered, at the middle of the north-western wall, and appeared to be connected with this level. Most probably, these are remains of a *mihrab*, later converted into a passage (?). [41]

Thus, archaeological data seem to provide full support for the data with regard to the conversion of the mosque into a Christian cathedral referred in the Portuguese chronicles. At any rate, two periods connected with this structure are registered : (1) « Islamic », when a *mihrab* existed in the north-western wall ; (2) « Christian », characterised by considerable reconstructions, a rise in the floor level, the destruction of the mihrab (or its reshaping into an additional entrance), and the arrangement of an « altar » at the north-eastern wall.

Apparently, there was no reverse conversion of the structure following the withdrawal of the conquerors. At least, there is no archaeological evidence that there was. D.B. Doe quotes a witness statement by Master Boughton, the captain of the vessel « Peppercorn », who visited a deserted old church in 1615 and found in it « an Altar with Images, and a Cross upon it ». [42]

Shinnie found here a number of ceramic fragments. For the most, these are local Socotran vessels. However, there are fragments of imported pottery : Islamic glazed pottery and Chinese celadon. All datable ceramics go back to the 16th-17th centuries. [43]

Remains of another Christian church or chapel were found in the wādi **Qalisan**, in eastern Socotra. In all probability, this monument emerged and functioned much earlier than the church at Suq. D.B. Doe, who was the first to presume the equivalence of the name Qalisan and of the Greek word *ekklesia*, found it possible to connect this equivalence with the 4th century and the missionary activity of St. Thomas. [44]

In the wādi Qalisan, the scene of the island's most beautiful full-flowing wellspring, the ruins of a small ancient settlement are registered. However, their chronological definition is difficult. In 1983, V.V. Naumkin and V.S. Shinkarenko discovered and described the ruins of a small church. Built of dressed and undressed stones, this small structure is clearly orientated with respect to the four cardinal points. The entrance is from the west, the altar in the

40. DOE, *Socotra*, p. 46.

41. DOE, *Socotra*, p. 45-46.

42. DOE, *Socotra*, p. 46.

43. SHINNIE, « Socotra », p. 105.

44. DOE, *Socotra*, p. 91.

eastern part. The structure is rectangular in plan with an apsidal eastern wall : it is 5 m wide and 5 m long.

D.B. Doe believes that the ruins of an ancient church are to be found 0.2 mile south of Hadibo in a place called **Tsinifiroh**, on the western bank of the wādi Manifu. This is the location of a group of structures, apparently remains of a settlement, and north-west of them lies a small cemetery with grave structures resembling rectangular fences. D.B. Doe thinks it is possible to compare one of the structures of this complex, which seems to have an apsidal wall in the northern part, with the layout of the Byzantine churches in Ravenna and Rome. [45]

Vitalij V. NAUMKIN
Alexander V. SEDOV
Institute of Oriental Studies
Russian Academy of Sciences

List of photographs

Photo 1. Socotra island. 1 : Dragon tree ; 2 : frankincense trees.

Photo 2. Socotra island. 1 : aloe ; 2 : Rakuf cemetery, grave 4.

Photo 3. Socotra island. 1, 2 : Rakuf cemetery, well-preserved burial structure.

Photo 4. Lower Rökib settlement. Stone wall of courtyard.

Photo 5. Lower Rökib settlement. Ruins of the structure.

Photo 6. Mathöbo settlement. Stone wall of structure.

Photo 7. Mathöbo cemetery. Surface structure of the grave.

Photo 8. Gyuzuf cemetery, grave 1. The burial chamber.

Photo 9. Collective tomb near Qallansiya. The interior of the burial chamber.

Photo 10. Hajrya settlement. Ruins of the defence wall.

Photo 11. Hajrya settlement. Ruins of the south-western building.

Photo 12. Hajrya settlement. Remains of the filled well.

Photo 13. Hajrya cemetery. Surface structure of the grave.

Photo 14. Hajrya. Surface structure of the islamic grave.

Photo 15. Mt. Hawari fortress. Remains of the stone structure.

Photo 16. Mt. Hawari fortress. Remains of the bastion.

Photo 17. Suq church. General view of the ruins.

Photo 18. Suq church. Remains of the stone columns.

---

45. DOE, *Socotra*, p. 42-43.

GENERAL INDEX

Abbreviations

Achaem.	Achaemenid
Akk.	Akkadian
anthrop.	anthroponym
arch. Afghan.	archaeology of Afghanistan (sites, finds, etc.)
arch. Gulf	archaeology of the Persian Gulkf (sites, finds, etc.)
arch. Ind.	archaeology of India (sites, finds, etc.)
arch. Soc.	archaeology of Socotra (sites, finds, etc.)
arch. Yemen	archaeology of Yemen (sites, finds, etc.)
distr. Ind.	district of India
Egy.	Egypt
Gr. aut.	Greek author
Gr. myth.	Greek mythology
Ital.	Italy
Ind.	India
Ind. aut.	Indian author
Ind. dynast.	Indian dynasty
Ind. lit.	Indian literature
Ind. myth.	Indian mythology
loc. Soc.	locality in Socotra
Myc.	Mycenean
myth.	mythology
Pak.	Pakistan
peop.	people
Per.	*Periplus of the Eryhtraean Sea*
Rom.	Roman History
Rom. aut.	Roman author
Skrt	Sanskrit
Skrt lit.	Sanskrit literature
Soc.	Socotra

Index

Athens, Aden, Arikamedu
New Delhi, 1994
index, p. 251-272

Greek Index

Mycenaean